HORROR NOIRE

From *King Kong* to *Candyman*, the boundary-pushing genre of the horror film has always been a site for provocative explorations of race in American popular culture. In *Horror Noire: Blacks in American Horror Films from the 1890s to Present*, Robin R. Means Coleman traces the history of notable characterizations of Blackness in horror cinema, and examines key levels of Black participation on-screen and behind the camera. She argues that horror offers a unique representational space for Black people to challenge the more negative, or racist, images seen in other media outlets, and to portray greater diversity within the concept of Blackness itself.

Horror Noire presents a unique social history of Blacks in America through changing images in horror films. Throughout the text, the reader is encouraged to unpack the genre's racialized imagery, as well as the narratives that make up popular culture's commentary on race.

Including a comprehensive chronological survey of the genre, this book addresses a full range of Black horror films, including mainstream Hollywood fare, as well as art-house films, Blaxploitation films, direct-to-DVD films, and the emerging hip-hop culture-inspired horrorcore Black horror films. *Horror Noire* is, thus, essential reading for anyone seeking to understand how fears and anxieties about race and race relations are made manifest, and often challenged, on the silver screen.

Robin R. Means Coleman is Associate Professor in the Department of Communication Studies and in the Center for AfroAmerican and African Studies at the University of Michigan. Her previous books include *African Americans and the Black Situation Comedy: Situating Racial Humor* and the edited collection *Say It Loud! African Americans, Media and Identity*, both published by Routledge, and most recently the co-edited volume *Fight the Power! The Spike Lee Reader*.

HORROR NOIRE

Blacks in American Horror Films from the 1890s to Present

Robin R. Means Coleman

Routledge
Taylor & Francis Group

NEW YORK AND LONDON

First published 2011
by Routledge
711 Third Avenue New York, NY 10017

Simultaneously published in the UK
by Routledge
2 Park Square, Milton Park, Abingdon, Oxon OX14 4RN

Routledge is an imprint of the Taylor & Francis Group, an informa business

Library of Congress Cataloging in Publication Data
Means Coleman, Robin R., 1969-
Horror noire : blacks in American horror films from the 1890s
to present / Robin R. Means Coleman.
    p. cm.
Includes bibliographical references and index.
1. Horror films–United States–History and criticism. 2. African Americans
in motion pictures. 3. Race in motion pictures. I. Title.
PN1995.9.H6M43 2011
791.43'61640896073–dc22   2011004185

ISBN 13: 978-0-415-88019-0 (hbk)
ISBN 13: 978-0-415-88020-6 (pbk)
ISBN 13: 978-0-203-84767-1 (ebk)

Typeset in Bembo
by Glyph International Ltd.

For Rosalind Cash and Spencer Williams, Jr.

CONTENTS

LIST OF ILLUSTRATIONS

All images courtesy of Photofest.

FOREWORD

QUESTION: Why are there no Black people in horror movies?
ANSWER: Because when the ominous voice says, "GET OUT!," we do!

And, the movie will be over ... unlike the frail little White girl who hurriedly lights a candle and slowly descends the darkened steps to see where that voice is coming from ... True or not, this joke was once an offhanded justification to help explain the virtual absence of Blacks in horror movies made before the 1970s, a genre of film that has always been very popular in the African American community.

Although Blacks make up only 13 percent of the population, surveys have shown we generate over 25 percent of total box office receipts. This, despite the fact that there have been times when Blacks are rarely seen in movies of any genre, and if we are on the screen the images portrayed are nothing to be proud of.

Much has been researched and written on the history of Blacks in the cinema, but until now our presence or absence in the horror genre has mostly been relegated to a single chapter or several footnotes. This book is a complete and in depth examination of the images, influences, and societal impact that Blacks have had in horror films from the 1890s to present.

Making a 180-degree turn from her earlier book, *African American Viewers and the Black Situation Comedy: Situating Racial Humor*, professor and award winning media scholar Robin Means Coleman has compiled an impressive array of films and their bevy of dark skinned victims who lend their blood, if little else, to the plots and storylines of these even darker themed movies. This book is an indispensable examination of Black participation in the horror genre that not only adds to the wealth of cinematic research, but also highlights and celebrates the role Blacks have historically played in this very lucrative arena of motion pictures.

Perhaps for the sake of awareness we should consider the intrinsic differences in the societal impact of "on-screen" horror as opposed to "real-life" horrors. Motion pictures are a powerful tool for manipulating facts, information, and images that often affect people's perceptions, beliefs, and mental attitudes toward the subject presented. Early portrayals of Blacks in films such as *A Nigger in the Woodpile* (1904), a comedy, actually contained elements of what could be considered low level horror, in this case in both its racist title and on-screen representation of Blacks, which in reality were performed by White actors in blackface. As comedy, this film was not intended to terrify or frighten in the classic sense, but it did attempt to warn White people against one particular race of people that they do need to be afraid of.

Even more despicable were the countless "real-life" horrors inspired by D.W. Griffith's notorious film *The Birth of a Nation* (1915). While Whites were trying to escape the fictitious on-screen dangers of the ravenous Black masses rising up to get them in a post-slavery Amerikkka, outside the movie theater, Blacks were actually dying from the factual horrors of being lynched, shot, dragged, raped, beaten, castrated, and burned by White supremacy groups and other enthused racists who "drank the Kool-aid" and bought into that film's hate inciting message. It is one thing to be vicariously thrilled or horrified by some gruesome act happening to someone else on the movie screen, knowing that the actor eventually washes off the fake blood and goes home, and another to actually feel the pain and experience the horrific and gruesome event in real life with real blood and no director to yell "cut."

Perhaps the most damaging aspect to the limited spectrum of roles portrayed by Black actors in early horror films is that there were no contrasting positive images for a sense of balance. To see a Black character bug his eyes and turn white when he sees a ghost might not have been so bad if his next role or his previous role had been as a doctor, a lawyer, or a successful business man. However, Hollywood films of that time relegated Blacks to subservient characters such as butlers, maids, and chauffeurs, or they appeared on the screen simply to entertain as stereotypical coons and buffoons.

Famed actor Willie Best was allowed to quiver his lips plenty in a series of spooky films, including *The Ghost Breakers* (1940) and *The Whispering Ghost* (1942). Other established funnymen such as Eddie Anderson and Mantan Moreland also became well known for their ability to bug their eyes and shake at the knees in times of panic and fear in films like *Topper Returns* (1941), and *Revenge of the Zombies* (1943), respectively.

For a much broader spectrum of on-screen images, audiences could always rely on all-Black cast films being produced specifically for a hungry Black market desperate to see themselves represented in this exciting, powerful, and relatively new entertainment medium. "Race movies," as they were called, were mostly produced by White owned companies who realized there was money to be made, but several Black film companies geared up to fill the need as well. Popular actor Spencer Williams Jr. wrote and directed a string of Black cast films in the 1940s that included the horror tale *Son of Ingagi* (1940), in which a research scientist keeps a creature from the African jungle in her cellar until it gets loose to stalk the inhabitants of the house. In producer Jed Buell's *Voodoo Devil Drums* (1944), movie audiences saw for the first time "The Virgin Dance of Death!" and "The Altar of Skulls!" Unlike in White cast films, where Blacks were used mostly as comic relief, in all-Black cast films such as these, each character on the screen, the good and the bad, the high and the low, were all representative of a complete darker hued world that actually existed in real life, but was seldom seen on the silver screen.

By the 1950s and 1960s African Americans were once again being virtually ignored by Hollywood, not only on movie screens, but now on the smaller television screen as well. Around that time, I was shocked and pleasantly surprised that "Ben," the Black lead in George A. Romero's classic horror film *Night of the Living Dead* (1968), was allowed to survive throughout the entire film, but the picture still refused to stray too far from the established trend of Blacks' demise.

However, in the 1970s film changed. "Say it loud, I'm Black and I'm proud!" had become the mantra as a new genre of film began lighting up the screens to usher in our new race pride and social awareness. The Blaxploitation era not only gave Blacks gritty urban street dramas like *Shaft* (1971) and *The Mack* (1973), but also gave birth to several interpretations of classic horror tales, such as *Blacula* (1972), *Blackenstein* (1973), and *Dr. Black & Mr. Hyde* (1976). As this short lived era of on-screen afro-enlightenment faded into oblivion it seems that the doors of mainstream horror began to creak open, but just enough to lead a few more token Negroes to the slaughter.

QUESTION: Why is the Black character always the first to get eaten by the monster?
ANSWER: Dark meat tastes great and is less filling!

It was in the 1980s when Hollywood entered into its "Kill a Nigga" phase. (Note: I do realize the National Association for the Advancement of Colored People [NAACP] has buried the "N" word, so I use it here purely for the sake of historical accuracy.) During this period, it seemed that if a Black character was allowed on the screen he or she was dead by the time the credits rolled. In *Wolfen* (1981), Gregory Hines got mauled by a wolfman; *Gremlins* (1984), Glynn Turman was lunch; *The Hills Have Eyes II* (1985), Willard E. Pugh got crushed; *Angel Heart* (1987), Lisa Bonet was sexually assaulted by a loaded gun; ... and on and on and on. Not only were the vast majority of Black characters killed off during this period, but they were often the first to die, and there is at least one website that tracks this phenomenon: www.blackhorrormovies.com/dyingyoung.htm.

My personal interest in the horror genre goes back many years and extends into my personal work. Based on my 1985 UCLA thesis project, "The Black Beyond," a *Twilight Zone/Outer Limits* type anthology series from a Black perspective, I was contacted by Warrington Hudlin of the Black Filmmakers Foundation in New York about participating in a forum on "Blacks in Horror, Sci-Fi and Fantasy." I drove up to New York from Philadelphia, where I was living at the time, anxious to participate and to see what other independent work was being done in the genre, only to find that at that time, in the mid- to late 1980s, it was only me.

I read somewhere that there has not been a horror film made that has lost money. Therefore, when I decided to do my first feature film, *Embalmer* (1996), I decided to go horror and ended up filing for bankruptcy ... I know, T.M.I. Regardless, that statement turned out to be quite accurate because the film *did* make a profit ... I just didn't get any of it. I produced *Embalmer* with a cast and crew of my Howard University students for a budget of under $30,000, financed mostly from a line of credit on my house. It grossed over $100,000 in the home video market, but the distributors, Yvette Hoffman and Toni Zobel of Spectrum Films in Mesa, Arizona, chose to go out of business rather than send me my royalty check.

I realized later that I was right on time with the concept as several other horror films were being produced by African Americans, including Rusty Cundieff's *Tales from the Hood* (1995) and Ernest Dickerson's *Tales from the Crypt: Demon Nights* (1995).

In the years that have followed, more and more Blacks have appeared in horror films, whether they are the first to die or not. The popular and financially lucrative *Scary Movie* series of films introduced by Keenen Ivory Wayans that sets out to spoof current horror flicks has added to the broad range of the genre, helping to make the box office receipts for these films stronger than ever. The straight-to-DVD market now has a mass of Black horror titles to choose from with varying degrees of fear, quality, and production budgets. And, with the new and advancing technology that makes moviemaking more affordable to the masses, and internet screening outlets such as Facebook and YouTube, many more Black people will die horrible deaths in horror films to come. Today's horror filmmakers, no matter their skin tone, know that there is only one color of blood on the screen, and one color of money at the box office ... green.

Steven Torriano Berry, Associate Professor and Filmmaker

Howard University

Washington, D.C.

August 2010

PREFACE

Rick Worland (2007), in his book *The Horror Film*, rather cheekily, though astutely, observes that horror film book authors have a propensity to include "more or less ironic declarations of whether their interest [in horror films] began in childhood or fairly recently, implicitly arguing that one's credibility to speak about the genre was somehow either enhanced or hurt by just when the writer's interest began."[1] Here, I join in this trite trend to offer my own declaration of interest—I got into horror films at a very tender age, perhaps as early as five years old. This revelation is about more than me confessing the "psychological jungles" of my slightly insane childhood.[2] My coming clean about consuming horror— and liking it!—is offered to give you some sense of my unique experiences with horror. It is my hope that this glimpse into my psychosocial world will help you to understand where, in part, my interpretations of Blacks' representations in horror films are coming from.

Confessions of a Horror Kid

I write this book flush with a sense of entitlement. I was born and raised in Pittsburgh, Pennsylvania. For you truly diehard horror film fans, I need not say more, as you already fully understand how I can claim this book to be my destiny. For those of you who need a hint: my birthplace is home to the Hercules of horror, George "*Night of the Living Dead*" Romero, as well as to special effects creator extraordinaire Tom "Godfather of Gore" Savini.[3]

As a pre-teen, I was keenly aware that I was quite literally walking in the footsteps of Romero and Savini in my favorite Pittsburgh shopping complex— Monroeville Mall. The Mall (as we Pittsburghers call it) is the spatially and ideologically terrifying centerpiece of the 1979 Romero film *Dawn of the Dead*.

The film also featured the spectacular living-to-undead effects wizardry of Savini, who even appears in a substantial cameo role as a "biker zombie."

In 1979, at the age of 10, I very much liked doing what bored kids across the nation like to do—I hung out at the Mall. The teen character Flip Dog (Danny Hoch) in the movie *Whiteboyz* (1999) put this mundane, modern-youth rite of passage into perspective rather succinctly: "All they do is hang out at the mall every day ... and walk back and forth from Footlocker to Chi-Chi's, Chi-Chi's to Footlocker.... Those are whack fucking activities."[4] Whack indeed. It was kids of my generation who shamelessly started the trend of ditching sand lots and playgrounds, opting instead to walk the wings of shopping malls like zombies.

But Monroeville Mall back in the 1970s was really something rather special. For one, its main floor was then made up of an indoor ice-skating rink. With the rink enclosed in Plexiglas, it looked much like the Civic Arena (a.k.a. the Big Igloo), home to the Pittsburgh Penguins. One could sit at the adjacent Pup-A-Go Go, a restaurant modeled on a hotdog stand, and watch little future Mario Lemieuxs awkwardly speed up and down the ice while little future Michelle Kwans kept to the center of the rink, cross-cutting and jumping. A few years later, the Mall management, failing to heed Romero's missive on the dangers of mass production, would tear out the one-of-its-kind ice rink and Pup-A-Go Go combo. A cookie-cutter (pun intended) Mrs. Fields is now where center ice used to be.

I saw *Dawn of the Dead* with my grandmother and mother at the Greater Pittsburgh Drive-In Theatre, which often featured late night horror movies. Though a decade after *Night of the Living Dead*, Romero's *Dawn* seemed to attract its fair share of Black viewers. There are, perhaps, two intersecting theories about Black folks' affinity with the *Dawn* film. The first explanation is that a decade earlier many of the theaters that showed *Night* were located in inner cities, serving a predominately Black audience.[5] Perhaps access contributed to Blacks' initial love affair with Romero. However, I think that proximity was just one part of what brought Black viewers to subsequent Romero films. The other key enticement was that *Night* had Ben! Ben (Duane Jones)—a complex, emboldened Black starring character who was calm under fire, competently took charge of a deadly situation, and who surprisingly kicked some (White) butt and took names (after all, Ben does slap around and shoot a White man).

We, two women and a kid, rode out to that drive-in to see if Romero's *Dawn* would again deliver to us another non-shuffling, anti-exploitation, empowered Black hero. Romero did not let us down. He provocatively provided a Black conqueror and more, through the hardy character Peter (Ken Foree), who survives the zombie plague and seeks safety along with a relative stranger—a very pregnant White woman (gasp!), Francine (Gaylen Ross). Would Peter and Francine find hope and a zombie-free life elsewhere? Who is going to deliver Francine's baby (double-gasp!)? Be it 1968 with *Night*, 1979 with *Dawn*, or even today, such representations of race, sex, and gender relationships still remain a big deal.

If memory serves, my trip to the drive-in with my folks was made all the more sublime when *Night* came on after *Dawn* as part of a special Romero double-feature. I kept my sleepiness at bay so that I could again take in *Night* (I'd seen it before) with the "mature" eye of a 10-year-old. I saw the flesh-eating as "nasty." However, I was indescribably, deeply affected by *Night*'s infamous ending that served, in my mind, then and now, as a powerful indictment on race relations. In the heart-wrenching, closing scenes of *Night*, after Ben has beaten all odds to survive the night against the cannibal zombies, he is (symbolically) lynched by a mob of shotgun toting White men. The film reflected directly upon the social climate of its time. The assassination of Dr. Martin Luther King, Jr. occurred the very day—April 4, 1968—Romero was driving *Night* to New York City for distribution. For many Black folks in 1968, on the heels of Dr. King's assassination, it was plausible to question if a self-assured Black man like Ben could at least safely exist on the big screen. Though Romero's film was fantastical with its flesh-eating zombies, it was still a film of significant realism. He directed the attention of the film's audience, demanding that we take account of how in the real world of Black men White mobs are far more deadly.

I recall my grandmother being willing to place her hand on a stack of bibles and swear that she recognized one of those "gun toting, Black-man-killing, so and sos," as she called them, featured in the film. I hate to say it, but she may have been right. Real-life Pittsburgh area police and other locals appeared as extras in the pivotal *Night* scene which decided Ben's fate. What we saw in *Dawn* and *Night* were truly *our* Pittsburgh experiences on that screen.

Pittsburgh, like many U.S. cities in the 1960s and 1970s, made it easy to be hesitant about its progressive potential (particularly for minorities). Pittsburgh was, and is, a segregated city. Its neighborhoods are culturally rich, but they also serve as de-facto racial boundaries. The Bloomfield neighborhood is predominately Italian. The Polish Hill neighborhood speaks for itself. On the north side of the city, Black folks, especially those living in the segregated remote elevations of the Northview Heights housing project, have to go through great efforts to reach Pittsburgh's downtown. They must get down from atop the city's steepest hills, cross over the "flats," and make their way across bridges over Pittsburgh's famed three rivers—the Allegheny, the Monongahela, and the Ohio—to get downtown, also known as Pittsburgh's "cultural district." The cultural district happily plays host to touring Broadway shows, conventions, and, even on occasion, a classic horror film festival. To connect with those Black folks living in, for example, the altitudes of the city's east side requires comparable effort. Hence, not only is interracial connection a bit of a challenge in the old Steel City, *intra*racial uniting is not all that easy either.

In 2005, Romero made his fourth entry to the *Dead* film series with *Land of the Dead*. *Land*'s social commentary is all about boundaries—corporate vs. public, rich vs. poor, insiders vs. outsiders—and location, particularly how those darn three rivers reinforce all manner of divides and separation. I cheered while watching *Land* as the Black gas station attendant turned zombie rebel faction leader took the very long walk down out of his neighborhood. He dove into the Point—where the three rivers meet—and marched across the water's murky bottom with his army of dispossessed compatriots to express his dissatisfaction, in his own 'special' way, about the values of those on the other side of the racial, class, and corporate tracks in the cultural district. Romero does get Pittsburgh so very well.

Pittsburgh has also, dubiously, afforded me some additional horror cultural capital to draw on. In 1982, the horror film *White Dog* told the story of a vicious German shepherd dog trained by a White racist to kill Black people. When people remark on the fantastical storyline of *White Dog*, I remind them of Dolpho, an Alsatian police dog. In a Pittsburgh suburb, in 2002, Dolpho had three official complaints lodged against him by Blacks for unprovoked attacks. Things came to a head when the dog opted to rip into a nine-year-old Black boy rather than pursue, upon its White handler's command, a nearby, fleeing White drug suspect.[6] Dolpho was suspended from the force.

At present, Pittsburgh is also home to a vampire "Meetup" group (but then, isn't every city?) and it is working to expand its werewolf group for people like "Nicole," who posts on the werewolf.meetup.com message board, "hi everyone. I'm 20 yrs old, female, and a werewolf. That's about all." The city also boasts the Pittsburgh Ghost Hunters Association (PGHA) that has been investigating paranormal activity in the area since 2002. The "hunters" of the PGHA claim to be particularly knowledgeable about instrumental trans-communicating (ITC). That is, they record messages "coming from the beyond" (think Michael Keaton in *White Noise* [2005]).[7]

So, yes, that I hail from Pittsburgh, and that I am a horror fan from way back, means that I bring a novel relationship to, and unique perspective on, horror films.

Racing Horror

My interest in horror flicks and their narratives on race certainly does not begin or even end with Romero's films. Films like *King Kong* (1933), with its "ooo-gaa boo-gaa" chanting dark natives who are enamored by white skin, are extraordinarily useful in putting a spotlight on how we understand the role of race, as well as (imagined) cultural practices. And, do not get me started on hip-hop culture inspired movies such as *Bones* (2001), with their neo-Blaxploitation themes set to a rap soundtrack. The tie that binds all of the films I will examine here is their ability to inspire provocative treatments of race and to offer unique lessons and messages about race relations.

I will show in this book that there are a great many horror films that contribute to the conversation of Blackness. I believe it is particularly important to understand that there is a wealth of horror films, often presented by Black film-makers such as Spencer Williams (*The Blood of Jesus*, 1941), Bill Gunn (*Ganja & Hess*, 1973), and Ernest Dickerson (*Def by Temptation*, 1990), that feature Black themes, Black cast members, and Black settings that contribute novel content to the genre.

Horror has something to say about religion, science, foreigners, sexualities, power and control, class, gender roles, sources of evil, an ideal society, democracy, etc. These topics take a compelling turn when examined through the lens of Black culture. My point is: the story of Blackness, as told through horror, is a complex and interesting one. While horror has at times been marred by its "B-movie," low budget and/or exploitative reputation, one cannot discount its unique skill at exposing the issues and concerns of our social world, to include our racial sensibilities.[8]

"One way of denigrating the horror genre," writes Hutchings, "is to denigrate its audiences ... by arguing that the only people who could actually enjoy this sort of thing are either sick or stupid (or sick and stupid)."[9] I do not want to give short shrift to what is, for some, a troublesome "bee in their bonnet" about horror films. Many of these movies are, indeed, rife with gore (the sick) and thin on scripting (the stupid). Horror films are rarely *Festival de Cannes* top-prize material, but their audiences may be far more astute than critics and some scholars give them credit for. They understand that the whole of the genre is not inane, and that horror filmmakers reveal something much, much more horrifying: that our world and relationships are really being held together with little more than spirit gum.

Night of the Living Dead is now a cult classic. Most aficionados agree that it is one of Romero's greatest contributions to the genre, and to the medium. However, it has been over 40 years since *Night* demanded that we ask ourselves what is scarier, flesh-eating zombies, or what we are doing to each other on a daily basis.

So, there you have it. Clearly I believe the horror genre has great revelatory promise, and that is what moves me to explore its myriad definitions of Blackness, as well as what the genre reveals about relevant Black character types, and about Blacks' levels of participation in film and Blacks' contributions to our social world.

ACKNOWLEDGMENTS

Over the years, a host of friends, colleagues, and even strangers helped to push this project forward by offering their support and contributing their insights. I regret that I cannot identify each and every one of you here. However, do know this: I am truly, truly grateful for your gifts of wisdom.

To my mother, Patty—the woman who helped me to understand that lessons in good and evil, moral consciousness, and cultural awareness are to be found in the most unlikely of places. Patty remains one of the best, most interesting, movie dates ever.

I cannot begin to detail here the tremendous support my husband, Randy, afforded me. He read every piece of research. He scoured archives. He watched every movie. He critiqued my arguments. He was unbelievably heroic in his efforts, giving of himself with extraordinary personal and professional sacrifice. Randy, to paraphrase Billie Holiday: "Fish got to swim and birds got to fly. Can't help lovin' that man of mine."

Routledge Publishing has an incredible team of people working hard to ensure that scholarship such as this is presented in its very best form. I am indebted to Matthew Byrnie, Senior Editor of Media and Cultural Studies, for seeing great promise in this book. I cannot thank Matthew enough for his advocacy. Likewise, I must thank Carolann Madden, Editorial Assistant, and Stan Spring, (former) Senior Editorial Assistant, and Gail Newton, Production Editor, for managing this book project. To Lisa Williams, Copy Editor: I cannot thank you enough for helping to make this book "sing!" Your exacting attention to detail is enviable. I really enjoyed working with you. To those who worked on the production of this book, I thank you.

I am particularly grateful to Photofest for assisting me in acquiring the images that appear in this book. This is the fourth book project Photofest has helped me with. It is wonderful to work with such efficient professionals.

Of course, I am especially grateful to the three anonymous reviewers of this book for their careful, attentive reading and astute feedback. Their suggestions were spot-on, thereby making this effort all the stronger.

My heartfelt thanks go to my colleagues in the Department of Communication Studies and in the Center for AfroAmerican and African Studies (CAAS) at the University of Michigan. I want to expressly thank my department chairs, Susan Douglas (Communication Studies) and Kevin Gaines (CAAS), for their encouragement and support. The Department of Communication Studies very generously provided funding for this project through the Constance F. and Arnold C. Pohs Research and Technology Endowment Fund for the Study of Communication and Social Change. CAAS, likewise, was quite generous by providing office space and a research assistant.

In fact, the University of Michigan is just chock-full of people willing to give of themselves in support of this research. I wish to thank Lester Monts, Senior Vice Provost for Academic Affairs, for the 2010 Harold R. Johnson Diversity Service Award. Thanks to Evans Young, Assistant Dean for Undergraduate Education, for recommending the awesome book title. To Evans Young, Catherine Shaw, Assistant Vice Provost for Academic Affairs, and the Women of Color in the Academy Project crew (Robin Wilson, Mieko Yoshihama, Ixchel Faniel), thanks for simply understanding … everything. A very special thanks to Rebecca Sestili, Author–Publisher Liaison. Rebecca, I am at this moment because of you. Philip Hallman, the Screen Arts and Cultures Film Librarian, was tireless in his hunt for some of the more rare, obscure, or banned horror films that are discussed here. Similarly, Jeffrey Pearson, Askwith Film Librarian, was also an incredible resource for acquisitions. Jeff is a true horror fan, and the University of Michigan may have one of the finest horror collections in the country thanks to Jeff's attention to the genre. I would also like to acknowledge Michael McLean for sending me away with dozens of horror movies each week to view. University of Michigan staff members Elizabeth James, Chaquita "Quita" Willis, Faye Portis, Chris Gale, and Orlandez Huddleston were all inventive and diligent in helping me to secure the resources I needed to bring this book to its successful conclusion. Their laughter and love is deeply appreciated.

Will Youmans, a doctoral candidate in the Department of Communication Studies at the University of Michigan, helped me to push my thinking in new directions. Charles Gentry, a doctoral candidate in American Culture, is an incredible intellectual. The depth and breadth of his Black popular culture knowledge are unmatched. To Charles: Robeson and Poitier would be proud!

To Mark H. Harris, creator of BlackHorrorMovies.com. You cannot imagine how awesome and helpful your website is! It is *the* "go to" site for anyone who claims to be a fan of horror. Yes, Mark, without fail I do say a prayer to the patron saint of Black death, Scatman Crothers.

A special thank you to my dear friend and shero Bambi Haggins, Director of Film and Media Studies at Arizona State University. I *wish* having "NAAA" was my problem!

And to you, dear reader—thank you. Now, look into that mirror, and say it with me: "Candyman. Candyman. Candyman. Candyman … Candyman!"

INTRODUCTION

Studying Blacks and Horror Films

:01 second into *Jurassic Park* (1993): unnamed Black guard #1 is charged
with moving a velociraptor into a holding cage [Oh no. Be careful Black
guard #1!] :04 seconds later, Black guard #1 is pureed by the velociraptor.

Jurassic Park may have been thrilling science fiction entertainment to some in that
darkened Columbia, Missouri movie theater, but for me this early scene of Black
annihilation promised a *horror* show. I recall spending several minutes mourning Black guard #1 (Jophery C. Brown), whose death was witnessed for the
singular purpose of evidencing what we all already know—that a velociraptor is a
bad-ass monster. To be sure, filmmakers such as Steven Spielberg savvily toy
around with audiences' expectations, to include figuring out that there is no
better way to demonstrate someone's, or some*thing*'s, extreme deadliness than for
it to secure a bloodbath victory over a Black man with a big black gun.

As those around me in that theater tittered with laughter at the antics of
children meeting dinosaurs, I was feeling oddly uneasy … perhaps because I was
now looking at the bloody stump of Jurassic Park's (Black) engineer Ray Arnold
(Samuel L. Jackson). The dinosaurs had gotten him too. Ray was not the unlikable lawyer, the corporate-secrets thief, or even the big game hunter, who were
all, deservedly, eaten by the reptiles. Like Black guard #1, Ray Arnold was an
innocent; as such, the only two Black characters in the film were united in that
they experienced gruesome, absolutely unwarranted deaths.

The purpose of this recollection is to reveal that, at times, Blacks have a rather
unique relationship with American film's presentation of Blacks. Some may
bring to, and take away from, their film viewing experience culturally specific
expectations—what Kozol calls "the racial gaze"[1]—in which they hope to see

themselves as whole, full, and realized subjects rather than simply "window dress-ing on the set"[2] or human meat to up a bloody body count.

In *Horror Noire: Blacks in American Horror Films from the 1890s to Present*, I am interested in what horror films can reveal, through representations, about our understandings of Blacks and Black cultural tropes, or Blackness, as well as what kinds of sociopolitical discourses these films contribute, and what meanings they might provoke. More, I speculate about the impetus for some of horror's racial-ized imagery and narratives. In my effort to rehistoricize and recontextualize the horror film, I note how the genre "speaks" difference. That is, marking Black people and culture as Other—apart from dominant (White) populations and cultures in the US. The book's main title, *Horror Noire*, functions as a sort of double-entendre. It simultaneously hails the "dark," or the "noire" (as in *bête noire*), while also offering a nod to horror's complex relationship with good and evil, right and wrong, much like another genre, film noir, grapples with these issues as well. However, this book does not take film noir as its focus. Rather, *Horror Noire* is a title that works to hail and join the wealth of popular culture forms offered focusing on Black Americans—who also appropriate the French "*noir(e)*" to describe "black"—such as: Noire Digerati, a technology organization that focuses on the inclusion of Blacks in game design, mobile computing, and interactive media;[3] or the book *Black Noir* featuring African American crime fiction writers;[4] or netnoir.com, a news and politics web portal "from an African American perspective."[5]

Horror is a genre, according to Mark Reid in *Black Lenses, Black Voices: African American Film Now*, that demands scrutiny when "difference demonizes charac-ters and creates or resists static notions of good and evil."[6] This is not to say that the *only* horror films worthy of study are those which lay bare, or address, our social inequities or debate our hypocrisies. For horror novelist Stephen King, that which is buried beneath the horror fantasy is sufficiently worthwhile; as he states, "we understand that fiction is a lie to begin with. To ignore the truth inside the lie is to sin against the craft."[7] To be sure, horror's intrinsic "fantastical quality has produced more imaginative, innovative and provocative (as well as tortuous and confused) insights than is sometimes apparent in those areas of representation more bound by the demands of realism."[8] Through its imagination, innovation, and push toward provocation, horror does not just comment on Black culture, rather it, as Clover puts it, "tells on" mainstream media as well, noting its lapses in convention, representational and cultural vision, and courage.[9]

What I seek to avoid here is treating the horror genre like "long chains of immutable codes" in which significant historical shifts are disregarded as "little more than minor variations."[10] Other scholars have effectively and influentially worked to identify and organize the treatment of Blacks, over time, in popular culture and media. For example, Brown categorizes Black character types frequently seen in early twentieth century mainstream literature, such as the "content slave" or the "wretched freeman."[11] Clark[12] contributed a typology organized around Black participation, or the lack thereof, in media. He identifies recurring portrayals and trends such as "nonrecognition" (or absence) and "ridicule." Nelson[13] and Coleman[14] focus on television situation comedy to provide a rubric that elucidates the sociopolitical impact of media discourses that includes "separate-but-equal" and "assimilationist." In *Horror Noire*, I have come to appreciate these and other important organizational contributions, while I innovate my own historical accounting—decade by decade—of Blacks' participation in the horror film genre.

Still, I have taken great care to not forcibly shoehorn this history of horror films into decades. However, *a posteriori*, my analysis did indeed reveal a cycle of representations that coincides with the rise and fall of sociopolitical trends in particular decades, and I present my understanding and interpretation of events here. Though delineated by decade, the horror genre features both long-lasting, cross-era trends as well as temporary ones. I work hard to note examples from each.

Horror as a (Resistant) Genre

The immediate question becomes, given the simultaneously stable (e.g. fear and violence) and flexible (e.g. taste and aesthetics) nature of the genre, "what, then, constitutes a horror film?" It is worth stating upfront that arguing what falls within and outside the confines of a genre is a decidedly complex, if not an impossible and at times fruitless, process. Today, especially in the age of multimedia and new media technologies, purist generic boundaries are extraordinarily difficult to define. Is a horror film only a horror *film* on, say, the Hollywood big screen, or do we now accept that horror film has found its home on increasingly smaller screens (e.g. portable digital technologies)? Can horror films be made not only by big studios, or independents, but also by one or two individuals with a digital camera, little semblance of a script, and no budget? Is *Jurassic Park*, for example, adventure, science fiction, a comedy, or all of the above? In keeping with the *Jurassic Park* example, does the film now approach the horror category because of its killer monsters, the feelings of fear it aroused, and because it was received and interpreted as horror by at least one audience member based on her belief that the very, very low mortality rate Blacks regularly have on film is terrifying? These questions reveal that even bringing together medium, production, and reception does not a clear definition make.

Hutchings, in his book *The Horror Film*, is correct in his observation that definitions are elusive: "which films are horror and which films are not remains as distant as ever ... perhaps the most striking and exciting feature of horror cinema in this respect is that, like one of its own shape-shifting monsters, it is always changing, always in process."[15] However, accepting inconclusiveness is unsatisfying here, as it is useful to at least broach some understanding of what horror films are, and those that are not, within the purview of this book.

Certainly the notion of genre, and the practice of assigning typologies, especially within horror, is a "particularly contested one."[16] Today, our understanding of genre extends beyond early Aristotlean/*Poetics* and Northrop Frye/*Anatomy of Criticism*[17] notions of teasing out art forms' separate and distinct formulas and conventions to create classificatory schema. Rather, genre is as much about the heuristic power surrounding naming a "thing" as it is about sociopolitical euphony. On "naming a thing," Gateward is useful here in revealing the depth of the problem; as she points out, "there are so many vampire films in fact, with so many shared conventions of iconography, theme, and character, that the vampire film has become a genre in itself."[18] The same can be said of Blacks in film. That is, there are so many films featuring Blackness, with so many shared conventions, that Black film has become a genre in itself.[19]

In the end, marking, or naming a thing, is inherently dangerous in that it may further subordinate that thing (e.g. mother vs. welfare mother). However, naming a thing has the potential to be politically powerful, and can work to expose material qualities that may be otherwise rendered invisible. There have been useful, inventive categories of film introduced in recognition of the kinds of leitmotif and roles available, for example, for Blackness. To illustrate, in dubbing certain films "Blaxploitation," this moniker is as much about exposing a category of film imbued with stereotypes of race relations, gender roles, sex, and violence as it is a critique of those who created the stereotypes, the political economy (financial investments, distribution, and marketing) behind such efforts, and reception and the great cultural impact the images had within and outside of Blackness. Additional categories, driven by cultural consensus, social impact, subject matter, style and technique, or quality continue to emerge all the time, such as "hood movies" like *Boyz in the Hood* (1991) or *Menace II Society* (1993). Understandably, many would eschew categorizing films through some sort of raciology. Such slotting runs the risk of an overdetermination of all manner of variables of difference, such as world view, class, sexuality, gender, etc. Nevertheless, David Leonard makes a compelling and persuasive case for delineating Black film to facilitate study in *Screens Fade to Black*: "it is important to examine Black cinema as a phenomenon in its own right—as something having its own history, cultural traditions, and expressive norms (Africanism, oral tradition, narrative style, spirituality, syncretism, hybridization)."[20]

So, what then is horror as conceptualized here? I draw on Phillips' discussion of horror definitions in his book *Projected Fears: Horror Films and American Culture*.[21] Here, he offers that horror as a genre is marked by that which is instantly recognizable as horrifying; that which meets our collective understandings and expectations of what is horrific; and that which is talked about and interpreted as being part of a genre of horror. Isabel Christina Pinedo, in *Recreational Terror: Women and the Pleasure of Horror Film Viewing*, capably synthesizes the range of horror considerations, defining the genre according to five key descriptors: (1) horror disrupts the everyday world; (2) it transgresses and violates boundaries;

(3) it upsets the validity of rationality; (4) it resists narrative closure; and (5) it works to evoke fear.[22] Indeed, in this book, I believe it is most productive to approach our understanding of horror films through a collection of considerations. In doing so, I attempt to avoid the traps and limits of fixing categories, while giving credence to a textual openness and ambiguity, or polysemy.

There is much to consider when exploring horror, and there are some limitations to my examination. In my critical-cultural/critical race approach, I notably omit the psychoanalytic as well as the aggression and violence emphases that have worked to define horror film scholarship. My query into cultural identity and mediated messages presents a different interest from those questions focusing on the effects of terror and violence on viewers' real-life psychology or blood lust. While my disengagement with psychoanalysis is guided by my culturally focused research questions, Hutchings presents a more pessimistic view of psychoanalytic readings, describing such film criticism as "deeply problematic" in great part because of its struggle with "notions of the collective, the economic, the technological, the historical, and race and class"[23] Jonathan Lake Crane, in *Terror and Everyday Life*, similarly expresses doubts about focusing on "screen violence ... libidinal desire or some other variation of psychic upheaval."[24]

Another hallmark of the horror genre is its complexity. Just as it can contribute the most rousing, heroic, and imaginative narratives, it can also generate films featuring chilling, abhorrent, unspeakable violence. It cannot be ignored that physical and emotional violence are often central to the horror film genre. While (hyper)violent dramatic films out of the crime, thriller, and war genres such as *Pulp Fiction*, *Saving Private Ryan*, and *No Country for Old Men* have been met with some critical acclaim and are often spared the scholarly detour through experimental effects research on aggression and psychological disturbance, horror's reliance on violence as a key narrative device cannot be overlooked. There is an acknowledgment here that it is not simply the bloodshed that makes a horror film a horror film, rather "it is the nihilistic context in which this violence occurs" that makes the horror film.[25] It is easy to see how horror's violence has come to be seen as lacking in any illuminating value. Perhaps we have the slasher-splatter films of the 1980s to thank for that (e.g. *Prom Night* [1980]). However, what is observed here is that in many instances violence in Blackness and horror function together to provide important discursive inroads, such as violence as exhibiting a sort of "return of the re/oppressed." Here, violence, be it gratuitous or declarative, will not overshadow the revelatory Blackness narratives that horror has to offer.

Blacks *in* Horror Films (vs. *Black* Horror Films)

This book contributes to the horror genre dialogue by offering two additional categories to the lexicon. The first is "Blacks *in* horror" films, and the second is "*Black* horror" films.

"Blacks in horror" films present Blacks and Blackness in the context of horror, even if the horror film is not wholly or substantially focused on either one. Nevertheless, these films possess a particular discursive power in their treatment of Blackness. These horror films are often major studio products, though certainly not universally. These films have historically, and typically, been produced by non-Black filmmakers for mainstream consumption. "Blacks in horror" films present some of the most important images in understanding how Blackness is represented. Examples of "Blacks in horror" films that will be discussed in this book include *King Kong* (1933), *Night of the Living Dead* (1968), *The Serpent and the Rainbow* (1988), and *Candyman* (1992). The tie that binds many of these films, first, is that they tend to provoke a consensus agreement of what makes horror films—they disrupt our notions of a rational, fear-free, everyday life. Second, these films have contributed significantly to discussions and debates regarding not only Blackness, but also its proximity to interpretations of what is horrifying and where it is embodied. These are films that often "code the monster as racial Other associated with a powerful savage religion."[26] Indeed, we see the racial Other in films such as *Candyman*, and Black religion as powerful and savage in the ilk of *The Serpent and the Rainbow*. In addition, these films are "now more hyperbolically concerned than ever with the question of difference" (cited in Grant 2).[27]

What is not included in this book are those horror films that do not provide significant insight into the legacy of Blackness' relationship to the horrifying. I exclude those films where Black characters are incidental or token and where a commentary on Blackness—except to say that it has fleeting relevance—is absent. Insertions of Blacks in films such as *Firestarter* (1984) or *Wishmaster* (1997), in which they are relegated "to the status of victims, largely undeveloped expendable characters,"[28] are omitted from this analysis. Still, there are cases included here of films that speak quite loudly about Blackness, even through its exclusion. The wholesale omission of Blacks and Blackness reveals much about our American culture at different points in history. For example, there are intriguing reasons that there are few or no Blacks in the 1980s suburbs which monsters Freddy Krueger and Michael Myers haunt and where they hunt. This means that a film need not have a Black character to have something to say about or against Blackness. Included will be discussions of films that seem to offer metaphors of race as well. *Creature from the Black Lagoon* (1954), in particular, is a film that lacks a significant on-screen Black presence but merits attention, as it contains the modern, Western White hero whose mission is to protect a similarly situated White woman from a primordial black monster.[29]

It is also worth considering film's notion of what good and evil look like. This means, in one instance, that there are some donors to "Blacks in horror" films that merit attention because of their significant contributions to our understanding of Blackness-as-monstrosity. The pro-Ku Klux Klan, Civil War epic

The Birth of a Nation (1915) is one film that soundly casts Blacks as horrific figures—they are monstrous, savage boogeymen (often, literally men) with troublesome cultural practices. Thus, in this book the "Blacks in horror" films definition at times reaches beyond traditional expectations of what would typically constitute a horror film to reveal how—in form and process—that which horrifies is solidified in the imagination.

Inevitably, someone will wonder why one film or another did not make it into the book. The criterion for inclusion employed here is one of salience in exemplifying the historical eras and themes that the films themselves have worked to create and inform. There is no goal to be encyclopedic.

Black Horror Films (vs. Blacks *in* Horror Films)

There is a second kind of film addressed in this book, and that is "Black horror" films. Black horror films are informed by many of the same indicators of horror films, such as disruption, monstrosities, and fear. However, Black horror films are often "race" films. That is, they have an added narrative focus that calls attention to racial identity, in this case Blackness—Black culture, history, ideologies, experiences, politics, language, humor, aesthetics, style, music, and the like. Black films, Cripps writes (and cautions):

> have a black producer, director, and writer, or black performers; that speak to black audiences or, incidentally, to white audiences possessed of preternatural curiosity, attentiveness, or sensibility toward racial matters; and that emerge from self-conscious intentions, whether artistic or political, to illuminate the Afro-American experience.... If we were to bring this definition to a fine pinpoint, we should argue forever over who has the right to dance on the head of the pin.[30]

In short, Blacks may appear in all manner of horror films, but the films themselves may not be *Black*, per se, in their relation to the filmmaker, audience, or the experience they present. It is worth noting Yearwood's point that the complexions of the filmmaker and the audience are not sufficient measures of Black film, horror or otherwise. Black film is about Black experiences and Black cultural traditions—a Black cultural milieu and history swirling around and impacting Blacks' lives in America. As tough as Black film is to define, this does not mean it does not exist, only that it is a dynamic thing out of which new aesthetics and boundaries emerge.[31]

In this book, *Def by Temptation* (1990) is a "Black horror" film. It is offered by Black image-makers: James Bond III is writer, director, and producer, and Ernest R. Dickerson is cinematographer. It presents an all-Black cast, including Bond, Kadeem Hardison, and Samuel L. Jackson. It hails a Black audience as it features R&B singers Melba Moore and Freddie Jackson, and draws on specific tropes of Black culture—it invokes Southern Black church rituals, Black urban spaces, Black masculinity performances, and Black vernacular, music, style, and other aesthetic features. Though, it should be noted that not all these features need to be present for a film to be "Black."

By contrast, there are horror films that turn attention to Blackness but fall short of being Black films. The film *The People Under the Stairs* (1991) is offered by a non-Black image-maker (Wes Craven). It is notable for its character "Fool," a Black child-thief, as the film's protagonist. But, the film also co-stars a White incestuous couple, "Mom" and "Dad," who are the grotesque antagonists. *The People Under the Stairs* implicates Mom and Dad as slumlords in an impoverished predominately Black neighborhood. Beyond Black thieves and the Black poor, the narrative focus is on Mom, Dad, and a White "daughter," Alice, who has been abducted and subjected to abuse. As such, *People Under the Stairs* is a rather Whiteness affair with a predominantly White cast, crew, and textual thrust. By my measure, it is a Blacks *in* horror film effort. However, where both films, *Def* and *People*, are similar is that, as Tony Williams argues, like many other horror films they contain "themes highly relevant to audiences occupying marginal positions in society."[32]

Another Craven-directed film, *A Vampire in Brooklyn* (1995), was written by African Americans Eddie and Charlie Murphy and Vernon Lynch. The film stars, in addition to Eddie Murphy, Black actors Angela Bassett, Allen Payne, Kadeem Hardison, and John Witherspoon. The film connects the Caribbean to a Black neighborhood in Brooklyn, presents Black arts forms, and relies on culturally derived humor. Here, *A Vampire in Brooklyn* is treated as a *Black* horror film. It is worth remembering, then, as film scholar Ed Guerrero writes in *Framing Blackness*, that "no Hollywood film of any Black image is the result of a single individual's inspiration or effort, but is a collaborative venture in which aesthetics, economics and politics share (sometimes antagonistically) influences."[33]

Together, "Blacks in horror" films and "Black horror" films offer up an extraordinary opportunity for an examination into how race, racial identities, and race relationships are constructed and depicted. Perhaps most interesting for both types of films is when and how they variously position Blacks as the thing that horrifies, or as the victim or that which is horrified. The horror genre's unique narrative, aesthetic, and commercial qualities provide for the notion that "the genre, now more than ever, is proving 'useful' in addressing the dilemmas of difference."[34] Certainly horror has always been attentive to social problems in rather provocative ways. However, this moment in American social politics—at the intersections of media globalization, identity formation, performance, and circulation, understandings of race (Blackness in particular and the notion of a post-racial era), and the access to and use of new technologies—is one ideal moment for digging into this filmmaking, race-making, and ideology-making phenomenon.

Epistemological Flow

Horror Noire is guided by several basic assumptions. The first is that the study of race continues to matter. In W.E.B. Du Bois' 1920 tome *Darkwater: Voices from Within the Veil*, Du Bois offers that he finds himself, in focusing on race in America, (sadly) again writing on a theme "on which great souls have already said great words."[35] The theme of race fails to exhaust itself for Du Bois for the very same reasons that pressed him into writing about race in the first place—the ever-present problem of the color line. The "strange meaning of being Black" at the dawning of the twentieth century when Du Bois was writing has followed us into the twenty-first century as well. That "strange meaning" of being Black in this millennium continues to be, in part, about "the problem of the color line" (contrary to recent proclamations of a "post-racial" society). It is a problem that is still exacerbated by a "sense of always looking at one's self through the eyes of others, of measuring one's soul by the tape of a world that looks on in amused contempt and pity."[36] For film historian Thomas Cripps, Hollywood film "from its very beginnings" played a role in sharpening the distinction of the color line, while working effectively to circulate society's racial beliefs and angst.[37] This book also takes on a number of "-isms." It interrogates the consequences of racism, sexism, classism, heterosexism, separatism, notions of the masculine and masculinity, and of feminism and femininity. Noted feminist scholars Patricia Hill Collins and bell hooks demand that we tune into interconnections and intersections between dominant discourses around race, class, gender, and sexualities. As such, this is a Black/feminist informed project in which Blacks are identified as subjects, not only objects (which is also the case in many of these films); the historical reality of Blackness according to film is defined and exposed; and the Black horror film story is told from the vantage point of empowerment and with a goal of consciousness raising.[38]

This book also extends Clover's essay "Her Body, Himself: Gender in the Slasher Film"[39] and Pinedo, who, in *Recreational Terror: Women and the Pleasures of Horror Film Viewing*,[40] argues that there is much more to horror films than misogyny and violent, voyeuristic gazes. While these, and other troubling instances of "-isms" are found in the films, this book argues that there are also opportunities, if not wholesale efforts, within some of these films to disrupt or eviscerate our assumptive, dominant views of each others' place in the world. Troubling issues of taint, darkness, or buffoonery are *not* the singular purview of this book. Rather, horror has also been a vehicle to take up all sorts of topics of empowerment, revolution, and rewriting the sites for heroism and evil. "Although direct parallels between social forces and popular culture are risky at best," presented here are two distinctive understandings of how Blacks' participation in the horror film functions.[41] In the first instance, Blacks have been rendered deficient—childlike, carrying taint, lower in socioeconomic standing, a metaphor and catalyst for evil, and demonized, even though not always cast, physically, in the role of demon. In the second understanding, this book works to reveal how the horror genre has the potential to shed encumbrances of African American representations rooted in, and derived from, a sort of "fin-de-siecle minstrelsy."[42] Rather, Blackness can be seen as mature, God-fearing and otherwise resistant to evil, whole and full, wise and aged, in full combat against evil, and at or near the center of constructions of goodness.

A Century of Black Horror

Chapter 1, "The Birth of the Black Boogeyman: Pre-1930s," begins with silent films and "anthropological" shorts such as 1895's *Native Woman Washing a Negro Baby in Nassau* to situate how Blacks were represented and Blackness was understood in film's earliest years. This chapter describes how early (Black face) films such as 1904's A *Nigger in the Woodpile* were presented as comedy shorts for non-Black audiences, but could also be interpreted as horror with their depiction of violent, lawless assaults against Black communities. These films not only reflected the sensibilities of the time, but also presented devastating lessons in turn of the twentieth century racial hierarchy and White supremacy. This chapter also examines the use of horror conventions by filmmaking innovators George Méliès, an illusionist and filmmaker who introduced one of the earliest "Blacks in horror" films on record, and D.W. Griffith, a film director who offered one of the most insidious and long-lasting understandings of Blacks as, quite literally, *bêtes noires*, or black beasts. This era in filmmaking is also noteworthy for its seminal contributions to entertainment media by this country's pioneer Black filmmakers who sought to challenge the myriad, damaging discourses of Blackness-as-evil.

This chapter reveals that Black filmmakers, such as John W. Noble and Oscar Micheaux, through *The Birth of a Race* (1918) and *Within Our Gates* (1920), respectively, worked to counter racist imagery by presenting Blacks on the big screen as complex, developed figures.

Chapter 2, "Jungle Fever—A Horror Romance: 1930s," reveals horror's fascination with predatory primates, as well its troublesome narrative tendency to identify apes and Blacks as being virtually inseparable on the evolutionary scale. Apes and Blacks in these "Blacks in horror" films are linked, as some have correctly observed with the representation of *King Kong* (1933). Also, during this period they are explicitly (literally and figuratively) linked through biology—that is, Blacks and apes are presented as procreating (bestiality), thereby producing progeny of Blacks/apes who are indistinguishable in their primitiveness. The chapter then turns to the island of Hispaniola, and the country of Haiti. Haiti saw African slave laborers bring with them cultural practices that were thought to be at best foreign, at worst deficient, by French, Spanish, U.S., and British colonists. African folkways and religions were imagistically exoticized and distorted during this decade in seminal films such as *White Zombie* (1932).

In the third chapter, "Horrifying Goons and Minstrel Coons: 1940s," I examine the transition horror films make from marking Blacks as a deadly serious symbol of evil (e.g. wicked Voodoo practioners) to adopting a stance of Blacks as a people to be dismissively laughed at and ridiculed. Exploring the presence and use of Blacks as comic relief in horror, this chapter focuses on the contributions of character actors such as Willie "Sleep 'n' Eat" Best and Mantan Moreland and their minstrelsy-informed performances (e.g. *King of the Zombies* [1941]). Next, the chapter attends to the quantitatively growing, qualitatively powerful presence of "Black horror" films. These films reveal a reliance on cautionary morality tales that define immorality as a gateway to supernatural evil. The films of, for example, Spencer Williams (e.g. *The Blood of Jesus* [1941]) are used to illustrate how the monstrous is defined when (race conscious) image-makers are at the creative helm.

Chapter 4, "Black Invisibility, White Science, and a Night with Ben: 1950s–1960s," tells the story of how Hollywood shifted its attention from supernatural evils toward technological ones. Enter the Atomic Age, and with it came horrifying themes of how science and technology can go astray when experimentation and discovery are left unchecked. As Americans found science laboratories to be the wellspring of things most terrifying (e.g. the fusion bomb), Hollywood deemed these spaces of intellectual and inventive achievement out of reach for Blacks (that is, in the media's imagination, Blacks could not be the analytically erudite). As a result, Blacks were omitted from the genre or relegated to the supporting role of snack food for mutant insects. *Monster from Green Hell* (1957) epitomizes this trend. In this chapter, I also detail the great cultural significance of director George Romero's cult-classic film *Night of the Living Dead* (1968), a film which directly and overtly addressed 1960s America's social problems and racial climate.

Blacks return to horror films with a vengeance (pun intended), as detailed in Chapter 5, "Scream, Whitey, Scream—Retribution, Enduring Women, and Carnality: 1970s." Here, I note the return of Blacks to horror, both "Black horror" and "Blacks in horror," through an influx of films offered, not entirely surprisingly, during the rise of the Black Power movement. Both types of horror films were deeply influenced by these times of Black nationalism, as well the lingering, graphic "television war" of Vietnam and national violence (i.e. assassinations and riots). In this chapter, I detail films which are notable for their anti-assimilationist ideologies, themes of revolution and revenge, and heroic "enduring," resilient Black women who defeat the monster and live on, ready to fight another day. I also observe how Voodoo is reclaimed in these films as a powerful weapon against racism (e.g. *Scream, Blacula, Scream* [1973] and *Sugar Hill* [1974]). Horror films from the 1970s also do not escape the label of "Blaxploitation"—the prevalence of financial, and culturally exploitative films featuring Blackness during the decade. Here, Blaxploitation-era horror films frequently advanced the notion of Black empowerment through violent revolution (e.g. *Soul Vengeance* [1975]), while simultaneously presenting anti-human rights narratives which were variously heterosexist and homophobic, hyper-masculine and misogynist. It is also noted in this chapter that though there were many horror films featuring Blackness, often they are derivative of the classics—*Blacula* (1972), *Blackenstein: The Black Frankenstein* (1973), and *Dr. Black, Mr. Hyde* (1976), all borrowing from *Dracula*, *Frankenstein*, and *Dr. Jekyll and Mr. Hyde* films.

Chapter 6, "We Always Die First—Invisibility, Racial Red-Lining, and Self-Sacrifice: 1980s," reveals a marked decline of the Black Power-inspired film themes seen in the 1970s. In the 1980s, in a notable reversal, Blacks enter into supporting relationships with (monstrous) Whites in that they display a value system of loyalty and trust that is generally disproportionate and unilateral. Notably, this loyalty is measured through the ultimate act of Black sacrifice— giving of one's own life (e.g. *The Shining* [1980]). This representational trend of Black self-sacrifice and devotion to Whites rears its head most prominently in "Blacks in horror" films. That is, Blackness is depicted as most valuable when it harkens to the value system and ideologies of (a stereotypically monolithic) Whiteness. In this chapter, I also detail how the decade of the 1980s gentrifies and segregates its Whiteness—moving White monsters and prey to the suburbs, places viewed as inaccessible to Blacks. These included suburban or rural settings such as Elm Street, Haddonville, Illinois, and Camp Crystal Lake, as represented in horror series beginning with *A Nightmare on Elm Street* (1984), *Halloween* (1978), and *Friday the 13th* (1980), respectively. Finally, in this chapter I note the return of the horror movie "short" with Michael Jackson (e.g. *Thriller* [1983]).

Chapter 7, "Black Is Back! Retribution and the Urban Terrain: 1990s," hails the return of "Black horror" films defined by the reintroduction of autonomous Black subjectivity, and the recognition of resilient, empowered characters—they represent the new race films. This chapter describes how Blackness is once again displayed as whole and full, diverse and complex, and therefore seen in horror roles and situations that have been largely elusive for Blacks over the decades. The most notable of these is *Def by Temptation* (1990), which recalls Spencer Williams' morality tales of the 1940s. Black horror films in the 1990s also offered a unique reversal of racial majority/minority roles. If Whites were presented at all, they were the ones seen in the role of sidekick or as incompetent, comic relief. During the 1990s, particularly in "Black horror," it was Whiteness that became the symbol of deficiency. In these films, there is often a self-consciousness in the narrative that makes it plain to audiences that the disruption and reversal of type is purposeful—part retribution, part forced atonement. This is most obvious in Black director Rusty Cundieff's *Tales from the Hood* (1995), in which he provides cautionary tales about protecting and saving the 'hood—Black inner-city enclaves. In all, this era describes a period in which Black characters' survival and/or demise does not rise or fall on the will and favor of non-Blacks. Films of this era additionally present the battle over good and evil as being played out *within* the confines of predominately Black, lower/working-class urban centers. So fearsome is the inner-city in the 1990s, that odd entities of all manner, such as the Predator of *Predator 2* (1990) and the children of *Children of Corn III: Urban Harvest* (1995), pay the urban centers a visit.

I conclude the book with, "Catching Some Zzzzzs—Blackz and Horror in the Twenty-First Century." Here, I present an analysis focusing largely on "Black horror" films which are inspired by hip-hop culture. This chapter details the (potentially) troublesome exaltation of Blaxploitation in films by Black film-makers, such as *Bones* (2001), directed by Ernest Dickerson and starring rapper-turned-actor Snoop Dogg. These new millennium "Black horror" films continue to present a spatial allegiance to the 'hood as seen in the 1990s. However, in the 2000s, an explicit rationale for such a geographical focus is the historical and aesthetic credibility such places promise. Films targeting the hip-hop generation quantitatively prevail at this time (e.g. *Bloodz vs. Wolvez* [2006]), and are often set, quite literally, to a hip-hop beat (e.g. *Now Eat* [2000]).

There is no dearth of "Black horror" films during this period, some of which evidence great imagination and creativity and others a great banality, due to the proliferation of underground and low-budget films earmarked for a stunningly expanding straight-to-DVD market (e.g. *Dream House* [2006]). The possibilities of liberation from the commercial mainstream and the possibilities of alternative modes of distribution are considered. I identify film production companies such as Maverick Entertainment as independent filmmakers and industry innovators who are making and distributing well-produced Black horror films. This chapter also presents a final discussion that teases out the "red thread" that runs through the preceding chapters by giving prominence to those points that work to answer the difficult questions, what does horror mean for Blackness, and what does Blackness mean for horror?

The horror film is fascinating if for no other reason than that it prides itself on snuggling up next to the taboo, while also confounding our sense of good and evil, monstrous and divine, and sacred and profane. It is one of the most intrepid of entertainment forms in its scrutiny of our humanity and our social world. It is my sincere hope that *Horror Noire: Blacks in American Horror Films from the 1890s to Present* is not regarded as the final word on Blacks' contribution to horror films. Rather, my intention and hope are to set off fierce debate, provoke incredible dissension, and to trigger even more exacting, nuanced explorations.

1

THE BIRTH OF THE BLACK BOOGEYMAN

Pre-1930s

> One only has to look up "black" in the Oxford English Dictionary to see the range of such associations as they were established by the sixteenth century; the word is used as a synonym for, among other things, malignant, sinister, foul, dismal, etc. Most tellingly, "black man" could mean either a Negro or the Devil.
>
> —Lively (14)[1]

Beginning in the mid-1800s, White men from occupations as diverse as scientist, eyeglass maker, and magician were beginning to explore film's technological boundaries and to press its storytelling ability.[2] In Europe, filmmakers were proving that whatever came out of their imaginations, film could handle. This included giving birth to (presumably) the world's first horror film proper— a two-minute, silent short entitled *Le Manoir du Diable* (*The Haunted Castle*), presented on Christmas Eve, 1896, at the Théâtre Robert-Houdin in Paris by French theater performer/magician Georges Méliès:

> A large bat flies into a medieval castle. Circling slowly, it flaps its monstrous wings and suddenly changes into Mephistopheles. Conjuring up a cauldron, the demon produces skeletons, ghosts, and witches from its bubbling contents before one of the summoned underworld cavaliers holds up a crucifix and Satan vanishes in a puff of smoke.[3]

This was the era of the silent film (late 1800s to late 1920s), a period in which the moving image could not yet be coupled with synchronized sound for mass reproduction and theatrical playback. This was also a time when to be a film-maker meant that one either had access to the (often experimental, self-invented) equipment necessary to capture a series of still images and make them move (e.g. "magic lantern" zoetropes), or possessed the capability to capture moving images using a film camera.[4] The filmmakers created what were then called "photoplays," with many of them initially only mere seconds or minutes long, thereby earning the moniker film "shorts." Films were initially watched through viewing machines such as the Kinetoscope which accommodated one viewer at a time. However, advancements in film technology rapidly evolved and the projection of moving images for large, paying audiences was accomplished in 1893. Although the films of this period were silent, it was not uncommon for them to be accompanied by live orchestral music and sound effects. "Intertitles," or stills of printed text or transcribed dialogue, were edited into the films to detail plot points while actors pantomimed their dialogue. In 1926 the first feature film with pre-recorded, synchronized sound was introduced.[5] In 1927, *The Jazz Singer* included, music, sounds, and, importantly, dialogue. From that moment on, "talkies" were a mainstay.[6]

In the early years of film, Blacks were portrayed by Whites, performing racist stereotypes while in blackface. One of the earliest known treatments of Blacks in what might be considered a horror film proper (though the term "horror" was not widely used at that time) was in the French film *Off to Bloomingdale Asylum* (1901).[7] The film was made by magician and illusionist Georges Méliès, known for his stage performances and approximately 500 short films which include themes of the supernatural and the macabre. *Asylum* is rife with ghostly figures as described in Méliès' catalog:

> An omnibus drawn by an extraordinary mechanical horse is drawn by four Negroes. The horse kicks and upsets the Negroes, who falling are changed into white clowns. They begin slapping each other's faces and by blows become black again. Kicking each other, they become white once more. Suddenly they are all merged into one gigantic Negro. When he refuses to pay his car fare the conductor sets fire to the omnibus, and the Negro bursts into a thousand pieces.[8]

The film's "Negroes" were performed by White actors in blackface, who were charged, seemingly, to depict the violence around crossing racial boundaries, the tensions around racial masquerade, and finally the brutish end to the metaphorical White man's burden with the destruction of the Negro.

American audiences were hardly left out of the early film experience. An early reference to Blacks in association with a spooky theme was in 1897 when the American film company Biograph offered a short, very likely a comedy, with the offensive title *Hallowe'en in Coontown*, thereby linking Blacks to the frightful holiday.[9] *Hallowe'en* joined the ranks of dozens of "coon" films, such as the *Wooing and Wedding of a Coon* (1907) or *Coontown Suffragettes* (1914), in which Blacks, portrayed by Whites in blackface, were comically ridiculed. The short film *Minstrels Battling in a Room* (circa 1897–1900) was narratively on the complex side. Here, Black men and women (portrayed by White men in blackface) are in what may be a nightclub, where they turn rowdy. The "Blacks" even go so far as to turn on a White man.[10] The fate of the Blacks in the film for "battling" a White man is unknown—but in fiction of the period there are dire consequences for Blacks assaulting Whites. The film's deteriorated state makes a firm conclusion impossible.[11] Indeed, many films of the pre-1950s period have been irreparably damaged or lost. The deterioration of film can be attributed to the manner in which the film itself was made—using highly flammable nitrate. G. William Jones, in *Black Cinema Treasures: Lost and Found* details the problem:

> Nitrate was used universally for 35-millimeter theatrical films until World War II. Nitrate's chemical composition is very close to the composition of gunpowder, and this sped up a transition to non-flammable acetate stock so that nitrate could go to war. … because nitrate stock has a tendency to destroy itself. First, such films become covered with a fine, yellow-brown dust as the backing begins to break down. Then, the images begin to stick to the next turn, so that unreeling the film does further damage … Finally, the film becomes a mixture of sticky, semi-solid masses awash in a puddle of dust. Estimates are that almost fifty percent of the world's pre-1950 film heritage is now gone forever—most of it due to nitrate decomposition.[12]

Some films did survive. For example, in 1898 directors Edwin S. Porter and George S. Fleming, working under the auspices of the Edison Manufacturing Company, filmed *Shooting Captured Insurgents*. This was real footage of four White soldiers executing four Black men. In doing so, Edison's company may have produced one of two of America's earliest, grisly horrifying shorts. The second is the 1898 short documentary *An Execution by Hanging*. The film company, Biograph, hailed *Execution*, which documented the hanging death of a Black man in a Jacksonville, Florida jail, as the only live hanging ever captured on film. Butters describes the scenes as "explicit" and "ghastly":

> the executioner adjusts a black cap over the prisoner's head. The noose is placed over his neck. After the man is hung, his body quivers and shakes from the tension. The nostalgic claim of the innocence of early silent cinema is clearly broken by this film. The death of an African-American man is clearly on the screen. His crime is never announced; his punishment is all the spectator understands.[13]

"Real" Blacks, not Whites in blackface, were frequently seen in silent, ethnographic films which were defined by scenes of people going about their daily lives while a White, male "adventurer"/filmmaker documented their activities. These representations were hardly "real," however, as they served the function of casting Blacks as Others—curiosities and oddities so markedly different from Whites that their most mundane habits must be documented and exhibited as if Blacks were animals in a zoo. The footage appears, at times, to be surreptitiously shot, unbeknownst to its Black "star," or at other times the films' subjects seem to go about their business conscious of, but in spite of, the camera trained upon them. In 1895, shorts such as *Native Woman Coaling a Ship at St. Thomas*, *Native Woman Washing a Negro Baby in Nassau*, and *Native Woman Washing Clothes at St. Vincent* all present Blacks going about routines, as selected by the filmmaker. Musser warns that these images did not present "a kind of primitive, nonracist innocence," as they are far from benign documentaries.[14] These perspectives of Blacks as odd and primitive would become a mainstay in horror over the next century, particularly in films which depict Blacks as savage, deadly natives (e.g. *Black Moon* [1934]).

Often, the films focused on a narrow range of Black activities, many of which were set up by the filmmaker. For example, there was *The Watermelon Contest* (1895), featuring a group of Black men prompted to race one another to finish a large piece of the fruit. Edison (1898) and German émigré Sigmund Lubin (1903) both produced films called *Buck Dance*. Lubin described his version as featuring "a number of smokes dancing for their favorite watermelon."[15] Oddly, the films of the early twentieth century spoke volumes about what White filmmakers obsessed over as it pertained to Blacks—watermelon and chicken (e.g. *Watermelon Feast* [1903]; *Who Said Chicken?* [circa 1910]). Over the coming decades horror would appropriate such stereotypes, with Blacks' love for melon and chicken being depicted as a powerful distraction from the monsters chasing them. To illustrate, years later, in the comedy-horror film *Boys of the City* (1940), the Black character Scruno (Ernest "Sunshine Sammy" Morrison) would halt his quaking with fear over a ghost just long enough to sing the praises of, and to eat, watermelon.

The Black world, according to the early film shorts, was quite narrowly defined in class, status, and contribution. Blacks were often depicted outdoors rather than in homes. Their work, when they did it, was of a laboring kind. Intimate images of the Black family were elusive. Lubin offered *In Zululand* (1915), described as "cartoon humor," in which Black women dress up as ghosts to frighten a relative from marrying a "good-for-nothing-nigger."[16] Lloyd Ingraham's *Hoodoo Ann* (1916) also has a wedding theme. A woman, Ann (Mae Marsh), enlists her maid, Black Cindy (Madame Sul-Te-Wan), to help her rid herself of a curse so that on her wedding day "the wedding of Ann is the funeral of the hoodoo."[17] Viewers were given no hint that there were Black intellectuals such as W.E.B. Du Bois, Booker T. Washington, Ida B. Wells, James Weldon Johnson, and Nannie Helen Burroughs. In these shorts, there were no poets, politicians, journalists, Harvard Ph.D.s, college presidents, or human rights activists. Still, perhaps an absence of references to Blacks would have been preferable given the alternative, as evidenced by the representation of the Black clergy in 1904's *A Nigger in the Woodpile*.

A Nigger in the Woodpile was not inscribed with the tropes of the horror genre. However, it can be interpreted as horrifying all the same. In the film, a Black church deacon (played by a White actor in blackface) is depicted as the frequent purloiner of a White farmer's firewood. Hoping to put an end to the theft, the farmer replaces a cord of wood with sticks of dynamite. As expected, the deacon comes along to steal the wood, and unbeknownst to him, picks up the explosives as well. The deacon is shown returning home, stopping to greet his wife (also a White male actor in blackface for gender annihilation, as well) who is cooking in the kitchen, and then placing the "wood" into their fireplace. The home explodes around them, leaving the couple, charred from the fire, to stagger about the ruins of their home. Then, the White farmer arrives, joined by a White male helper. They take hold of the deacon, dragging him off. Perhaps the farmers plan to take the Deacon to the proper legal authorities for charges (as if the bombing of his home was not punishment enough); however, the real-life 1904 context of the film belies imagining such a conclusion. Rather, this was a period when lynchings were rampant and militant White supremacists terrorized Blacks.

For much of the early 1900s, the generic qualities of horror went uncharted. The concept of a "horror" film did not enter into the popular lexicon until the 1930s. However, the generic elements of horror are visible from film's start, to include the fantastical, battles between good and evil, disruption of the everyday and rationality, and, of course, the invoking of fear. How Blacks secured their place in the genre and the nature of those representations requires an exploration into the early days of American film, during which the notion of Blackness-as-monstrous was introduced.

Though such representations of Blackness were first conceptualized outside of the horror genre, such images made a significant contribution to horror, and continue even today to figure prominently in American cinema's notion of what is most horrific in our society. They function as key reminders of the little value placed on Black life, and could be interpreted as horrifying. Butters notes that the actions depicted in films such as *A Nigger in the Woodpile* can be easily dismissed by some: "one can argue that violent depictions of African Americans were simply part of the slapstick tradition of comedy that dominated early screen portrayals. Slapstick comedy … involves cruel humor and violence."[18] However, the film also exploits anxieties about Blacks and stereotypes of Black criminality to evoke fears among Whites about the unsettling presence of the "niggers" among them.[19]

The filmmaker Lubin, known for his stereotype-laden Sambo and Rastus film series introduced around 1909, united horror and slapstick with real Black actors as stars to offer one of the first "Black horror" films. The 1915 horror-comedy production *The Undertaker's Daughter*, directed by Willard Louis, is a short, silent film starring John Edwards and Mattie Edwards. According to Lubin's publicity material, *Daughter* told the following story:

> Mattie Cook, the Undertaker's daughter, loves John Scott, who has no job, but father wants her to marry Sime Sloan, who has one and it takes all of Mattie's persuasive power to overcome Dad, but she is equal to the occasion. She gets rid of Sime and Bime [other suitors] by promising to marry them if they will prove their love for her. One must sleep in one of her father's coffins and the other sit by it all night. [With the help of noise and John, she gets rid of them.] In their fright they run through the meeting house presided over by Dad, who gets a couple of spills. He finally decides that John is the most sensible and can help in the under-taking business.[20]

The stars of the film, John and Mattie, who were part of the "Negro stock company of the comedy section of the Lubin Company," would appear in two other films together. Mattie would go on to make appearances in two films by the Black director Oscar Micheaux.[21]

D.W. Griffith and *The Birth of a Nation*: Making Blacks Horrifying

> It is the racist who creates his inferior.
>
> —Fanon (93)[22]

D.W. (David Llewelyn Wark) Griffith was born in 1875 in La Grange, Kentucky, to a Confederate Army officer turned state legislator. During Reconstruction in 1885, while the Griffith family was experiencing significant financial hardship, the family patriarch died. After dropping out of school to help support his family, Griffith eventually turned his sights to becoming a playwright. Both theater and film were acceptable career paths for Griffith, and he pursued writing and acting for both the stage and screen. Griffith was said to be a marginal writer, and his scripts were often rejected. In 1907, after a move to California, Griffith failed to sell his scripts to Edwin Porter, the famed director under (Thomas) Edison Manufacturing. In 1908, Griffith went to see Sigmund Lubin for a job. Griffith's application was rejected. Griffith then traveled to New York, finally landing an acting job with Biograph Company in 1908. Shortly thereafter, Griffith was permitted to direct at Biograph, and over the next five years made an astonishing 450 short films in which he honed his camerawork and editing skills, including techniques like cutting, cross-cutting, and close-ups. In 1913, as a productive, successful director, Griffith left Biograph to start his own

Reliance-Majestic Studios. It was through his Reliance studio that Griffith made *The Birth of a Nation*.

D.W. Griffith's *The Birth of a Nation* (1915) did not showcase his writing skills, or the lack thereof. Rather, the film's script was primarily based on two Thomas Dixon, Jr. pro-White supremacy, terrorist-themed novels, 1901's *The Leopard's Spots: A Romance of the White Man's Burden* and 1905's *The Clansman: An Historical Romance of the Ku Klux Klan*. Dixon was described favorably in a magazine as a "preacher, lecturer, novelist, and Southern country gentleman long known for the earnestness, we might say fanaticism with which he deals with ... the Negro problem."[23]

Griffith paid Dixon a few thousand dollars, as well as a portion of the profits, in return for Dixon's stories and consultation. In return, Dixon also became integral to the promotion of the film. It was Dixon who got the film screened in the White House for President Woodrow Wilson, who said of the film, in part, "And my only regret is that it is all so terribly true."[24] Together, Griffith and Dixon earned millions from the film.

The Birth of the Black Boogeyman

The film *The Birth of a Nation* tells the story of two families—the Southern Camerons and the Northern Stonemans—during the Civil War and Reconstruction period. The drawn-out film plot, at three hours, is rather straight-forward. The first part of the film tells Griffith's version of the history of the end of the Civil War and President Abraham Lincoln's assassination. The second part of the film is about "race and revenge," with Southern Whites, good-hearted Northerners, and loyal Black servants bonding.[25]

The Camerons live in the town of Piedmont, and are former slave owners. Theirs is a distinguished family full of war heroes and doting, supportive women. The Stoneman family are their friends from Pennsylvania, who are led by the family patriarch, Congressman Austin Stoneman (Ralph Lewis). Stoneman is an abolitionist who, in spite of being an influential politician, is also depicted as weak and demasculinized—he is sickly, wifeless, possesses a clubfoot which gives him a pronounced limp, and is depicted as an integrationist who has been ideologically duped by Blacks. The Cameron family includes three sons who all join the Confederate army. Two of the Cameron sons are killed in the Civil War. One son, Ben (Henry Walthall), becomes a war hero and is dubbed "the Little Colonel." The Little Colonel (as he is referred to for the remainder of the movie) is sent to a Northern hospital to recover from his wounds, where he meets Elsie Stoneman (Lillian Gish) and falls in love. The Stoneman family has two sons who join the Union. One son is killed, the other son falls in love with Margaret Cameron (Miriam Cooper), whom he meets during a visit to the Cameron home. Liberal Northern politicians such as Stoneman are depicted as being displeased with the South for attempting to secede from the rest of the country. Stoneman even imports to Piedmont a "mulatto" named Silas Lynch (George Siegmann) to assist in the integration effort.

According to film historian Ed Guerrero, *Birth* was the first true feature-length film made in America, setting the "technical and narrative standard for the industry" while carrying on the Hollywood trend of uniformly devaluing African Americans as "buffoons, servants, and a variety of subordinates."[26] The principal Black characters in *Birth* are presented by Whites in blackface. They include: Gus (Walter Long), a Union soldier who is lynched by the Ku Klux Klan for making advances at Flora "Little Sister" Cameron (Mae Marsh), a very young girl; Silas Lynch, a corrupt politician; Lydia (Mary Alden), a wicked "mulatto" woman who kidnaps and ties up Elsie because Lynch desires the White woman; and Mammy (Jennie Lee) and Tom (Thomas Wilson), two former slaves who are diehard loyalists to the Cameron family and remain as servants. These characters are joined by a host of extras, some of whom are played by real Black actors, portraying corrupt politicians, robbers, would-be rapists, arsonists, cheats, and (attempted) murderers.

The Birth of a Nation's definition of Blacks and Blackness is extraordinarily troublesome. Viewers' initial introduction to Blackness, and the prompt to associate Black culture with monstrosity, comes when Black Union soldiers arrive in the town of Piedmont as a marauding gang, looting and bringing destruction, as they "enter the town like *monsters*," preying upon the White innocents.[27] They are contrasted with the White confederate soldiers, who are beleaguered and war-torn, as well as honest and committed to protecting their (White) land and (White) families. While the violence of the Civil War was terrifying, its true horror, according to the film, came after in the form of unchecked, freed Black men. For example, in one scene, the Little Colonel is standing on a sidewalk. Blacks bully their way through, forcing the Little Colonel to cede the sidewalk by jumping out of harm's way. At this spectacle, Lynch proclaims, "This sidewalk belongs to us as much as it does to you, Colonel Cameron." However, as Griffith depicts the scene, there can be no expectation that any viewer would find the behavior of the Black men, or Lynch's reaction to it, equitable. As such, Griffith portrays Blacks as wolves overtaking the sheep.

If Blacks are the wolves in Griffith's movie, they are not averse to eating their own. In one scene, when Mammy meets the Black Northern servant of the Stonemans, she kicks him in his butt while proclaiming: "Dem free Niggers fom de North sure am crazy." In another, much more violent scene, when the loyal ("Uncle") Tom character refuses to side with the interloping Black Union soldiers, they string Tom up by his arms in a tree and whip him, evoking powerful lynching symbolism. When a White man tries to rescue Tom, the White man is shot by the Blacks.

Blacks also have a taste for booze and chicken, as Griffith depicts in a scene entitled "The Riot in the Master Hall—The Negro Party in Control of the State House of Representatives." The scene, at first, is to be understood as sadly comical. A collection of Black men (depicted by Black actors) are assembled in the legislature; they begin misbehaving—one sneaks bites of chicken, another takes off his shoes, plopping his filthy bare feet atop his desk, yet another sneaks gulps from a bottle of booze. The men are to be viewed as pitifully inept. That is, until they pass legislation permitting interracial marriage. With White men and women witnessing the vote high in the Whites' section of the hall's balcony (a sort of reverse Jim Crow segregation as depicted by Griffith), the Black men turn to look upon the White women. The scene has the Black men now less interested in the flesh of chicken and more excited about the flesh of White women.

However, it is in the film's most startling and infamous sequence, "The Grim Reaping," that Griffith works to solidify the idea that Black is horrifying. Gus "the renegade," as he is called in the film, is eager to take advantage of his recent freedom as well as the new interracial marriage law. He settles on a child, the youngest Cameron daughter, "Little Sister." Little Sister is shown playing alone in the woods, as Gus stalks her. Finally, he approaches and says: "You see, I'm a captain now and I want to marry," and then touches the girl's arm. The chase is on as Little Sister breaks away and runs, panic stricken. With Gus in pursuit, Little Sister flees deeper into the woods until she reaches the edge of a precipice. Seeing Gus as a fate worse than death, Little Sister throws herself over. Shortly thereafter, in her dying breath, Little Sister reveals to the Little Colonel that Gus was her tormentor. That Gus is to be viewed as a Black male sexual predator advancing on White womanhood is clear. In Dixon's book *The Clansman*, rape is actual, not implied as in the film, with the Black male predator associated with a monster: "the black claws of the beast sank into the soft white throat."[28] The film was made during a time when a Black man merely looking at a White woman ("eye rape") resulted in a lynching. The impact of these racist scenes housed in one of America's most technologically important films is a wicked bell that cannot be unrung. Even today, Black representations draw from those created and popularized by Griffith (and Dixon). Blackness was effectively transmogrified, with Blacks becoming one of the most loathsome and feared of all creatures.

Griffith's attack against Blackness did not stop there. Griffith continued to play on the "myth of the Negro's high-powered sexuality" and the idea that "every black man longs for a white woman" through the character of Lynch.[29] When Lynch goes beyond merely touching a White woman's arm, as Gus did, to holding hostage and groping Elsie there could be no confusion that Griffith sought to indict all Black men (even "mulattoes") as dangerous rapists. The actions of the likes of Gus and Lynch justify the rise of the Ku Klux Klan— "Brethren, this flag bears the red stain of the life of a Southern woman, a priceless sacrifice on the altar of an outraged civilization"—and the hate group does not disappoint as they lynch Gus and (off screen) Lynch.

FIGURE 1.1 Gus meets his doom at the hands of the KKK in *The Birth of a Nation*
David W. Griffith Corp./Photofest

Bogle (1993) confirms that Griffith's construction of the Black man as beast was purposeful:

> Lillian Gish's comments in the January 1937 issue of *Stage* verify the fact that Griffith was well aware of the contrast and that he used it to arouse his audience. Said Gish: But one day while we were rehearsing the scene where the colored man picks up the Northern girl gorilla-fashion, my hair, which was very blond, fell far below my waist and Griffith, seeing the contrast in the two figures, assigned me to play Elsie Stoneman.[30]

Only six years old, the NAACP Civil Rights organization faced the challenge of getting the film banned. Dixon ran an end run around the NAACP, taking the film to the White House to screen for President Wilson and his family, as well as the Supreme Court and members of Congress.[31] After viewing the film, President Wilson, a historian, said, "it's like writing history with lightening."[32] With the President's famous endorsement of the film, distributors charged a premium $2 admission price to an estimated three million people in New York City alone, over 11 months and 6,266 screenings.[33]

Griffith was not done imagistically abusing Blacks. In 1922, he made a comedy-horror film with Black characters entitled *One Exciting Night*, about a haunted house. "The black characters," writes Cripps, "were strikingly off the mark. The central character, an improbable detective, was a 'Kaffir, the dark terror of the bootleg gang.' The remaining Black roles were played by blackfaced Whites as traditional servile flunkies, who trailed through the plot."[34] Peter Noble adds to this description while indicting Griffith:

> This comedy is a noteworthy instance of how a director steeped in anti-Negro prejudice can influence his audience. The Negro character in *One Exciting Night* [played by a White actor in blackface] commenced the long line of those well-known screen puppets, the cowardly Black men whose hair turns white or stands on end when they meet danger in any form. We know them well by now; they are afraid of the dark, of thunderstorms, of firearms, of animals, of police, and so on. ... In *The Birth of a Nation* he portrayed the coloured man with hatred, and seven years later, in *One Exciting Night*, with contempt.[35]

In spite of protests against his films and even an unpleasant encounter with his Black maid—who said, "it hurt me, Mr. David, to see what you do to my people,"—Griffith refused to acknowledge the harm caused by his films.[36]

Gus as (Frankenstein's) Monster

To borrow a phrase from Carol Clover, author of *Men, Women, and Chain Saws: Gender in the Modern Horror Film*, "but where exactly is the horror here?"[37] To understand *The Birth of a Nation*'s racialization of Blackness as horror, it is useful and illustrative to compare the film's infamous sequence "The Grim Reaping," with Gus as a monster in pursuit of a White girl resulting in her death, with that of a similarly notable scene in an undisputed horror film, *Frankenstein* (1931), in which the Monster kills a White girl.[38] Though the films appear nearly 15 years apart, spanning the silent and sound eras, such a comparison is apropos as both films capably center the audience's attention on a dangerous thing, highlighting and signifying monstrosity through the juxtaposition of a triumvirate of purity—Whiteness, womanhood, and child. What becomes central is how these films variously treat their monsters and how they ask the audience to feel about them.

In *Frankenstein* (there are no Blacks in this movie) a young medical scientist, Dr. Henry Frankenstein (Colin Clive), recreates a man out of scavenged body parts and animates him with electricity. Dr. Frankenstein creates the man (henceforth "the Monster") over the objections of his fiancée, Elizabeth (Mae Clarke), and his former professor, Dr. Waldman (Edward Van Sloan). The cultured, enlightened Frankenstein has a helper, Fritz, who is lacking in both culture and enlightenment. Fritz (Dwight Frye) is marked as aberrant by his deformities (a hunched back and facial scars), and cruelly delights in torturing the Monster (Boris Karloff).

The Monster is hidden away in the cellar of Frankenstein's laboratory, but is unprotected from Fritz, who torments him with a flaming torch. When the Monster's fear of fire is misinterpreted as unfettered rage, Frankenstein and Waldman decide that the Monster must be restrained. The Monster is then confined to the cellar and put into chains. While chained, the Monster is again threatened by Fritz and in self-defense kills his attacker. Discovering the murder, Frankenstein and Waldman drug the Monster, and Waldman prepares to disassemble the creature. Just as Waldman is about to begin the surgery, the Monster awakes and in another moment of self-preservation, he kills Waldman. The Monster escapes the confines of Frankenstein's laboratory, and sets out to explore the world. The Monster encounters Maria (Marilyn Harris), a young girl playing alone near a lake, who invites him to join her in play. The beast and the girl engage in a game of tossing pretty flowers into the lake to watch them float. The Monster, thinking all beautiful things float, picks up Maria and tosses her into the lake, discovering too late that he has made a deadly mistake. The gaff is devastating:

> the Creature was not acting with evil intent. He errs in logic but not in feeling. His actions are the natural consequence of trying to figure out how he should play with the girl. He meant to treat her as delicately as she treated the lovely mountain wildflowers. She perishes, and the Creature is doomed for the crimes of being both a monstrosity and a child murderer.[39]

The Monster goes to Frankenstein's home and peers into Elizabeth's bedroom, where she is frightened enough by his looking upon her to scream and faint. Her screams send the Monster fleeing into the countryside. In the meantime, Maria's peasant father has recovered her body, taking it to the doorstep of Frankenstein, whom he holds responsible for the girl's death. The father is followed by a mob intent on destroying the Monster. In the film's final scenes, the Monster is surrounded and trapped in an old mill. The Monster, who is miserable and distraught over what he now understands himself to be, directs his anger toward Frankenstein. The Monster grabs the doctor and throws him to his death. The mob then sets fire to the mill, thereby destroying the Monster. What made the Monster unique, and thereby dissimilar to *The Birth of a Nation*'s "monsters," such as Gus and Lynch, was the narrative technique of demanding that the audience sympathize with the beast and its miserable plight because "a monster who loathes his own life and contemplates existence with a downcast eye exhibits troubling parallels with depressed humans."[40] Unlike the Monster, Gus and Lynch are far from sympathetic characters. Their predicament is the arrogantly presumptuous belief that a power grab, as well as a literal grab of White women, is within reach. More, Gus and Lynch's "failing," which

FIGURE 1.2 The Monster and Maria in *Frankenstein*
Universal/Photofest

functions to raise ire, is their inability to see their monstrousness, or Blackness, as problematic.

Where Gus, in particular, and the Monster are the same is in their grotesque bodies, which become a "locus of contradictions."[41] The Monster is an outsized atrocity with an assemblage of body parts. His flesh is corpse colored and lacks living vibrancy; with life coming from an electric shock, there is no blood pumping through the Monster's undead, reanimated body. And yet, this freak of nature does not invite viewer abhorrence, only pity. It is Dr. Frankenstein, a wealthy, über-intellectual who, with his God-complex, is to be scorned.

Gus appears most monster-like. His uniform is filthy and ragged. Gus himself is swarthy and at times appears to creep rather than move about proudly erect like the Cameron men (or even the Monster). His monstrous look is heightened due to the use of blackface. As a result, Gus' bulging white eyes appear frantic and wild, his skin a muddy, streaky grey-black. After Little Sister kills herself rather than "marry" Gus, he further secures his fate when he shoots and kills one of his White pursuers. Though the Monster's body is supposed to be every bit as problematic, the Monster's sullen eyes mark him as soulful. The Monster becomes more human than Gus can ever be as he does not kill his pursuers (the mob of peasants); rather, in torment, he kills his creator—a symbol of man and science gone wrong—in effect saving humanity from such hubris.

Gus and the Monster reveal disparate horrors even as they both promise to provide "particularly intense moments" of birth, entrance, transformation, destruction.[42] Both are depicted as being born out of the imagination of privileged minds. The Monster is a creation of Dr. Frankenstein, and Gus and Lynch are born out of a social liberalism gone wrong. Both Frankenstein and Stoneman are viewed as mad scientists embarking on an irrational, dangerous social experiment, or, as Butters put it: "Thus, as Dr. Frankenstein makes his monster not fully realizing what he is doing, Stoneman makes Lynch."[43] Gus, Lynch, and the Monster's entrances into the world reveal that each, whether he knows it or not, possesses a reliance on his (White) master. The Monster is child-like and vulnerable in his entrance. By contrast, during Reconstruction Gus and Lynch enter the White world with their power uncontained and behaviors unchecked. For the Monster, Gus, and Lynch their transformation into the monstrous comes when each are fully absent from their masters. But only the Monster learns important lessons and becomes a new "man" because of it. Even as the Monster is a triple murderer, having killed Fritz, Dr. Waldeman, and Maria, his necessary demise is a sad mercy killing. Importantly, the Monster is not viewed as monstrous because of lust. That would be the purview of Gus and Lynch since they do not mistake young White girls for flowers, but sees them as potential lovers. As Williams notes, the hallmark of a monster is its sexual difference—an aberration—from the "normal" male.[44] More, Gus and Lynch cannot be "normal"; rather, their attempt at race mixing is a sexual transgression that is marked very clearly as dangerous.

In *Birth*, there is never any move to hold Stoneman responsible for his creation. In fact, when Lynch turns a romantic eye to Elsie, Stoneman's daughter, Lynch is marked for destruction by his creator, Stoneman himself. In doing so, Stoneman is recentered within Whiteness, seemingly freeing himself of his misguided trust in Blackness, or even snapping out of his temporary insanity. In the end, there are no Blacks in *Birth* to pity or identify with.

In borrowing from Dixon's and Shelley's novels, *Birth* and *Frankenstein* adopted literature's age-old contribution of tales of good/virtuous/light versus evil/corrupt/dark. However, film's reach as a mass medium, the allure of film as a new technology, as well as *Birth*'s startling imagery, took Dixon's racist stories to new heights. *Birth* was the first film to be screened in the White House. The film has been credited for cycles of resurgent interest in the Ku Klux Klan.[45] It has since been used as a piece of propaganda and as a recruitment tool for White supremacy movements and groups such as the Ku Klux Klan, the neo-confederates, and neo-Nazis.[46] *Birth* has been honored by the Library of Congress with inclusion in its National Film Registry (1992) and celebrated by the American Film Institute, which ranked it the 44th most important film of all time. In 2004, the popular African American DJ and music producer DJ Spooky kicked off a world tour for capacity crowds at venues such as the Lincoln Center (New York) and the Vienna Festival, presenting his "re-mix" of the film, which he retitled *DJ Spooky's Rebirth of a Nation*. DJ Spooky set the film to a hip-hop beat and inserted colorful graphics into the film.

To be sure, *The Birth of a Nation* is not part of the horror genre. Nevertheless, it introduced, and secured in the American popular imagination, a character of quintessential horror that would become a recurring, popular narrative device for instilling fear. In presenting Gus, as well as other Black men, as malevolent, *Birth* has the dubious distinction of introducing the loathsome "brutal buck" character into film. The brutal buck is a vicious Black male, and all the more dangerous because he is so single-minded and unrelenting in his evil doing. He cannot be reasoned with, as he lacks rationality. The character is so base and primal that he can only be understood as animalistic. Donald Bogle famously discusses the damage Griffith has done in presenting Black men as brutal bucks: "always big, baadddd niggers, over-sexed and savage, violent and frenzied as they lust for white flesh. No greater sin hath any black man. ... Griffith played hard on the bestiality of his black villainous bucks and used it to arouse hatred."[47] And, indeed, variations on the theme continue to resurface in media such as the infamous Willie Horton "Weekend Passes" (1988) political campaign television ad, in which a Black convicted murderer and rapist is featured, and in films such as the "Blacks in horror" film *Candyman* (1992), in which Black men, exuding sexuality, hold White women captive.

Blacks Take on Fright-Films

In response to *Birth*, with the goal of counteracting its effects, Black films—that is, films starring Black actors and featuring Black stories, and (ideally) made and distributed by Blacks, immediately began to appear "in earnest."[48] Black filmmakers correctly anticipated the power of Griffith's representations, and did not sit idly by while their race and culture were being imagistically soiled. Black films were produced to respond to *The Birth of a Nation*. For example, George and Noble Johnson, through their Lincoln Motion Picture Company, founded in the summer of 1915, released *The Realization of a Negro's Ambition* (1916) in an effort to present a positive contrast to the portrayals of Blackness in *Birth*. Then there was the Frederick Douglass Film Company, formed in 1916 by Dr. George Cannon and Rev. Dr. W.S. Smith with the specific goal of countering the effects of *The Birth of a Nation*. The Company's first film, *The Colored American Winning His Suit* (1916), depicted African Americans as hard working, and their ability to engage in self-help was a dominant theme.

Acclaimed novelist and filmmaker Oscar Micheaux, through his Micheaux Book and Film Company (1919), offered the feature *Within Our Gates* (1920). *Gates* is most memorable for its attempt not only to counter Griffith's epic, but to reimagine the infamous "Grim Reaping" scene. In *Gates*, it is a Black woman[49] who is being pursued by a White man who wants to rape her.

One benefit of the increase in Black stories, Black produced or otherwise, was the introduction of a wealth of diverse Black images, presenting complex, multidimensional characters, as well as a broad range of narratives, including fright-films. For example, the Unique Film Co. offered the three-reel, all-Black cast "Black horror" film *Shadowed by the Devil* (1916). *Devil* is a morality tale, focusing on three characters—"the good, the bad, and the ugly,"[50] and what it means to be a "good [Black] man."[51] The film "contrasted the characteristics of three individuals—a spoiled 'princess,' a man possessed by the devil [literally], and Everett, 'a good industrious son of poor parents, a quiet and sober young man, a loving husband and ... father [who] shows the traits of his early learning'."[52] As intriguing as the film sounds, *Shadowed* came and went almost as quickly as Unique itself, as the company put out only one other (non-fright) film before its fast demise. The paucity of Unique's output was not unusual as "the economic vulnerability of Black and White independent film companies in the silent era meant that most companies only had one or two films to their credit."[53]

Indeed, the economic difficulties faced by film companies were very real. For example, Richard Norman, the White owner of Norman Film Manufacturing Company, detailed the monetary and resource challenges he faced in a letter to Anita Bush, a Black actress in the silent Black fright-film *The Crimson Skull* (1921). For her work, Bush requested a greater salary, and in response Norman explained his financial constraints: "as our picture will be produced for colored theatres only, it will have a possible distribution in about 120 theatres; 85% of which have an average seating capacity of but 250. These figures are no comparison with the 22,000 white theatres in which our product will find no market."[54] Bush did not receive her salary bump, but she did sign on with Norman to star in *The Crimson Skull*, joining her former theater co-star, the Black actor Lawrence Chenault, in the film.

The Crimson Skull was advertised as a "baffling western mystery photo-play" featuring the "Skull" and his stick-up gang the "Terrors," who, while cloaked in a black costume painted with a white skeleton, play on superstitions by haunting, terrorizing, and robbing their victims. The film was so well received when screened in Baltimore, Maryland, at the Carey Theater that it was "continued for two days."[55]

Like Norman Film Manufacturing, the Ebony Film Company (1915), despite what its name seemed to promise, was not Black-owned. As some White-owned film companies of the day did, it made its stereotypical contributions to representations of Blackness through films such as *Money Talks in Darktown* (1916) and *Shine Johnson and the Rabbit's Foot* (1917). Though the company was White-owned, it was managed by front-man Luther J. Pollard, its only Black officer, and it kept a sizable cadre of Black stock company performers. Ebony Film Company produced a number of fright-films, bringing their catalog to a numerically impressive collection of two-dozen films. Ebony featured Blacks in a whopping *five* comedy-horror short films between 1917 and 1918.

The five were: (1) *Devil for a Day* (1917); (2) *Ghosts* (1917); (3) *Mercy, the Mummy Mumbled* (1918); (4) *Spooks* (1918); and (5) *Do the Dead Talk?* (1918).[56]

The films were screened for both Black and White audiences, even though they were primarily marketed toward Whites, as this 1918 company advertisement in *Motion Picture World* reveals: "colored people are funny. If colored people weren't funny, there would be no plantation melodies, no banjoes, no cake walk, no buck and wing dance, no minstrel show and no black-face vaudeville. And they are funny in the studio."[57]

In response to Ebony's offerings, Black viewers were offended, as "Mrs. J.H." wrote in a Letter to the Editor of the *Chicago Defender*:

> I consider it my duty, as a member of the respectable class of theater patrons, to protest against a certain class of pictures which have been and are being shown at the theaters in this district. I refer to pictures being exploited by the Ebony Film Company, according to the advertisements, and which make an exaggerated display of the disgraceful actions of the lowest element of the race. It was with abject humiliation that myself and many of my friends sat through the scenes of degradation shown on the screen, and if they were meant for comedy, the meaning certainly miscarried. When beastly actions of the degraded of our people are flaunted before our eyes in places of amusement it is high time to protest in the name of common decency.[58]

The Black press was similarly scathing in its reviews of Ebony films. The *Chicago Defender* pointedly advised: "when you see one of these so-called 'all-colored comedies' advertised, keep your money in your pocket and save the dime as well as your self-respect."[59]

Such was the general tenor of fright-films—scared "Negroes" bugging their eyes for laughs—for nearly the first two decades of the twentieth century. However, Oscar Micheaux would wipe smiles from faces and reign supreme in offering "Black horror" films.

Oscar Micheaux: Master of the Macabre

Oscar Devereaux Micheaux was born in 1884 to former slaves, and reared in Kansas. At approximately age 26, in March 1910, he wrote to the Black-owned and operated weekly newspaper the *Chicago Defender*, describing his life as a "resident, pioneer and landowner" in the predominately White Gregory County, South Dakota. While homesteading (he did not embrace the identity of "farmer"), Micheaux began filling notebooks with the semi-autobiographical tales of the (barely) fictional character "Oscar Devereaux," ultimately turning his notes into one of his first self-published and distributed books, *The Conquest: The Story of a Negro Pioneer*. This would be the first of his six novels.

Micheaux's move into film began in 1918 when George Johnson of Lincoln Motion Picture Company reached out to the author after seeing an advertisement in the *Chicago Defender* for his book *The Homesteader*. Lincoln was interested in acquiring the rights to the book for the purpose of adapting it for the big screen. A flurry of communication between Micheaux and Johnson resulted in Johnson trying to "convince Micheaux that he had more expertise in 'the picture game,' and promising that he could mold the book 'into a first-class feature.'"[60] However, Micheaux was insistent that his novel, at 500 pages, was worthy of a feature-length, six-reel film, not the usual two to three reels typically produced by Lincoln, and common for Black films at the time. Negotiations broke down, as Micheaux became determined to produce *The Homesteader* himself under his Micheaux Book and Film Company. Micheaux Book and Film Company would indeed produce only features, a nod to Micheaux's ambition to make lengthy feature films.

In 1919, with the silent drama *The Homesteader*, Micheaux became the first Black American to make a feature-length film. Micheaux continued to write and also worked to adapt his novels for the big screen. The filmmaker "wrote himself into history" by drawing upon his now-famous biography to create works which offered a sociopolitical take on Blackness not seen before in popular culture.[61] These stories became the basis of some of his most famous works, such as the silent films *Within Our Gates* (1920), *The Symbol of the Unconquered* (1920), and *Body and Soul* (1925). Micheaux was the epitome of an independent filmmaker, drawing on the kindness of his network of Black friends who let him "shoot films in their living rooms and set up chairs there for screenings."[62] The result—over a 30-year career Micheaux made approximately forty films.

Among those films, at least three were silent fright-films which more closely resemble the horror genre of today. Micheaux did not indulge in comedy-horror. His films went about the very serious business of storytelling. One such film, a dramatic fright-film, *A Son of Satan* (1924), nearly failed to see the light of day due to some slippery business maneuverings on the part of Micheaux himself.

Noted Micheaux scholars Pearl Bower and Louise Spence, in their book *Writing Himself into History: Oscar Micheaux, His Silent Films, and His Audiences*, explain that to save money and to maximize profit, the filmmaker turned crafty distributor. He would not submit his films, as required, for licensing until he had already booked the film and advertised. The tactic saved Micheaux the time and resources associated with securing licensing only to be told to cut some material to meet the requirements of licensing boards' censors. Instead, Micheaux attempted to move the boards to act in his favor, quickly and with little hassle, by explaining that theaters were waiting for delivery of his films, and the censors need not worry about his films' content since they would be seen only by Black audiences.[63] To cajole the board, "his letterhead during this period listed all the films he had in distribution and described his firm as "Producers and Distributors of High Class Negro Feature Photoplays."[64]

When the Virginia Board threatened the release of *A Son of Satan*, Micheaux booked the film anyway, without approval, in Attucks Theatre in Norfolk, and circulated ads and other promotional materials for the film. Only then did the Board hear from Micheaux, who had been ignoring their demands for changes to the film. Ultimately, his strategy was a brazen feat:

> His tardy reply illuminates how he manipulated the system to make it work to his advantage, while avoiding the undesirable consequences of his own misdemeanors. Setting the scene for a melodrama, and playing the role of the trickster, he struck a note of "contrition," saying he had been traveling in cinder-infested Jim Crow cars throughout the South all summer and "was just so tired and distracted half the time" that he never felt composed enough "to set down and explain the why of." Playing to the paternalism of the board, he pleaded poverty and reminded them that these films were only shown to Negro audiences, anyway.[65]

The state levied a twenty-five-dollar fine, the minimum penalty, and rejected the scenes of miscegenation for "reasons of discretion."[66]

The seven-reel *A Son of Satan* included Lawrence Chenault, of *The Crimson Skull* fame, in its cast. According to ads, the film featured "a powerful supporting colored cast" performing an adaptation of a Micheaux story, *The Ghost of Tolston's Manor*.[67] The film is about a man who, on a bet, agrees to spend the night in a haunted house, and was described as "a hair raising story of adventure in a haunted house, where rattling chains and walking ghosts are as common as parrots and puppies."[68]

The film was not, however, without its controversies. Micheaux's film was met with some scorn for its depiction of Blacks drinking, gambling, and shooting dice. The Motion Picture Commission of the State of New York rejected the film, thereby withholding its license for such depictions, as the Commission states in its letter to Micheaux:

> The picture is filled with scenes of drinking, carousing and shows masked men becoming intoxicated. It shows the playing of crap for money, a man killing his wife by choking her, the killing of the leader of the hooded organization and the killing of a cat by throwing a stone on it. There are many scenes of crime. The film is of such character that in the opinion of the commission, it is "inhuman" and would "tend to incite crime."[69]

The film, by the day's standard, was particularly stereotype-filled, as it portrayed Black men in all manner of "carousing," while White men were portrayed as savage Klan members. As such, the film evidenced how Micheaux could be "unabashedly defiant to both white and black America."[70] Still, *A Son of Satan* was generally well received. The *Chicago Defender*'s D. Ireland Thomas wrote of the film:

> some may not like the production because it shows up some of our Race in their colors. They might also protest against the language used. I would not endorse this particular part of the film myself, but I must admit that it is true to nature, yes, I guess, too true. We've got to hand it to Oscar Micheaux when it comes to giving us the real stuff ... I do not want to see my Race in saloons or at crap tables. But it is not what we want, that gets the money. It is what the public clamors for that makes the coin jingle.[71]

Micheaux's next fright-film, *The Devil's Disciple* (1925), again counts among its stars Lawrence Chenault. It is described in the *New York Amsterdam News* as "intensely gripping and dramatic" as it tells the story of the dangers of big city life, in this case Harlem, for young women. In the film, the danger takes the form of a man, a disciple of Satan, who seduces and exploits "women of the streets." One woman believes that she can change the man, but instead becomes a victim of degradation herself. According to the *Pittsburgh Courier*, "what ensues makes a story of such nerve-tingling suspense and dramatic situations that you are gripped in an ecstasy of entertainment from which you are not released until the end is flashed before your eyes."[72]

Micheaux was still not done with his spooky offerings. *The Conjure Woman* (1926) was based on Charles Chesnutt's 1899 short story collection of the same title. The collection presented seven short stories, all set in Patesville, North Carolina, centering on the act of conjuring—a hoodoo magic[73]—by Blacks (slaves and free) resisting the cruelties inflicted upon them by violent, racist Whites. Micheaux wrote Chesnutt outlining his ideas for adapting the first story of *The Conjure Woman* for a "photoplay":

> I think you could develop a good synopsis from the first story of *The Conjure Woman*. Write the case of the man and woman into a good love story, let there, if possible, be a haunted house, the haunts being intriguers to be found out near the end, the heroine to have ran off there and in hiding—anything that will thrill or suspend, but have a delightful ending and give opportunity for a strong male and female lead (Oscar Micheaux to Charles Waddell Chesnutt, 30 October 1921, Charles Waddell Chesnutt Papers, Western Reserve Historical Society, Cleveland, Ohio).[74]

This film, however, did not make much of a splash, for unknown reasons. What is known is that the film was not extensively promoted and it saw very limited screenings.[75]

Micheaux's films have been understood as "race movies" and morality tales which have the dual goal of circulating a positive, uplift-the-race message while showing Blacks as complex and human—loving and good, flawed and weak, evil and forthright. Micheaux also had a good eye for a compelling story. His fright-films were provocative, psychological thrillers (not merely "bump in the night" spooky movies). His work would open the door for the likes of Black actor/director Spencer Williams and his "Black horror" morality-themed films of the 1940s. Until then, however, Blacks' participation in horror would be marred by imagistic mistreatments almost exclusively in "Blacks in horror" films.

Conclusion

It was against this early twentieth century backdrop, when W.E.B. Du Bois would famously lament of Blacks "measuring one's soul by the tape of a world that looks on in amused contempt and pity," that Blacks entered into filmmaking.[76] They sought to offer up entertainment from their own vantage point of Blackness while countering the prevailing contemptuous representations being circulated by those who were particularly invested in preserving pure notions of Whiteness. Certainly, for these Black filmmakers, the profit potential did not hurt either. However, Griffith's falsehoods proved strong motivation for Blacks to enter into the field—quickly and in great numbers. Independent Black film companies and Black theaters began to spring up. By the late 1920s, an impressive 700 Black theaters were serving Black audiences (proving that "renaissance" was not just a Harlem phenomenon).[77]

Still, the life of the Black filmmaker was far from easy. Censorship, distribution, access to resources (e.g. equipment, actors, payroll), and seeing a return on their investment were significant, often unconquerable problems. As a result, non-Black filmmakers still ruled the industry, and their visions of Blacks and Black culture prevailed. There seemed to be no stopping depictions of Blacks as monstrous or the race-baiting comedy-horror films, in which Blacks were the victims of violence at the hands of Whites. More, the bugged-eyed, spooked Negro was just beginning to have its day, reaching a fevered pitch in the coming decades. The next decade, the 1930s, did see blackface performance ebb, providing more opportunities for "real" Black actors. However, the roles open to Blacks, particularly in the horror genre, which was being formalized in the 1930s, were dreadfully regressive. The decade also saw increased participation of Black women—no longer would they be depicted by White men in blackface, and, increasingly, roles were written for Black women, albeit frequently to portray a half-naked Voodoo witch or a fully clothed Voodoo practicing maid.

In the coming decade, there were still more representational problems on the horizon for Blacks. "Jungle films"—films about the uncivilized lives of Blacks in places such as the continent of Africa or on the island of Haiti—became more popular during the 1930s. These films' contribution to the horror genre was profound and the tropes of these films remain popular today. Blacks as savage, evil Voodoo practitioners chanting "ooo-ga boo-ga" while whipping themselves around in a frenzied Voodoo dance to the cadence of jungle music (drumming) rivaled the grotesqueness of a Gus or a Lynch. More, Whites would still be depicted as superior and enlightened ... and still the protectors and saviors of White womanhood, which continued to be imperiled by Blacks. There was little to counter such images as the 1930s was a decade of "Blacks in horror" rather than "Black horror."

2

JUNGLE FEVER—A HORROR ROMANCE

1930s

Voodoo and zombies. Kid's stuff, right? Grade B-movies. Well, that's wrong. Just one hour plane ride from Miami is the Caribbean country of Haiti, and this country is literally being held hostage by Voodoo priests who can and do turn people into zombies.

—Bill O'Reilly (20)[1]

In 35 short years (1895–1930), in America, film went from being the expensive, experimental hobby of inventors to a full-blown commercial industry— "Hollywood." By the mid-1930s, film production was hailed as a leading industry in the US, with $2 billion in financial worth. The average weekly attendance at theaters rose steadily from 40 million in 1922 to 48 million in 1925 and 110 million in 1930.[2] The 1930s was also when the term "horror film" finally entered into the lexicon.[3]

Nearly every mainstream film company began producing horror films; however, Universal Studios can be credited with innovating this "Golden Age" of horror films with their now-classic string of monster movies—*Dracula* (1931), *Frankenstein* (1931), *The Mummy* (1932), and *The Invisible Man* (1933).[4] Universal's monsters were joined by other popular Universal horror films such as *Murders in the Rue Morgue* (1932), as well as a string of sequels such as *Bride of Frankenstein* (1935) and *Dracula's Daughter* (1936). Thanks, in part, to the efforts of Universal, the 1930s remain one of the most celebrated periods in film history. Unfortunately, Blacks were largely absent from Universal's monster movies, with the rare exception of the Black actor Noble Johnson, who had small parts as the servant "Janos the Black One" in *Murders in the Rue Morgue* and as the servant "the Nubian" in *The Mummy*. One writer with the Black newspaper the *Pittsburgh Courier* believed Universal had little respect for Black audiences during this time.[5] Indeed, Blacks were experiencing filmic slights, but they were not only coming from Universal.

Black filmmakers had little opportunity to inform the film industry during this time. The advent of sound, a costly technological innovation, and the occurrence of the Great Depression, which brought economic collapse to global markets, made for a deadly mix for Black filmmakers. Already teetering financially, many saw their companies completely fail. Black films became White scripted, owned, produced, and distributed, featuring Black actors (and still on rare occasion Whites in blackface), for a White target audience. Blacks' representation in film, whether inside or outside of the horror genre, was remarkably static. Social realism in film often took a back seat to depictions of happy Black folks in servitude to Whites, as seen in the dramas *So Red the Rose* (1935), *Rainbow on the River* (1936), and *Gone with the Wind* (1939).

Horror was no different, even finding a way to insert some jovial singing (e.g. *Black Moon* [1934]). Blacks during this decade were not depicted as progressive "New Negroes" as celebrated through the era's Harlem Renaissance. Instead, they were presented as rather devolved and child-like. In several instances, home was still a White-owned plantation, though the plantation setting was not the antebellum South but rather some wicked Caribbean jungle which threatened to encroach on the civilized space carved out by Whites. Evil Voodoo magic figured prominently, as did monstrous animals—particularly the ape, who also had a particular fondness for blonds. Against this odd assemblage of generic themes, one constant was a narrative of romance, begging the question, would the jungle, Voodoo, or even the ape, complicate the quest for White love?

Conquering the Black World

1930s horror displayed an obsession with "out of Africa" tales in which Whites "conquer" Africa. It was a preoccupation that may be attributed to the early twentieth century adventures of President Theodore Roosevelt (1901–1909). Roosevelt was a published historian (he was named President of the American Historical Association); he was a naturalist, conservationist, and explorer (he is credited with discovering the 625-mile uncharted river the Rio Roosevelt); he worked with the Smithsonian, the National Museum of Natural History (D.C.), and the American Museum of Natural History (New York).

Roosevelt may have been one of the first "media" Presidents as his voice, delivering a political speech, was the first to be recorded for mass circulation. Roosevelt also allowed his image to be recorded through a collection of silent film clips. There are many scholarly and nonfiction writings authored by Roosevelt. Together, these media artifacts made Roosevelt one of the most publicly accessible leaders of the early twentieth century.

As a result of Roosevelt's willing presence in mass media, Americans were provided with ample coverage of his life's travails, including his African safari escapades. In 1909, he visited the then-Belgian Congo for an expedition with the purpose of acquiring animals for U.S. museums. He and his team returned with a trove of over 11,000 specimens (e.g. elephants, hippos, rhinos, insects) for preservation and/or mounting. In the public's mind, Roosevelt had "conquered" Africa.

Roosevelt contributed to his own myths through his writings about his safaris, and regularly portrayed himself as a kindly, rational figure. He wrote that he had *almost* pitied the Black African porters on his expedition as they had only their clothes, one blanket, and a tent; that is, until he met the Kikuyu, who only had a small blanket, but no clothes and no tents. It was then that Roosevelt assuaged his guilt by proclaiming "how much better off" his porters were "simply because they were on a White man's safari."[6] Such experiences were well documented thanks to a robustly publicized, massive compendium project of Roosevelt's speeches, quotes, and writings. The compendium project began in 1928 and was finally completed in 1941, corresponding with the great proliferation of America-taming-the-jungle films.

Love in the Jungle … with Apes … That's Nasty!

> Occasionally a hoax of some kind will win a front page story, but it's best if newspapers can be "let in" on the stunt.
>
> —*The Encyclopedia of Exploitation* (138)[7]

"Animalistic, 'wild' sexuality." Patricia Hill Collins, in her book *Black Sexual Politics*, observes that Black women cannot seem to shake such sexual stereotypes. Hill Collins writes of "Western perceptions of African bodies," noting that the "mélange of animal skins, … breast worship, and focus on the booty" remains ubiquitous.[8] Hill Collins notes that from Sarah Bartmann (the perjoratively dubbed "Hottentot Venus") to Josephine Baker to Destiny's Child, the attraction—or, more precisely, the marketability—of these Black women's bodies has been tied to such hypersexual primitive figures, colloquially referred to as "freaks." Importantly, it is Black women's *sexuality*—not Black romance or love—that captured the attention and imagination of image-makers during the 1930s horror cycle.

The 1930 "Blacks in horror," jungle film *Ingagi* is all about Black women's animalistic sexuality. Set in the Congo, the film is said to be influenced by the travels of Roosevelt in the country. *Ingagi* is one of the more sickening horror films, not because of the expected horror tropes of blood and gore (there is none of that), but due to its disgusting attack on Black sexuality.

Ingagi tells the story of White research scientists who travel deep into the jungles of the Congo to investigate the odd rituals of a Congolese tribe that both reveres and fears gorillas, or "ingagis." The Congolese give their virgin women to the beasts. The film's story is one of White enlightenment. Appalled by the natives' ritual sacrifice, and unable to tolerate it a moment longer, the scientists work to rescue a young Black woman victim from the clutches of an ape-beast. In the course of saving the woman's life and killing the animal, the men, and therefore the film's audience, are led to believe that the woman was not simply saved from being pummeled and/or eaten by the animal. Rather, she was rescued from enduring a highly erotic encounter with bestiality. To bring this point home, at the film's end another semi-nude woman emerges from the jungle thicket holding a human baby, but its skin is covered in fur. The infant is described as "a strange-looking child, seemingly more ape than human."

Ingagi was not originally marketed as a horror movie by its director William Campbell or its producers Congo Pictures, Ltd. Instead, it was promoted as a true and factual documentary film. That is, Campbell claimed that *Ingagi* was simply the edited, but otherwise unadulterated footage shot by the expedition members. He promised audiences that the members of the expedition and the activities by the tribe were real, and that nothing was staged. In promotional materials, tag-lines encouraged film-goers to believe the events depicted in *Ingagi*: "You Have Heard of Such Things But You Doubted Their Reality … But Here in This Amazing Film Are Shown for the Very First Time These Amazing Facts," and "A Million Thrills … An Authentic Record of African Adventure!," and "Myths And Legends Of Darkest Africa Reduced To Reality Through Astounding Camera Records!" The hit film was soon popularly referred to as "the gorilla sex picture," broke box office records, and even spawned a tune called "My Ingagi."[9]

A human engaging in intercourse with a gorilla was never shown on-screen. Rather, the audience was literally kept in the dark as distant camera work and dim lighting only allowed inter-species copulation to be implied, and obstructed the view of the White actresses in blackface portraying some of the native women.[10] However, the poster art for the film explicitly (figuratively and literally) promised bestiality as the ape is shown fondling a Black woman. The poster depicted an ape, standing erect, abducting a bald Black woman, her breasts exposed. The ape is holding the woman in its two "arms" and is squeezing one of the woman's breasts between its fingers. As such, *Ingagi* alludes to an "aggressive Black male sexuality in the form of the gorilla" on the prowl for lascivious Black women.[11] Here, Black women are implicated in a complicated scheme of aberrance in which they are simultaneously hypersexual and available, but are not at all feminine, beautiful, or sexy (by traditional, Western standards). Promotional material also included the question, was Darwin right? Hence, *Ingagi* suggested a direct link between the genetics of Blacks and the "super-masculine black beasts."[12] The result was a film that invited audiences to associate Black sexual practices with bestiality and provoked disgust toward Blacks' unique ability to breed with an animal. As such, the film was all about binary dichotomies, working to effectively separate civilized (human) Whites from savage (beastly) Blacks, thereby distinguishing Whites as examples of racial supremacy.

The controversy around *Ingagi* did not stop there. According to *LA Times* reporter Andrew Erish, who wrote a lengthy special feature on the film, several months after the film's release suspicion began to emerge about its authenticity. *Ingagi* included scenes and stock footage from older, well-known jungle films such as *Heart of Africa* (1915) (another purported "documentary" about safaris in Kenya). Many of *Ingagi*'s gorilla scenes were shot in a California zoo. It was proven, by a signed affidavit, that actor Charles Gemora portrayed the offending gorilla while clad in a gorilla suit. Someone recognized one of the "African" women in the films as an often-cast extra in Hollywood films. The *Los Angeles Examiner* reported that regular "Central Avenue Negroes" were cast as the tribesmen. Still, when pressed, the film's director and others involved in making the film insisted that *Ingagi* was authentic, and cities continued to book the film as such. Three years later, after the film had its day in theaters, and after the film's production company boasted about profits in excess of $1 million, the Federal Trade Commission (FTC) said the filmmakers could no longer promote the film as authentic.[13] As part of their case, the FTC noted that "ingagi" was a made-up word.[14]

In all the controversy, no one seemed to care about the attack on Black sexuality. In spite of the establishment of a governing code for morality and decency in the film industry, which included the rejection of female nudity, real or implied, if serving a prurient interest, Black women's bodies did not rate. The Black "native" body, neither moral nor decent, "was at once made an acceptable site for sexual titillation and sanctioned racial degradation."[15] Sadly, there were no *Birth of a Nation*-type campaigns to boycott the film. In the end, *Ingagi* went down in history, according to a *New York Times* review summary, as "one of the most outrageous hoaxes ever perpetrated."[16]

On the immediate heels of *Ingagi* came 1932's *The Monster Walks*. This "Blacks in horror" movie is mundane (certainly compared to *Ingagi*). Greed motivates a pair of housekeepers to try to do away with Ruth (Vera Reynolds), the daughter of their recently deceased employer. Ruth has just inherited her father's wealth and his mansion, which also happens to house an ape in the cellar. The housekeepers put on ape costumes and plan to kill Ruth, pinning the murder on the animal. However, just in the nick of time, Ruth is saved by her heroic fiancé Ted (Rex Lease).

Monster delivers several horror clichés which had been developing over the years—scary animals, the gothic, spooky mansion, the beautiful White victim, the White savior, romance, and, interestingly, the comic-Negro. *Monster* features the (in)famous character actor Willie Best, appearing under the obviously offensive stage name Sleep 'n' Eat, in the role of Exodus. In the film, Exodus is Ted's driver and butler. Exodus is child-like, rambunctious, and always profoundly and comically scared by everything—lightning, the dark, big houses, noises, and even a bearskin rug. The film is a rather serious fright-fest, except when Exodus appears in a scene. The film even ends comically. Exodus and ape finally come face to face. His meeting with the animal is supposed to give credence to the Darwinian theory that (Black) man comes from ape (as also theorized in *Ingagi*): "You mean that he's related to me?! ... Well, I don't know. I had a grand-pappy that looked something like him. But he wasn't as active."

Importantly, Exodus also illustrates a trend around how audiences were prompted to understand Blacks in America in opposition to those from other parts of the non-Westernized world. When portrayed in domestic settings, the dominant representation of Blacks during this period was comedic. The representation aligned with the safe, happy-go-lucky, subservient, and desexualized representations seen in films such as *Gone With the Wind*, which harkened back to a more stable and orderly time in American history. However, when Blacks (played by African American actors) were transplanted to foreign settings, they were presented as dangerous, hypersexual savages who posed a considerable threat to Whites. *Ingagi* and a host of other jungle films (e.g. *Tarzan, the Ape Man* [1932], *Black Moon* [1934]) lend credence to this theory.

The King of Ape Love

Ingagi's popularity and box office success proved that the formula of "dark" primitives, and "light" superiority would continue to work well and profitably. It was *Ingagi*'s success that convinced the film studio RKO to green-light the "Blacks in horror" film *King Kong* (1933), in which a giant ape, Kong, falls for, pursues, and abducts a White woman.[17]

If *Ingagi* prompted audiences to consider the repulsive sexual mores of Black women, then *King Kong* (1933) extended the assault to metaphorically implicate Black men through the imagery of the big black ape in pursuit of a White woman. It is an instance, as Snead persuasively argues, of "the coded Black" in which Blackness is implicitly carried in the form of an ape.[18] Kong is "blackened," or racially coded, when juxtaposed against the presence of Whites in the film. Kong is the color black, emerging from a "lower," primitive culture in which he is surrounded by Black natives—or mini-Kongs when they dress up like apes to worship their big Kong. The soundtrack that accompanies scenes with Kong and other Blacks in the film consists of drums, an auditory cue that is typical of jungle films and the appearance of Black natives.[19] The film also continued to confine understandings of Blackness to wildness, and its sexuality to savagery, adding fears of the big black phallus. In doing so, *King Kong* piled on another reason for the dark Other's termination—his body is far too endowed in comparison to the more modestly appointed White man. Kong is chained, shipped to the US (his middle passage), where he experiences a bit of slavery before being executed for going on a rampage in pursuit of a White woman.

King Kong did not stray far from the *Ingagi* film-within-a film narrative device—a kind of "optical colonialization."[20] In *Kong*, a White American filmmaker and crew sail to Skull Island, somewhere in the Indian Ocean (around Indonesia), to make a movie featuring a beautiful, blond White woman against the backdrop of a "real" primitive island which has been untouched by evolution.

Upon their arrival on the island, the crew mounts an expedition and encounters a tribe made up of Black (not Indonesian) natives. Bogle (2005) reports casting for Kong included hiring "everybody they could find," as long as they were not light-complexioned. The studio was looking for extras with a "dark complexion, big lips, and kinky hair."[21] The use of Black actors to portray Indonesians illustrates a typical racial impulse by Hollywood to conflate anyone with dark skin as Other.[22] The natives are clad in bits of animal cloth, carrying spears, with their faces painted and wearing Afro wigs. The "native's chief," a bit part, is played by the Black actor Noble Johnson. The tribe (and this should sound very, very familiar) offer their silent, submissive semi-nude virgin women as "brides" to Kong to remain on the ape's good side.[23] The brides' portrayal uniquely combined the wild and savage with bowing servitude.

Upon the arrival of the White crew, the Chief and his tribe spot the young, blond "beauty" Ann Darrow (Fay Wray). The natives immediately conclude that her White skin makes her quite special. The Chief's jubilant exclamation, "Look at the golden woman!" (translated into English by the ship's Captain, who just happens to speak "native"), enjoins the Black male gaze with the ape's, with Kong similarly fawning over Darrow once he sees her. When the aspiring filmmaker Carl Denham (Robert Armstrong) responds, "Yeah, blondes are scarce around here," the character's observation works not only to elevate Whiteness, but also to dismiss the possibility of beauty being found in Black womanhood. And then the Chief proposes a troubling trade—he will hand over *six* Black women to the Americans for Darrow. The plan is to sacrifice Darrow, with whom the Chief and his tribe theorize Kong will be infinitely more pleased. Of course, the Chief's offer is refused. As Greenberg elaborates, this confrontation is racial myth-making at its worst:

> According to this debased view of other lands and people, one of "our" women must be worth six of theirs. And although "their" men are capable of the most heinous aggression, one of "our" men can still take on and whip half a dozen of theirs in a fair fight … *Kong* then, is the epitome of the White man's daydream of the brute black, the heartless, mindless foreigner, feasting on violence and rapine.[24]

Later, the natives sneak aboard the ship and kidnap Darrow, an event described in broken English by a Chinese cook, Charlie (Victor Wong), "Crazy Black man been here." When Charlie asks to go ashore—"Me likey go too!—his request is summarily dismissed, and Charlie neither makes it off the boat nor is seen again. Indeed, this is a war between Blacks and Whites only.

After the tribe kidnap Darrow, they deliver her to the giant Kong with great ceremony. Certainly, it is worth questioning, "what the monster would do with the girl if he had a chance to keep her … given the obscure nature of his desire and genital apparatus."[25] However, *Ingagi* has previously implied that anything is possible and that the rescue of Darrow from the animal means saving her from a most unimaginable encounter with a 50-foot beast.[26]

The film also asserts that, unlike his past encounters with Black women, Kong's reaction to Darrow is unique in that he does not consume her; rather he falls in love with her and wishes to keep her around. Indeed, Kong's profound desire for such a "human" partner is not shown when he is offered Black women. Rather, his sexual desire becomes humane and humanized more fully when he settles on Darrow. His affection is displayed by his protective heroism and in the gentle stroking of her striking blond hair—hair, the film's audience is reminded, that the ape has not seen before among the Black inhabitants of Skull Island.

Eventually, Darrow is rescued from the ape's clutches by Driscoll. However, it is the tribe which suffers the consequences of Kong's loss of his White "bride." Kong goes on a rampage, destroying the village and killing scores of natives. He bites off their heads, beats them, eats them, and stomps them to death. In one scene, deleted from most prints, he tramples the infants in the village.[27] Kong is captured, enslaved by the Americans, and put on exhibition on a New York City stage while in shackles; he thereby bears a startling similarity to the undressed slave on the auction-block showcased for fetishistic, visual dissection.

FIGURE 2.1 Kong's next victims in *King Kong*
RKO Radio Pictures/Photofest

Kong escapes his captors to search for Darrow. Much like the Monster in *Frankenstein*, Kong, the big black ape, makes the fatal mistake of entering the bedroom of Darrow, and taking her away for what will be a final moment together. The implicit narrative goal is to keep the beast out of the (White) boudoir.[28] There is little disagreement that Kong represents masculinity and sexual dominance, as there are "few images of male domination in all of Western art more outlandish and unforgettable than the giant ape holding [Darrow] like a prize atop the delirious deco-phallicism of the newly constructed Empire State Building."[29] Comparing the infamous images of domination displayed by Gus and Silas Lynch in *The Birth of a Nation* to *Kong*, Young writes, "King Kong provides one version of this overdetermined racist cultural fantasy" while also reinforcing "the more muted historical 'realism'" of *Birth [of a Nation]*."[30] Not surprisingly, Kong is ultimately shot down and killed, executed by military forces, effectively ending his rampage across the Big Apple in pursuit of a White woman.

The primitive ape/beautiful White woman love story would continue to enthrall filmmakers and audiences for decades to come. In 1976, John Guillermin remade *King Kong*, initially advertising for a "well-built" Black man for the role of Kong.[31] Ann's name was changed to Dwan and the purpose of the expedition was changed from filmmaking to a crew working for a petroleum company exploring an "undiscovered," albeit fully inhabited, South Pacific island for oil. Much of the remainder of the film remains true to the original. Though this is a post-Civil Rights/Black Power movement release, there is little evidence of racial sensitivity in the film. The representation of South Pacific islanders as primitive Blacks remains, as does the notion that the islanders believe six Black women are equivalent to one White woman.

In 2005, when Peter Jackson offered up the third major studio remake of *King Kong*, the release reignited long circulating debates about the big black African ape as a metaphor for Black male depravity, in contrast to Western White superiority and desirability. Jackson's *King Kong* is also fairly faithful to the original 1933 film. However, Jackson works to reimagine a few key scenes, as they pertain to Blackness. The Black natives of Skull Island (many of whom are further blackened up with make-up while their teeth are filed to points) are the horror in this movie—they are filthy, terrifying, hostile, and violent. Hordes of them swarm over the White filmmaking team, spearing and clubbing many of them immediately after they land on the island. The natives are depicted as monsters who, inexplicably, shake and shudder and growl as their eyes are rolled back in their heads. This performance of possession allows the viewer to get a better look at these wicked people, who are pierced with bones and adorn themselves with charms made of skulls.

Jackson's other principle representation of Blackness is displayed through the self-sacrificing character Ben Hayes (Evan Parke), a World War I veteran who serves as the ship's trusted and resourceful first mate. The character is spared from sharing a scene with the ghoulish, blacked-up natives as he happens to stay aboard ship to repair it while the others go ashore. When the natives attack, Hayes appears on the island but only after the natives have scattered from gun fire offered by the ship's captain. Hayes adopts the role of a protective father figure to a White teen named Jimmy, who is a member of the ship's crew. The bond between Hayes and Jimmy becomes so profound that Hayes turns sacrificial when the expedition, of which Jimmy is a part, comes under attack by Kong. In Hayes' final scene, about mid-way into the movie, he draws Kong to him screaming, "Look at me!" and warning the others, "Go back. Back across the log. Get Jimmy out of here. You gotta run Jimmy. Do as I say. Run!" Kong kills Hayes, and Jimmy lives to see another day.

When Kong is forced to perform in America, his unveiling is preceded by blacked-up, afro-wig-wearing natives in a lively song and dance number. The character Hayes' death works to remove the awkward dilemma of the modern Black confronting the Black primitive in the script. Jackson's *Kong* won Academy awards for special effects and sound, and earned over $650 million in ticket and DVD sales, making it one of the highest-grossing movies to be distributed by Universal Pictures.

The Legacy of the Ape—Beyond the 1930s

Science fiction films such as *Planet of the Apes* (1968) extended the theme of White superiority over racially coded inferior species such as apes. *Planet of the Apes*, which launched four sequel feature films, a remake, and two television series (one of them animated), tells the story of a group of American astronauts who travel through space from the year 1972 to the year 3978 and crash land in an "upside down world" in which apes (gorillas, orangutans, and chimpanzees) rule over mute, primitive humans. Race figures prominently in *Planet of the Apes*, where even the apes invoke a racial caste system. The astronauts are a team of three. There is the Col. George Taylor (Charlton Heston), a square-jawed, blond White male who takes charge of the mission. Taylor leads his two crew-mates as they try to figure out where, and when, they are. Landon (Robert Gunner) is also a White astronaut, but his more timid manner and humanistic approach to the world render him subordinate to Taylor. A third man, Dodge (Jeff Burton), rounds out the team. He is Black and is hailed as being a serious scientist by his colleagues. When the men are attacked by the verbal, gun-toting, clothed apes, Taylor is injured but survives. Landon is lobotomized, though not killed. Only Dodge is killed. A taxidermist stuffs him, and he is put on display in a museum.

A fourth astronaut, a young, blond woman named Stewart (Dianne Stewart), has her life-support system fail during the space trip, and she dies long before the craft lands on the ape planet. In removing the White woman from the film at its very beginning, Stewart, a blond beauty or the "most precious cargo," as Taylor describes her, is also spared a close encounter with apes who in this film now possess the ability to examine and probe the human body. In the 1970 sequel, *Beneath the Planet of the Apes*, the obsession with blond beauties briefly rears its head again. When a gorilla soldier (the blackest and crudest of the apes in the ape world) stumbles upon the body of a platinum blond White woman, the ape is so enamored that he stops in his tracks to stroke her silky, blond locks.

Conquest of the Planet of the Apes (1972), a pointed allegory about race relations and oppression in the US, is the only film in the series to be closely associated with the horrifying: "Watch the screen explode as man faces ape in the most horrifying spectacle in the annals of science fiction."[32] Such a promotion signaled that *Conquest* was not family-friendly science fiction, as the previous films had been marketed. A prequel, set in 1991, the story centers on how apes, through armed revolution, come to dominate the Earth. Informed by the events of the Watts riots of 1965, Black narratives permeate the film. The Governor's assistant, MacDonald (Hari Rhodes), who is Black, is cast as a sympathetic, heroic figure by enduring and speaking out against a series of racial slights. In one scene, MacDonald is accused by a White police officer of loving apes, to which another officer responds, "Don't it figure." The audience is invited to view the officers as racist. MacDonald must also endure an ape slave auction scene where a chimpanzee is described as "in early prime and perfect physical condition" as well as "familiar, obedient, and docile," with bids beginning at $800. This reversal of apes as becoming more human-like (with humans becoming more savage) is highlighted in the film by linking apes to America's history of racial politics:

MACDONALD: How do you propose to gain this freedom?
CAESAR: (CHIMPANZEE): By the only means left to us—Revolution. … You above everyone else should understand. We cannot be free until we have power. …
MACDONALD: Violence prolongs hate. Hate prolongs violence. By what right are you spilling blood?
CAESAR: By the slave's right to punish his persecutors.
MACDONALD: Caesar. I, a descendant of slaves, am asking you to show humanity.

In the film's final scenes of apes revolting against slavery, they are armed with M16s and the filmmakers purposefully adopt a red, black, and green color scheme to heighten the sense of unrest (these also happen to be the colors associated with the Pan-African movement). In interviews, the filmmakers note that they were aware that they could not have a movie with the leader of the Watts riot as its star, but they could have an ape as a revolutionary leader.[33] There were even claims that Black audiences identified with the film's less than subtle message, with one magazine reporting Blacks could be heard cheering, "Right On!" as the apes battled "Whitey."[34]

In the 1930s, and spanning the twentieth century, film continued to obsess over White men in foreign lands conquering some "dark" place and its "dark" inhabitants. The preservation of White womanhood would also remain central, alongside the message that Blacks were primitive in their development and lesser in worth. The union of these two messages, the purity of White women and the animalism of Blacks, has proven to be so unrelentingly popular that in 2008 NBA basketball star LeBron James posed as the dangerous Kong with White model Giselle in the role of Ann Darrow for the April cover of *Vogue*, a fashion magazine. In reenacting a scene from the famous horror film, James and Giselle moved the link between Black men as lusty apes and White women as their prey a bit closer to the realm of the real.

Out of Haiti Comes Myth-Making

> But in Haiti there is the quick, the dead, and then there are Zombies.
> —Hurston (179)[35]

Haiti, at approximately 17,250 square miles, comprises the western part of the island of Hispaniola. Though a small country, over the last four centuries it has loomed large in history as being at the center of a tug-of-war between a number of foreign occupiers. Today, Haiti has only seven decades of freedom under its belt. Having (barely) survived an exploitative cycle of invasion and subjugation, and most recently suffering a catastrophic earthquake, the cost to Haiti has been high, giving it the distinction of being "the poorest nation in the western hemisphere."[36]

Haiti's troubles began in 1492 when Christopher Columbus landed on the island, "discovering" it and naming it Hispaniola, while also claiming the land and its inhabitants, the Taino Arawak, for Spain. Spain brought to the island sophisticated weaponry and disease, against which the Arawaks could not defend themselves. A generation later, around 1517, with the decimation of the Arawak, West African slaves from countries such as Benin (then Dahomey) were brought to Hispaniola to cultivate sugar. The slaves brought with them a variety of religious practices that were rejected by the Europeans. Unable to openly practice their faiths, Hispaniola's slaves mixed their beliefs and hid their rituals within the religion of their slave masters—particularly Catholicism, which offered a remarkably similar structure. This concealment of indigenous religions was not an uncommon practice. Dr. Bellegarde-Smith, a Haitian-born scholar of Haitian history and of Vodou, explains the history:

> Vodou is related to other transplanted African traditions such as Santeria, which took root in Cuba and Candomble in Brazil. In all of these places, Catholicism was the official religion of colonizers. Slaves and common people hid the spirits they knew inside their veneration of the

Catholic saints. To this day, many Haitians combine Vodou practices with Catholic devotion.[37]

During the late 1600s, the island again suffered violence as the French settled on its northern-most reaches and stripped it of its tobacco resources, thereby sparking conflict between France and Spain. Eventually, in 1697, the two European countries would take it upon themselves to divide Haiti, with France securing the western third of the country and naming it Saint-Domingue (which would later become Haiti).

In 1793, one of the island's most significant slave revolts occurred—the Haitian Revolution—which finally led to the abolition of slavery. The revolution leader, the Haitian-born slave Toussaint L'Ouverture, "a voodooisant or adept of voodoo" prayed for, or "called upon the spirits," to bring freedom to Haiti.[38] The spirits apparently responded with some measure of favor, as L'Ouverture and his army also ran off the English who were trying to gain a foothold on the island. L'Ouverture, in becoming Haiti's new leader, created a constitution and worked to repair the exploited island's economy for its citizens. For approximately five years (1798–1802) Haiti understood a freedom and self-governance it had not experienced for three centuries.

Haiti's independence was threatened again when L'Ouverture moved to rid the country of all European control, a condition that Haiti's remaining European plantocracy opposed with help from 30,000 French troops. To remove some measure of resistance, L'Ouverture was arrested. Held against his will, L'Ouverture eventually died from pneumonia after being denied medical care. In his place, the African-born slave Jean-Jacques Dessalines stepped in, leading Haitians to beat back the French, famously tearing the white pane out of the French *tricolore* to declare the country a Black republic, and to (again) pronounce Haiti independent in 1804. France would try again to take the island in 1825, instead leaving with a treaty in which France would recognize Haiti as independent, but at a cost of 90 million francs for the impoverished country.

In the meantime, some 10,000 Haitians and slaves, as well as French colonists, fled the turmoil, landing in New Orleans, Louisiana (lured by its similar plantations), thereby having a dramatic impact on the city's cultural landscape. This migration proved important to myth-making about the Caribbean, which came to be viewed as a "fatal, promiscuous place" whose cultural products "travel willy-nilly around the world, mutating as they do at each point of arrival."[39] Indeed, in the US, Vodou would become "Voodoo" (though some resisted the spelling as vulgar). Even one horror film *The Love Wanga* (1936), explained that Haiti's religions came to be *"known to White men* as VOODOO" [emphasis mine].[40]

The US refused to acknowledge the country's independence until 1862.[41] Haiti's rise in the world was further complicated by leadership coup after leadership coup, fueled by outsider interests.

In 1915, U.S. President Woodrow Wilson ordered yet another occupation of Haiti. For 19 years, from 1915 to 1934, the United States possessed Haiti, a preemptive seizure purportedly motivated by World War I concerns that Germany might want the island for its own militaristic advantage. The US' occupation of Haiti, led by the Marines, took the form of a dictatorship, marked by an extreme violence in which all forms of political dissent met with enormous bloodshed. The violence was also punctuated by deep-seated racism on the part of the U.S. military: "The highly placed Marine officer Smedley Butler referred to the leaders of the peasant resistance as 'shaved apes, absolutely no intelligence whatsoever, just plain low nigger [sic].'"[42] In 1932, under President Roosevelt, it was announced that the Marine's time in Haiti was to officially come to an end by way of staggered mass departures. The last Marine exited in 1934, waving good-bye to a country left in a social, political, and economic shambles.

It is likely no coincidence that the departure of the Marines from Haiti that started in 1932 coincided with the release of the first American Voodoo-inspired zombie horror movie *White Zombie* (1932), with Haiti as its setting. Indeed, the Marines brought back fantastic stories of the Haitian people's purportedly odd folkways, including the use of black magic (deadly spells and poisonings).

In the Beginning, There Was *White Zombie*

Depictions of Voodoo in film have been around nearly as long as the medium itself.[43] Often, if there was a jungle film in the making, some representation of a witchcraft ritual was tossed in to heighten the sense of danger in a savage land, complete with snakes, partially nude natives dancing around rings of fire, and, of course, the fear-inducing soundtrack of those associated with the dark— drumming. Rhodes identifies some early treatments of Voodoo in film history beginning with the 1913 film *Voodoo Fires*, which promised the clichéd union of evil rituals and inferno. Sigmund Lubin's film company also took up the trend of casting Voodoo as vulgar in *Ghost of Twisted Oak* (1915). The film *Unconquered* (1917) depicted Voodoo as tied to ritual human sacrifice.[44] *The Witching Eyes* (1929), a White produced, scripted, and directed "Black horror" film, was an early entry into the popular trend of depicting how Voodoo could be used to disturb affairs of the heart.

There is much that can be written about what was present in these films, including the exploitative treatment of Blacks and Black religions. Yet, what is also notable about these early Voodoo films is what is absent from them— zombies. Indeed, Voodoo was depicted early on as a sort of pagan religion whose unique properties include rituals celebrating Black gods and black magic. However, the Voodoo film saw a dramatic change in 1932 with the film *White Zombie*, which focused on zombism, and the ability to raise the dead to do one's bidding.

White Zombie can be credited with spawning the prolific zombie horror film subgenre (e.g. *Night of the Living Dead* [1968]; *The Serpent and the Rainbow* [1988]). However, the primary influence for the film and the subsequent zombie genre is the William Seabrook travelogue *The Magic Island* (1929), about zombie-making in Haiti. While monsters such as Frankenstein or Dracula had a literary origin, the zombie purportedly came from nonfiction; depictions of Voodoo and zombies drew on first-hand accounts written by Europeans and Americans. Seabrook's book is by far the best known and cited. Written during the U.S. Marines' occupation of Haiti, *The Magic Island* functioned to depict the country as extraordinarily difficult, with Haitians and Americans at odds with one another in great part because of Haitians' lack of civilization and refinement (even the educated elite were found to be lacking). The Marines were understood to be racist, but their animosities toward Blacks were written off as understandable given the wickedness of the land.

Seabrook's book is based on his two-year stay with a Voodoo priestess. Written in a dramatically sensational style, accompanied by glaringly racist caricature illustrations by Alexander King, in it Seabrook wrote of witnessing Voodoo rituals:

> in the red light of torches which made the moon turn pale, leaping, screaming, writhing black bodies, blood-maddened, sex-maddened, god-maddened, drunken, whirled and dance their dark saturnalia, heads thrown weirdly back as if their necks were broken, white teeth and eyeballs gleaming.[45]

Seabrook worked to lend credibility to his work by citing sources such as *The Museum Journal* (1917) of the University of Pennsylvania on the savagery of Haitian Voodoo, which reported on how Haitians bite the heads off snakes, how they are taught "to hate the Whites" during their Voodoo rituals, and how Haitians eat "a goat without horns," that is, a human child, "raw or partly cooked."[46] Seabrook even claimed to present the secret formulas for bringing forth the undead, recipes which were found on the body of a "bocor" or sorcerer:

> *To call up the dead.* Go to a cemetery on a Friday night at midnight, one where shootings have taken place. Go to a man's grave, taking along with you a white candle, one leaf of wild acacia, and a fully loaded gun. On arrival you will make this appeal: "Exsurgent mortui et ad me veniunt. I require of you dead that you come to me." After saying these words you will hear a stormy noise; you do not take fright, and then fire one shot. The dead will appear to you; you must not run away, but walk backward three steps, saying these words: "I besprinkle you with incense and myrrh such as perfumed Astaroth's tomb," three times. *Sending back a dead spirit after you*

have called it. Pick up a handful of dirt, which you will throw to the four corners of the earth saying: "Go back from where you came, from dirt you were created, to dirt you may return. Amen."[47]

Seabrook would go on to write more nonfiction books about his first-hand observations of devil worship in Africa, his foray into cannibalism (tastes like veal), and his study of witchcraft practices from around the world.

White Zombie did little to discount the stories about Haiti as presented by Seabrook; rather, the film used the book as its template. The "Blacks in horror" film, which is also about trickery and love, tells the tale of Charles Beaumont (Robert Frazer), a wealthy White businessman residing in Haiti who meets a White couple—Neil (John Harron) and Madeline (Madge Bellamy) from New York. The couple plan to marry, and Beaumont persuades them to have their wedding on his property in a remote jungle area in Haiti. Beaumont's motives, of course, are not pure, as he has fallen in love with the blond Madeline and hopes to lure the couple to his home where he will abduct Madeline, keeping her on the island for himself. Beaumont enlists the assistance of a (obviously named) White sugar plantation owner, Murder Legendre (Bela Lugosi), who has mastered the power of Voodoo and controls a horde of zombies who do his evil bidding. When Murder sees Madeline, he wants her too, thereby setting off a wicked tug-of-war for the only (White) woman on the island (Black women are largely absent from the film). Murder and Beaumont zombify Madeline and try to force her to murder Neil; then Murder turns Beaumont into a zombie as well.

White Zombie is noteworthy for its introduction of the zombie monster, which had not been seen in film before. Hence, as the film title promises, the focus is on *White* zombies enslaved by Murder. In Murder's sugar mill, Black and White zombies toil side by side in perilous conditions, with Murder explaining, "They work faithfully, they are not worried about long hours." This premise recalls Seabrook's chapter entitled "Dead Men Working in the Cane Fields," which similarly introduces the zombie as

> a soulless human corpse, still dead, but taken from the grave and endowed by sorcery with a mechanical semblance of life … and then make of it a servant or slave, occasionally for the commission of some crime, more often simply as a drudge around the habitation or the farm, setting it dull heavy tasks, and beating it like a dumb beast if it slackens.[48]

It is a fantasy of post-slavery docility—ageless slaves laboring in the sun and under deadly conditions forever and without complaint. Murder has dozens of such drudges, but prizes his possession of five White, French zombies, all formidable foes before he took their souls. There is a captain, a thief, the island's Minister of the Interior, and the hulking high executioner, who, Murder explains, "almost

FIGURE 2.2 A zombie with Murder in *White Zombie*
United Artists/Photofest

executed me." The fifth zombie is Murder's greatest trophy, a fellow who he describes as "once my master"—a powerful White witchdoctor who Murder had to torture at length before his Voodoo secrets were revealed.

The real horror in this film, though, as with many horror films before and since—from *King Kong* to the more recent *Candyman* (1992)—is the threat made against a White woman. Madeline joins Kong's Ann Darrow as the archetypal female victim. Both women suffer rather similar fears, to include engaging with the Other. For Madeline, her encounter with the Other comes from those who inhabit Haiti, and the threat she faces is similar to Darrow's—a kind of White slavery through forced prostitution. In the end, like all monsters, Murder and Beaumont pay for their lustful treachery with their lives, leaving Madeline to finally unite with Neil. Rhodes writes, "all men—zombies, fiancée, betrayer all want to sexually possess the women."[49] On the issue of desire, the film was cited in a July 29, 1932 *New York Times* review for using zombies as monsters because "they make good servants. They can carry off blondes without getting ideas in their heads, which helps in these mad days."[50]

In the upside down world of Haiti, White men can become evil Voodoo practitioners, beguiled White women can be moved to the brink of murder, and powerful Whites can be turned into slaves. It is Haiti's impact on Whiteness that has spawned the horror. In one catch-line related to the film, it is asserted that Haiti was always wicked but it did not merit attention until it turned on Whites: "They knew that this was taking place among the Blacks, but when this fiend practiced it on a White girl ... all hell broke loose."[51] Although this is a horror movie that assigns the tropes of horror mainly to Whites, White Zombie is an indictment on Blackness. The audience learns that the island is "full of nonsense and superstition," and is inhabited by natives participating in an odd "death cult" who "use human bones in their ceremonies." These practices were "brought here from Africa," the purported wellspring of evil. The sparse representation of Blacks in the film does not spare Blacks from stereotyping as they are described as monstrous all the same, as when Neil thinks Madeline is "in the hands of natives," and proclaims that she would be "better dead than that!"

Indeed, with Haiti as the film's setting, it is surprising how few Black characters there are in Zombie. Black women are nearly excluded from Zombie, while Black men are present, but none in central roles. Still, a few Black representations are noteworthy, offering one of the earliest effective depictions of Blacks in the genre. The film presents a funeral scene in which the camera lingers for a moment on a group of (non-zombie) Black pallbearers. The men do not speak (as they should not), but they are memorable. They are striking— smartly dressed, polished from their well-manicured haircuts to their tuxedos. They are consequential for what is not portrayed in their depiction; there are no "coon" antics or other deficiencies, just appropriately subdued elegance.[52]

However, the most notable Black portrayal in White Zombie occurs in the first few minutes of the film and comes from a cameo appearance by the Black actor Clarence Muse (uncredited) as "Coach Driver." Muse's character (the Driver) is charged with driving Neil and Madeline to Beaumont's mansion. When the coach comes upon a large group of Black men and women digging in the road, blocking the carriage's path, the Driver explains succinctly why Haitians bury their dead in the road: "It's a funeral, mademoiselle. They're afraid of the men who steal dead bodies. So they dig the graves in the middle of the road, where people pass all the time." Here, the influence of The Magic Island upon the movie is again apparent as Seabrook writes of road burials: "why, so often, do you see a tomb or grave set close beside a busy road or footpath where people are always passing? It is to assure the poor unhappy dead such protection as we can."[53] In another scene, as the Driver moves Neil and Madeline closer to their destination, he spots some White zombies. In response, the Driver yells, "Zombies!," and urges the horses on at full speed to put more distance between the coach and the monsters. Frightened, Neil demands, "Why did you drive like that you fool? We might have been killed!" The Driver delivers a soliloquy in a measured timbre that sounds more like a professorial lecture: "Worse than that, monsieur. We might have been caught. ... They are not men, monsieur. They are dead bodies ... Zombies. The living dead. Corpses taken from their graves who are made to work in the sugar mills and the fields at night." The Driver drops the couple at Beaumont's mansion. He again sees the monsters and warns, "Look, here they come!" and then flees the scene (thereby exiting the film).

His is not a stereotypical scared-Negro-feets-don't-fail-me-now routine, but he departs expeditiously given the coming danger.[54]

Muse's portrayal of the Driver, albeit brief, contradicted much of what Hollywood was presenting about Blackness. Five years after *White Zombie*, it seemed the industry had learned little, as Robert Stebbins observed in *New Theatre*, July, 1935:

> The Negro's activity in the Hollywood film is confined to fleeting shadows of him as a lazy servant ... or a coachman who has been made to look ridiculous ... He is also ... a voodoo-maddened villain bent on exterminating the White race in "Black Moon," or at best a benighted prisoner intoning the ubiquitous spiritual in the death house while the hero is prepared for his walk along the "last mile."[55]

Muse himself can be implicated in this indictment against Blacks' representations in film, as his participation in the "Blacks in horror" film *Black Moon* (1934) presented a devolution in representational progress.

Black Moon focuses on Juanita (Dorothy Burgess), a White woman sent away to the US from her home in San Christopher by her uncle, Dr. Raymond Perez (Arnold Korff), a plantation owner, and by Perez's overseer, Macklin (Lumsden Hare). The two White men are "alone" in San Christopher surrounded by over 2,000 "natives" who are described as mostly "bandits" from nearby Haiti. The natives have brought Voodoo with them to San Christopher, which includes blood worship and human sacrifice on behalf of their "Black gods." Juanita cannot shake her connection to the island, and even takes up playing "native drums" in her spare time. It is revealed that when Juanita was a child, after the natives murdered her parents, she was provided with a Black caregiver who secretly inculcated her in Voodoo, filling her "with the sound of drums and the sight of blood." Hence, the horror in this film is the idea that Voodoo can creep out of the jungle and into a White home and a White woman at any time.

Longing for home, Juanita returns to San Christopher with her daughter Nancy (Cora Sue Collins) (with her husband to arrive later). She is welcomed by the hordes of natives, who shower her with flowers and have to be beaten back by her uncle, who also has a reputation for whipping and killing the natives. Yet, over the course of the movie, it is the natives who are depicted as relishing murder—Macklin, Anna (Nancy's White nanny, Eleanor Wesselhoeft), and a Black man who, under orders, summons Juanita's husband to save her from evil are all killed, as is a Black woman who is offered as a human sacrifice. It is clear fairly early on that Juanita is far too tainted by the natives to be saved. She drums, slips into trances, and dances sensually in Voodoo rituals (surrounded by approximately 500 African American dancers in native costumes).[56] Juanita leaves her daughter unattended to sneak off in the middle of the night to be with the

FIGURE 2.3 The taint of a Black man's shadow in *Black Moon*
Columbia Pictures / Photofest

natives, a transgression that is met with utter repulsion by her uncle as he washes his hands of her. Juanita eventually becomes so submerged—so "blackened" through her brush with Black natives and Black Voodoo—that she tries to kill her husband and her daughter. For these sins, Juanita is killed, by her savior husband.

Here again, the depiction of Haiti's effect on a White woman may be rooted in early "true" reports about the Caribbean. Joan Dayan (175, 178) in *Haiti, History, and the Gods*, writes that White women's taking on Blackness was a recurrent theme in many writings by colonial historians of the Caribbean. Dayan writes that these historical tomes asserted that "Whites' gradual taking on of the traits of Blacks was seen not as imitation but infection." While Blacks tried to assimilate White culture, when Whites took up Black culture they were described as having "caught a disease, as if they were too weak-willed or amoral to resist the contagious attraction of loose living, scanty dress, and languorous talk. … Unbearable heat and numerous Blacks contributed to the inevitable pollution of civility and grace."[57]

Black Moon, then, becomes more than a horror tale about the abominable blackening of a White woman; it is also a stark, violent warning against integration.

The Black "problem" in the film does not end with Juanita's death. Enter Clarence Muse, as "Lunch," the owner of a schooner who hails from

Augusta, Georgia. Lunch shuttles people from San Christopher to Haiti, entertaining them with a song while they sail. It is through Lunch that both Caribbean Blacks and U.S. Blacks are marked as backward on a scale of deficiency. Lunch refers to the island Blacks as "monkey chasers," explaining that monkeys like coconuts, and so do the natives, who chase the monkeys to steal their fruit. It is also through Lunch that it is revealed that the natives have to be kept under a watchful eye and scolded because they prefer sleeping instead of working. In fact, at the film's end, the Whites get away from the bloodthirsty natives because some have fallen asleep during their attack, permitting Lunch to lead the Whites to safety. But Lunch is also a comic-negro and Uncle Tom stereotype. He is alternately bug-eyed scared and fiercely loyal and sacrificing for the Whites. The scenes are an obvious pitting of Blacks against other Blacks, with Black Americans slightly superior to those from San Christopher, "the site of unending violence, named for the patron saint of lost causes."[58]

Muse was emotionally torn by his portrayals of such characters, talking and writing about them often (e.g. his self-published work *The Dilemma of the Negro Actor*, 1934). In an essay mournfully titled "When a Negro Sings a Song," Muse writes of the predicament Blacks confronted in the limited singing and comedic roles offered in Hollywood films: "There are two audiences to confront in America—the Black and the White. The White audiences definitely desire buffoonery, songs and dances from the Black man, while the Negro audience wants to see and hear the real elements of Negro life exemplified."[59] The dignity Muse brought to his acting was most apparent in Black films and in his script writing, further revealing a tension between Black films and White films.

Muse's indications of "self-respect and Black self-awareness" aside, he was still held accountable for his more troubling performances.[60] Bogle described Muse's roles as depicting a "humanized tom," far from a Stepin Fetchit comic performance or a full-blown Uncle Tom, but troubling all the same.[61] However, Muse is also known for bringing depth and complexity to his performances that were also distinct for their relative lack of stereotype (given the time).

For example, in 1941 Muse was featured in a substantial supporting role as Evans the Butler in the "Blacks in horror" film *Invisible Ghost*. Again teaming up with Lugosi who played Dr. Kessler, Muse's Evans is also the manager of the Kessler estate, which includes supervising its White employees (e.g. cooks, groundskeepers). As murders begin to plague the Kessler home, Evans is presented as intelligent and informed, and participates in a rather civil interview with the authorities as they hope he can help them. Evans becomes central to cracking the mystery, ultimately aiding in securing the arrest of the culprit, Kessler.

Nevertheless, these better-crafted roles for Blacks were not sufficient to draw film away from Black places such as Haiti. Blacks found themselves forever associated with Voodoo, black magic sorcery, and zombies, in the horror genre.

If Loving You Is Wrong, I Don't Want to Be Right

Movies such as *King Kong* and *White Zombie* were really glowing love stories. Thanks to the threats from natives and an ape, in *King Kong* Ann appreciated her true love and savior, Jack Driscoll (Bruce Cabot), all the more. Likewise, if Madeline had second thoughts about marrying her Neil, all that was settled when she saw her other choices, Voodoo-tainted White men. *The Mummy* (1932) also took up love, mixed-raced identity, and the one-drop rule, but there would be no tragic mulatto here. In this film, Helen (Zita Johann) is half Egyptian/half English, but marks herself as quite separate from African countries, including her mother's birthplace of Egypt. For Helen, gazing out at the pyramids from an English club, the country looks "beautiful" even as it is a "dreadful" place. Her father, the governor of Sudan, left her in Egypt for a trip back to the "beastly, hot" country. Suddenly Helen is mesmerized, coming under the spell of Ardeth Bey/Imhotep (Boris Karloff), a 3,700-year-old resurrected Egyptian priest who was mummified and buried alive for the sin of abusing magic by trying to cast a spell to bring his true love back to life after her death. Imhotep recognizes that Helen is "of our blood" and then reveals to her, through magic, that Helen was his beloved in another life. In fact, blood figures prominently in Imhotep's world. When the Nubian (Noble Johnson), a servant to a White "master," comes under Imhotep's spell as well, the Nubian's susceptibility to the magic is explained in the film as being based on his Black blood: "The Nubian! The ancient blood. You made him your slave." The Nubian becomes Imhotep's slave, just as Nubians had been in ancient Egypt, as seen in a flashback. It is from the forlorn Imhotep that Whites must rescue Helen. But they are doing more than retrieving her from a monster; they are freeing her from "an oppressed and backwards ethnic other" by seeing her as sufficiently White.[62] Helen is also able to escape Egypt's myths, with its superstitions and polytheism, when her love, Frank (David Manners), who talks emphatically about the value of scientific reasoning, saves her.

White women were not looking for love in all the wrong places, but it seemed as though Black women did all the time. *Ingagi* was a grotesque reminder of how that could happen. The biggest mistake a Black woman could make, however, was to choose a White man as her suitor. If getting it on with a monkey was implausible, then trying to woo a White man was wrong ... dead wrong.

In the "Blacks in horror" film *The Love Wanga* (1936) the setting is Paradise Island, just off of the coast of Haiti.[63] There resides Klili Gordon (Fredi Washington), a biracial (Black/White) plantation owner who is in love with Adam Maynard (Philip Brandon), the White owner of a neighboring plantation. In this "true" story, in which the "names have been changed," the problem is that though Adam has treasured a very close friendship with Klili, he cannot bring himself to love her because, as he explains, the "barrier of blood that separates us can't be overcome." Klili, who is phenotypically as light as Adam, cannot ever be White enough as somewhere in her blood line there is African ancestry. Hence, she is tainted by the one-drop rule, in which just a bit of Black blood makes one instantly and forever Black. When Adam chooses (predictably) Eve (Marie Paxton), a pure White woman, for his bride, Klili is enraged with jealousy. She holds up her arm next to Eve's proclaiming, "I'm White too. As White as she is!" The tragedy of skin color and blood is textbook tragic mulatto stereotype, in which her proximity to Whiteness makes her beautiful while the irreconcilability of her situation makes her a danger to herself or others, and ultimately leads to insanity.[64] Klili resorts to Voodoo, first using a death charm to send Eve to the brink of death (from which she is miraculously saved). Klili is then moved to raise 13 zombies, undead Black men, to kidnap Eve and put her into a trance so that Klili can kill her.[65] Here, the zombies are slightly reimagined from earlier portrayals. They are still reanimated empty vessels under someone else's control. However, *The Love Wanga* removes from the audience's memory colonial and occupation discourses in favor of what Dayan describes as a new idiom dismantling the US' culpability in forced labor.[66] The new construction places Blacks at the center of forcible servitude as well as death since White massacres are not exposed.

However, the film is most notable for its attention to racial identity. Fredi Washington, a Black actress with a very fair complexion and green eyes, was type-cast as the tragic mulatto, and her most notable role was as the "passing" Peola in *Imitation of Life* (1934). *The Love Wanga* continued its color play by casting the White actor Sheldon Leonard as LeStrange, the Black overseer of Adam's banana plantation. Leonard is an odd choice to play a Black man; however, his casting may have been a preemptive move on the part of the filmmakers, as Washington ran into trouble with censors in the non-horror film *The Emperor Jones* (1933), also set in Haiti. In *Jones* Washington kisses the Black actor Paul Robeson, which censors feared looked too much like a White woman kissing a Black man.[67] To remedy the problem, Washington was instructed to wear darker make-up to appear more Black. In *Wanga*, make-up was not a feasible solution to the race dilemma as Klili must look "as White as" Eve. Perhaps it was better for a White-appearing woman to be seen in an embrace with a White male actor than for her to be seen with a Black one. In *Wanga*, then, it is dialogue, not appearances, that must mark LeStrange (a rather apropos name) as Black. He refers to Adam as "my master," and there is this proclamation:

LESTRANGE TO KLILI: You're Black. You belong to us. To me.
KLILI: I hate you, you Black scum!

Like Klili, there can be no mistaking LeStrange's Blackness because of his proximity to evil. He is just as adept at Voodoo, and as wicked, as Klili. LeStrange steals a Black woman's dead body, dresses it in Klili's clothes, and hangs the body from a tree as part of a Voodoo curse against Klili for rejecting his love.

Klili's undying love for Adam is depicted as impossible but not surprising as she and her taste become part of the well-trod myth about "mulatto" women liking the very best of things: "Numerous European accounts of the mulatto women dwell, in particular on their exquisite taste, their love of finery, and their special attachment to lace, linen, silks, and gold."[68] Of course, liking and having are two very different things, and Klili can never have Adam. For all that she has done, Klili becomes a hunted woman. In the end, when LeStrange's Voodoo curse does not deliver death upon Klili quickly enough, LeStrange chokes her to death with his bare hands.

Apart from its treatment of racial identity, *The Love Wanga* took the route of most other horror films that included an attention to Blackness. Black Voodooists abound on Paradise Island, working fervently on their craft in a place where the people are otherwise, according to the film, unhurried and primitive. There are plenty of Bocours (witch doctors), Loas (spirits), and zombies, as the film explains their existence: "the lifeless bodies of murdered negroes reanimated by the Bocours for evil purposes." Everyone, good or evil, seems to know how to craft an ouanga (wanga) or charm, which can be alternately used to spark love or to prompt death. When not engaged in some sort of magic, the Blacks on the island spend a considerable amount of time throwing dice, gambling, and dancing. *The Love Wanga*, of course, does not deny Blacks a beat to dance to, and the ever-present beat of Voodoo drums, or "Rada," is heard. The drums are described in sensuous terms—they present a "throbbing" and "pulsating" beat—while the camera lingers on the shirtless, muscled chest of a Black man fervently beating the instrument.

In 1939, *The Love Wanga* was remade starring an all-Black cast in the "Black horror" film *The Devil's Daughter*. Written by George Terwilliger and directed by Arthur Leonard, this was a film scripted, directed, and produced by Whites, but which targeted Black audiences.

The film's opening scenes function to establish just how different Black folkways in the Caribbean are. In a lengthy sequence, a large group of shabbily dressed banana plantation workers are seen singing and dancing in a clearing. This is also the site for gambling and cock-fighting. It is also revealed that the workers believe in Voodoo as an evil magic that can be manipulated for all manner of immoral ends.

The film tells the story of two half-sisters from Jamaica. The first is Isabelle (Nina Mae McKinney), whose mother was a Haitian Voodooist. Isabelle has been running the family plantation and has the love and support of its Black and Creole workers. The second sister is Sylvia (Ida James), who left Jamaica years ago to pursue higher education in the United States, and became a refined woman in Harlem (the time period coincides with the Harlem Renaissance). When the siblings' father dies, he leaves the plantation and the wealth that comes with it to the more cultivated Sylvia, while the more coarse Isabelle gets nothing. Sylvia returns to Jamaica to manage the property, while enlisting the help of an overseer named Ramsey who claims to be in love with her, but does so only to steal her money. Ramsey is played by the White actor Jack Carter. Though the White actor Sheldon Leonard was "blackened" in his dialect in *The Love Wanga*, here Carter is not. Rather, his race is not addressed in the film at all. The color-coding may also be a bit of politically clever casting, as Ramsey is revealed to be a liar and a thief. Two other principal Black male characters are recognizable as such. There is John (Emmett Wallace), who loves Sylvia and in the end wins her love. There is also Percy (Hamtree Harrington), Sylvia's butler from Harlem, who believes Blacks from Jamaica are lacking and, with comic effect, learns they can be duplicitous when he is tricked into believing they have stored his soul in a pig (which is later eaten).

The film's primary focus, however, is on the dissimilarities between the two sisters, which actually functions to complicate U.S. vs. Jamaica comparisons, and brings some depth to the portrayals. Isabelle is depicted as the rough and tumble sister doing the hard work of running the plantation, while fawning over John, who is not interested in her. Sylvia is depicted as having returned bourgeois, touring the plantation in fancy dresses by chauffeur. The divide between the sisters is at the line of the urban and urbane versus the rural and unsophisticated. However, even this contrast is recast through a caution about the dangers of leaving home, becoming uppity, and losing touch with one's people. Harlemites Sylvia and Percy are exposed as gullible due to their geographic and cultural separation from "home." More, while plantation work is seen as rudimentary and inelegant, being cultured and well read is cast as rather useless.

Isabelle devises a plan to win back the plantation—she exploits prevailing superstitions by reminding Sylvia and John that her mother was Haitian, implying that she can perform Voodoo. Isabelle instructs her workers, many of whom practice Voodoo, to beat their drums in the jungle with more vigor than they have in the past, moving Sylvia to observe that the drums sound even more "menacing" than she remembered from her youth. Sylvia believes she has become the victim of a Voodoo ritual when Isabelle drugs her and pretends to prepare her for a sacrifice. The film presents a rather lengthy Obeah (black magic) ceremony over which Isabelle presides, offering incantations. Isabelle is revealed to be faking her power—if she truly was magical she would not need to rely on drugs. John rushes to Sylvia's rescue, while bringing up blood mixture: Isabelle is not Haitian "enough" to effectively do Voodoo. Isabelle and Sylvia make their peace. Sylvia turns over the plantation to Isabelle as she comes to understand, "I don't belong."

Chloe, Love Is Calling You (1934) is a racially intriguing, if controversially themed "Blacks in horror" film that takes on not only the tragic mulatto, but also Jim Crow-era racial violence. It is a tale in which a poor, elderly Black woman and Voodooist, Mandy (Georgette Harvey), seeks revenge for the lynching of her husband, Sam. Mandy is "mammy" to a young adult daughter, Chloe (Olive Borden, a White actress), who appears White and must suffer harassment from both Blacks and Whites for her tainted blood. Chloe has two male suitors. The first is Jim, a long-suffering, doting "colored" man (portrayed by the White actor Philip Ober) with a drop of Black blood in his veins, whom she does not love. The second is Wade (Reed Howes), a White man, who has just arrived in town to oversee the nearby turpentine plantation and who initially mistakes Chloe for a White woman. In casting all three characters with White actors, there can be no censor concerns of a White woman being seen in the arms of a Black man.

Chloe desperately loves Wade, but runs from him because of her racial secret. For dreaming of being with Whites, she is accused by Jim of listening to her "White blood speaking." Chloe thereby presents the classic tragic mulatto tale in which she is tormented by being trapped in Blackness, even though her body gives little hint of it. The Black population claims to see Black in Chloe, as evidenced in a scene when a Black man attempts to assault Chloe by remarking, "High yellow, they always was my meat." Likewise, when two White women look at her, they remark, "She's so dark."

The twist here is that Mandy swapped her dead Black baby for Chloe in revenge for Chloe's White father, the Colonel, ordering the lynching of Sam. By Mandy's side, all see Chloe as Black and treat her as such. The lesson in race prejudice is presented, even as it falls short. When it is confirmed that Chloe is indeed White, she (like Tarzan) gives credence to the innate superiority of Whiteness. In this Cinderella story, Chloe has absolutely no difficulty in settling into the (rich) White world. Newly Whitened, the young woman asks that "Chloe" never be referenced again, and confidently proclaims, "I am Betty Ann." She moves easily through her mansion home, dons lavish white gowns, and ably entertains the White elite. Her new home is the epitome of ostentatiousness in that it is as colossal as it is ornately appointed. It seems apropos, then, that this Big House, towering over a plantation, would be the site of Black resistance. Such houses, with their "monumental staircases," a "maze of huge doorways, halls, and gigantic rooms," and with uniformed house servants gliding "silently about their tasks," were cruel symbols of histories and myths of servitude.[69]

Mandy seeks to punish both the Colonel and Chloe for their betrayals by sacrificing Chloe in a Voodoo ritual. There are the booms of the Voodoo drums, fire, and native dancing. Mandy is dressed as the Voodoo spirit Baron Samedi. But all fails ... for Blacks. Jim attempts Chloe's rescue from Mandy's clutches, but is mortally wounded, leaving her to be saved by Wade. Chloe as Betty Ann and Wade finally find love as a pure White couple.

Chloe, like *The Love Wanga*, and *The Devil's Daughter* are lacking in true scares. However, they do take up the subject of racial politics head on. *Chloe*, in particular, stands out in its attention to racial violence. Films of this period were critiqued for failing to address such racism, as revealed in *The Harlem Liberator*'s column "Camera Eye" (1933): "Hardly a word appears about lynching, peonage, share cropping or chain gangs. And when these subjects are treated they are glossed over."[70] However, *Chloe* provides rare attention to lynching. Mandy's Voodoo "sure is talking" when she returns to Louisiana, the state in which Sam met his fate: "Thar' is. Thar' is. That old hangman's tree. Where them White folks killed my Sam and the bloodhounds tore him to pieces. Here I is, Sammy. Here is your Mandy come back to put curses on the Colonel and them White folks." In the film, Sam's death, as ordered by the plantation owner, the Colonel, is not disputed, but it is dismissed: "I fired Sam. Don't remember what for." There are different ways of reading the Colonel's account of Sam's death. His coldness works to implicate him in a racism which holds Black life as inconsequential. Or, the reading is a literal one given the time—Black life was regarded as absent value. The Colonel goes on to explain that in response to his firing, Sam slugged him. For this, the Colonel matter of factly explains, "Sam was lynched." It is this injustice that Mandy focuses on throughout the film, "It won't be long now Sam … 'Cause I'm a work my Voodoo. The thunder's gonna growl and the lightning's gonna rain. And the devil's gonna walk on a White man's grave." However, the film does not go much farther in its interrogation of Blacks' Jim Crow-era treatment. Mandy is depicted as crazy, hence her obsession with Sam's lynching becomes easily dismissed. At the film's end, the Colonel orders the immediate arrest of Mandy, who is fleeing her crimes, explaining, "We don't want any lynching." The line "don't want any lynching" implies that if Mandy continues to flee, then the Whites of the community will have to bother themselves with her lynching too.

The film's other central Black character, one that undermines even the illusion of a revolutionary moment in the film, is the Colonel's house servant Ben (Richard Huey). A textbook Uncle Tom characterization, Ben is a happy, doting servant who is undyingly loyal to his White employer, even going so far as to spy on Mandy and other Blacks on the plantation to report their deeds to the Colonel. It is Ben who reveals to the Colonel that Mandy has returned to Louisiana to "put Voodoo on you." Ben even breaks into Mandy's shack, along with the Colonel and Wade, to rifle through her belongings. Bug-eyed and scared with fright, Ben roots through Mandy's "Voodoo bag," finding baby clothes once worn by the Colonel's daughter, thought to be drowned. Finally, when a doctor seeks to confirm that Mandy's Black baby was the infant who had died, not the Colonels' White one, he takes Ben to dig up the baby in search of conclusive evidence. The doctor triumphantly reports back: "The hair is kinky."

Conclusion

Love was in the air in the 1930s, but this was the horror genre and the road to passion, expectedly, was full of deadly detours. Apes, Voodoo, natives, and zombies had a tendency to disrupt affairs of the heart. Part of the horror was that it was affairs of the White heart into which these monstrosities were interjected. Monstrous characters like Kong, Murder, and even the Mummy knew how to ruin date night for Ann, Madeline, and Helen, respectively, even as they tried to win the affections of fair ladies. This was a serious, scary business as the mainstream (White) public would "find the enslavement of White Christians by dark-skinned natives extremely abhorrent. Furthermore, because the victims of Voodoo sorcery are most often female these early, largely racist narratives … would prey upon deep-seated racial paranoia."[71] Thank goodness for White knights who rode in to save the day, and to rid their betrothed of their wickedness. The lesson here was that in being a victim of some uninvited dark evil, sexual and racial purity were challenged, but ultimately restored.

Indeed, no greater love hath man (or ape) than a pure White woman. But woe is the one who trades on and delivers evil; to be sure one can have no greater sin. Implicated in this sordid affair were the Klilis, Mandys, and the Juanitas. These three wicked women had done far too much to go on living. Interestingly, though all three lived by the metaphorical Voodoo sword, none died by it. Rather, men decided the fate of these women. Klili was strangled by a (Black-ish) man, Mandy was hunted down by White men, and the bullet in Juanita's back was delivered by a White man. These women, with their black hearts, were further blackened by their connection to Voodoo. However, the most pointed disdain and contempt was reserved for Juanita, a White woman, who willingly submitted to and sided with the Black world.

Certainly some would say that the horror has to be located somewhere and in these films it just happens to be among Black people and in Black places. However, in the films of this period the focus is not so much on horror (or love) as it is on casting Blacks as dreadfully horrible, and that is an especially important difference. These are not modern horror films in which monsters come to slash and torture; rather these are horror films in which it is not enough to locate horror in the monster (e.g. an ape), the monster has to also be blackened. Additionally, if that monster … blackened … has its way with native Black women, the effect is more than a good "Boo!"; rather it speaks to the disgusting nature of Blacks. The Black evil being thrown around, the Uncle Toms, mammies, and coons, all are used as fodder for racial ridicule and to assure White supremacy. That is the real horror of these films.

Representationally, over the coming years, things would get no easier for Blacks. In the longer term, for example, Haiti and zombification would be further abused in popular culture. In the press, Haitians continue to be cast as wicked and tainted with refrains that the "boat people" (seeking political and economic freedom) are coming, importing not only Voodoo to the US, but also disease (tuberculosis and AIDS).[72] Horror continued to implicate Blacks in zombification, throwing in a bit of satanism (e.g. *Angel Heart* [1987]) and cannibalism (e.g. *Zombiez* [2005]) as well.

In the next decade of the 1940s, progress continued to be slow for Blacks in horror films. In fact, the genre was regressing, casting Blacks as buffoons and comic relief, and giving even more prominence to the coon performance in spooky films such as *The Body Disappears* (1941), featuring Sleep 'n' Eat, and *King of the Zombies* (1941), boasting Mantan Moreland. There were glimmers of hope for Blacks with the return of a Black film director, Spencer Williams. Williams' "Black horror" films had monsters, the devil, and a healthy dose of lessons in morality to go with them. But first, there would be another ape film to contend with in Williams' half-man, half-ape film, *Son of Ingagi* (1940).

3

HORRIFYING GOONS AND MINSTREL COONS

1940s

In staging this orgy of terror
That leaves you in dread of the dark,
The movies are making an error;
They're all overshooting the mark.

—Jaffray (174)[1]

Horror had come into its own very quickly, and a multitude of filmmakers happily jumped on the horror bandwagon, either specializing in horror or diversifying their portfolios by adding horror films to their oeuvre. This exploding interest in the genre soon meant that a horror film glut was at hand, and audiences who once lined up to get a taste of horror began to bend under the (often crude and formulaic) oversupply; in response audiences turned scarce.

As 1940s horror films were greeted by rather anemic box office returns, the film industry responded to dwindling ticket sales with a two-tiered film production and distribution system. There were A-list movies, with impressive budgetary support, and "B movies," such as horror, which garnered lower budgets and promotion.[2] The two types of films, A and B grade, were at times marketed as part of a double-bill so that when audiences queued up for a quality "A-film" like the Academy Award-winning *All the Kings Men* (1949), they might also take in a horror movie such as one of the many, many mummy "B-flicks" in circulation: *The Mummy's Hand* (1940), *The Mummy's Tomb* (1942), *The Mummy's Ghost* (1944), or *The Mummy's Curse* (1945). Frequently, two B movies would make up the double-bill so that patrons might, perhaps, enjoy an evening of monster movies. Even with such clever double-feature marketing, horror continued to struggle. Perhaps the atrocities of World War II, the most repulsive of which targeted civilians, such as the Holocaust and the atomic bombings of Hiroshima and Nagasaki, were far, far more horrifying and inescapable.[3]

Horror was just gaining its momentum, and already it was under considerable threat. The famed Universal Studios' monsters became embarrassingly derivative, with the comedy duo Bud Abbott and Lou Costello "meeting" many of the monsters in slapstick films. RKO, the studio that produced *King Kong* (1933), under the direction of Val Lewton, offered more original horror film fare, such as *Cat People* (1942). *Cat People* was a rare horror innovation for the time as much of the horror fare of the 1940s was man-in-a-monkey-suit drek such as Monogram Pictures' *The Ape* (1940).

While the horror genre was unraveling, Blacks' representational treatment in the films, particularly in "Blacks in horror" films, saw no improvement. After 50 years of participation in the genre, Blacks were still relegated to roles such as that of the primitive, jungle native or servant to Whites. The most dramatic change to Blacks' portrayals in horror during the 1940s simply added insult to injury, as late nineteenth and early twentieth century minstrelsy was resurrected to create comedy-horror films in which Blacks were presented as deathly afraid coons—absurd, comic figures whose intellectual deficits, such as speaking in malapropisms, cultural inferiority, such as chasing chickens, and physical antics, such as bugging their eyes, invited laughter and ridicule. Unlike the native or the servant, who was often cast as a mere extra in horror films, moving about silently in said films, the scared comic-Negro roles (as they have come to be called) were substantial co-starring parts that were central to the plot. When horror paired with comedy the genre turned to Blacks, with comic actors such as Mantan Moreland and Willie "Sleep 'n' Eat" Best called in to perform their very "best" coon antics.

Importantly, "Black horror" returned during this decade, and thanks to filmmaker Spencer Williams Jr., the horror genre saw some of its most compelling stories, unique characterizations, and thoughtful treatments of Black life and culture. Williams' films focused on the battle between good and evil, delved into Black religiosity, and centered their stories on women. Williams' films begged the question, how could Black filmmakers, excluded from Hollywood and operating on a shoe-string budget, bring to the genre something so markedly inspiring? In sum, this was the dilemma regarding Blacks' participation in horror films of the decade: abysmal, but prominent portrayals, or promising portrayals, limited in their reach.

Monster Mash

The "Blacks in horror" films released over the course of the decade evidenced how dire things were for Blacks. *I Walked With a Zombie* (1943) is set on the Caribbean on the island of postcolonial St. Sebastian, on a sugar plantation and in its surrounding jungle.[4] For the Blacks in the film, St. Sebastian is an island built on death due to its past love affair with slavery. The film begins derisively with a White woman, Betsy (Frances Dee), casually and uncritically dismissing the atrocities of slavery while in a conversation with a Black man, a descendant of slaves:

COACHMAN (CLINTON ROSEMOND, UNCREDITED): The enormous boat brought the long ago fathers and mothers of us all chained to the bottom of the boat.
BETSY: They brought you to a beautiful place, didn't they?
COACHMAN: If you say, Miss, if you say.

Though the film works to assert that slavery's history and effects remain at the fore for Blacks and their existence on the island, this particular scene works to illustrate how filmmakers could not help but to dilute such messages with a postcolonial fantasy of primitive exoticism and beauty. St. Sebastian may be crying from Blacks' spilled blood (as Ti-Misery, the masthead salvaged from a slave ship, symbolically does in the film), but the film works hard to convince viewers that the Caribbean is still a very lovely place to vacation. Humphries, explains Betsy's incomprehension scene in this way: Betsy "can only see beauty around her, beauty of the kind constructed by colonial discourse for the benefit of those who live off the fruits of slave-labour. ... It would be difficult to represent and sum up social and economic blindness more cogently."[5] The way in which Betsy first sees St. Sebastian is reminiscent of *White Zombie* (1932) when the engaged couple Neil and Madeline are surprised that Haiti is not going to be the wedding paradise that they expected. Betsy's (and Neil and Madeline's) ability to be among so many Blacks without knowing them provides startling insights into the repression of cultures and histories.

I *Walked With a Zombie* features an assortment of Voodoo-practicing Blacks who spend quite a bit of time "frightening" Whites by beating Voodoo drums and engaging in rituals. This restriction of Blacks to stereotype means that the films most interesting turns focus on "the psychological problems of White people" rather than any kind of consideration of, or engagement with, the Black characters.[6]

In *Zombie*, there is, expectedly, a zombie among the Blacks—Carre-Four[7] (Darby Jones). Carre-Four skulks around silently and ominously, never really a threat except for when he is ordered to enter the home of the White plantation owner and snatch away a White woman. Of course he does not fulfill this part of his mission, as Black men can only look (which is presumably menacing enough), but they cannot touch. Carre-Four is not the only zombie on the island; there is also Jessica, a White woman who may or may not be a true zombie. There is much to be known about Jessica as the White protagonists battle to regain her soul, and the White men battle for her love. However, Carre-Four's story does not merit exploration, and no one is interested in restoring his soul.[8] There is also Alma (Theresa Harris), who keeps up with the tradition of her slave ancestors of mourning when a Black child is born, but making "merry at a burial." In the film, Alma's tears (which are not seen) are aligned and even supplanted by Ti-Misery's, the masthead-turned-garden-water-fixture on the plantation, that appears to be weeping when its water flows. In the film, the story of the island's slavery history is represented through Ti-Misery. The film denies the living a chance to fully recount this slave history. Instead, Ti-Misery, through symbolism, filters and carries living Blacks' slave narratives of St. Sebastian. Rounding out this odd group, who are viewed "through the confused eyes of the film's White protagonists,"[9] is an omniscient Calypso singer portrayed by Lancelot Pinard a.k.a. Sir Lancelot. Lancelot's contribution to the film is to weave gossip, stories, and an ominous warning about one's fate into his Calypso songs.

What is clear in this film is that Blackness is so infectious that it imperils Whites, particularly White women, who are weakened by their brush with it. In this film, two White women fall victim to Black culture. The first becomes obsessed with the myths and power of Voodoo and she in turn zombifies another defenseless White woman. *New York Times* film critic Bosley Crowther dismissed

FIGURE 3.1 Only a Black man's shadow can enter the White boudoir in *I Walked with a Zombie*
RKO/Photofest

I Walked With a Zombie, snidely remarking the film "drains all one's respect for ambulant ghosts."[10]

Two years later, in 1945, RKO (absent Val Lewton) introduced a sequel to *I Walked With a Zombie*, entitled *Zombies on Broadway*. This horror film took a comedy turn, as so many films did during the 1940s, by centering on the antics of Jerry Miles (Wally Brown) and Mike Strager (Alan Carney), who are Abbott and Costello-type buddies. The film is about the efforts of Jerry and Mike to find a real-life zombie for the opening of a New York club called the Zombie Hut. The duo travel to San Sebastian and are welcomed to the island with a song by Sir Lancelot as the Calypso singer who summarizes their coming fate through lively rhyme. The actor Darby Jones is also back in the role of the silent, gliding zombie, though his name has been changed to Kolaaga and he has a new master in Dr. Paul Renault, played by Bela Lugosi. Lugosi's presence provides a bit of humorous inter-textuality for horror fans as he delivers the line "You've seen me create a zombie [before]," thereby paying clever homage to Lugosi's turn in the first zombie horror film, *White Zombie* (1932). Kolaaga is portrayed seriously, without comic effect. It is explained that Kolaaga was "taken" by Renault, and is now being forced to kidnap victims for zombification, as well as do a little house-keeping work around Renault's spooky mansion. In this film, Kolaaga actually does grab a White woman, delivering her to Renault, who opts not to turn her into a zombie after observing her beauty. More, in this film, Kolaaga is far more empowered as he turns on his master, refusing his orders to kill others and ultimately killing Renault (with a shovel) instead. The film shows natives as half-clothed primitives and makes reference to Voodoo drums with their "death beat" that drives the Whites crazy; the "hill natives" also dance around a fire, with spears. The comedy in the film is performed largely by Jerry and Mike, with Mike even appearing in blackface (which fools the natives into thinking he is Black).

The "Blacks in horror" film *White Pongo* (1945) stood out for its use of more than a dozen Black actors during a period when roles were decreasing due to the budgetary constraints of B movies. Here, the majority of the Blacks are cast as extras—partially clothed natives with no speaking lines. They guide a team of White scientists across the "dark continent" and through land "unexplored by White men" in search of a great anthropological find, a prized white gorilla, or "pongo," believed to be the intelligent missing link. A violent black gorilla—who attacks the pongo but loses the fight and pays with its life—is undesirable, and is tossed back into the jungle by the White men when it is accidently trapped. When the natives do get to make a sound, it is only for brief moments, such as when they fawn over European clothes or when they are screaming as pongo stomps them to death. Only one very lucky adult male native, Mumbo Jumbo (Joel Fluellen), gets to say "Bwana" and offer himself as "#1 porter boy."[11] In the film, Mumbo Jumbo, like Carre-Four, also has an opportunity to touch a White woman, but does not dare. And like Carre-Four and Kolaaga, there is little else known about Mumbo Jumbo as he joins the ranks of the many Blacks who are treated as (work) objects rather than subjects in these films.

To view *White Pongo* as a B movie is generous. The film is cheaply made, relying on a good bit of old stock footage of animals drinking water to pad a convoluted, badly conceived script. However, *Pongo* looked like A-list, award-worthy fare next to its film doppelgänger *White Gorilla* (1945). The bulk of *White Gorilla* is a jumbled mix of stock footage and scenes from the 1915 silent, short nature film *Perils of the Jungle*. This messy movie is essentially a race-war film between a black gorilla, Nbonga, who makes a rare white gorilla, Konga, an "outcast" in the jungle because it is different.[12] The two fight over the course of the film, with the black gorilla, "the monster with his huge chest filled with hate," the instigator. Predictably, the film's location was some African "bad country" where natives "hated the White man" and where Whites are scared of the tones of the natives' drums. When the white gorilla is killed by an interloping White man, the ape is eulogized at length, with the black ape Nbonga even implicated in the mourning of a noble, fallen White warrior who was simply fighting on behalf of his race and in "a battle for jungle supremacy":[13]

> You know I feel kind of sorry I had to kill that white gorilla. He seemed almost human. … His death seemed to cast a spell of loneliness over the jungle … a silent tribute to his passing … I can almost see him [the black gorilla] as he discovers the white outcast laying there as though sleeping. His efforts to make him do battle. And then the change … His bewilderment as he looks at the motionless figure. A sort of human emotion that comes over him. Then the slow realization, the outcast is dead. Then the animal instinct returns, the instinct to cover up and hide the remains of a fallen one from the scavengers of the jungle. A gesture for forgiveness as a chance of death call for the outcast for his race—the white gorilla.

In the end, the audience came to know much more about the white gorilla than about Carre-Four, Kolaaga, and Mumbo Jumbo combined.

Reforming Hollywood, Reinventing the Black Image

Gearing up for a new decade of films, in December 1939, Spencer Williams and a who's who of Black horror film stars, including Clarence Muse (*Black Moon, White Zombie, The Invisible Ghost*), Laura Bowman (*Drums o' Voodoo, Son of Ingagi*), and Earl Morris (*Son of Ingagi*) met to discuss how to rein in the "derogatory types and stigmas" inflicted on Black characters in film across genres.[14] Independent filmmaking, Black or otherwise, had all but disappeared for the time being; hence the bulk of the representations of Blacks was coming out of Hollywood. Demanding change, however, was a tricky proposition as Hollywood was the dominant employer and the industry had already shown it could and would work around a Black presence, as Williams' "knew they spoke from weakness, from the ranks of the Bs [i.e. B movies], from still prevalent servile roles."[15] Many Black performers were already keeping quiet "about their dissatisfaction or anger over the lack of decent roles. Like the White stars, they knew bad-mouthing the industry got them nothing except a one-way ticket back to wherever they had come from."[16] The other alternative was to forge ahead with their work in Hollywood, acting as change-agents when and where they could.

Several Blacks opted to speak up about their treatment by Hollywood. On December 28, 1940, actor Clarence Muse published his hope for a new year filled with improved imagery for Blacks:

> SOMEHOW, SOME WHERE, WE MUST HAVE A MAJOR NEGRO PICTURE. THIS IS a serious resolution ... A great Negro story, big enough, good enough, to be released by a major company like any other picture ... Uplifting, daring, entertaining and true to Negro life in all its elements ... I have resolved to do my best to encourage this ... And if it happens ... What a happy New Year![17]

Still, Blacks' treatment in and outside of horror was troublesome, and after much deliberation, the NAACP attempted to corral Hollywood—its writers, producers, directors, publicists, casting directors, and the like—by getting them to agree to a plan which would improve Blacks' standing in the industry. After significant resistance from Hollywood, which had so far refused even to listen, in 1942 the Civil Rights organization finally got its audience with film producers and studio executives, and urged them to liberalize the roles offered to Blacks.[18] However, Blacks were also blamed for their own plight; a Columbia Pictures studio representative said, "as long as there are colored persons ... willing to play Uncle Tom roles or through buffoonery ... to barter the dignity of their race" the portrayals will continue.[19]

Absent what Cripps called a defined "Black aesthetic," it was difficult to identify what exactly constituted improved imagery.[20] The film industry had its "Code" which prompted them to consider whether the images they were creating were appropriately moral or exploitive. The Code was clear on what it found off limits; things such as lustful kissing, profanity, sexual perversion, and miscegenation. Imagining such a "Code" for racial imagery was difficult, though the best minds kept trying to develop some strategies for handling Hollywood. Lawrence Dunbar Reddick was one of the more well known and respected of those who worked to forge a plan of action. Reddick earned a doctorate from the University of Chicago in 1939 and that same year assumed the position of curator of the (today) Schomburg Center for Research in Black Culture as part of the New York Public Library. During his tenure there (1939–1948), he wrote and presented his ideas on the treatment of Blacks in all media, such as textbooks, radio, print, and film. In 1944, he published his ideas for handling Hollywood in a lengthy scholarly essay in the *Journal of Negro Education*. Reddick suggested that censorship boards, such as the Hays Office which administered the Code, should be worked with to "include treatment of the Negro in films" as part of the codes.[21] More, to protect the interest of performers, Reddick proposed that "Negro actors in particular must be supported when they refuse to accept 'Uncle Tom' and 'Aunt Jemima' roles." He even asked the government's Office of War Information to ban racist language such as "nigger," "darky," "pickaninny," "Smoke," "sambo," and "coon" from film on grounds that such language could be exploited by America's enemies.[22] Reddick continued to circulate his ideas on reform. The NAACP continued to call meetings, with uneven success. Those in Hollywood who were more liberal-minded made changes that they thought were appropriate. However, film was slow to progress. Black actor Spencer Williams, Jr. took it upon himself to effect change by moving forward with his own plan to offer up representations for Blacks, by Blacks.

Making Over the Ape Film

Williams' first contribution to the cause came in 1940 with a "Black horror" film he wrote and starred in. However, the film's title—*Son of Ingagi* (1940)—was cringe-worthy. Horror audiences had heard of these mythical "ingagis" before. In 1930, director William Campbell presented the infamous, highly controversial "Blacks in horror" film *Ingagi*, about apes or "ingagis" and the Congolese women who bear their children. *Ingagi* was originally offered as a real and true documentary recording the strange, beastly practices of Black women in the jungle. *Ingagi* ended with a native woman cuddling a half-ape, half-human baby.

Was Williams imagining *Son of Ingagi* as a sequel? Why would Williams imply a link with the earlier film through such a similar film title? The two films are not connected; however, *Son of Ingagi*, made by the White director Richard Kahn, has a couple of minor overlaps with the original film. *Son of Ingagi* is about a scientist who travels to Africa and brings back an ape, a "half-man, half-beast," as the film's promotional poster describes the creature. In addition, the film also subtly advances the notion of interbreeding; after all, where exactly did the ape–human offspring come from? Thankfully, the similarities end there, with *Son of Ingagi* taking a novel turn toward a focus on the Black middle class.

The film's first significant imagistic contribution is that the scientist who recovers the ingagi is both Black and a *woman*—Dr. Helen Jackson (Laura Bowman), an aging, wealthy, brilliant researcher boasting talents in chemistry, anthropology, and animal behaviorism. Through Dr. Jackson, the White male on safari is recoded, though the exploitative nature of such missions is not so easily dismissed even in a Black and female body. Dr. Jackson is a neighbor and family friend to a young, up-and-coming newlywed couple, Robert and Eleanor Lindsay

(Alfred Grant, Daisy Bufford), who celebrate their nuptials with similarly aspiring friends. Here again, Williams breaks ground, depicting a Black bride and groom and their wedding.[23] The film includes a musical number by the Lindsays' buddies, portrayed by the real-life quintet the Four Toppers. The film also includes the portrayal of the competent "prominent" attorney Mr. Bradshaw (Earl Morris) and Mr. Nelson, a detective played by Williams.

On Robert and Eleanor's wedding night, the factory that Robert works at burns to the ground, leaving him jobless and fretting over how they will survive. Dr. Jackson takes the young couple under her wing, bequeathing to them her home and all of her possessions. After the scientist dies in an encounter with the rampaging ape, the animal breaks free of his confines to roam the house, unseen, thereby frightening the Lindsays, who have moved into Dr. Jackson's home. They then phone the police to investigate. Unbeknownst to the couple, Dr. Jackson has $20,000 in gold hidden in her home, along with the now murderous ape. Though the ape in *Son* walks upright and wears pants and a tunic, the film does not explore the ape–human connection, dealing with the monster simply as a beast on the prowl. Thanks to an "all-star colored cast" and the film's setting in an all-Black community, the Lindsays' saviors are not White men riding in to defeat the savage beast, as seen in so many colonial-themed ape films. Instead, the Black community rallies around to support the Lindsays.

FIGURE 3.2 Dr. Jackson prepares to meet her end at the hands of her ingagi
Sack Amusement Enterprises/Photofest

Detective Nelson (Williams) arrives to solve the mystery of the murders in the home, which now includes the murder of the attorney, Bradshaw, who while visiting the home is secretly strangled by the ape. However, the ape proves elusive as well as a trickster—when Nelson completes making a sandwich for himself, the ape steals it while Nelson's back is turned, leaving the detective befuddled. Thus, Williams brings a bit of comedy to his performance, revealing some of the comedic skill that he would use in the (controversial bufoonish) role of television's Andrew "Andy" Hogg Brown in the situation comedy *The Amos 'n' Andy Show* (1951–1953). However, in the film Williams is no coon. He is shown both serious and comical. Notably, with Nelson asleep, it is Eleanor who stays on alert listening for prowlers, and it is finally Eleanor who discovers the ape—though she faints and has to be rescued by Robert since Nelson is knocked out by the animal. In the end Nelson redeems himself by recovering the hidden wealth and turning it over to the Lindsays so that they may happily pursue their lives, and the American dream, together.

Son could be thought of as a double "B" film—low budget, for Black audiences, two rather deadly box office traits. However, the film did succeed in making an initial step toward recuperating the race film and Blacks' portrayals in it. The effort spoke to Williams' personal mission of changing Blacks' treatment in entertainment film.

FIGURE 3.3 Spencer Williams, Jr. (with hat)
CBS/Photofest

Taking on Hollywood, the Devil Can't Defeat Me

Well, let me see, there was once a Black cinema. Spencer Williams performed there and made relevant films. And there was an audience for that. ... It was a culture—film culture, Black culture—where serious, relevant films were made.

—Charles Burnett, filmmaker[24]

A native Louisianan, Spencer Williams, Jr. entered into show business full-on as an adult, in his mid-thirties, after a stint in the military and work around theater circuits as first an aide and then a bit comedy actor who also contributed some comedy material for theatrical performances. He got his start in those race films whose content targeted Black audiences but which were made by non-Blacks. Williams appeared in a diversity of genres, including musical shorts such as *Brown Gravy* (1929), westerns such as *Harlem on the Prairie* (1937), and crime dramas such as *Bad Boy* (1939). He was also a writer with writing/screenplay credits for films such as the 1929 comedy short *The Lady Fare*, as well as *Harlem Rides the Range* and *Son of Ingagi*, films in which he also stars.

In 1983, 14 years after Williams' death in 1969, some of Williams' films were found and recovered from a warehouse in Tyler, Texas (about two hours outside of Dallas), by film and video archivist G. William Jones of Southern Methodist University in Dallas. Williams had a special relationship with the city of Dallas, filming there and working in partnership with Dallas-based Sack Amusement Enterprise for financial, distribution, and production support. Sack permitted Williams to make movies outside of the Hollywood system, which would have excluded him anyway, while maintaining creative control of his product.

The 1940s was Williams' decade. He directed 12 films, all of them between 1941 and 1949. Notably, he wrote, produced (under his company Amegro), and directed *The Blood of Jesus*, a "Black horror" film, in 1941. The film, which marks Williams' directorial debut, has been hailed as "the most popular race movie ever produced."[25] *Blood* was never marketed as a horror film; rather, it shirked generic classification, being described at times as fantasy and other times as religious drama. However, if Sobchack is correct, that the horror film deals with "moral chaos, the disruption of natural order," particularly God's order, and "threat to the harmony of hearth and home," then *The Blood of Jesus* is the quintessential horror film.[26] The film is heavily inspired by Christian religiosity and centers on the theme of free will—choosing a path of righteousness or one of sin. Threat to hearth and home is introduced when the church-going, God-fearing "Sister" Martha (Catherine Caviness), who lives in a close-knit rural town, cannot persuade her husband Razz (Spencer Williams) to attend church or to witness her baptism. Razz is deemed a sinner because he chooses to go hunting instead and, in a brief comic scene, he hunts on his neighbor's farm, claiming two hogs as his prize. Chaos ensues when Martha, upon return from her baptism and while praying in their bedroom, is accidently shot when Razz's rifle falls to the ground. The rifle discharges, with the shot traveling through the bedroom wall and striking Martha and her picture of (a White) Jesus. She is mortally wounded, leaving Razz devastated. But this is horror, and disruption of the natural order is, well, in order. Razz finds himself praying in sincere earnest over Martha, who is dead but who has not yet been assigned her place in Heaven or Hell. Interestingly, it is Martha, not Razz, whose faith is challenged. Here again, Williams distinguishes himself by placing a Black woman, just as he did in *Son* with Dr. Jackson and Eleanor, at the center of his narrative. Martha brings even greater depth to the representation of women. She is the antithesis of Razz, a louse of a husband, who would easily fall prey to the Devil. Hence, Martha is the one that must be rendered vulnerable to be sure that she is righteous rather than *self*-righteous.

While in death, Martha is greeted by an angel who takes her to the Crossroads, the junction between Hell and/or Zion. Martha assuredly chooses Zion, but the Devil (James B. Jones, complete with horns and a cape) intercedes, sending in a "false prophet," the charmingly seductive Judas Green (Frank H. McClennan) as "temptation" to entice the right-living Martha to witness a side of life she has never seen. He directs her attention away from Zion to a cityscape ablaze in bright lights and full of people and lively music. Judas becomes the "bête noire of the Black bourgeoisie" as his flash, smooth talk and connection with the urban make him excessively evil.[27] Judas' terrain is markedly different from the dust-filled, far from sparkling rural life Martha is accustomed to; thus he is able to lure her with fancy clothes, while leading her down the path to Hell, which is filled with swing bands and couples dancing to a "little jive." In defining piety and sin in this way, the film makes no pretense; it is a straightforward view of religiosity, "all surfaces" in its treatment of good and evil.[28]

Judas first takes Martha to the 400 Club, a classy venue for more well-heeled Blacks. However, Martha is there only briefly before the real plan is revealed. Judas secretly sells Martha for $30 to a fellow named Brown (Eddie DeBase) who is at the club waiting to pick up this latest young catch. Hence, Williams' narrative, already a cautionary tale, adds an additional warning for young women metaphorically "just off the bus" from the safety of the homely rural to the treacherous urban. Brown takes Martha to a seedy, dangerous juke joint in which women receive money to dance with men (and perhaps a bit more).

While horror has attended to Black women before, often by way of the wicked Voodoo priestess, Black women infrequently get to be central and *feminine*. Black women are not eligible for the symbolic pedestal upon which White women are placed by men, to be romanced, gazed upon lovingly, and to see their bodies, emotions, and even their beauty protected. These moments of sheer adoration tend to be for Whites only, such as Ann Darrow in *King Kong* (1933). However, Martha is a Black character who comes close to being placed on that pedestal. Razz longs for her, praying over her relentlessly. The last time a Black woman had a man attend to her with such verve she was strangled to death by him (i.e. Klili in *The Love Wanga* [1936]). More, Martha is also depicted as a Black Southern "lady"; hence she is a real prize for the Devil. When Judas is sent in to tempt her, he does so by placing her on a pedestal, thereby exploiting Razz's failure to fully recognize the value of not just this woman, but what she represents as a lady. Here, Judas acts as trickster, confusing Martha by conflating sex (sexiness, sexual attraction) with the feminine. This is a subtle and important difference, distinguishable in great part by comparing Judas' performance of masculinity, which is modeled on desire and sexual urges, with Razz's perform-ance late in the film, which focuses on love and intimacy. In fact, Martha's dilemma is presented as a war over what kind of femininity she will embrace, the "lady" or the sexpot in fancy clothes and shoes (before she is "turned out"). Manatu argues that Black women have been, and continue be, denied access to and participation in the feminine. As a result, Black women are not afforded the opportunity to fight for, or opt to escape from, a feminine performance, including the proverbial pedestal.[29] Notably, the femininity that Martha chooses—to be a respectable, God-fearing lady—is what gets her love and romance (Razz) and firmly secures her on the pedestal.

While trapped with Brown in the juke joint, Martha falls to her knees in prayer, begging God for forgiveness, and in return a Black female guardian angel helps Martha escape her fate. Feeling restored and empowered, Martha (now in an angelic, flowing dress) flees back toward the crossroads. As Martha runs, the Devil's minions from the juke joint appear, chase her down, and attempt to stone her to death. The next sequence is one of the most dramatic and highly stylized in the film. Cripps calls the imagery in the film "unlike that in any other Afro-American movie."[30] In the next scenes, just as Martha arrives at the sign marking the crossroads, the sign is transformed into a towering cross bearing the image of Jesus. Martha, lying prone beneath the cross, is literally washed in the blood of Jesus as blood runs from Jesus' body, which is nailed to the cross, and over hers. As stunning as the scene is in appearance and symbolism, it is also meaningful as it speaks to Martha negotiating a complex state of abjection. That is, she finds herself in a state and space between object and subject. Martha represents several levels of abjection, as she occupies a liminal position between the living and the dead, and also between compromised saint, but not quite a sinner. Martha reveals how physically and emotionally traumatic it is to confront her condition of being separate from her body (object) and being absent of her humanness/humanity (subject).

Martha's final choice, to side with God, thereby expelling that which she does not want as part of her subjective self, is a lesson in rejecting the "improper" and "unclean," replacing them with the "clean and proper self."[31] Restored by the blood of Jesus, Martha suddenly awakens at home. She and the now God-fearing Razz are reunited under the watchful eye of the angel.

Williams took great care with his first film, striving for exacting detail to accommodate the most discerning audience members who might scrutinize his religious message. He presents the (real-life) Reverend R.L. Robertson and his Heavenly Choir while offering an authentic glimpse into the Black church, from sermons to songs to prayers. Indeed, the first three minutes of the film make clear that this is a production that is taking religion and its iconography quite seriously. The congregants talk of following the "10 original commandments accepted as civilized law" and that religion should be "practiced with honest sincerity." Bibles, crosses, and portraits of Jesus abound. Hymns such as "Good News" and "Go Down Moses" are sung by the choir. Rev. Robertson performs an authentic riverside baptism while the choir sings and parishioners pray and engage in praise and worship.

The Blood of Jesus also popularizes several themes that would take center stage in more modern "Black horror" films beginning in the 1990s. Williams' themes of choosing between being good and evil, being tempted by the fast way of (Northern) urban life versus that of the humble, honest (Southern), rural life, and a woman as moral arbiter and savior figures prominently in films such as *Def by Temptation* (1990) and *Spirit Lost* (1997).

Hallelujah! Eloyce Gist

While Williams' messages and film style would be oft-duplicated in horror, Williams' own films did not emerge in a cultural vacuum. Oscar Micheaux's *The Scar of Shame* (1927) used the urban, secular music, and all that comes with the lifestyle such music supports, as a warning to stay close to one's own (Southern) roots. Following Micheaux's lead, the wife and husband filmmaking duo Eloyce and James Gist made two circa 1930 films, *Hellbound Train* and *Verdict Not Guilty*, which took up themes of good/South and evil/North. *Hellbound Train*, here a "Black horror" film, is particularly seminal. Williams' *Blood* closely resembles *Hellbound*'s story, which centers on a journey, and messages of choosing the path to righteousness. The Gists' silent, short film's iconography may have also informed Williams' film as the two share Devil, crossroads, and damnation imagery. While there is no evidence that Williams saw the Gists' films, it is clear that Williams is applying to his films a style seen in the efforts of Micheaux and the Gists.

Gloria J. Gibson provides the most insightful pieces of research into the Gists' life, particularly Eloyce's.[32] According to Gibson, Eloyce Gist was born in Texas in 1892, with Washington, D.C. becoming her home not long after the turn of the century. She attended Howard University. Eloyce's thinking about religion is said to reflect her own beliefs in Baha'i and that of James, her Christian self-ordained evangelist husband. Eloyce worked in partnership with her husband, and his contributions to their filmmaking are undisputed, if not precisely known. However, the silent film *Hellbound Train* is viewed as being significantly Eloyce's as the script is largely hers, as are several scenes which she arranged the shooting of. The Gists made films, not for entertainment, but as a teaching tool to aid in their ministry.

The duo traveled from Black church to Black church, by auto, with their films and equipment.[33] When Gibson interviewed Eloyce's 82-year-old daughter, Homoiselle Patrick Harrison, in the early 1990s, Harrison recalled how the couple screened their films: Eloyce would play the piano and lead the congregation in hymns. Then, the film would be shown, followed by a sermonette by James Gist. Tickets were either sold in advance, or a collection was taken at the close of the service, with the Gists and the church splitting the money.[34] The Gists' films were well received, even drawing the attention of the NAACP in 1933, when the organization contacted the couple to offer their endorsement of their efforts.

Thanks to the efforts of film scholars Gibson and S. Torriano Berry, who have been reassembling and digitizing the film's fragments, the film's story is fairly discernible. *Hellbound Train* begins with the title card "The Hell-Bound train is always on duty, and the Devil is engineer," followed by a message from the Devil, "Free admission to all—just give your life and soul. No round trip tickets—one way only." The film then shows a group of sinners queueing up for their train tickets: "no round-trip tickets, one way only [signed] Satan." The train has dedicated cars for all kinds of sinners, a storyline presented through title cards made by Eloyce.[35] For example, those who dance at parties and in clubs have their train car because "the dance of today is indecent," with Eloyce aligning dancing and music with the more sinful side of life. Those who sell alcohol have a car as well: "there's room in hell for BOOTLEGGERS and their followers." Alcohol is depicted as leading to all manner of trouble for women. One woman is shown being encouraged to drink by a man, who then guides her into a private room. "Mislead by the whisper of a man," she is next shown, alone, watching over her newborn. Interestingly, there is also a scene that attends to reproduction in which a woman dies in spite of a doctor's best efforts. The card reads, "She has taken medicine to avoid becoming a mother. SHE'D better get right with GOD, for it's murder in COLD BLOOD."[36] There are other sins identified, such as gambling and murder, as well as being a crook and liar. The Devil has a car for "backsliders, hypocrites and Used to be Church Members."[37] The implication is that this is a very long train with lots of cars to accommodate all evil-doers; none will avoid judgment and Hell.

Unlike Williams' film *Blood*, the audience is not shown that a return to righteousness is possible after one has sinned. Rather, the sinful remain that way and embark on their train journey, with the train moving rapidly toward the "Entrance to Hell." According to Gibson

the train bursts Hell wide open (it enters a tunnel), crashing and exploding into flames. The Devil circles the train to further torment the victims. … In the final scene a man, perhaps James Gist, states, "Thus I've demonstrated to you this picture which I painted as a vision from hearing a sermon in a revival meeting." Behind him is a large poster or flowchart of the hell-bound train's journey. This scene may have functioned as a segue to Gist's sermonette after the film.[38]

After the death of her husband, Eloyce continued to tour, "traveling with the films, a projector, and an assistant for a while, but soon realized she couldn't shoulder the diverse responsibilities alone. The work of programmer, manager, and exhibitor was too taxing."[39] More, sound had made the silent film obsolete, making way for efforts such as Williams'. Eloyce died in 1974. The magnitude of her accomplishments can be measured today by the condition of her films. According to the Library of Congress, showing the films so often took their toll: "The movies were so widely shown that they literally fell apart along the splices and were received by the Library in hundreds of short fragments."[40]

The Gists and Williams' religious-message/"Black horror" films act as a purposeful intervention into the film discourses swirling around Blacks in the 1930s and 1940s. Horror films gave dichotomous attention to Blacks' religious practices in that they were depicted either as evil Voodooists or as (ideally) faithful Christians. Interestingly enough, neither the Gists nor Williams explored Black religions more broadly, beyond Christianity. Williams in particular had a model for dealing with Black religion through the 1934 Sack Amusement film *Drums o' Voodoo*, which examined Voodoo and Christianity equally.

In the film, believers in Voodoo and in Christianity co-exist in the same rural Louisiana community. The films' opening title card initially casts Voodooists as evil with their incessant drumming "on the eve of a sacrifice." However, no such event pans out. Rather, the evil introduces itself in the form of a cool slickster, obviously named "Tom Catt" (Morris McKenny). Here, Catt is much like Williams' Judas who is in pursuit of Martha, as Catt wants a young woman named Myrtle (Edna Barr) to work as eye candy in his juke joint. The problem is that Myrtle wants nothing to do with either Catt or his juke joint. Others are opposed to Catt getting his claws into Myrtle, including her minister uncle (the oddly named) Elder Amos Berry or Elder Berry (Augustus Smith), Ebenezer, the grandson of the local Voodoo witch Auntie Hagar, and Auntie Hagar (Laura Bowman) herself. Hagar works her magic to protect the minister's niece. Importantly, she has the minister's support, as he announces, "I believe [she] is the only one 'round here that can drive Tom Catt out of this community." In fact, Hagar has the support of the entire community—Christian and Voodoo alike—who want Catt's disruptive ways to end. It is Catt who has drawn people away from the church, but it is the work of Hagar that brings them back into the fold when she begins to wage war against Catt. Catt is struck blind, inside the church, by Hagar's magic. In the end, stricken by Hagar, Catt falls into quicksand and dies. All is well again thanks to the teaming up by Christians and Voodooists, with the Voodooists presenting a different, but hardly deficient Black religion.[41]

Perhaps Williams knew his audience and had settled on a strictly Christian formula that he knew would work. *The Blood of Jesus* proved popular and profitable enough that Sack Amusement threw their support behind a second Williams film with a rural, Southern religions turn.[42] Williams' next religio-horror film, *Go Down, Death* (1944), focuses on Big Jim Bottoms (Williams), who is a far from comic character. Rather, Jim is the owner of a nightclub that is also the playground for men and women of low morals. The story closely parallels *Drums o' Voodoo* in that Jim regards as his enemy Jasper, a young preacher (Samuel H. James) in charge of Mt. Zion Baptist Church, who is "ruining Sunday business" at the club. Jim enlists three "fly chicks," or prostitutes, to set Jasper up. As the minister presents the women with bibles and reads them scriptures, they surround him, press a drink in his hand, and quickly kiss him just in time for Jim to snap a picture.

Before Jim can "expose" Jasper and ruin his reputation, Jim's (adoptive) mother Caroline uncovers the scheme and confronts her son. Caroline, a Christian and devoted church-goer, demands the photos. Caroline also begs Jim to acknowledge Christ so that their family can all "be together in the hereafter." Instead, Jim mocks her and dismisses her pleas. To strains of the song *Nobody Knows the Trouble I've Seen*, Caroline talks aloud to her dead husband Joe asking Joe to talk to God about Jim. Caroline is stunned to see Joe's ghostly image appear leading her to a safe in which Jim has stored the scandalous picture and all of its copies. Joe's ghost opens the safe for Caroline, and she removes the pictures.

Williams' use of Joe's ghost is much like his use of Martha in *The Blood of Jesus* as they both return from the dead to speak to and about Black people's experiences. So rarely is the living story of Black people spoken in popular culture that it is often represented as being told by the dead. The efficacy of such communication rises and falls, literally, on where the dead speak. "In modernity," writes Holland, "'Death' can no longer occur in the midst of the living, and to achieve the separation between the happy (living) and the miserable (the dying/almost dead), the hospital was created."[43] In these Black films, the talk of the dead or dying is, notably, delivered at home. Martha's lessons of religiosity are delivered from her bed, at home, as she is attended to, watched, and prayed over by Razz at her bedside.[44] Similarly, in Williams' film, Joe comes to Caroline and is able to be heard only at "home" and during prayer.

Jim catches Caroline before she is able to get away with the photos and fights with her, accidently killing her. The film's title, *Go Down, Death*, comes from the 1926 James Weldon Johnson poem/funeral sermon of the same name, and it is this sermon that is delivered at Caroline's funeral while Jim listens on guiltily, having blamed Caroline's death on a robber. In the sermon, words of assurance are offered, which include a promise that Caroline is not quite in death but has passed on to an afterlife.

During his mother's funeral, Jim begins to get his punishment. When Jasper preaches, "Grief-stricken son—weep no more," Jim hangs his head in shame and begins to hear a voice—his conscience talking to him. After the funeral, Jim's mental condition worsens. The devilish, disembodied voice screams at him, "You killed, you killed, killed your best friend!" and "The Lord has no mercy for killers." Jim runs in fright, but the torment worsens. Jim runs, but falls to the ground as the voice promises, "I'm going to show you where you're going home to … Hell!" However, Jim cannot see Hell alive and upright. Instead, he is stricken down, though not yet dead, to receive the visions of his fate.

As is Williams' trademark, illustrated in a hauntingly stylized sequence, Hell is revealed to Jim through shocking visuals of writhing undead tortured souls in a lake of ice, and a horned Lucifer violently consuming souls. The sequence is borrowed from the frightening silent film *L'Inferno* (1911), an adaptation of Dante's Inferno, the first part of the fourteenth century epic poem *Divine Comedy*, directed by Francesco Bertolini and Adolfo Padovan. Williams' budget constraints moved him to become creative, turning to one of the more frightening allegorical presentations of good and evil for archival footage. The film depicts a downward, spiraling journey to the inferno of Hell in which sinners endure never-ending tortures. The Devil is present, abusing and even eating the wicked. Soon after being exposed to the visions, Jim is found truly dead, having gone to the quintessential "Terrible Place" (not simply a haunted house or spooky tunnel) that is a requisite and even celebrated element of horror.[45]

However, these types of films were not sustainable. In 1968 and 1970 film scholar Thomas Cripps interviewed Alfred and Lester Sack, of Sack Amusement Enterprises, distributors of *The Blood of Jesus* and *Go Down, Death*. According to Cripps, before the war *The Blood of Jesus* (by way of example) "had amounted almost to folk art among [Williams'] Southern rural clientele; its lack of artifice had seemed a charming flaw rather than a crippling wound."[46] However, the Sacks revealed that the film's setting in "those days … almost gone" was met with loud laughter in the North in the war years and beyond.[47] More, so-called "all-Colored cast films" were competing with films in which Blacks were cast as co-stars, not simply extras, alongside Whites. In the horror genre, unfortunately, co-starring roles for Blacks meant performing as the comic-Negro sidekick. Williams would have to share his decade of achievement with the likes of Mantan Moreland and Willie Best, whose popularity was built on cooning.

"Ain't Nobody Here But Us Chickens"

> Are Hollywood producers mindful of their harmful acts,
> Or are they just plain ignorant and do not know the facts?
> They show us all as comics, wasters, gangsters, and slowpokes,
> Don't they know colored people are just like other folks?
>
> —Razaf (16)[48]

Film had a half-century of image-making under its belt; however, if one were to consider the depictions of Blacks during this time, the offerings resembled something out of the nineteenth-century minstrel stage. During the 1800s' slavery and post-antebellum periods, theater performances had much to say about race relationships by offering an opportunistic depiction of the White master–Black slave relationship. Whites were portrayed as patient, paternalistic caregivers to their squirrelly, inept but otherwise content human property. This racial relationship between superior Whites and happy "darkies" was a powerful fantasy supplanting the reality of the brutalities of chattel slavery.[49] These fantasies were initially played out on stage by Whites in blackface who performed in black voice – a malapropism-laden, simpleton manner of speaking. While it was hard to imagine that Blacks would participate in their own subjugation on the theater stage, in the late 1800s they were cast in the darkey role, with some appearing in blackface. To draw White audiences from White minstrel performances, Black actors claimed to be the real deal, "true plantation slaves, not an 'imitation' like Whites in blackface."[50] Film simply lifted these kinds of performances from the theater stage (often also borrowing its actors), and placed them on celluloid.

For example, theater actor Harold Lloyd found fame in film, appearing in approximately 200 comedy films. One of his better-known films was the 25-minute silent comedy-horror film *Haunted Spooks* (1920). *Haunted* and films like it were dubbed "thrill comedy" films, which coupled tense, thrilling scenes or knee-knocking frights with broad humor.[51] In this "Blacks in horror" film a young man, "the Boy" (Lloyd), helps his new wife, "the Girl" (Mildred Davis), earn her inheritance, a sprawling mansion. The Girl cannot claim the home unless she lives in the home for one year. The Boy chases off the Girl's greedy Uncle (Wallace Howe), who "haunts" the house in an attempt to drive the Girl away. The film features a large cadre of Black actors (approximately 10) in the capacity of house servants who are told by the Uncle that "grinning ghosts of the dead scream from their graves and roam these rooms." The film depicts the servants as quite gullible, spreading the tale (through the use of title cards) in malapropism-laden black voice, "An' de whole graveyard turns upside down! Gassly, spookey ghosts come heah to room dese roams." As the Uncle "haunts" the house, a child servant (Ernest "Sunshine Sammy" Morrison") dives into a bin of flour, emerging white and petrified. The butler (Blue Washington) is depicted as being so terror-struck that he can only tap dance in place while sweating black ink which coats his face. The depiction of Blacks was so abysmal in the film, one could easily assume that the "spooks" in the film's title was a hateful slur deployed to describe the Black characters.

Hollywood was notably prolific in presenting such comedy-horror offerings, with these films dominating the genre during this decade. The humor that Blacks affected, a "hybrid minstrelsy," was still White-oriented, with Blacks employed to validate and veil the racism.[52] This was an era marked by an obsessive representation of Blacks as "cultural inferiors," in which Blacks became the White man's burden as Blacks were shown as lacking, but here in America to stay.[53] Blacks were increasingly depicted as being American (either from the South or from New York, most often Harlem), rather than almost singularly natives in Africa or the Caribbean. The representational shift was a bit of propaganda as the Office of War Information's (OWI) Bureau of Motion Pictures claimed it was in the nation's best interest to present a unified (though not necessarily integrated) America.[54] Still, Hollywood's horror films continued to insult. For example, in the "Blacks in horror" film *The Ghost Breakers* (1940), Bob Hope as Larry talks of traveling to "Black Island" to (in a double-entendre joke) "get acquainted with the spooks." The prevalence of such films was, in part, the outcome of incomplete censorship plans which easily identified and demanded a deletion of the most egregious, vicious stereotypes, but overlooked those couched in humor. As a result, racist comedy-horror became a tour de force, and it all worked to further enforce Whites' ascendancy.[55]

A Sin and a Shame

> "I got an urge that I want to leave, but my legs won't cooperate with me."
> —Birmingham Brown, Charlie Chan's *The Scarlet Clue* (1945)

Willie Best marketed himself as Sleep 'n' Eat. Nellie (Wan) Conley became Madame Sul-Te-Wan. Ernest Morrison was known as Sunshine Sammy. Mantan Moreland did not need such gimmicks, as his name sold itself. When Moreland's name appeared on a promotional bill, audiences could rest assured that they were going to hear his best one-liners and see him bug his eyes and quiver with fright. The characters that these performers played, and what they did to their reputations and to that of Blacks, have been described in the most scathing terms. However, some of the most ferocious contempt has been reserved for Moreland. Film scholar James Nesteby described the roles that Moreland took as "the sunshine friend, the coon who turned coward at the first sign of distress, or the coon who could not motivate his feet when the rest of him was shivering."[56] The British film journalist and historian Peter Noble (181-182) wrote brutally of Moreland, "no Negro actor has ever rolled his eyes with such abandon as Moreland, no coloured actor has ever tried so hard to revert to the Stepin Fetchit subhuman characterisation. He is the accepted U.S.A. idea of the Negro clown supreme, and performs before the cameras like a well-trained monkey."[57]

Born in Louisiana in 1902, Moreland began his career as a traveling performer, making his way to the vaudeville stage in his twenties. Appearing in over 100 films, Moreland's claim to fame was his comedy. He was credited with being a comedy craftsman, displaying an "arsenal of gestures and grimaces that actors had traditionally used to steal scenes and develop characters."[58] His spirited performances were perfect for comedy-horror.

FIGURE 3.4 Mantan Moreland
Toddy Pictures Co./Photofest

In the "Blacks in horror" film *King of the Zombies* (1941), set during World War II, Moreland plays Jefferson "Jeff" Jackson, a Harlemite and valet to his White master, Bill "Mr. Bill" Summers (John Archer). The pair, along with their pilot, James "Mac" McCarthy (Dick Purcell), crash land on an island in the Bahamas. There, the trio locate the mansion of Dr. Miklos Sangre (Henry Victor), an Austrian scientist. Sangre is also a "secret agent" for an unnamed "European government." He is using the power of Voodoo as an interrogation tool to drag war secrets out of an American admiral so that America's enemies (who communicate by radio in German) may have militaristic advantage. The scientist's scheme relies on the powers of Tahama (Madame Sul-Te-Wan), an aged Voodoo High Priestess who doubles as his cook. Despite his diminutive size, Moreland is a scene stealer as he widens his eyes while delivering one quick quip after another at the expense of his own Blackness. For example, just before crash landing he shudders, "Oh oh!!! I knowed I wasn't cut out to be no blackbird." And, when his character Jeff realizes he has survived the crash he proclaims, "I thought I was a little off-color to be a ghost." Jeff's purpose in the film is to be frenzied with fright, while the Whites around him are calm and reasoning, reinforcing dichotomies of Black emotionality and White rationality.[59]

Nearly every line delivered by Jeff is (albeit rightly so) about the dangers on the island and the trio's urgent need to leave. As such, Jeff is cowardly, the White men serious and heroic. But, of course, Jeff does not run, opting to stay close by the side of his Mr. Bill. In another scene, Jeff is assigned a bed in the servants' quarters, away from Mr. Bill. He is to be escorted away by the eerie butler Momba (Leigh Whipper). Out of both fear and loyalty Jeff asks, "Oh, Mr. Bill, does I has to, can't I stay up here with you?" Jeff does not simply turn his humor on himself, but implicates other Blacks in deficiency by describing the Black zombies on the island as "too lazy to lay down."

In 1943, Monogram Pictures, the same studio who brought audiences *King of the Zombies*, introduced the sequel, *Revenge of the Zombies*. While the two films have generally the same premise, the narratives do not connect and the second film makes no mention of the first. *Revenge* is set in Louisiana, with Moreland back as Jeff. Madame Sul-Te-Wan returns, but this time in the role of Mammy Beulah, a cackling, elderly housekeeper. They are joined by a host of silent zombies that include James Baskett (Academy Award winner for *Song of the South* [1946]), as the overworked zombie slave Lazarus.

The premise of *Revenge* is similar to *King*, but it is more overt in its anti-German/Nazi propaganda. Dr. Max Heinrich von Altermann (John Carradine), who greets his German compatriots with a click of the heel of his boots, is experimenting with a drug made from "swamp lilies" which will help him create an army of zombies: "I'm prepared to supply my country with a new army, numbering as many thousands as required ... an army that will not need to be fed, that cannot be stopped by bullet. That is, in fact, invincible."

When his (White) zombie wife goes missing, von Altermann assembles the Blacks in his kitchen for interrogation. Most interesting about this scene is the disregard the Black characters are portrayed as having for the German. When von Altermann accuses his maid Rosella (Sybil Lewis) of knowing where the zombie went because she is "always under foot listening and watching," Rosella responds in a defiant tone: "I ain't seed nothing, I ain't heard nothing." Next, a scornful Mammy Beulah chimes in, challenging her master, "You sho' you don't know where she is master, you sho' you can't guess?" When von Altermann replies, "Would I be asking you if I knew?" Mammy Beulah snaps back, "Well, you might master, if you wanted to *pretend* you didn't know." On the whole, this is an amazing exchange given representations and real-life race relations of the time. The Black characters are not "sassy," rather they are oppositional. It is a powerful scene of American propaganda depicting Blacks unified in their derision for this German. In films of this era, Blacks are not depicted as rising up in opposition to Whites in this way, and certainly not with impunity. Black zombies or Voodooist natives, then, were not the only monsters of the war era. Filmmakers distributed monstrosity a bit farther afield, and zombies became representative of a kind of anti-democratic social and mind control that more fascist regimes might find use for.[60]

Mantan Moreland and Flournoy Miller, as Washington and Jefferson, respectively, teamed up in the Black horror-comedy film *Lucky Ghost* (1942). *Lucky* boasted a Black cast and targeted Black audiences. It was directed by

William Beaudine, a White man who, with over 350 films under his belt, was known for making B movies in two weeks or less. The film was distributed by Ted Toddy's Dixie National Pictures, Inc. (later Toddy Pictures Co.). Toddy, a White man who supported several films starring Moreland, built his fortune on producing and distributing films featuring Blacks such as *Harlem on the Prairie* (1937), *Mantan Runs for Mayor* (1947), and *House-Rent Party* (1946).

Lucky Ghost tells the tale of two down-on-their-luck men, Washington (Moreland) and Jefferson (Miller). We learn that the men have been in trouble with the law from a judge telling them to "get out of town, and keep walking," which the not-too-bright men do, literally, walking for days on end. Washington cannot write and he does not know the days of the week, but is a master at throwing dice. Jefferson plays the straight man to Washington, who throws out one-liners and engages in slapstick antics. Their comedy does nothing to distance Blacks from long-lingering stereotypes. For example, the men have a built-in radar for chicken. As Washington enters a coop to steal chickens he is caught by the owner, who yells "Who's in there!?" giving rise to the popular colloquialism offered by Washington: "Ain't nobody here but us chickens!" As Washington flees the coop, the owner shoots him in the butt. In 1915, the Lubin Manufacturing Company produced a cartoon film, *A Barnyard Mix-Up*, which focuses on a "'chicken-thieving Rastus' who escapes the farmer's buckshot but is finally laid low by an axe, although he is resurrected in an unusual manner by an explosion of dynamite."[61] *Lucky* served as a reminder of how pernicious the "Blacks love chicken" stereotype is.

The pairs' luck changes when Washington wins in a craps game a stack of cash, a car, chauffeur, and clothes from two monied passers-by headed for an illegal afterhours club (inside of a mansion). Washington and Jefferson go to the club and while there Washington wins the entire club by playing dice. The club turns out to be haunted by a family who is displeased their "no good nephew" has turned their home, now owned by Washington and Jefferson, into a place where sinful "jitterbuggin', jivin', and hullabalooin'" is going on. Their hauntings provide Washington ample opportunity to alternately be frozen with fright or engage in a "feets don't fail me now" routine.

Moreland's trembling act as the "coon who turned coward" was not confined to comedy-horror. [62] In the mystery *The Strange Case of Doctor RX* (1942), in the role of Horatio Washington, his hair turned white with fright. When he was cast in the *Charlie Chan* comedy-mystery film series as chauffeur Birmingham Brown from 1944 to 1949 he often delivered quips such as: "I got an urge that I want to leave, but my legs won't cooperate with me!"[63]

Cedric Robinson, in *Forgeries of Memory & Meaning: Blacks & the Regimes of Race in American Theater & Film before World War II*, works to rehabilitate Moreland's legacy,[64] describing him as "no fool" and as someone who employed a kind of subterfuge in which he teased and mocked Whites for not being as superior as they let on. Robinson specifically cites *King of the Zombies* (1941) as a film in which Moreland carved out some Black comeuppance. For example, Robinson sees in Jeff intellectual capabilities which are purportedly evidenced through Jeff's use of words like loquacious, kosher, and prevaricator. Indeed, Jeff uses such words, though in Jeff, whose speech is also littered with malapropisms, such talk is to be viewed as comical.

And as for Moreland's depiction as Birmingham Brown, Robinson even finds hope there, observing that Brown turned the Chan household into something more "diverse, lively, daring, and comic."[65] Moreland's inclusion is certainly lively and comical, though more prop-like than bringing racial diversity.

It is difficult to see how, as a whole, these comedy-horror films do more than continue to cast Blacks as inferior. As Moreland's characters stay by the side of his White masters, stuck like glue, the films communicate that all is well between Blacks and Whites. Such depictions accomplish a "view of racial harmony by presenting to its intended audience an image of Blacks as humorous (they can't be unhappy; they make us laugh), mistaken (you see, they do need us to guide them), and eager to please (we obviously merit their concern)."[66] These films are also unique because the violence in them is so trivialized. In more traditional horror films, violence is ubiquitous, but hardly trivialized. When a mummy strangles or an ape pummels, these actions are understood as violence. When Moreland's character is shot in the butt as he scrambles away or when Eddie Anderson's character, Eddie the chauffeur in *Topper Returns* (1941), is repeatedly head-butted by a seal and nearly drowned, the consequences of violence upon Black bodies (in this Jim Crow era, no less) are muted.

Willie Best was the 1940s other comedy-horror icon. He, too, entered acting at an early age, "with the tall, thin Negro going through all the hackneyed rigamarole of the vaudeville black-face comedian."[67] Bogle writes, in partial jest, that Best was Stepin Fetchit's (Lincoln Perry) "step-chillun," with Best appropriating Perry's comic, shuffling, dull-witted moves and characterizations, and taking the roles which might have gone to Perry.[68] Best was not nearly as good a performer as Perry and could not get at the lazy, slow-moving coon performance with the same ingenuity. He simply was not as accomplished an actor. In *The Ghost Breakers* (1940), Best appeared alongside Bob Hope, hanging his bottom lip while enduring lines such as "You look like a blackout in a black-out. If this keeps up, I'm going to have to paint you white." Best was always the same, not quite funny, just simply a dimwit who played a sidekick but did not react to insult or, like Moreland, fire back with the occasional zinger. Best notoriously hung his lower lip, bulged his eyes, and shuffled through "Blacks in horror" films such as *The Monster Walks* (1932), in which he considered his kin-ship to an ape, and *The Smiling Ghost* (1941), in which he adds crossing his eyes and out-running a team of stampeding horses to his scared-Negro performance. Best would be called in again and again to do little more than quake with fear and jump at shadows in other comedy-horror films such as *The Body Disappears* (1941), *Whispering Ghosts* (1942), and *The Face of Marble* (1946).

FIGURE 3.5 Willie Best
RKO Radio Pictures/Photofest

Scared-Negro ... Puppets?!

> "If I'm yella' you's colorblind,"
>
> —Scruno, *Spooks Run Wild* (1941)

The great proliferation of comedy-horror films seemed to almost smother
the achievements of Spencer Williams. Even *The East Side Kids* film series
(1940–1944) with the young Scruno (Ernest "Sunshine Sammy" Morrison) got
in on the scared-Negro act. In *Spooks Run Wild* (1941) as Scruno trips through a
dark, haunted mansion, he is scolded by his pals, "The next time you come
out of the dark, put a coat of whitewash on, will ya?," to which Scruno replies,
"I'm so scared I'm turnin' white now." In *Ghosts on the Loose* (1943), another
William Beaudine quickie, Scruno, quaked and sputtered, "Who dat say who dat
when I say who dat," as Emil (Bela Lugosi) a Nazi spy stalked him.[69] It comes as
no surprise that Hollywood would move from infantilizing men to implicating
children—real and cartoon alike—in the scared-Negro act.

George Pal created stop-motion films featuring wooden puppets, or
"puppetoons." Pal's most infamous films are his series of Jasper short films
(1942–1947) starring the puppet Jasper as a "little pickaninny" (as Jasper was
called in promotions) drawn like a blackface caricature—bug eyes, wide, bright
smiling lips highlighted against coal black skin—who lives with his "Mammy" in

a decrepit shack. Jasper and those around him speak in black voice. Across the series, Jasper's love for watermelon is a constant, and the source of many of his troubles, sending him into horror film territory, with Jasper experiencing "frightening violence" highlighted by gloomy scenes, darkly lit, that mark the mood as ominous and foreboding.[70] In *Jasper and the Watermelons* (1942) Jasper steals watermelons out of a forbidden watermelon patch. The film then turns to a "haunting sequence with [the] frightened child chased by threatening figures."[71] As the film changes from day to night, enormous watermelons appear singing, "Gonna be trouble in Watermelon land tonight," as the melons turn into snarling monsters in pursuit of Jasper. The monster melons turn cannibalistic as they do their best to consume Jasper, all the while Jasper narrowly escapes each one, running and leaping and fighting his way out of their mouths. A swirling watermelon juice waterfall finally gives Jasper the edge he needs, as the rapids carry him back home to Mammy ... who offers him a slice of watermelon. In *Jasper and the Haunted House* (1942) it is not watermelon, though it usually is, that gets Jasper in trouble, but gooseberry pie. On Mammy's order, Jasper is to carry the pie to Deacon Jones, but ends up in a haunted house. Jasper's shadow turns and runs, leaving Jasper behind. Here, in special effects, Jasper's eyes are made to bug and flutter from fright, at the speed of sound. There is a musical interlude in which a ghost plays a little jazz piano and haints dance around.[72] Eventually, Jasper escapes the home, and while running away gets stuck in a billboard that reads, "Next time try Spooks gooseberry pie."

Jasper came out of the imagination of Pal, who was born in 1908 in Hungary and died in 1980 in the US. During his career, his animation work earned him an Oscar, as well as six other nominations. Pal claimed to have no racial animus in mind when he created Jasper and that he was "simply bringing to life a truly American Black folk character, and harbored no racial prejudices himself."[73] Never mind that the series was built on a soup of Black stereotypes and dysfunction with abject poverty, a single-parent home, absent father, mammy, and an "idle, trouble-making" Black male, who steals watermelons no less, at its center.[74] It mattered little what the maker's intent was, the reception by Blacks was poor. *Ebony* magazine ran an article, "Little Jasper Series Draws Protest from Negro Groups," lamenting the depiction of a Black boy who loves watermelon as much as he is spooked by haunted houses.[75]

Richard Neuert draws parallels between the Jasper films and, interestingly, those of Spencer Williams, writing, "however, it is worth noting as well that some of Pal's Jasper themes, such as urging rural folks to stay put, respect the old traditions, and avoid stealing, also turned up in 1940s live-action race movies like Spencer Williams' famous *The Blood of Jesus*, made by and for African Americans."[76] However, Williams' religious/horror themed films were unmatched, becoming a sort of genre unto themselves, "pristinely Black in [their] advocacy, locale, point of view, social ethic, and ... resolutely non-Hollywood folk technique."[77] There was nothing about Jasper that reflected Blackness, and it certainly did not take up the additional aims of advocacy or of privileging Black bourgeois values. Williams presented value systems, class positionings, rituals and behaviors, love relationships, and ideologies of uplift that had not been seen during this cycle of horror films. Pal's films not only failed to speak to these views, but were symbolically devastating. In fact, nearly two decades after Pal introduced Jasper, Black groups were still trying to keep such stereotypes away from viewers. A Portland, Oregon, television station had to be cajoled by the Urban League in 1959 to cancel the series due to its obvious stereotypes. The Black press—the *Los Angeles Sentinel*, the *Chicago Defender*, and the *Afro-American* (Baltimore), among others—reported that the Urban League wrote to Portland station KOIN about the portrayal of Jasper, which "serve[s] to perpetuate false notions about the peculiarities of Negroes as a race." The appeal to KOIN went on to say: "it is tragic that Jasper and his associates are continually presented in ways which solidify false notions and cater to an assumption of racial superiority on the part of White viewers."[78]

Conclusion

Spencer Williams' films were not technically complex. After all, one film (*The Blood of Jesus*) did present the Devil as a man in a Halloween-type costume. Some critics might even say that his oversimplified lessons in piety did not correspond with the deadly times within which they were delivered. Still, Williams literally stepped out on faith to create popular and successful "Black horror" films steeped in (Southern) Black culture for Black audiences. His films proved that there are interesting Black stories to be told. Unfortunately, Hollywood turned a blind eye to such evidence as it continued to mine for formulaic, stereotypical narratives.

Still, a host of right-minded individuals and organizations would continue to appeal to Hollywood, asking it to revolutionize its treatment of Blacks. Joel Fluellen (*White Pongo* [1945]) and Betsy Blair (actress and wife of Gene Kelly), in 1946, appeared before the Screen Actors Guild (SAG) and proposed that the Guild advocate for its Black membership: "NOW, THEREFORE, BE IT RESOLVED that the Screen Actors Guild use all of its power to oppose discrimination against Negroes in the motion picture."[79] In 1947, Boris Karloff (*The Mummy* [1932]), as a member of SAG's anti-discrimination committee, noted the challenges SAG faced and the incremental change the organization was pursuing: "And if we insist that producers write roles for Negroes according to certain patterns, they may well leave out Negro roles altogether. However, what we plan to do is fight for the inclusion of Negroes in all crowd scenes. We plan to insist that in all scenes at least ten per cent of the characters be Negroes moving about ordinary business the same as other people."[80]

The proliferation of comedy-horror drowned out and undermined calls for change. In these fictions, Blacks are alternately and/or simultaneously "naturally," authentically docile and savage, nurturing and monstrous. Such treatments begged the question of whether Blacks would ever get to play the day-to-day monster in horror, or creatures reflecting on mythology, or be featured in a psychological horror. Could horror create a Black monster without indicting the entire race as monstrous, and perhaps image a Black character as brave or as a savior? The Gists and Williams began to answer these questions in the affirmative with few resources. While imaging Blacks' whole and full participation in the horror genre was proven easy, the film industry continued to fail to act over the coming years for a number of social (and some financial) reasons.

Horror film exited the 1940s just as it had entered, under threat. Calling some of the films produced in the coming decade "B movies" was terribly generous as horror filmmakers of the 1950s were lucky if they could hire actual humans to slip into rubber suits to play their monsters. Increasingly, horror sank into laughability as monsters became inflatable brains (e.g. *The Brain from Planet Arous* [1957]), rubber and paper mache tree stumps (e.g. *From Hell It Came* [1957]), or mangy puppets on a string (e.g. *The Giant Claw* [1957]). This made it even easier for television, which began broadcasting nationally in 1948, to become a formidable competitor to film. Though television was much more strictly regulated by the Federal Communications Commission (FCC), if a viewer wanted to see frightening fare, television had it, by either airing horror films or creating thriller programming (not quite horror, but some sci-fi) such as *Alfred Hitchcock Presents* (1955–1965). If the comic-Negro was desired, television had that covered as well, with Black "TV minstrels"[81] appearing in programs such as *Beulah* (1950–1953) and *Amos 'n' Andy* (1951–1953).

As for horror films, invisibility and ridicule are the best terms to describe what lay ahead for Blacks over the next *two* decades (1950s–1960s). In the 1950s, science fiction and horror would wed to create monsters malformed by atomic energy bombs. Unlike Spencer Williams, who imagined a Black woman scientist, Hollywood could not do the same. Since Hollywood could not imagine Black scientists in laboratories where bombs and chemicals were created and where experimentation went awry, there could be no Blacks in movies attending to such themes. Blacks were rendered largely invisible in 1950s horror; that is, unless some scientist needed to take an African safari. Otherwise, Blacks would rear their heads again for a bit of that hybrid minstrelsy in the 1960s (e.g. *The Horror of Party Beach* [1964]). It would not be until 1968, nearly 25 years after Williams' films, with *Night of the Living Dead*'s Black lead character Ben, that the genre would finally catch up with Williams' vision.

4

BLACK INVISIBILITY, WHITE SCIENCE, AND A NIGHT WITH BEN

1950s–1960s

I am an invisible man. No, I am not a spook like those who haunted Edgar Allan Poe; nor am I one of your Hollywood-movie ectoplasms. I am a man of substance, of flesh and bone, fiber and liquids—and I might even be said to possess a mind. I am invisible, understand, simply because people refuse to see me.

—Ellison, 1952[1]

It looked like something from outerspace, and it seemed like a weird nightmare, not part of me.

—Mamie Till Bradley, mother of 14-year-old Emmett Till, who was murdered by White racists[2]

Something was wrong. In the sleepy, affable small town of Santa Mira, the idyllic 1950s peace was being disturbed by a dangerous "them" which worked to intrude upon the community's "us." The town began reacting swiftly, albeit controversially, to the threat. When interstate buses delivered outsiders to Santa Mira, the interlopers found themselves ominously met by the town's sheriff, immediately placed into the back of his patrol car, and taken away, never to be seen again. Control and conformity were Santa Mira's new preoccupation; hence, its inhabitants would no longer tolerate visitors (outside agitators) who possessed the potential to ask questions and to influence others with their differing agendas. With each passing day, its citizenry tightened the reins, eliminating all manner of variance. A swing/jazz band who had arrived just months earlier to play in one of the town's popular restaurants, thereby marking Santa Mira's flirtation with progress—"We're on the way up"—was, in this new climate, let go. The band was replaced by a pre-programmed jukebox. On the whole, this was a lamentable

America, one that was repressing its citizens' humanity: to be "mechanical" in this way was to be "a walking zombie!"[3]

The horror/sci-fi film *Invasion of the Body Snatchers'* (1956) fictional town of Santa Mira served as a metaphor for the many threats that 1950s America struggled with—change, (atomic/cold) war, foreign invasion, communism, and racial integration. It evidenced, as did many films of the 1950s and 1960s, a "strong resonance between the elements in the film and various anxieties existing in the broader culture."[4] In the film, that the notion of safety-in-sameness happened to be delivered by otherworldly (illegal) aliens did not obscure the fact that Americans were happy to secure insularity and stability by any means necessary. *Invasion*, a horror film without any Black characters, evidenced how some Americans came to believe that while the road to cultural fascism could be unpleasant—a sort of standing in front of the schoolhouse door to ward off individualism—the end was certainly justifiable.

Invasion stands today as not only a fan cult-classic, but one of America's most celebrated films.[5] The film is a tale about how extraterrestrial seedpods land on Earth, bringing with them the ability to fully duplicate humans, then kill them, to produce emotionally neutered clones, or "pod people."[6] Metaphorically, *Invasion* can also be regarded as the bellwether for the treatment of anything deemed as a threat to White conformity in horror films of the 1950s and 1960s. Pointedly, there was little representational variation in the horror genre over the two decades of the 1950s and 1960s, as Blacks were often rendered invisible as Santa Mira's outsiders.

The Invisibles

As the 1950s emerged, Black characters were a very scarce commodity in horror. What had in the past constituted "Black" labor, such as domestics or plantation workers, became less necessary in an era of film preoccupied with more scientific and extraterrestrial threats. For these challenges, White and, notably, often female characters would assume the role of aides. For example, in the 1957 film *The Giant Claw*, a (laughable) gargantuan monster bird with an anti-matter energy screen is menacing Earth (the US in particular). Though science's most deadly invention, the atom bomb, cannot exterminate this alien, scientists remain undaunted, working to theorize a solution. In this film, there is little need for Blacks carrying bags or serving meals. The bird is a dilemma for intellectuals and the spaces that such people work in are laboratories or research centers. In this work context, Blacks can, presumably, serve no purpose.

In the film, "Miss Caldwell" (Mara Corday), a White female mathematician and systems analyst, takes on the duties of aide. Though she promises to be a learned person, she is unable to map the basic flight pattern of the bird (that is, analyze its system). Instead, Caldwell becomes one who takes orders and affably tolerates sexual harassment—she is referred to as "mother, dear mother" and ordered by a workmate to "kiss me and be quiet," which she eagerly does. This kind of notably "severe repression of female sexuality/creativity," writes Wood, not only attributes passivity, subordination, and dependence to the woman, but "in a male-dominated culture ... woman as the Other assumes particular significance."[7] Though her primary job is to look beautiful and to serve as a sort of housemaid, bringing the men refreshments, Caldwell is able to take notes and keep an eye on instrument panels—tasks presumably well beyond the reach of Blacks.

Even in the general absence of racial diversity, the use of racial symbolism was rife throughout the decade of the 1950s. The film *Bride of the Gorilla* (1951) similarly links difference to aberration. Here, the character Barney (Raymond Burr) is a rubber plantation foreman overseeing the management of a residence built deep in the Amazon jungle. Barney is a cruel manager, who reminisces fondly, "Oh, when they had slaves!" Filmmakers knew such jungle films had racial implications, and this one was no exception, with lines such as: "White people shouldn't live too long in the jungle." According to Thomas Cripps in *Making Movies Black*, a writer for the Maryland newspaper the *AfroAmerican*, Carl Murphy, "was called in to advise on ... *Bride of the Gorilla* [thereby] establishing a Black stake in issues other than the use of 'nigger' in the dialogue."[8] Indeed, slurs are absent from the film, but so too are substantive appearances by Blacks. In the film, Barney becomes covetous of his boss' wife Dina (Barbara Payton), and kills his boss to have her. The murder is witnessed by Al-Long (Gisela Werbisek), a witch, who curses Barney. Barney is plagued by hallucinations in which he believes he is transforming into a gorilla. The film features a short cameo appearance by the famed Black actor Woody Strode in the role of Nedo, a local policeman. Here, in his very brief appearance, Strode plays it straight. He is stoic and professional. His actions are largely centered on quickly searching Al-Long's room to see if she has hidden evidence related to the boss' murder. His principle function is to lend credence to the frightening power of Voodoo. Alarmed by the witch's powers, Nedo firmly scolds her: "I don't believe in Black magic ... But you keep away from my house. I don't want witches near my children." He then swiftly exits the scene (and the movie). The brevity of Strode's appearance is unfortunate, as it served as a reminder of what Black actors could bring to the genre—appropriate fearfulness without playing bug-eyed spooked. However, either kind of portrayal, spooked or generally normal, halfway into the twentieth century was still a remarkable rarity.

Another film during this cycle of horror films, *The Bride and the Beast* (1958), has apes/primitivism and civilization at its center. However, in this film Blacks again fade from the screen. *The Bride and the Beast* stars no Blacks, but still succeeds in casting the "dark continent" and that which comes out of it as creepily grotesque. In the film, Dan (Lance Fuller), a big game hunter, marries Laura (Charlotte Austin). Their marriage license cost $6.00, which prompts Dan to inexplicably enthuse, "I could buy six wives for that in the middle of Africa!"

Dan introduces Laura to Spanky, an African gorilla that Dan has captured and keeps in the basement of his mountaintop home in the US. In making Spanky's acquaintance, Laura exhibits an odd sexual attraction to the beast, gazing lustily upon the gorilla and, later, dreaming about the animal. In one shocking scene, Spanky visits Laura in her bedroom, where beast and beauty embrace, followed by the animal stripping Laura of her clothes. Dan kills Spanky on the spot. Under hypnosis, Laura's strange animal attraction is explained: In a previous life Laura was herself a gorilla, the queen of the gorillas to be exact. Laura and Dan, joined by their "houseboy" Taro[9] (played by the White actor Johnny Roth performing in brown face), whose vocabulary is limited to addressing Dan as "Bwana," make their way to Africa for Dan to resume his hunting. Here monster (black gorillas) and place (Africa) as overtly racialized are revealed. While in Africa, Laura's attraction to all things African—a sort of jungle fever—deepens, and Dan tries to cure her of her obsession. The film ends with an ebullient Laura being carried away, into the depths of the jungle, in the arms of a black gorilla. However, the scene provokes unease, showing Dan as the real victim, losing his love to a form of grotesque miscegenation, a mixing of species which produces a fear similar to that of the mixing of races. In short, animals and Blacks are all the same.

Black Is, Black Ain't

The 1957 "Blacks in horror" film *Monster from Green Hell* evidenced how Blacks could be effectively employed in the horror genre. The film is a standard horror/sci-fi B movie—low budget, with comical special effects. The film opens by asking the question, what happens to life in the "airless void above the Earth's atmosphere" in a "flock of cosmic radiation?" To find out, the U.S. space program sends a monkey, wasps, a crab, spiders, and a guinea pig into space via two unmanned rockets. Disaster strikes when a rocket is lost "just off the coast of Africa." Dan (Robert Griffin) and Quent (Jim Davis), two White American scientists working on the space project, soon get reports of mysterious wasp monsters wreaking havoc on central Africa and set off to do something about it. There, the men meet up with a White doctor, Dr. Lorentz (Vladimir Sokoloff), and his daughter Lorna (Barbara Turner), who treat the African natives with "real" medicine and whose additional mission is to disabuse Africans of their superstitious ways, which include traditional medicine and prayers to non-Judeo-Christian gods. The film takes a predictable turn, complete with the launching of a safari through the jungle staffed by shirtless, loin-clothed, silent natives walking in single file carrying baggage on their heads.

However, among the natives is a man named Arobi. Arobi is played by Joel Fluellen, a Black actor who was a tireless advocate for complex, noteworthy roles for Blacks in Hollywood. Fluellen's influence is clear, with his character Arobi nearly stealing the movie (assuming one is paying attention to such a character). Arobi is an upright and articulate character who is a far cry from an earlier horror turn by Fluellen as "Mumbo Jumbo," a bowing, mush-mouthed servant in the "Blacks in horror" film *White Pongo* (1945). Arobi is always impeccably dressed in Western safari clothes—starched khaki shorts, a safari hard hat, pressed shirt, knee socks, utility belt with ammo, and rifle. Though Arobi is often instructed by the scientists to work or "do"—such as the important job of rigging explosives— he is also often sought for his thoughts about the plan that they are pursuing. While the native guides are subservient to the White scientists, Arobi becomes an essential member of their team, contributing advice in professorial tones. He does not sleep with the natives, but around the camp—albeit near, but not alongside— with the Whites (there is, after all, a White woman on the team).

The movie concludes with the group watching the demise of the monsters, and a coda dialogue. The three White members of the team speak first. The two men, then the woman, speak very briefly. In the end, it is Arobi who delivers the moving, closing opus: "The death of the creatures will bring about the deliverance of my people. The gods have been kind. They've taught us, as Dr. Lorentz taught us, to have faith." The speech evidences a continued reliance on White wisdom. However, it also functions to restore some cultural value to Blackness. Much of the movie is about dismissing the native ways, but Arobi reasserts the notion of gods (plural). Because, indeed, it is not science that kills the mutants. Rather, it is Africa, in the form of one of its volcanoes, which destroys them, thereby restoring a balance in nature.

Monster from Green Hell is not without its problems, and the problems are significant. Arobi aside, it is still a movie that renders Blacks invisible. For example, one of the swiftest, most uneventful deaths comes a mere 2 minutes, 51 seconds after the film's opening credits. Here, a Black man named Makonga (uncredited), from one of the African villages, is found dead. His demise is unseen, and it is simply stated that the man met his fate at the hands of a monster in the jungle— "green hell"—who injected him with a massive amount of venom. The scene functions to set up what is lacking in Blackness and what is superior in Whiteness. Makonga's body is brought to Dr. Lorentz. Dr. Lorentz symbolizes modernity; the sophistication of White scientific and religious enlightenment. Makonga is autopsied in the shadow of a large cross hanging over his body in the doctor's makeshift hospital. Makonga's death also comes to symbolize all that is wrong with Africa—its "turmoil," as it is called in the film. Six months after his death the monsters have multiplied, but there is no sign of any form of African government, military, medical centers, industry, or modern cities—there is only the jungle. Africa is depicted as a wayward, primitive land invested in superstition, absent modernization or civilization. Hence, it is the Americans, whose experiments exposed the continent to danger in the first place, who fly in (literally, in the film they offer a plug to TWA airlines) to act as saviors. Dan and Quent enter Africa, in a manner that Sontag would call "strongly moralistic," to make all aware that they know the proper, humane use of science and that they, White men, are not really mad scientists.[10] As for the Black characters, apart from Arobi there are only male African "natives" serving as pack animals and as the hapless victims of the rampaging monsters. These roles—load-bearers and victims—are not necessarily mutually exclusive.

"I Do Love De White Women"[11]

Filmmakers continued to press a trend in offering up what Gonder calls "racially coded uncouth monsters," but some also added both overt and covert anti-miscegenation messages for good measure.[12] *Creature from the Black Lagoon* (1954) is to the 1950s what *King Kong* was to the 1930s, an obviously metaphorically raced, anti-miscegenation film. The film presents a team of White scientists/archeologists traveling through the Amazon in search of a primitive black sea-land creature—the Gill Man (Ricou Browning/Ben Chapman). As in *The Giant Claw*, the team includes a White female researcher whose main purpose is to act as eye candy and to shriek with fright when the Gill Man is spotted. Of course she is also the object of desire for the monster, who repeatedly attacks the team in an attempt to get at her. The researchers are led on their expedition by a crew of Brazilian men who, like the Africans in *Monster from Green Hell*, meet their desultory, gruesome demises quite early on in the film. The deaths of these men—the natives—are immaterial as only the loss of a scientist would be "a useless waste of experience and ability."[13] However, it is the monster itself that evokes a most troubling racialization.

In this film, the creature is violent and single-minded in its desire for a White woman. The Gill Man is Kong and Gus from *The Birth of a Nation* rolled into one impossible body. Bodily, the monster resembles a racist caricature—its lips are large and exaggerated, its skin is dark. It is seemingly feeble-minded. Its movements are shambling except for a swift, adept move it displays when stealing away with a White woman. The monster permits a counter-image to White evolution which is pictured as modern, intellectual, and civilized. That is, the film tells us that Whites—with men at the top of the hierarchy—have evolved, while, importantly, other races remain static and immobile in their progress. Hence the film also speaks to where, or among what places (the exotic, dangerous Amazon) and which populations (the Brown/Black Brazilians), inferiority can be located. When the monster meets its expected demise, in its own territory, at the hands of the White scientific elite, not only is its subordination assured, but it also becomes understood that such an Other had no place in, and could make no contribution to, the White world, and that its mere presence, even in its own non-White world is a nuisance—a sort of White man's burden.

Patrick Gonder, in his essays "Like a Monstrous Jigsaw Puzzle: Genetics and Race in Horror Films of the 1950s" and "Race, Gender, and Terror: The Primitive in 1950s Horror Films," presents a very close and detailed reading of *Creature from the Black Lagoon*, arguing that the film's function is not merely to reinforce White superiority and non-White inferiority, or monstrosity.

Rather, this is a film which also "taps into racist fears of desegregation" [14] as the Black monster, in leaving its proper place in the water and attempting to integrate among those on land, is a Darwinian reminder of why segregation is necessary.[15]

It is important to remember that *Creature* was not simply a tale about seismic action on the evolutionary Richter scale. Rather, this was a story in which the White male researchers are driven to destroy the Gill Man, as opposed to even studying it, because it has committed the ultimate sin of having eyes for a White woman.

Real life and art coalesced around the sexual threat to White womanhood. In August 1955, 14-year-old Chicagoan Emmett Till was murdered for whistling at a White woman while on vacation in Mississippi. The brutality of the boy's murder was horrific as he suffered beatings and blunt force trauma, the gouging of his eyes, and a bullet to the brain. His mutilated body was tied to a 100-pound piece of farming equipment and then sunk in a river. Emmett's mother, Mamie Till Bradley, demanded that the world pay attention to this atrocity as well as to the other horrors Blacks were facing in the US when she opened her son's casket, insisting that the Black press take pictures and print them in their periodicals.

Goldsby (250) wrote about the imagistic impact of Till Bradley's decision: "In a stunning move that recast the scope and direction of the case, she authorized a four-day memorial service open to all, and allowed the black press to photograph her son's corpse. Images of Till's mutilated body ran in such nationally circulated magazines and newspapers as *Jet*, the *Chicago Defender*, the *Pittsburgh Courier*, the *New York Amsterdam News*, and the *Crisis*."[16] The photographs of the heinously abused, bloated body of a child were the ultimate in horror imagery. In rapid succession, there were historic high-profile cases reasserting rights and justice for Blacks. *Brown v. Board of Education of Topeka, Kansas* (1954) and the case of the nine African American students who attended Central High School in Little Rock Arkansas (1957) were direct challenges to *Plessy v. Ferguson* (1896), which assured segregation in schools. Even here, the safety of White women was invoked—would young White women be safe from Black men in the integrated classroom? Till and the Gill Man suffered a similar fate as their bodies were battered in a variety of ways, and mortally wounded before seeing a watery grave. "White men not only lynched and tortured African American men in real life," writes Butters, "but they lived out these fantasies through violent cinematic attacks on Black men," whether they were real, in fiction, or metaphorical.[17]

A Ways to Go

There was not much of a discernible shift between the horror films of the 1950s and the 1960s. The 1960s opened the same way the previous decade had, with

White male doctors/researchers looking to intervene in nature's progression and with Blacks suffering measures of invisibility. The distance between Whites and Blacks was best illustrated in the horror film *The Alligator People* (1959). Set in "primitive, savage" Louisiana, in a plantation home that even a "conjure woman knows is evil," the film tells the story of a White scientist whose medical experiments turn humans into alligators, and who is now working to reverse the effects with radioactivity. This film includes appearances by two Blacks, Toby the butler (Vince Townsend, Jr.) and Lou Ann the maid (Ruby Goodwin). The odd medical experiments are conducted in a laboratory, which is a separate structure from the plantation house. Toby and Lou Ann's purview is the home where they clean, cook, and tend to other domestic affairs; only Whites and White human–alligator hybrids leave the house to enter the lab. In their brief appearances, Toby and Lou Ann do engage Whiteness, working to control an uneducated laborer, Mannon (Lon Chaney, Jr.), a violent, dirty, drunkard whose erratic behavior (e.g. attempted rape) threatens the research. However, their encounters are limited to when Mannon comes to the house or its front yard, as that is the confined purview of the pair. Mannon, by contrast, moves about at will, including entrance to the lab, a place that is out of bounds for the two Black domestics.

The Horror of Party Beach (1964), a very serious "horror-musical," is much like *The Alligator People* in its treatment of Blacks. Blacks do not figure in the narrative, except for a feisty, doting, but not-to-bright servant named Eulabelle (Eulabelle Moore) who is never seen outside of the home of her employer, a doctor/research scientist. When toxic waste monsters begin killing off young White beachcombers, it is Eulabelle who enters the scene to assert no less than three times to the doctor who has been asked to help solve the mystery that there must be some wicked Voodoo magic at work: "It's the Voodoo, that's what it is!" It is not. Still, superstitious Eulabelle functions to implicate Black religion as evil, even going so far as to carry a Voodoo doll around with her to curse the monsters, or, as she puts it, "one of dem zombies." The real culprit is illegally dumped radioactive waste that has reactivated the dead, whose bodies were in shipwrecks, bringing them back as half-human/half-sea monster. The implication is that even though the danger is White and man-made, Black Voodoo is the yardstick for all monstrosities.

However, Eulabelle's second contribution is far more interesting. In tune with all things domestic, it is Eulabelle who discovers that common household sodium can do away with the radioactive sea monsters. However, the manner in which Eulabelle discovers the solution reaffirms the notion that Blacks have no place in a laboratory. In the film, Eulabelle is frightened to be alone in the dark, and dares to venture down to the doctor's lab, where he is working on a chemical weapon to kill the monsters. While she is adept at carry trays, cleaning, and looking after the home upstairs, in the lab Eulabelle is a clumsy disaster. She knocks over chemicals and breaks beakers, and then shrieks out an apology. By happenstance, her accident leads to a solution—sodium. However, Eulabelle does not possess the intellectual capacity to say "sodium," so she refers to it as the "whatcha call it." *The Horror of Party Beach* proved troublesome on two fronts. First, indeed, it functioned to reinforce the belief that only Whites, qualified or not (be they wives or other doting women), should be in laboratory spaces. Second, for 1964, when the Civil Rights and Black Nationalism movements were complementing each other, it seemed regressive to see a mammy character resurrected.

Significantly, *The Leech Woman* (1960) presents a Black female principle character as adept and central to a White scientist's experiments. Paul Talbot (Phillip Terry) hopes to create a pharmaceutical fountain of youth, a drug which will not only stop, but also reverse, the aging process. Enter a 152-year-old Black woman named Malla (Estelle Hemsley), a former slave who bears, as she explains, "the brand of the Arab slaver who stole me and my mother from Africa and sold us across the sea 140 years ago." Malla's Africanness makes her mysteriously magical as, upon meeting Paul's wife, she (correctly) declares: "You will never divorce your husband. You won't have to. He will die. His death will give you life … you are the one in my dreams of blood." She also happens to have Nipea, an organic drug concoction that can slow the aging process. A smart, tough negotiator, Malla insists that Paul pay for her return to her African homeland, and only then will she provide him with the drug. Incidentally, there is a second substance that when mixed with the Nipea reverses the aging process, restoring the old to youth. The drug is housed only in Africa among the Nando people, a "savage, proud race … who have an undying hatred for Europeans." Paul pays for Malla's passage, but he and his older wife, June (Coleen Gray), who is in her late sixties, approximately 10 years old than Paul, secretly follow Malla to Africa to secure the second ingredient of the drug—the fountain of youth. They discover that Malla's tribe performs a ritual in which they kill to extract the pineal gland from men, mixing the secretion with the Nipea powder and ingesting it to reverse the aging process. Going through the ritual, Malla becomes the gorgeous "young Malla," played by popular actress Kim Hamilton. The film then shifts its attention to June escaping Africa (with stolen Nipea) and leaving all Black characters in the film behind, for a return to the United States. In the US, June—who is aged and deemed unattractive—kills those Whites around her for their glands so that she may concoct the fountain of youth drug for herself. The shift to the US is a necessary one, as June cannot prey upon African men, injecting their fluids into her body. The film carefully avoids any blood-mixing and miscegenation implications.

To *The Leech Woman*'s credit it was the very rare "Blacks in horror" film during this time to cast a *Black woman* in a central role. More, she is a feminist, asserting the value of women while protesting against ageism, noting that men's grey hairs are unfairly respected as a sign of intellect and maturity, while aging women are scorned or neglected. Malla was one of the more substantial Black characters of the genre during this film cycle, and was a marked improvement over the kinds of representation Blacks were experiencing in films such as

The Alligator People. Still, Blacks' inclusion in horror during this period remained uneven and confused.

Here We Go Again: Voodoo and Comic-Negroes

Horror films again adopted Africa and the Caribbean as their settings, places purported to be free of the kind of racial strife witnessed in America during the Civil Rights movement, and therefore places where stories could have Black characters without focusing on racial equality issues. The strategy was a return to the themes seen in horror films of the 1930s. As a result, zombies, Voodoo, and the jungle would get their second wind through films such as *Serpent Island* (1954), *Voodoo Island* (1957), *Voodoo Woman* (1957), and *Zombies of Mora Tau* (1957). But there would be few or no Blacks to appear in such films. Rather, for much of the 1950s and well into the 1960s, as evidenced by the film *Voodoo Bloodbath* (1964), "almost all of the horror films with a discernible racial component kept the Black presence contained within narratives featuring exotic island locales, white interlopers, and uninhibited natives ('savages') practicing voodoo and experiencing zombification."[18] For example, the horror film *Zombies of Mora Tau* (1957) had no Black characters, but that fact did not impede it from implicating Africa, a land that "time has forgotten," in evil Voodoo. In the politically tinged film, which critiques Western colonialism, it is revealed that in 1894 a crew of Americans sailed to the continent of Africa to loot its diamonds. The sailors succeed in locating the bounty, and get it loaded on their ship just as (unseen) Voodoo-practicing African natives curse the men, making them zombies and sinking their ship. As zombies, the sailors must guard the diamonds forever. Over the decades other treasure seekers try to recover the diamonds from their watery grave, but are killed by the zombies. Unlike the dominant representations of zombies, these White American zombies have no "master"; that is, these White zombies are not under the control of Africans. Rather, they are fairly autonomous creatures who are merely trapped in their undead bodies. American sailors again attempt to recover the diamonds. An aged White woman (the wife of the American sea captain who was zombified) reveals that if the diamonds are lost at sea forever, then the zombies can go to their final resting place peacefully. In the end, the diamonds are thrown away in the sea, thereby freeing the undead White men from zombism.

Returning horror to Africa often meant that horror continued to indict Blackness in rather novel ways. 1953's *Bwana Devil* had the potential to examine British colonial rule in Kenya and the road to resistance by Kenya's Kikuyu, a people who suffered hunger, due to British food rationing, overwork in deplorable conditions, humiliation, beatings, and executions at the hands of their colonizers. Protest ultimately culminated with the 1952 Mau Mau movement, an uprising opposing foreign rule. Instead, the film cast Kenya as an inherently savage land, even implicating Kenya's wildlife, specifically its lions, in a tale of racist victimization in which Whites are the injured parties. In the film, Kenyan lions have decided that the British are the killer cats' snack of choice.

Audiences were provided with a throwback horror film reminiscent of 1940s narratives, in which Blacks were spooked and abused for comic effect. The film *Spider Baby, or the Maddest Story Ever Told* (1968) tells the story of the Merrye family, stricken with the Merrye Syndrome. The inherited disease is the result of inbreeding and causes mental deevolution. One family member, Virginia (Jill Banner), is obsessed with spiders, and believing she is one, uses ropes as her web and butcher knives as her stingers. Mantan Moreland, cast simply as "delivery-man," opens the film and is dead within its first five minutes. The deliveryman climbs the porch of the secluded, decrepit mansion home of the Merryes and peers through a window, calling out to the home's inhabitants. The window slams shut, trapping him so that his head and torso are dangling in the house while his legs flail outside the house on the porch. Virginia appears, a butcher knife in each hand. She throws her "web" on the deliveryman, entangling him. Gleefully, Virginia yells, "Sting, sting, sting!" as she slices the deliveryman with her knives. The attack reeks of comic affect. A shot of the porch shows the deliveryman's legs kick about in slapstick manner. An interior shot reveals the deliveryman's upper torso pinned by the window and Virginia with his severed ear as a souvenir. The scene is easily standard horror fare, except Moreland resurrects his classic laugh-riot, bug-eyed performance. Moreland, in this cameo role, is included singularly for the purpose of recalling the comic-Negro suffering violence in a horror film.

Mantan Moreland may be regarded as one of the most explicit bridges between 1940s zombie-themed films such as *King of the Zombies* (1941) and *Revenge of the Zombies* (1943), and Black representations in horror. Moreland had been central to the creation of films about zombies (and other monsters) featuring Blacks. His appearance in *Spider Baby* marked the end of a long, dry season of race-free horror films. Additionally, Moreland's performances reminded horror movie audiences that Blacks and zombies were, for better or for worse, an interesting duo and the two together were very much missed. It was not much of a surprise, then, that the return of Blacks in horror was in a (far from funny) zombie film *Night of the Living Dead* (1968). *Night of the Living Dead*, which is worth discussing in some detail, would introduce one of the single most dramatic, provocative changes regarding Black participation in horror.

A Night with Ben

It was the night of April 4, 1968. Hours earlier film director George R. Romero had heard, along with the rest of the world, that Civil Rights activist and Nobel Peace Prize winner Dr. Martin Luther King, Jr. had been assassinated in Memphis, Tennessee. Romero was already anxious as he was driving from Pittsburgh to New York City with his[19] low-budget, independently produced horror film

Night of the Living Dead in the trunk of his car. Would he be able to secure a distributor for his film, a film that pressed the horror genre to new limits with its graphic, gory violence and bleak plot? *Night of the Living Dead*, a "Blacks in horror" film, presented as its star a Black character, Ben (Duane Jones), who heroically and singularly survives a relentless, night-long attack by cannibalistic ghouls only to be shot dead in the bright light of day by a posse of White vigilantes who then spear his body with hooks to lift it onto a bonfire. Certainly, in the context of the King assassination, this film might be seen as too inflammatory to secure backing. However, soon after his arrival in New York, Romero did secure funding for the film from Walter Reade Organization/Continental, and (appropriately) on Halloween 1968, *Night of the Living Dead* opened in theaters, thereby making film history for its dramatic reformation of the horror genre. *Night of the Living Dead* is a zombie movie the likes of which had not been seen before, and which has been copied thousands of times since. It has been credited with revolutionizing and solidifying the zombie subgenre in horror.

Night of the Living Dead opens in a cemetery in a small town just outside of Pittsburgh. There, siblings Barbara (Judith O'Dea) and Johnny (Russell Streiner) are visiting a grave. A man in a suit slowly approaches the pair, and from a distance he appears to be normal. However, as the man nears it is clear something is wrong with him—his walk is not slow, rather it is shambling; his stern face is not solemn, rather it has the empty look of the undead. The man attacks Barbara, and Johnny runs to her rescue only to be killed when the man pushes him down, his head striking a gravestone during the frenzied scuffle. Barbara flees the scene distraught and panicked, unable to help her brother as the "ghoul" or zombie chases her. Crumbling mentally from her inexplicable encounter, Barbara stumbles into a farmhouse, taking refuge there. Soon after, she is joined by Ben (the only Black person in the film), who is also trying to survive attacking zombies.

As Barbara slips into catatonia, Ben assuredly takes charge. He gets busy boarding up the farmhouse, blocking the zombies who are trying to gain entry. He locates a shotgun in the house and beats back the horde of zombies with bullets to their brains, blows to their skulls, and fire. It is Ben's last stand, and he is effectively and heroically winning. However, unknown to Ben and Barbara, a small group of survivors have locked themselves in the cellar of the house and are hiding in silence from what they believe are zombies traipsing in the house above them. Eventually, the group emerges. There is Tom (Keith Wayne) and Judy (Judith Ridley), a young couple. There is also the Cooper family—Harry (Karl Hardman) and Helen (Marilyn Eastman), and their daughter, ill, zombie-bitten young Karen (Kyra Schon), who remains in the cellar. Almost immediately an argument ensues between Ben, a highly competent, take-action kind of guy, and Harry, a sulky, angry man who wants authority and respect. Harry proposes that the group seal themselves in the cellar until help arrives. His suggestion is met with opposition all around. Tom sides with Ben and begs Harry to reconsider basement isolation—what Ben calls a "death trap" with no exit. Helen wonders why Harry must always be "right and everyone else wrong." For Helen, who knows Harry best, the issue is not necessarily the soundness of either plan, but that her husband wants to be boss. Ben Hervey, in his 2008 book *Night of the Living Dead*, argues: "Ben is no saint either; though he is more heroic, honourable and charismatic than Harry, he can also be less reasonable."[20] For example, when Harry continues to hide away in the cellar, leaving everyone who sided against him to die, Ben counters by refusing to let Harry take food with him to his child.

A news report on television reveals that the undead are everywhere, and in one of many sound bites scientists speculate whether the rise of the undead may have something to do with a probe sent from Earth to Venus that returned tainted with radiation. Unlike many horror films before and since, *Night of the Living Dead* did not implicate Blackness in the evil that is happening. These zombies are not Black, and do not emerge from Black places such as Africa, the Caribbean, or some Louisiana bayou; nor do they rise as a result of some odd Black Voodoo ritual. Rather, *Night* used the 1950s film habit of placing the blame on (presumably) White scientists and alien invasion. The news reports broadcast that shelters are being set up for any survivors. With the zombies still surrounding and attacking the house, Ben devises a plan for the group to get away in a nearby, but gas-less truck. Tom, Ben, and Harry—the men—work as a team to get the truck to a nearby gas pump. At the last minute, Judy runs to be by Tom's side as he fights his way to the truck to gas it up. The plan goes awry and the gas-soaked truck explodes, with Tom and Judy in it. Their death is a shocking twist—surely this young couple will be the face of America's future by surviving. No. The zombies have Tom and Judy's charred bodies for their dinner.[21]

Seeing the scene, Harry cowers inside the farmhouse, leaving Ben locked out to fight off the zombies. Here, the film cleverly sandwiches its hero, Ben, between two different kinds of monsters, both possessing diminishing humanity. This, too, is a unique turn in the film as the representation of monstrous difference typically functions to highlight the favorable, enlightened traits of White characters.[22] Here, the film reminds us that humans and monsters are not far apart and, indeed, can be one and the same. But the scene's tension is heightened by its racial component.

As Ben begs for Harry to open the door, Harry fails to move; he is both petrified of the zombies and upset with Ben. Harry alternately peeks out at, then hides from Ben. Eventually, Ben forces his way into the house. Once inside, Ben and Harry momentarily unite as they focus on repairing the breach in the house that Ben was forced to make. Still, Ben is irate, screaming, "I ought to drag you out there and feed you to those things." And it is assumed the younger, taller, more fit Ben could take on the older, dumpier Harry. But Ben does not. Instead, once the repairs are made, Ben batters Harry for trying to leave Ben to die. The racial anxieties are heightened as Ben does something that had not been done before by a Black character in a horror film (at least not without severe retribution for the character): Ben beats Harry to the ground, picks Harry up, and then beats him down again, leaving Harry bruised and bloodied. Indeed, up until this moment in 1968, it was rare for any film to depict a Black man beat a White man. Ben, who is no longer in immediate danger, beats Harry because he is frustrated and angry. It is a depiction that is not entirely out of line, but the race of the men amplifies the drama.

Much later, after Ben offers to carry Karen (Harry's daughter) a mile to safety, Harry is still more interested in getting Ben's shotgun and the power it promises. Helen warns Harry to leave Ben and the gun alone: "Haven't you had enough?" Harry cannot leave it alone, grabbing the shotgun and turning it on Ben. But Ben is able to wrestle it from Harry, shooting and mortally wounding him. Harry staggers to the cellar to find his daughter has died. The zombies begin to overrun the house, and Johnny, Barbara's now undead brother, and the zombie horde smash through windows and doors, taking her away to be consumed. Harry dies in the cellar. Karen reanimates and begins to dine on her father's corpse. She then discovers her mother cowering in the cellar, still alive. Karen brutally stabs her mother repeatedly with the edge of a shovel, so that she may snack on her as well. Ben is forced to "kill" them all again, and with the zombies rampaging through the house above he seals himself in the basement until dawn. As day breaks, Ben emerges from the cellar to the sound of human voices. The town's police and a posse of locals are rounding up the zombies and killing them. As Ben makes his way outside, he is suddenly shot in the head by the posse members, who mistake Ben for a zombie.

The filmmakers have been unwavering in their assertion that the casting of a Black actor as the star was happenstance—"he just turned out to be the best person for the part"—and that race had no import in the script, as evidenced by there being no mention of Ben's race in the film.[23] Though Romero was keenly aware that his film would be the "first film to have a Black man playing the lead role regardless of, rather than because of, his color," he also asserts that "even when Duane gets shot at the end, we weren't thinking any Black-and-White connotations." It was decades later when he realized "what it really meant."[24]

If it took Romero years to understand what Ben's role meant, some audiences seemed to understand right away. In the months after *Night*'s release, Romero was repeatedly peppered with questions about those "rednecks" who killed Ben—were they real people (as some of the extras in the film were "real," such as news reporter Bill Cardille playing himself in a cameo appearance), were they acting, or simply being themselves? In a 1970 review, Romero explains, "most of the people were actually from the small town we shot in … we had quite a bit of co-operation from people in the city—the police and city fathers … [they were] happy to have guns in their hands."[25] Of course labels of White "militia," "posses," "rednecks," and even "small-town" police bring up connotations of racism. As a result, the disgust the audience is prompted to feel about the characters is heightened and turned into real contempt and hatred, as it is understood that these are real people from Pittsburgh's real backwaters. More, in interviews, though Romero is careful not to alienate those who helped him so much by volunteering for his movie, he admits to not doing "much of anything" by way of directing their acting, as such "metaphorical fantasy confronts a barely filtered reality."[26] This collision between fantasy and reality becomes all the more real when in Romero's 1990 remake of the film the Black actor Tony Todd (of *Candyman* fame) is cast as Ben. Todd recalls the real suggestion of bigotry on the part of the extras playing the posse:

> Everybody in town wanted to be a zombie. And we shot in Washington, PA, which is not the most liberal place in America. You've seen *The Deer Hunter*. Strange things happen in Pennsylvania. And so, I'm surrounded by a bunch of zombies who were rednecks in another life … I knew it was going to be fucked up because they were all waiting to try to tackle me for real. Some of the tension you see is real, genuine stuff.[27]

In the original *Night*, that the posse was rooting out zombies with attack dogs further aligned them with all too familiar images of police dogs being urged to attack Civil Rights workers. Their rural dress of flannel and denim, their talk— "Beat 'em or burn 'em, they go up pretty easy"—and their accessories of bullets, cigars, and guns on the whole screamed, "Good ol' boys," which also represented danger to, and for, Blacks. The danger the men pose is represented in the perfunctory manner in which they take Ben out. Ben is hit with a bullet and knocked out of the frame, only to be seen again in a second long shot of his body slamming to the floor. The Sheriff matter-of-factly says, "Good shot" and "That's another one for the fire." Hervey writes, "That's it: there's no drawn-out death scene, no blaze of glory for this hero."[28]

Contrary to Romero's claims that race had not been considered, the actor Duane Jones (who by day worked as an English professor) rejected the idea that Barbara would somehow come out of her stupor to rise up and save him and herself from the zombies. For Jones, such an ending "would have been read wrong racially." Jones believed that "the Black community would rather see me dead than saved … in a corny and symbolically confusing way." Ben's death was shocking but was perhaps one of the most realistic moments in the film as he is shot dead by his "natural enemies, Pittsburgh cops and rednecks."[29]

Those who walked out of the theater before the credits rolled missed the handling of Ben's body. A series of grainy still images are flashed under the credits. They look like they could be the weathered photos of Emmett Till, shot in the head, being loaded onto the back of his executioners' truck to be transported to

FIGURE 4.1 Ben being thrown onto the pyre in *Night of the Living Dead*
    Ten/Photofest

the Tallahatchie River, where his body would endure more abuse. Instead, the stills are of Ben's lifeless corpse being impaled by meat hooks and lifted for transport to a pyre. Ben's body is then pressed down into the fire by wood and other debris. In the end, "our hero is not only dead but obliterated. There will be no record of his struggle, no burial or memorial, no hope of justice."[30]

There is much to be said about *Night*'s production, symbolism, and power. Richard Dyer, in his famed essay "White," draws attention to the color symbolism in the film, such as the black and white photography, in an era of color, to heighten and complicate understandings of good and evil. The night is dark (black), but the light of day brings more evil in the posse (white).[31] *Night* was also initially accused of presenting a "pornography of violence" with its unflinching scenes of zombies disemboweling their victims and then eating the entrails, prompting the Motion Picture Association of America to take a closer look at its ratings system.[32] And there are those who have written on the warring dysfunctional "family" in which the characters are unable to work together even in a disaster that transcends race and class.[33] However, less is known about *Night*'s reception among Black audiences—that is, apart from the fact that Blacks supported the film in great numbers, contributing to its popularity.

Night's impressive box office earnings—it cost approximately $115,000 to make but grossed $90,000 in the first weekend of its release, could be attributed to, in great part, its popular reception among Black audiences.[34] Kevin Heffernan points out the contribution of Black movie-goers to the box office success of *Night* in his book *Ghouls, Gimmicks, and Gold: Horror Films and the American Movie Business 1953–1968*, and his journal article, "Inner-City Exhibition and the Genre Film: Distributing *Night of the Living Dead."* He observes: (1) on the whole Black film-goers represented 30 percent of first-run audiences compared to 15–20 percent of the general population; (2) theaters in Black neighborhoods contributed to *Night's* success, as these theaters often struggled to get films (especially during the 3-D boom when it proved too costly to upgrade their theaters) and so *Night* was eagerly welcomed and for longer runs; (3) a film such as *Night*, with its implicit attention to race issues, straddled the fence as both a "prestige social problem film" and as a "exploitation item"; and (4) Black audiences lined up to see a film with a proud, smart, resourceful African American as its protagonist and star.[35] Heffernan also notes that when theaters in African American communities (e.g. in cities such as Philadelphia) secured first-run films (which was an infrequent occurrence), they were often horror films.

Indeed, if the Black press' attention during the 1950s and 1960s to the horror genre was any indication, the genre had favored status in Black communities. In newspapers such as the *Chicago Daily Defender*, the *New York Amsterdam News*, and the *L.A. Sentinel*, short articles and feature stories were frequently presented on horror films, notably when *no other* films or genres were mentioned. The *Daily Defender* was particularly prolific. For example, the *Daily Defender* ran an article in 1957, "Horror Films Debut Soon," promising that

> folks who like the blood-chilling type films will be well-satisfied soon with the arrival of a new series called "Shock." Fifty-two horror films from the archives of Columbia and Universal-International promise a whole year of blood-sucking entertainment ... watch out for these films—they'll give you a terrible treat.[36]

A 1960 article in the same newspaper proclaimed, "a triple bill of harrow films now playing the Royal Theatre are filling movie-goers with chills and chuckles that some have seldom experienced before. *A Bucket of Blood, The Giant Leeches,* and *Orders to Kill*, make up the electrifying screen program."[37] In yet another 1960 article, the *Daily Defender* detailed some horror clichés in promoting the film *Paranoia* at Chicago's Oriental Theatre:

> many great horror films revolve a plot around a beautiful victim who is alone and vulnerable to murder ... another technique in scary movies is letting the viewer believe the victim can escape ... one of the proven ingredients for horror is trying to drive the victim insane.[38]

Such stylized writing about horror films continued into the 1970s:

> Two excellent films of horror and suspense, shock and shiver that are scary
> and nervous even in quieter moments in their stories will open a first run
> double-feature program on Friday, (April 17) in over 30 neighborhood,
> suburban and drive-in theatres all over Chicagoland … Beware, however,
> this double-feature is not-for-the-weak-of-heart. Others who doubt the
> occult, who are nervous and fright-prone are doubly warned.[39]

Being aware of horror films' promotion and popularity in Black communities is
essential to understanding how, generally, the genre advanced due to Black
viewership, and how, specifically, *Night* saw such success. By the time *Night* hit
theaters, Walter Reade/Continental was ready to capitalize on the often-
mistreated Black market. "Many of the theaters that showed *Night of the Living
Dead*," writes Heffernan, "were in the inner city and served a predominately
African American audience," in part because neighborhood theaters or "nabe
houses" which catered to Blacks struggled to secure films.[40] These theaters
embraced non-blockbuster, indie, and eclectic programming. For example, *Night*
was paired with the Sidney Poitier drama *For the Love of Ivy* (1968) in its first run
at one Black nabe theater in Philadelphia, and at another it was on a double-bill
with a 1968 Jim Brown crime film called *The Split*.[41] In such theaters, *Night* was
put into heavy rotation.[42]

Night of the Living Dead was inducted into the US National Film Registry in
1999 and has been the basis for countless zombie movies, including a string of
sequels and derivatives, while earning cult-classic status among fans.

Dawn of the Dead

Romero would go on in his next three movies—*Dawn of the Dead* (1978), *Day of
the Dead* (1985), and *Land of the Dead* (2005)—to feature Black men in pivotal
central roles. *Dawn of the Dead* is set weeks after the undead first arise, and reveals
that the zombie plague has permeated every corner of society. Here, the des-
peration of the situation is revealed when zombies are seen wreaking havoc in the
tightly packed, highly populated city of Philadelphia. Predominately White, male
teams of SWAT officers (an urban version of the rednecks depicted in *Night*)
sweep through a tenement, caring little about distinguishing between zombies
and the building's Black and Brown human residents: "Blow all their Puerto
Rican and nigger asses right off!" A violent racial/ethnic and zombie cleansing
commences as the residents refuse to leave their homes as instructed.

As would be a continuing theme for Romero in his many *Dead* films, zombies
are metaphors for Whiteness, even as now some zombies are depicted as non-
White. In one scene, a Black zombie attacks a Black man. The zombie is not only
pale to mark its undead state, but it appears to be whited-up, a color contrast

"emphasized in a shot of the whitened Black zombie biting the living black man's neck."[43] Enter the Black hero, Peter (Ken Foree), a SWAT member who steps out against his White peers, demanding they end their slaughter of innocent citizens. When a member of the squad does not immediately stop, Peter kills him, just as he would a zombie, ceasing the man's kind of hyper-masculine, racial-domination performance. Peter is outside of, and above, both. Peter befriends another tactical officer, Roger (Scott H. Reiniger), a White male who possesses a similar distaste for the kind of violence they witness. Peter and Roger decide to try to escape the zombie/police madness by finding a refuge that is chaos-free. They join up with two others with the same intentions— a White couple, Stephen (David Emge) and his mistress Francine (Gaylen Ross), who are reporters for a news station and have access to the station's helicopter. Later, it is revealed that Francine is pregnant. The four find a safe haven in a shopping mall.

This film is a critique of American consumption and consumerism, as well as an engagement—thanks to the presence of the pregnant Francine—with the feminist movement and sexual revolution. By setting the film in a shopping mall, Romero continued to bring impressive change and innovation to the horror genre. This was important because decades of mad scientists, entranced women, plots of science gone awry, and settings of old houses laboratories had become

FIGURE 4.2 Peter readies to battle zombies in *Dawn of the Dead*
United Film Distribution Company/Photofest

"dull and routine."[44] The mall setting was thrillingly novel, as the group played among its wares.

In *Dawn*, theirs is a life of materialism, occasionally interrupted by interloping zombies. Likewise, Blackness does not interrupt (much). In one scene, jungle drums are the soundtrack as the group explores a gun shop rife with African safari pictures. While the drums and the "African" music typically signal Voodoo, there are no Voodoo zombies here, despite Peter's (inexplicable) aside that his grandfather was a Voodoo priest. Instead, this is a film about economic exploitation, which, according to Romero, means all Americans have become zombies mindlessly consuming—cannibalizing—commodities, most of which are not essential for sustenance and survival. One could not blame Black Voodoo for that.

Peter's life becomes dull routine, which, in a very unprogressive way, includes watching Francine "keep house," in an apartment that the group has set up in the mall. The smart and talented Francine is "Caldwell'd," as seen in *The Giant Claw*, cooking and cleaning for the men (although she demands to be consulted on plans and to be allowed to learn to shoot and to fly the helicopter). Otherwise, Peter's existence is inane, tied to chatting to his buddy Roger, who has been bitten by a zombie, until Roger eventually succumbs and Peter must shoot him.

Eventually, the group's relative peace is disrupted by a biker gang who wants in on the mall's bounty. The gang breaks into the mall, and swarms of zombies follow, overwhelming the place. The bikers become zombie food, and Stephen is killed and turned into a zombie. Peter and Francine—who, after months in the mall, is quite advanced in her pregnancy—are the only survivors. Francine flies herself and Peter away from the mall. The film ends inviting the audience to worry about the pair's fate. They are low on fuel, and have no idea where they should go. However, there is another unknown the film does not broach—can Francine deliver her baby alone? Will Peter, a trained officer, assist? What will their future be together? It is in these questions that Peter's Blackness and maleness and Francine's Whiteness and womanhood are most obvious.

Day of the Dead

Romero's third entry, *Day of the Dead* (1985),[45] lacked the political and, to some extent, the racial innovation of the two earlier *Dead* films. The film's time period is after "all the shopping malls are closed" (a reference to *Dawn of the Dead*) and it is set in an underground military bunker in Florida in which grotesque experiments are being conducted on the zombies by civilian scientists under the direction of the military. Above ground things appear rather hopeless, with little life left as the zombies have taken over. The remaining remnants of government and military hope that the experiments will reveal a way to end the zombies' reign. The film focuses on a zombie, Bub (Sherman Howard), who seems to be evolving and can sense the wickedness in the morally devolving scientist and military men around him. The scientists are aloof, at times callous. One of them experiments on undead soldiers, and even feeds them to other zombies. The scientists are "mad." The military men are a 1980s version of Romero's *Night* rednecks. The soldiers are revealed to also be sadistic, racist, and sexist. It is the military men who are monsters, ready to torture and kill humans and zombies alike. The men threaten to rape the lone female scientist, Sarah (Lori Cardille), and bully and even murder the other civilians on staff because they are different.

The requisite Black character in this film is John (Terry Alexander) a civilian-contract helicopter pilot who hails from the West Indies. In this context, John is a triple minority—Black, non-military/scientist, and foreign, as marked by his West Indian accent. John is also learned and civilized. John has fashioned a makeshift, but idyllic living space, which he calls "The Ritz," in the bunker, complete with a replica of a beachside cabana which he uses as a reading room. He easily shares his quarters with a forthright White civilian named William (Jarlath Conroy), a living arrangement which alludes to a more enlightened definition of masculinity that is not associated with the soldiers, who bunk with their guns.

In the film, things go wrong and Sarah, William, and John must fight a two-prong battle against the zombies, who overrun the bunker, and against the soldiers, whose bloodlust is equal to that of the zombies. Everyone is assumed to be expendable in this film except for John, because he is the only one who knows how to operate the helicopter, which can ferry survivors to safety. Though the military men need him, he is clearly despised. John has mocked the soldiers' primitive behavior and been unbowed by their threats. When he refuses to leave Sarah and William to face imminent death in the bunker at the hands of the zombies, John is to be beaten into submission—a clear allusion to slavery. However, John fights off the soldiers, rescues Sarah and William, and saves the day by flying the three of them away from the bunker and to a remote, deserted island that only he seems to know about. The film concludes with John peacefully fishing on a beach, joined by Sarah and William.

At a 2010 horror convention in Indianapolis, the actor Terry Alexander and the director, Romero, talked about the character John and, specifically, this final scene which depicts the three characters enjoying quiet survival. In noting the resourcefulness of the character John, Romero quipped that though there have been hundreds of other zombies-take-over-the-world films produced over the decades, perhaps audiences should believe that "Terry is *still* on that beach fishing," a hypothetical that Alexander enthusiastically embraced.[46] Romero's comments about the character John give subtle credence to Dyer's analysis that, "the point about Ben, Peter, and John is that in their different ways they all have control over their bodies, are able to use them to survive, know how to do things with them." Though Whites lose control while they are alive, and often "come back in the monstrously uncontrolled form of zombieness,"[47] these Black men, particularly John—who, unlike Ben, lives and, unlike Peter, is the one who actually pilots the group to safety—remain self-possessed while carrying on.

Land of the Dead

In 2005, Romero offered *Land of the Dead*. Here, Romero's political depth returns as he works to critique classism. In *Land*, there are three classes. The first is the upper class, consisting of wealthy humans who live in an exquisite waterfront, glass and steel high-rise which is protected on three sides by the city's three rivers and on the land-facing side by electrified barricades. Their lifestyle is maintained by a second class of people, professional foragers who scour the city's ruins, while fighting off zombies or "stenches" for commodities—food, fine wines, textiles, and other supplies. The foragers live, as do most of the surviving citizenry, in a chaotic, brutal wasteland. This second class is starving, dirty, and living and dying in the streets. The third, though perhaps not the "lowest" class, then, are the zombies, who roam free and, as humans die or are caught outside the fences, have plenty to eat.

One zombie, a Black man called "Big Daddy" (Eugene Clark), turns out to be especially evolved and cognizant of humans' continued brutalization of zombies. He becomes a leader of a zombie faction, learns to communicate through grunts and roars, and discovers how to use weaponry to bring down his human oppressors. He even teaches his compatriots to take up arms such as knives and machetes. In a pivotal scene, Big Daddy evidences a high order of rational thinking as he discerns his zombie army can get to the high-rise—an ostentatious symbol of exclusion even for the zombies—by walking on the rivers' bottom instead of risking electrocution by the fences. Indeed, the zombies invade, and Big Daddy seeks a particularly brutal revenge against the wicked owner of the high-rise. The film ends with a group of surviving humans, stars of the film, respectfully yielding the city to Big Daddy while the humans look for a new place to live. In return, Big Daddy seems to acknowledge this truce as he leads his zombie army.

On the whole Romero's films can be celebrated for their complex and even positive treatment of Blacks. Part of these characters' depth perhaps comes from Romero's belief that race did not figure prominently in the casting of actors Duane Jones, Ken Foree, or Terry Alexander.[48] However, their characters are certainly not free from the histories and politics that their skin color hails. Romero's Black characters are revolutionary in terms of cinematic represen-tations of race in America, whether human heroes or zombies. More, these Black characters *are* notably depicted as different from the Whites who surround them. Ben, Peter, John, and Big Daddy are all self-assured in their identities, and while they seek survival among others, theirs is not necessarily a message of integration but of co-existence—a subtle, but important difference. Their difference becomes clearer when, as Dyer insists, the characters' Blackness is understood in contrast to Whiteness. Through such an examination, it is obvious that the heroism of these four characters comes, in part, because they cast themselves as outside of the racial hierarchies and other dominant norms. It is through their rejection of these constraints and resistance to domination that it is "possible to see that Whites [or at least those invested in Whiteness] are the living dead."[49]

Conclusion

The decades of the 1950s and 1960s brought new meaning to the old saying "one step forward, two steps back." Hollywood was not ready to give up on a vapid formula of locating evil in Black places or among Black people. Recall, it is the Black maid Eulabelle in *The Horror of Beach Party* who randomly pronounces that a toxic waste monster must be the work of (Black) Voodoo. As such, in keeping with the impulse to understand evil and the monstrous as Black-inspired, Hollywood went back to Africa, avoiding Civil Rights-era Black America, for its horror. Africa, specifically tribal Africa, was an easy film target because it seemingly looked different from the US due to its lack of a dominant, identifiably Christian tradition or dominant capitalist practices.[50]

When seen—and it is important to note that Blacks were rarely seen during these decades—the representations of Blacks and Blackness did not press boundaries as Black servants carried the representational weight. Rare, inspired performances came from Joel Fluellen as the intelligent and resourceful Arobi in *Monster from Green Hell* (1957), Estelle Hemsley (old Malla) and Kim Hamilton (young Malla) as the commanding and clever Malla in *The Leech Woman* (1960), and Duane Jones as the authoritative and driven Ben in *Night of the Living Dead* (1968). These performances evidenced what could be done with Black American talent in horror films.

Nevertheless, the horror genre itself was making progress. Horror's recuperation included attending to the stories and issues that were already entering into Americans' homes by way of television news broadcasts. Narratives that queried capitalist, patriarchal rule, militarization, and social inequities and fears found their way, in a rather sophisticated manner, into theaters. The sort of sociopolitical metamorphosis that the horror genre was undertaking would make depictions of racial diversity virtually compulsory.

Night of the Living Dead was, by any measure, the breakthrough, mainstream "Blacks in horror" film that was all about a critique of the status quo and about upheaval. Certainly, there had been Black stars (importantly, men and women alike) in horror films in earlier decades thanks to the contributions of Spencer Williams, Oscar Micheaux, and the like. However, the presentation of Ben was ground-breaking, different and important, if for no other reason than that his encounter with and treatment of Whites was novel. There was no lusting after White women or bowing and shuffling. Nevertheless, *Night* was an unrelentingly pessimistic film on all levels. *Night* became a fictive reminder of Norman Mailer's 1957 assertion in his essay "White Negro" that "any Negro who wishes to live must live with danger from his first day, and no experience can ever be casual to him, no Negro can saunter down a street with any real certainty that violence will not visit him on his walk ... In such a pass where paranoia is as vital to survival as blood ... Knowing in the cells of his existence that life was war, nothing but war."[51]

It mattered little if the makers of *Night* were purposefully inscribing or encoding a racial message; the take-aways are what is central. Indeed, in *Night*, the allusion to lynching through the murder of the assumed monstrous Ben is quite stark. The film audiences who witnessed Ben's demise were reminded that Blacks' social, political, and economic disenfranchisement and violent victimization were a dreadful history from which it was difficult to escape. Together, Emmett Till's and Dr. King's deaths "exposed the limits of [America's] ideology of domestic order,"[52] and the fictional hero Ben was added to that reminder. The second key take-away here is that there was a real revolution going on in America with the Civil Rights movement and the subsequent Black Nationalism movement, but for nearly a decade and a half a genre built on violence and atrocity turned a blind eye to these exact things happening on American soil. It was only in the latter part of the 1960s that there was finally a revolution, with tensions around difference being overtly addressed in films such as *Night*.

In the coming decade of the 1970s, the real-world revolution and the theater revolution would align explicitly with horror centering itself on themes of Black empowerment. However, most notable was the reality that the genre took up a radically different tack than what *Night* offered. While *Night* revealed the difficulties in us "all just getting along," the 1970s focused on Black Power, nationalism, and self-reliance rather than the difficulties of cross-racial integration and cooperation. This would be a decade of "Black horror" rather than "Blacks in horror." The 1970s would even produce a few critically acclaimed "fubu" or "for us, by us" stories, such as the Black-written and directed horror film *Ganja & Hess*.

Heffernan makes a strong claim for the "incalculable" influence of *Night* on the coming 1970s horror films, noting that the film's artistic elements anticipated the trends which would become staples for Blaxploitation horror of the 1970s. More, according to Heffernan, *Night* revitalized the "inner-city nabe box office," importantly providing a home for Black horror films such as *Blacula* and *Abby* until such theaters were finally forced to close their doors for good in the mid- to late 1970s.[53]

As the 1970s took shape, some White horror films would continue with the nuclear threat theme (e.g. *The Hills Have Eyes* [1977]) and critiques on the (bourgeois) family unit (e.g. *The Last House on the Left* [1972]; *The Texas Chainsaw Massacre* [1974]) to the continued exclusion of Blacks. However, Blacks would indeed return, both with a vengeance and for revenge in Blaxploitation-era horror, which indicted "Whitey" for past discriminatory ills and for the continued exploitation of Black communities.

5

SCREAM, WHITEY, SCREAM—RETRIBUTION, ENDURING WOMEN, AND CARNALITY

1970s

> Entirely too many "black" films have been black in name only.... Half the time, the material not only isn't black, it isn't even original, as white material ready for the bone yard is given a hasty blackwash and sent on one last creaking go-round.... Are these films black? I don't know the answer, but I think it's time somebody asked the question.
>
> —Holly (127)[1]

In the 1970s, filmmakers took full advantage of the doors George Romero's brand of horror opened, as well as the disappearance of the Hays Code and the seemingly ever-in-flux, watered-down Motion Picture Association of America (MPAA) ratings system.[2] In just a few short years, gory, R-rated fright-fests such as *The Exorcist* (1973), *The Texas Chainsaw Massacre* (1974), and *Halloween* (1978) took hold of the genre, rendering the likes of *Dracula* (1931), *King of the Zombies* (1941), and *Creature from the Black Lagoon* (1954) bloodlessly attenuated. Though the genre saw rapid and dramatic changes in style and form, this is not to say that the classic horror films such as 1931's *Dracula* and *Frankenstein* did not continue to profoundly influence the genre. The old classics were updated with contemporary themes (and a good bit of carnage). This sort of refreshing, particularly on the heels of Romero's successful film *Night of the Living Dead*, starring a Black actor, opened up narrative space for many more Black characters. Reinventing the genre from the vantage point of Blackness often meant reimagining the classics. For example, *Dracula* became *Blacula* (1972), featuring the first Black vampire in American film. *Frankenstein* became *Blackenstein* (1973),[3] with the monster being a wounded Black Vietnam War veteran put back together by a White doctor. *Dr. Jekyll and Mr. Hyde* became *Dr. Black, Mr. Hyde* (1976), with the monster taking the form of a murderous white creature, laying waste the efforts of his Black better half. A lawsuit filed by Warner Bros. film studio charged that *The Exorcist* (1973), a story about a demon from Africa possessing a White girl, was stolen by the makers of the film *Abby* (1974). *Abby* told the story of a Black woman who becomes possessed by a Yoruba sex demon. Indeed, this was a "revisionist decade"[4] for the film industry in which, for the first time, "the studios produced Black-oriented film pitched directly at pleasing Blacks."[5] Indeed, over the decade, "Black horror" would thrive, with Blacks arriving in the genre as villainous monsters, anti-heroes, and monster slayers. Black women figured prominently as strong, resilient protagonists. Whites were represented as well, but in this decade they would be victims, paying dearly for trying to victimize Blacks.

To be sure, "Black horror" films were not the first to present well-trodden movie themes. Early silent (horror) film scavenged to the point of plagiarism "preexisting formats for lucrative plots and styles of presentation that could be feasibly adopted for the moving camera" while often only minimally altering the pilfered stories with new details.[6] While Black horror filmmakers did some poaching, the genre should be credited not only with dramatically reshaping the narratives, in some cases, but also with reappropriating "generic forms for more overtly political goals [such as] to critique the white power structure."[7]

The films were emboldened by Black Power ideologies—a range of belief systems espousing an awakening of Black pride, self-sufficiency, and empowerment which were prominent during the decade. The imagistic result was "screen images of black life reflect[ing] the new confidence of black people"[8] and a "veritable avalanche" of Black super-heroes and anti-heroes found their way to the big screen.[9] However, the influx was followed by a fresh assortment of problems, as Gary Null, in *Black Hollywood*, explains:

> What emerges, in fact is an altogether new set of black stereotypes. Perhaps derived from the movement toward black power, the cool, efficient black hero seems to have more in common with James Bond than with the political ideals of any black movement. Some of these movies pay lip service to black separatism, Afro-American culture, and local control.[10]

The Horrors of Blaxploitation

Lamenting the representations in and quality of 1970s film featuring Blacks, Ellen Holly of the *New York Times* wrote in 1974, "one of the penalties of being black and having limited money is that we seldom control our own image. We seldom appear in media as *who we* say we are, but rather, as *who whites* say we are."[11] The economic conditions under which Black films were made gave rise to the moniker "Blaxploitation"—a portmanteau uniting the concepts of "Black" and "exploitation"[12]—to define the decade's Black films, horror and non-horror alike. Blaxploitation describes an era of Black film offerings which often drew their inspiration from Black Power ideologies while presenting themes of empowerment, self-sufficiency (though not always through legal means), and consciousness-raising. In "Black horror" specifically, mainstream or White monsters, such as Dracula or Frankenstein's the Monster, were purposefully transformed into "agents" of Black Power.[13] Blaxploitation films also often had an anti-establishment message, challenging "the Man's" or "Whitey's" exploitation of Black communities (e.g. importing drugs, running prostitution rings, rogue cops), though the critique rarely rose beyond indicting a few wicked individuals.

Blaxploitation's attempt at political engagement was not without its critics. Rhines explains:

> these films were released during the height of the Civil Rights/Black liberation movement, yet their subject matter of sex, violence, and "super cool" individualism was the antithesis of what contemporaneous Black political organizations like SNCC, the NAACP, or SCLC supported for Black people.[14]

The films were "condemned by Black opinion leaders across the political spectrum for [their] criminal stereotypes and rightly identified as mainly the product of white studios, writers, and directors," even as the movies proved to be popular, particularly among Blacks who enjoyed seeing Black characters and communities on the big screen.[15] Moreover, the films were notoriously exploitative of women, as a hallmark of Blaxploitation films was the subjection of their female characters to misogynistic treatment, abuse, and rape. Blaxploitation later came to be thought of as a film genre in and of itself boasting drama/action classics such as *Sweet Sweetback's Baadasssss Song* (1971), *Shaft* (1971), *Super Fly* (1972), *Coffy* (1973), *Foxy Brown* (1974), *The Mack* (1973), and *Dolemite* (1975), as well as "Black horror" films such as *Blacula* (1972).

Nineteen seventy-two's *Blacula* was the decade's gold standard for recreating a (White) horror classic in the image of Blackness, while also tackling issues of Black pride and empowerment. Directed by the Black filmmaker William Crain and starring William Marshall, this "Black horror" film presents a compelling take on the vampire story while exploring the effects of racism alongside the loss of Black history and identity.

Blacula begins its story in the year 1780 with Mamuwalde (William Marshall), an African prince, traveling with his wife, Luva (Vonetta McGee), to Transylvania for a dinner meeting with Count Dracula (Charles Macaulay). In the meeting, Mamuwalde presses Dracula to renounce the slave trade, from which the enormously wealthy Dracula, seemingly, has been profiting greatly. Dracula is not only a vampire, but it turns out he is a virulent racist ("It is you who comes from the jungle") as well. *Blacula* rather self-consciously included hateful rhetoric to expose its diminishing effects and to actively rebuke such offenses. In this film, and in a great many Black horror films of this decade, "lingering racist tropes … were now readily identified and exposed."[16]

Dracula bites Mamuwalde, thereby infecting the prince with vampirism. Mamuwalde is renamed "Blacula"—a variation of his White vampire "master's" name, which marks him as an Other, even among vampires. Given a slave name, he is robbed of his (African) identity. Dracula then entombs Mamuwalde, leaving him to suffer forever, as the undead, from blood thirst. Luva is not tainted with vampirism, though she presumably dies almost immediately.[17]

Mamuwalde-turned-Blacula remains entombed for nearly two centuries, until 1972 when Dracula's abandoned Transylvanian castle has its property put up for public sale.[18] Still in his coffin, Mamuwalde makes a much belated trip through the Middle Passage. Thus, Mamuwalde finally makes his appearance in the new world—enslaved by vampirism and auctioned off.

Two Los Angeles collectors, one Black, the other White, both gay men, buy some of the castle's contents, which include, unbeknownst to them, Blacula. The men, who are in a loving relationship, are depicted as stereotypically sissified, and effete in manner and dress. When Mamuwalde emerges from his coffin, ravenous for blood, he transforms from a stately man to a hairy man-monster and quickly feeds on the two men, permitting glimpses of sensuality through implications of an interracial/homosexual encounter. When Mamuwalde feeds on Billy (Rick Metzler), the White collector, he feeds on Billy's cut arm while pushing Billy's face (neck and lips) far from him. When Mamuwalde feeds on Bobby (Ted Harris), the Black collector, he first chokes him into unconsciousness and then violently bites, feeding on the lifeless body in anger. Mamuwalde's taking of the men, then, allows only a glimpse of homoeroticism before quickly shifting to a homophobic, heterosexist stance signaled by rage and violence.

Mamuwalde is initially satiated, and, remarkably, does not turn his attention to avenging his own "death" or that of his beloved Luva at the hands of Whites. Instead, in spite of its politically inspired narrative beginnings, *Blacula* becomes a horror love story in which Mamuwalde begins an unrelenting pursuit of a woman, Tina (also played by McGee), who reminds him of Luva. Mamuwalde's actions, then, align with that which has "always [been] explicit in Dracula's reign of terror in England … the search for romantic love and the desired recuperation of normality."[19]

Romantic love in *Blacula* is narrowly defined as heterosexual. In the film, the brave, savvy Dr. Gordon Thomas (Thalmus Rasulala), with the help of his medical assistant/girlfriend Michelle (Denise Nicholas), uncovers Mamuwalde's secret. Together they are a good team, and also in a loving relationship. Yet, Bobby and Billy, who are similarly doting on one another, and even equal partners in a thriving business, are reduced to "two faggot interior decorators" in the movie. Later, when Bobby's body disappears from a funeral home because he has turned into a vampire, police raise the question, "Who the hell would want

FIGURE 5.1 Blacula in full rage in *Blacula*
         AIP/Photofest

a dead faggot." And, in yet another scene, a racist stereotype, "they all look alike," is shifted to gay men, furthering the film's dismissive, heteronormative rhetorical violence.

Sharrett describes such *Dracula* films as a parody of Freud's *Totem and Taboo* (1913), a collection of essays attending to themes such as the importance of the father-figure, obsessions with the magical realm, and illicit carnality.[20] Sharrett writes, "Dracula [is] the tyrannical father incidentally violating all sexual taboos, including those against homosexuality."[21] Though 1970s Black films (both horror and non-horror) presented characters (such as Bobby and Billy) outside the boundaries of heteronormative sexuality, their depiction was rarely with positive, innovative effect. Gays, lesbians, bisexuals, the transgendered, and others who violated "traditional" gender roles reminded audiences that sexual identities are not always stable. However, such "instability" was often severely punished. For example, a gay man is sodomized with a hot curling iron in the non-horror Blaxploitation film *Black Shampoo* (1976). Wlodarz, in "Beyond the Black Macho: Queer Blaxploitation," finds that heterosexuality anchors representations of "authentic" blackness (and heroism), while queerness gains a certain threatening representational power." This means diverse sexualities are not absent from Black film. Quite the contrary, there are a great number of, at least, queer characters. However, "the films themselves admittedly remain anxious and often phobic in their handling of these characters."[22]

Presenting an "authentic" Black, masculine ideal, Mamuwalde's amorous feelings for Tina, which she quickly reciprocates, can be viewed as motivating Afrocentric nostalgia for a complete and full Blackness. "Tina's willingness to be his partner, to become a vampire," argues Gateward in "Daywalkin' Night Stalkin' Bloodsuckas: Black Vampires in Contemporary Film," is her attempt to recuperate the nobility of African culture, during a period in American culture when the idea of Africa as a mythic homeland was prevalent in both the political and expressive cultures of Black Americans and the Diaspora as a whole."[23] Likewise, Mamuwalde's name and nobility "link him to the Afrocentric cultural politics adopted by some branches of the Black power movement."[24] Tina is persuaded to believe, by Mamuwalde, that she is the key to recuperation through a play on Africa-as-motherland rhetoric: "We are of the Abani tribe, you and I. Northeast of the Niger Delta. Our people are renowned as hunters.... You are my Luva recreated." Even when Mamuwalde must say goodbye to Tina, he does so in Kiswahili.

However, in the film the connection between noble Africans and African Americans is (perhaps unintentionally) illusory. Mamuwalde lands in a predominately Black section of L.A. But it is clear that these are not his people. Mamuwalde is of a different time and caste. It is as if, as James Baldwin so eloquently wrote in *Notes of a Native Son* of African/American relationships, "they face each other, the Negro and the African, over a gulf of three hundred years—an alienation too vast to be conquered in an evening's goodwill."[25] Certainly it does not help that Mamuwalde preys upon the Black Americans he encounters, making him little different from anyone, or thing, that had been known to victimize Blacks and their communities.

These slippages aside, *Blacula* has been credited with being revolutionary. Elizabeth Young, in *Black Frankenstein: The Making of an American Metaphor*, credits the film for capitalizing on the "freedom for political fantasy that horror films could afford."[26] Leerom Medovoi, in his article "Theorizing Historicity, or the Many Meanings of *Blacula*," observes, "the figure of Mamuwalde recalls, for instance, the eulogizing of Malcolm X throughout the late 1960s as the 'shining black prince' of African-America."[27] While Harry Benshoff, in his article "Blaxploitation Horror Films: Generic Reappropriation or Reinscription?," draws upon *Blacula* to argue that films of this period critically comment upon White racism (both institutionalized and personal) and are "steeped in African American culture of the early 1970s; references to the Black Panthers, Afrocentric style, [and] soul food."[28]

American International Pictures

Blacula met with enough box office success—grossing over $1 million by the end of its theatrical run[29]—that its production company, American International Pictures (AIP, 1954 to present), sought to continue to court the Black horror film. AIP had been known for their low-budget, exploitation fare targeting the youth audience, be they monster movies or "beach" films such as *Beach Party* (1963) and *Beach Blanket Bingo* (1965). AIP could not be credited with being a film trailblazer. Rather, they cautiously watched from the sidelines per their policy to "observe trends in emerging tastes."[30] Only then did they jump on bandwagons; they "always waited for someone else to test the water first."[31] In the case of Black films, one litmus test was *Sweet Sweetback's Baadasssss Song* (1971) offered through the production company Cinemation, which earned impressive box office returns grossing over $11 million.[32] The other was the film *Shaft* (1971, MGM), with its $17 million domestic gross.[33] Together, the success and acclaim of these films moved AIP in 1972 to release *Blacula* as well as the non-horror 1973 gangster film *Black Caesar*.[34] Theirs was an effective business strategy:

> Initially, it may seem hard to imagine two groups of films more disparate in tone, style, content and audience than AIP's beach films and blaxploitation movies; yet the studio's prioritization of the urban black audience from 1972 to 1975 serves as a compelling lesson on how the same formula employed in its exploitation of the beach a decade earlier could be updated and relocated to a new racial geography so as to produce similar results with a sharply different demographic. In its spate of films aimed at Black audiences, AIP [realized] the studio's greatest box-office returns.[35]

AIP continued to follow through with its decision to advance such niche products with horror offerings starring Black actors, such as *The Thing with Two Heads* (1972), *Scream, Blacula, Scream* (1973), *(The Zombies of) Sugar Hill* (1974), *Abby* (1974), and *J.D.'s Revenge* (1976). All were fairly low budget as it was also AIP's policy to "produce with prudence, avoiding expense for what won't show on-screen."[36] Following AIP's lead, Exclusive International released *Blackenstein*, and Dimension films offered *Dr. Black, Mr. Hyde*.

Fight the Power

Hoping to capitalize on the success of *Blacula*, Exclusive International's *Blackenstein* (1973) was "a product of White Hollywood, made by a White director, William Levey, and a White writer, Frank Saletri[; the film was] crude and sloppy, a failure even by low-budget standards.[37] *Blackenstein* evidenced a coalescence of sociopolitical concerns as it adopted an anti-(Vietnam) war stance, questioned the contribution of Blacks to what may be perceived as a colonialist war effort, and explored the continuing tensions around Black/White race relations. The film focuses on Eddie Turner (Joe De Sue), a Black man, whose body is severely damaged by a land mine during the Vietnam War.

Limbless, Eddie is essentially a head without a body. Upon being shipped back to the US, Eddie is sent to a Veterans Administration (VA) Hospital. While there, the helpless Eddie is bullied by a White orderly in an exchange which works to highlight struggles around bigotry and White supremacy. First, the orderly (Bob Brophy) taunts the armless man: "Why don't you reach over there and have a nice, cool drink of water." The scene dramatizes a racial hierarchy that is "inseparable from the setting of a VA hospital during the Vietnam War—Black Power and other activists frequently criticized the Vietnam War as a conflict run by white men but disproportionately fought by black men."[38] Next, the orderly reveals that he tried to enlist but, to his great embarrassment, was deemed unfit for service. The orderly then transfers his lack onto Eddie: "Big deal you laying there, you know it's my taxes, my friends' taxes that's gonna keep you there. We gotta take care of you." Eddie is summarily dismissed as being a fool for falling for the "scam" of patriotism, while also reduced to a welfare case—Whites must "take care" of him.

Eddie's fiancée, Dr. Winifred Walker (Ivory Stone), gets Eddie transferred out of the hospital and into the care of the kindly, White Dr. Stein (John Hart). Dr. Stein, as in the classic *Frankenstein* (1931), works out of his castle-like home, which is complete with a basement laboratory. However, Eddie is not turned monstrous by Dr. Stein; rather, his fate is sealed by Malcomb (Roosevelt Jackson), a jealous Black assistant to Dr. Stein, who wants to sabotage Eddie and Winifred's relationship. Malcomb tampers with Eddie's drugs, turning Eddie into a fully restored and mobile, but psychopathic hulking monster. Here, much like *Blacula*'s failure to directly engage White oppressions, a White country which first forced him to fight, *Blackenstein* "vitiates one of the main political contributions of the Frankenstein story: its focus on the origins of violence [thereby diffusing] the targets of its monster's anger."[39] The White orderly meets his expected gruesome demise. However, just like Mamuwalde, Eddie is also happy to kill off innocent, unsuspecting Black people. When Eddie opts to disembowel a Black woman, he does so only after the audience is provided with a lengthy "money-shot" of her jiggling, exposed breasts.

The scenes of slaughter are tempered, however, by the film's low budget. Eddie's murderous rampage is shot in poor lighting, and acted out amid shadowy darkness. As a result, the film takes on an unanticipated atmospheric, moody hue and tone. The effect is a unique one as the on-screen violence that is the hallmark of horror films takes a back seat to that which can be heard—the anguished moans of a monster moved to kill when he does not really want to, perhaps just as he (as a man) did during the war. Eddie's fate is not at all dissimilar to one narrative of disabled American war veterans. He returns to his country unaccepted and unable to fit in; impaired by (prescription) drugs, he turns to a life of crime, and is killed by law enforcement (police dogs maul Eddie to death). Though he is able to survive war in a foreign land, it is his return home that finally defeats him.

The Thing with Two Heads (1972) and *Dr. Black and Mr. Hyde* (1976) drilled down more explicitly on the themes of race relations and medical experimentation. *Heads*, named one of the 50 worst movies ever made, is a story of Black comeuppance in the face of White bigotry.[40] The film, more farcical than horror, tells the story of Dr. Maxwell Kirshner (Ray Milland), a famed surgeon and racist, who is dying and wants to live on by transplanting his head onto a healthy (White) body. The NFL football player Rosey Grier portrays "Big Jack" Moss, a Black death row inmate, who though innocent of his crimes, offers to donate his body to science rather than die in an electric chair. Unbeknownst to an unconscious Kirshner, his surgical team transplants Kirshner's head onto Jack's body. Both awaken surprised to see their heads on Jack's body—hence, the thing with two heads. The movie's premise had (ridiculous) comic consequences. "They transplanted a White Bigot's Head onto a Soul Brother's Body!" screamed the movie's ads and poster art, which perhaps served as a not so subtle metaphor for the treatment of Blackness by White image-makers.[41]

Dr. Black and Mr. Hyde, with Black director William Crain again at the image-making helm, took race and medical experimentation far more seriously, with Dr. Pryde (played by former NFL player Bernie Casey) as a caring

FIGURE 5.2 *The Thing with Two Heads*
American International/Photofest

Black doctor treating the Black poor of Watts. Dr. Pryde's name is an obvious double-entendre about Black pride (he is never called Dr. Black). In the film, Dr. Pryde is experimenting with a cure for hepatitis and cirrhosis.

Dr. Pryde develops what he believes is a promising treatment for the deadly diseases that are afflicting members of the Watts community, particularly its female prostitutes. The women are presented in gratuitous scenes of exploitation. They are frequently topless and occasionally nude. The film later reveals that the impetus for Dr. Pryde's search for a cure is that his own mother (though not a prostitute) died from liver damage. Indeed, this storyline is an interesting tale of achievement and commitment. Dr. Pryde has reached the heights of education and, importantly, returned "home" to do good work, despite his troubled upbringing. In fact, the film presents two "homes" for Dr. Pryde. The first is where he works, his hometown of Watts. However, he does not live in Watts. Rather, he lives in an upscale, suburban community in a sprawling mansion home. It is revealed that Dr. Pryde's boyhood home was a brothel for "ladies of the evening," in a (presumably) predominately White community.[42] There, his mother was a live-in maid in the home, where it was her responsibility to "clean up the filth." The job took its physical and emotional toll, moving Dr. Pryde's mother to drink and ultimately develop "this liver condition," which proved deadly. Hence, his residing outside of Watts is not about escape, but is a symbolic act of reclamation.

Eventually, Dr. Pryde tests his drug on himself, with the expected disastrous results. The drug turns Dr. Pryde into a "White dude"—a white, ashen-faced, blue-eyed killer monster (presumably Mr. Hyde, though he is never called this in the movie). Dr. Pryde makes his way (in his Rolls Royce) to the inner-city, making Watts his killing ground, where he unleashes his repressed hatred of prostitutes and pimps.

On the doppelgänger's hit list is Linda (Marie O'Henry), a prostitute that Dr. Pryde has fallen for. As law enforcement hunts for the killer, Linda is initially mistrustful of the police and is openly conflicted about leading them to Dr. Pryde. Here, the film is exposing a well-known tenuous relationship between law enforcement and Black communities; the film overtly addresses the issue of Blacks steering clear of police: "In the Black community, nobody knows nothing, nobody sees nothing, and nobody hears nothing." The film also speaks to the real-life quandaries Black women face when imperiled by a violent relationship—involving the police is not always an easy choice. The National Association of Black Social Workers summarizes the fears:

> Women of African ancestry often do not call the police for fear of police brutality against their mates or against themselves.... Women of African ancestry often do not report domestic violence for fear that such reporting would be a betrayal of the race or would contribute to negative stereotypes.[43]

Eventually, Linda comes face to face with her tormentor. He attacks her in his monstrous state, but does not kill her, eventually releasing her (perhaps there is some of Dr. Pryde left in him). The police arrive and, as in *Blackenstein*, release police dogs on him, harking back to 1960s television images of police dogs attacking Civil Rights movement activists. Fleeing, the monster climbs to the top of the Watts Tower, with helicopters circling overhead, recalling the climactic scene of *King Kong*. Police shoot the Dr. Pryde monster—in a hail of bullets he plunges to his death. The allusion to Blacks and apes in the film's ending is a curious one, as it does not appear in the original 1886 novella *Strange Case of Dr. Jekyll and Mr. Hyde* by Robert Louis Stevenson, or in the subsequent approximately half-dozen mainstream film adaptations since the novella. However, the Black monster-ape emerges more explicitly in the 2006 film *The Strange Case of Dr. Jekyll and Mr. Hyde,* starring Black actor Tony Todd of *Candyman* (1992) fame. In the film, Dr. Jekyll first morphs into the evil Eddie Hyde. As Hyde becomes more crazed and lethal, he (oddly) transforms into a primate, attempts a rooftop escape, and is shot down like Kong, plunging to his death.

The film *Fight for Your Life* (1977) presented the "worst" of both Black and exploitation film worlds. A low-budget rip-off of *The Last House on the Left*, the film follows three sadistic escaped male convicts: an Asian, a Mexican, and a White self-appointed "boss" of the trio. Hiding from police, the men take refuge in a predominately White, small town. The home they choose to hide out in belongs to a Dr. Martin Luther King, Jr.-like Black minister, Ted Turner (Robert Judd), who preaches on themes of Black passivism, peace, patience, and the meek inheriting the Earth.

The Turners are the embodiment of an integrationist family. In addition to living in a largely White community, their recently deceased son (as a result of an earlier car accident) had a White fiancée, Karen (Bonnie Martin), who still visits the family. Karen is a friend to the family's young adult daughter Corrie (Yvonne Ross). The youngest son in the family, a pre-teen named Floyd (Reggie Rock Bythewood), has a White best friend, Joey (David Dewlow), the son of a local police officer. A central plot line in the film is whether peace or (armed) resistance is more tenable in the face of cruel racism. Ted's ideology is embraced by his wife, Louise (Catherine Peppers), but rejected by "Granny" (LeLa Small), a feisty, wheelchair bound woman who spouts Black nationalist rhetoric: "Black power is where it's at!" In the film, Jesse (William Sanderson), the White convict who refers to his partners in crime as "chink" and "spic," terrorizes the Turner family. He forces them to engage in acts of degradation—"Say, 'All us Black ass coons is hungry'"—and showers them with racial epithets. Eventually, the horrors increase as Karen and Joey are killed. Ted is beaten into unconsciousness with his own bible. Corrie is gang-raped. Finally, the family rises up by arming themselves, and killing their tormentors. However, it is Ted who is at the center of the climactic finale, in which he is not only in a showdown with Jesse, but dramatically renounces his ideology of peace and meekness for Blacks through an act of vengeance. Ted cruelly taunts Jesse, calling him a "faggot" and asserting that he is less than a real man for giving in to homosexual rape in jail. He then blows away Jesse, the last of the convicts, with a gun. *Fight for Your Life* was high on a principal message—ideologies of turn-the-other-cheek integration were no longer sustainable. However, it was also a lowly exploitation movie in which such ideologies, as well as racism, sexism, and even recidivism were cheapened, reduced to a moment in a family's life which is resolved through vigilantism.

The problem with this decade of industry exploitation of the Black film market was that occasionally a low-budget, but compelling horror film would be offered, but was unable to stand apart from the lowest dross. *Soul Vengeance* (a.k.a., *Welcome Home Brother Charles*) (1975)—directed by Black director Jamaa Fanaka—presented one of the more shocking storylines seen in horror: a Black man wills his penis to grow to abnormal lengths and to gather impossible strength so that he can use it as a weapon to kill White bigots. While *Soul Vengeance*'s horror twist may provoke incredulity, the film is possibly the most provoking response to: (1) the fear of the Black male phallus; (2) the performance of masculine gender roles; and (3) police brutality.

Soul Vengeance begins by focusing the audience on a lasting, divisive issue in race relations—White police brutality upon Black bodies. Charles Murray (Marlo Monte), a drug dealer, is picked up by "the Man"—two White Los Angeles Police Department (LAPD) officers. The officers drive Charles to an alley to beat him. One of the officers, Jim (Stan Kamber), attempts to stop his partner Harry "Free" Freeman (Ben Bigelow) from inflicting more abuse on the handcuffed Charles, but his efforts fail. Though terrorized and beaten by Harry, Charles is unbowed during the encounter and his defiance is severely punished—Harry castrates Charles with a straight razor. However, this particular punishment is motivated by something unknown to Charles: Harry's wife is having an affair with a Black man because Harry is "not enough of a man" with his "shriveled up thing." The castration, then, is a complex narrative around bigotry, penis envy, and the protection of White womanhood.

Charles is then incarcerated, with little reference made to the damage that has been done to his body. While in prison, Charles is consumed by thoughts of revenge that are played out in dreams and other visions. The depiction of Charles' mental state echoes the (in)famous writings of Black nationalist Eldridge Cleaver in *Soul on Ice*. Cleaver describes his state of mind while in jail: "I, the Black Eunuch, divested of my Balls, walked the earth with my mind locked in Cold Storage."[44] After three years in prison, Charles is released and returns to his Watts home only to discover that much of his life is unrecoverable. He is faced with the fact that recidivism looms large given his dramatic reduction in social status as an ex-con. Legitimate employers want nothing to do with him—"I can't even wash a car."

Here, the film sets aside its horror leanings to embark on an extended, dramatic exploration of the bleak life of 1970s Watts for men like Charles.

Charles struggles to maintain a masculine gender performance. He enters into a loving relationship with a woman, Carmen (Reatha Grey), but theirs is a rocky union largely because Charles laments his inability to financially support her.

Charles catches a television news report about Harry being recognized for his highly effective police work. Charles' anger over the denial of his performance of masculinity on social and economic fronts, as well as over the celebration of a rogue cop, is manifested in the film's return to horror tropes and through a focus on Charles' mutilated penis. His penis, it turns out, was not completely dismembered by Harry. Rather, it healed with aberrant musculature.

Charles talks his way into the home of the police officer who brutalized him, as well as that of the lawyer who prosecuted him. Once in their homes, Charles drops his pants, quite literally mesmerizing each man's White wife with his bewitching penis. Again, the film's narrative aligns with some of the controversial political discourse of the time:

> Many Whites flatter themselves with the idea that the Negro male's lust and desire for the White dream girl is purely an aesthetic attraction, but nothing could be farther from the truth. His motivation is often of such a bloody, hateful, bitter, and malignant nature that Whites would be hard pressed to find it flattering.[45]

In the first act of Charles' revenge, he has sex with the women while they are entranced. While they are under Charles' spell, he implants a demand into their psyche: they must open the doors to their homes for him later in the evening, when their husbands return home from work. The women do as ordered, and Charles catches the men off guard, killing them.

However, the viewer is not initially sure how the murders have been carried out, as "what lurks outside the frame or unclearly within it, generates uncertainty about what one is seeing."[46] Finally, in the murder of the lawyer, Charles' power is fully revealed. Charles is able to will his penis to grow to lengths of several feet, which he then loops around the neck of the other character, strangling him. This scene is a fascinating one as Charles' desire to have the White men choke on "it" cannot be fully realized in the literal sense, as that would require a far more homoerotic encounter than is already presented. Still, in wrapping a Black penis around White men's throats, a highly erotic, but clear visual reference to lynching is established. As such, while the White male is rendered impotent—by a cheating wife or by having to pay for sex—the Black man becomes a "super stud"[47] and the White man "a victim of his own Frankenstein monster."[48]

Charles' murderous deeds are finally uncovered, he is pursued by police and, like so many Black monsters discussed earlier, he is cornered on a rooftop. The police bring Carmen to the site, asking her to talk him down. In the film's final, dramatic scene, Carmen defiantly yells to Charles, "JUMP!" The film ends abruptly. Now that Charles has molested, murdered, and has been outed as possessing an unusual physical attribute, it is expected that his life is on a very short clock. During this era, "no one wanted to see a black hero defeated";[49] hence a death in which a Black man has control of his destiny is better than handing himself—his life—over to Whites. The audience is left to assume Charles has indeed jumped.[50]

Enduring Women

Over the decades, women's roles have become increasingly central and innovative in horror. In non-Black horror films, women have triumphantly battled against monsters (e.g. Laurie Strode in *Halloween* [1978]) and have been frighteningly evil (e.g. Pamela Voorhees in *Friday the 13th* [1980]). While audiences had seen wicked women before in the form of the vamp, temptress, succubus, and Voodoo queen, the *heroic* female in horror was just beginning to make revolutionary inroads during the 1970s.

Carol Clover, in *Men, Women and Chain Saws: Gender in the Modern Horror Film*, theorizes on the form and function of the female heroine in horror, describing her as the "Final Girl." The moniker captures the meaning—she is the one who, in the end, does not die. Indeed, the Final Girl is *the* survivor—surviving the monster's attack and often the only one to do so (e.g. Ripley in *Alien* [1979]). As Clover explains, "she alone looks death in the face, [and] she alone also finds the strength either to stay the killer long enough to be rescued (ending A) or to kill him herself (ending B)."[51] The Final Girl is also *a* survivor—smart, resourceful, and a fighter in the face of evil. Again, as Clover elaborates, the films of the 1970s began to present "Final Girls who not only fight back but do so with ferocity and even kill the killer on their own, without help from outside."[52]

What is important here, in part, is the absence of a male savior. In the absence of a male savior, it is the female who gets to take on and bring down the monster. As Clover asserts, what is key is the qualities of the Final Girl, "the quality of the fight and qualities that enable her to survive."[53] For example, in *Halloween*, when Laurie Strode (Jamie Lee Curtis) in penned down in a closet by the deadly Michael, she does not whimper and collapse, awaiting death. Instead, she moves into fight mode, even quickly fashioning a weapon out of a clothes hanger (the only thing on hand) to take on the evil. Likewise, (Ellen) Ripley (Sigourney Weaver) in *Alien* displays her tough leadership qualities when the crew is faced with the unstoppable alien monster. While a Black male, Parker (Yaphet Kotto), wants to attack headlong—"You're gonna let me kill it, right?"—it is Ripley who understands such an approach is unworkable, and takes control by screaming: "Shut up and let me think!" Final Girls tend to be White. When their fight with the monster is over, their lives return to stasis. Ripley sleeps peacefully after she ejects the alien. Laurie Stode's quiet, suburban life can return to normal.[54]

However, 1970s horror films featuring Black women handled the Final Girl with noteworthy variation. White Final Girls were generally unavailable sexually and were masculinized through their names (e.g. Ripley) and through the use of (phallic) weaponry (e.g. butcher knives or chainsaws). By contrast, Black women were often highly sexualized, with seduction serving as a principal part of their cache of armaments. Much like the White Final Girl, Black women stare down death. However, these Black women are not going up against some boogeyman; rather, often their battle is with racism and corruption. In this regard, there is no going to sleep once the "monster" is defeated, as the monster is often amorphously coded as "Whitey," and Whitey's oppressions are here to stay.

With no real way to defeat the evil (systems of inequality) that surrounds them, Black women in horror films could be described as resilient "Enduring Women." They are soldiers in ongoing battles of discrimination, in which a total victory is elusive. The Black woman's triumphant walk into the sunset promises to take her, not toward a life of peace, but back into the midst of rogue police, sexist men, and "the Man" who is exploiting her Black community.

The Enduring Woman, unlike the (asexual) Final Girl, often fights not only for her own life, but also on behalf of men. For example, in the non-horror Blaxploitation film *Foxy Brown* (1974) the character Foxy (Pam Grier) takes on "the Man," seducing her foes before killing them, while also exposing herself to beatings and rape, all because she wants to avenge her boyfriend's murder. The 1974 "Black horror" zombie film *Sugar Hill* presents a similar motivation for its Enduring Woman. The provocatively named "Sugar" (Marki Bey) wants to avenge the death of her boyfriend Langston at the hands of a "Whitey" crime boss. Sugar uses her good looks and sensuality to get close to her foes; hence she is denied the opportunity to enter into battle like other Final Girls. She does not set aside her sexuality, or have a "masculine" name or posess her own "masculine" weaponry, rather she has lips and hips, but no chainsaw. Likewise, *Scream, Blacula, Scream*'s (1973) Enduring Woman, Lisa (Pam Grier), is called into battle to save not one, but two men—one from the vampirism that is coursing through his veins, the other, a former love, from an attacking vampire.

The acclaimed art-house movie *Ganja & Hess* (1973) (winner of the Critics' Choice prize at the Cannes Festival),[55] directed by Black director Bill Gunn, presents the story of a tormented man and a wicked Enduring Woman. The "Black horror" film centers on Dr. Hess Green (Duane Jones of *Night of the Living Dead* fame), an attractive, highly successful archeologist. The monied Hess is "an elegant and sophisticated man by his clothes, Rolls Royce, and magnificent mansion, where a servant meets his every need."[56] Hess' socioeconomic status is purposeful, as the director's strategy was "anti-stereotype" filmmaking, thereby reflecting an "earnest desire to transcend debilitating blaxploitation clichés."[57] Hence, Hess was offered as the antithesis of depictions of the urban underclass or of those securing illicit profits through underground economies as seen in a host of Blaxploitation films.

In the film, Hess is employed by the Institute of Archeology and is provided with an assistant, an older Black man, George Meda (Gunn). In a moment of privacy, while Meda is in a reception area waiting to introduce himself to Hess, he passes the time by pointing a small pistol at his reflection in a wall mirror. This is the audience's first glimpse at Meda's insanity.

Hess invites Meda back to his estate, and while there Meda reveals a crude side, offending the prim and proper Hess with vulgar jokes. Meda then sneaks away from Hess, fashions a noose, and climbs a tree on Hess' property, threatening to hang himself. Hess comes to understand that Meda is drunk and "neurotic," a volatile combination of instability. Hess asks Meda not to kill himself on his property because, as Hess reasons, "that will give the authorities the right to invade my privacy with all sorts of embarrassing questions.... I am the only colored on the block ... and you can believe the authorities will drag me out for questioning."

Meda then attacks Hess, viciously knifing him "for the father, son, and Holy Ghost." The weapon Meda happens to use is a dagger of the Myrthia people, an ancient blood-drinking caste of Nigeria, which is part of Hess' extensive private collection of prized artifacts. Having "killed" Hess, Meda commits suicide. However, the infection from the blade means that Hess awakens undead and bloodthirsty. Hess stores Meda's body in a cellar freezer rather than call the police, thereby evidencing that even the Black elite, not just prostitutes such as *Dr. Black, Mr. Hyde*'s Linda, continue to fear (White) police.

Hess then goes blood hunting, traveling far from his sprawling estate to a ghetto to prey upon the poor. The wealthy Hess takes blood from a clinic's blood bank. He kills a prostitute and her pimp for their blood. Another prostitute, who is caring for her newborn, meets a similar fate, though he leaves her baby untouched and abandoned, crying near its mother's body. In this regard, *Ganja & Hess* became emblematic of films of the 1970s that were "constantly challenging the legitimacy of capitalist, patriarchal rule ... , the monster became an emblem of the upheaval in bourgeois civilization."[58]

Soon Meda's wife, Ganja (Marlene Clark), arrives in search of her husband, who has "disappeared before" during bouts of psychosis. Just as Ganja's name promises (the psychosomatic drug cannabis), Hess becomes completely addicted to the beautiful, but uncouth woman. Ganja eventually discovers her husband's body and soon after she marries Hess. Her rationale is simple: She would rather be married to an extremely wealthy crazed man than be the widow of a poor one.

Eventually Hess reveals his secret to Ganja, transforming her by stabbing her with the knife so that they may live together "forever." Together, they represent addictive personalities—both to blood lust and to their own carnal indulgences. They work to satiate their insatiable lusts frequently—killing and having sex, sometimes simultaneously—until Hess concludes that such an existence is untenable.

FIGURE 5.3 Hess and Ganja in *Ganja & Hess*
Kelly/Jordan Ent./Photofest

Hess searches for, and discovers, a cure. He must accept Jesus as his personal savior, and then stand before a cross with the cross' shadow over his heart. Only then can Hess die, and perhaps even go to Heaven. The film concludes with Hess going to a church to cure himself. He then returns home to Ganja to die, begging her to join him in a peaceful death. However, Hess goes to his death alone.

Ganja opts to endure as infected, and as a sexy succubus, continuing on alone masquerading as high class and cultured. She stays at Hess' estate, among his wealth, while having her share of male lovers and victims. Ganja not only survives her encounter with the monster, but happily chooses to become one. Ganja is also an Enduring Woman in that she is sexy and sexual, she finds her victory in the death of her two husbands, and, now fully independent (free of husbands and flush with money), she indulges her every whim. She is no longer bound or terrorized; rather, she happily terrorizes (men) herself. She does not expect a knight in shining armor to come to her rescue; as such, she has developed ways to ensure her own survival, and even to thrive.

Ganja & Hess was initially "suppressed" by its producers because it was far from the typical Blaxploitation fare that had become so familiar during this decade. "The producers," write Diawara and Klotman, "wanted a film that would exploit black audiences—a black version of white vampire films. However, the producers withdrew the film when Gunn went beyond the vampire genre to create an original product."[59]

Pam Grier: Exploiting the Enduring Woman

Pam Grier became a Blaxploitation-era icon, starring in seven films for AIP alone.[60] She became, as Dunn describes in *"Bad Bitches" and Sassy Supermamas*, an AIP and Black cinema muse, "helping to establish Grier's sex goddess screen imagery."[61] However, Grier was not offered up by AIP as a sex goddess in the tradition of White actresses Ava Gardner, Elizabeth Taylor, Hedy Lamarr, or Lauren Bacall. Rather, she was confined to the role of a hot mamma—a "controlling image," as Hill Collins describes it, of Black female sexuality in which Black women become a symbol of deviant female sexuality, while White female heterosexuality becomes the "cult of true" womanhood.[62] Such imagery relegated Black women to the "category of sexually aggressive women," thereby providing justification and yawning narrative space for sexual abuses.[63] For example, in *Foxy Brown* (1974) Grier's character Foxy is drugged and gang-raped (by White racists). The horrific encounter is presented as a necessary hurdle as it allows Foxy to exact revenge upon those who wronged her boyfriend. In *Coffy* (1973) Grier as Coffy offers herself as an undercover prostitute—which requires her pimp to "test her out."

The hallmark of a Grier film was her partial nudity. The film camera lingered on her exposed, buxom bosom and long legs while she endured all manner of sexual exploitation. Writes Dunn:

> The exhibition of women's sexual bodies [was] enabled by the general relaxation of traditional Hollywood restrictions regarding violence, sexual content, and profane language. However, in the case of Grier, this exhibition is deeply tied to … AIP's insistence on depicting Black female resistance and empowerment primarily through the pornographic treatment of their star.[64]

Though sexual readiness does not immediately exclude a "feminist edge," the treatment of Grier and other Blaxploitation starlets was distinctly hypersexual ever available for sex, no matter how horrifically violent.[65]

Notably, Grier is removed from these misogynistic images in the "Black horror" film *Scream, Blacula, Scream* (1973). *Scream* is the sequel to *Blacula*, which was directed by Black director William Crain and starred the acclaimed (Broadway) theater stage and screen actor, director, and jazz and opera singer William Marshall. Perhaps Grier's far-from-pornographic treatment could be attributed to Marshall's influence and earlier insistence that *Blacula* avoid stereotype. Novotny Lawrence, in *Fear of a Blaxploitation Monster: Blacks as Generic Revision in AIP's Blacula*, details Marshall's influence:

> While *Blacula* was in development, William Marshall collaborated with the producers to ensure that the image of the first black horror monster

contained a level of dignity. In the original script Blacula's straight name was Andrew Brown, which is the same as Andy's in the blackface white comedy team of Amos and Andy. Marshall criticized the name commenting: "I wanted the picture to have a new framing story. A frame that would remove it completely from the stereotype of ignorant, conniving stupidity that evolved in the United States to justify slavery" ... Marshall eventually persuaded the producers to incorporate his suggestions, and the first black vampire emerged as a regal character.[66]

Marshall's demeanor, stature, and oeuvre tended to present Blacks outside of exploitative tropes (e.g. on stage he portrayed Othello, Paul Robeson, Frederick Douglass, an opera singer, and a doctor). It would seem that he would not participate in a role where he would play an (sexual) abuser. Hence, given her treatment in other films, it is perhaps worth noting that Grier's *Scream* character Lisa remains clothed, conservatively dressed even. Largely absent is the heavy makeup, revealing clothing, and large, silky wigs that were Grier's typical costume. Rather, her natural hair—a short afro—was on display in *Scream*. And, she is often seen in pantsuits with high collared tops, thereby denying the viewer the objectifying look at her cleavage and legs. Lisa strikes a serious, even professional pose in the film, bringing a rare air of dignity to the often maligned Voodoo religion. Confronted by naysayers, Lisa and others define Voodoo as an "exceedingly complex science" and as a "religion based on faith." In one scene, Lisa goes to a funeral home to pray over a deceased friend. She lights candles, assembles a small altar, and settles in to pray quietly—there is no stereotypical, frenzied dancing, drumming, or chanting. Her prayers are more akin to thoughtful meditation.

Where *Scream, Blacula, Scream* is particularly innovative is its inclusion of Lisa as a smart, heroic, Enduring Woman. In the film, the vampire Blacula is resurrected through a Voodoo ritual. Blacula is resurrected by Willis (Richard Lawson), the selfish, angry brother of Lisa, his adopted sister. Willis wants to use Blacula to exact revenge on Lisa, whom he refers to as a "jive ass bitch," and other members of their Voodoo cult for failing to elect him their leader or "Papa Loa." However, Blacula is unhappy about his forced return. When he is called by his real, princely name "Mamuwalde," the anguished vampire screams, "The name is Blacula!" Tormented by his fate, Blacula asks Lisa to use her Voodoo skills to rid him of the vampire curse and send him to his death where he can rest in peace. Here, Lisa is cast as hero and savior. However, there is a key limitation to such a representation, as Clover explains: "On the face of it, the occult film is the most 'female' of horror genres, telling as it regularly does tales of women or girls in the grip of the supernatural. But behind the female 'cover' is always the story of a man in crisis."[67]

Indeed, the pressure on Lisa to heal Blacula is heightened when he threatens to kill Lisa's ex-boyfriend Justin (Don Mitchell), with whom she is still friendly.

Lisa now must save both men. Unlike her male hero counterparts who "get the girl," Lisa does not get either man even as she bravely saves them both. "If anything," writes Bogle, "these action heroines pointed up the sad state of affairs for Black women in the movies. Very few films attempted to explore a Black woman's tensions or aspirations or to examine the dynamics of sexual politics within the Black community."[68] In surviving her encounter with a vampire, when others have not, protecting her ex from death, and in saving Mamuwalde's soul, Lisa possesses the foremost traits of the Final Girl: "she is the one who encounters the mutilated bodies of her friends and perceives the full extent of the preceding horror[; she will show] more courage and levelheadedness than [her] cringing male counterparts."[69] Lisa's triumph is not simply about succeeding without the intervention of a/her man. Rather, she also presents an Enduring Woman figure. Her battle is not over. For example, her struggles against sexist men and against stereotypes (Voodoo as a cult) will continue. The Enduring Woman knows that significant challenges remain for her, and for her community.

Abby (1974), too, was one of the more intriguing (copyright infringement suit with makers of *The Exorcist* notwithstanding) of the "Black horror" films due to its unique focus on sexual diversity.[70] It begins with archeology professor and theologian Garnet Williams (William Marshall) accidentally releasing an evil spirit during an archeological dig in Nigeria. The sex demon makes its way to the US and into the staunchly Christian home of Garnet's daughter-in-law, Abby Williams (Carol Speed). Abby is married to Rev. Emmett Williams (Terry Carter), and is employed at her husband's church as a marriage counselor. Where *Abby* takes a bit of a novel turn is that possessing Abby is the *male* demon Eshu (voiced by Bob Holt), a Yoruba god "steeped in a Western, sex-negative Christian ideology."[71] With the theater poster art boasting, "Abby doesn't need a man anymore," the film presents a compelling multi-sexuality narrative: a male spirit seeks sexual conquests while in a female's body. For example, through Abby the male demon asks a man, "You wanna fuck Abby, don't you?" The demon has sex with his (male) victims, and at the height of the act, he kills. The film lays bare and complicates heteronormativity as men are attracted to the outward appearance of the female Abby, who oozes sexuality and has little problem seducing her prey.

Along the way, the film capitalizes on the characterization of Garnet as a professor/theologian/minister (and the authoritative demeanor William Marshall brings to his roles) by inserting educational commentary on Eshu: (1) he claims credit for natural disasters; (2) he is one of the most powerful of all earthly deities, more than the powerful Orisha gods; and (3) Eshu is a god of sexuality, a trickster, creator of whirlwinds and chaos. Finally, through a Yoruba-informed exorcism Abby is freed of her possession. The effect is presenting a Black religion in a markedly different manner than, say, many Voodoo-themed horror films which cast the religion as singularly odd, ahistorical, and evil.

Apart from these intriguing plot points, *Abby* was rather standard low-budget horror fare, with the *New York Times* calling it "silly."[72] Abby is no Final Girl or

FIGURE 5.4 The monster Abby in *Abby*
American International Pictures/Photofest

Enduring Woman as she is saved from a fanciful life of sex and partying (and killing) by her father-in-law, husband, and police officer brother while being restored to favor with her male (Western) God.

As boundary pressing as (Black) horror films are, they have not been as innovative in disrupting traditional narratives about sex and sexualities. For example, with few exceptions, films focusing on monster-apes or vampires have as their backdrop heteronormative love stories. It is not surprising, then, that Abby-as-sexual-predator must be defeated, not just because of her possession and because she kills her prey, but because "transgressive sexuality is defined as monstrous."[73] Still, Abby's performance is (perhaps unintentionally) independent, sexually liberated, and confident. While possessed, Abby is gregarious and strong in personality as well as physical strength. Were she not a killer, she could be interesting fodder for readings of a person free of gender and sex role encumbrances.

Sexpot Sistas: Same as It Ever Was

Voodoo has become so expected in horror films that one periodical reported disappointment when this facet of Black culture was not presented in horror movies. The Black culture magazine *Jet* questioned why Black horror films should

FIGURE 5.5 Sugar's cleavage invites more stares than her zombies in *Sugar Hill*
American International Pictures / Photofest

be based on the Christian Dracula legend "when there was Voodoo in the Black experience."[74] The "Black horror" film *Sugar Hill* (1974) attempted some reclamation of the Voodoo. If most Blaxploitation celebrated a "'bad Nigger' who challenges the oppressive White system and wins,"[75] then *Sugar Hill* celebrated the "Baad Bitch"[76] who did the same, albeit through Voodoo. In *Sugar Hill*, Blacks—specifically shackled slaves from Guinea who end up in New Orleans—are the zombie undead. The zombies are summoned by Mama Maltresse, a Voodoo queen (Zara Cully), on behalf of Sugar (Marki Bey), to exact bloody revenge on a "Whitey" crime boss, Morgan (Robert Quarry), and his thugs who have killed Sugar's boyfriend.

The silent, but lethal army of zombies has among its members a loquacious, discerning, thinking leader—Baron Semedi (Don Pedro Colley).[77] Semedi acts much like a union leader, negotiating the terms under which he and his zombie peers will work. Semedi quickly spies that his targets are irredeemably evil—killers, racists, and shake-down artists. As a result he and his horde happily kill Morgan and his crew. The zombies are heroes. Identifying with the monsters in *Sugar Hill* makes for "a pleasurable and a potentially empowering act"[78] as the zombies come to represent a pro-Black cadre of Black men doing away with "Whitey"—indeed, "Black heroes were winning and community identification was intense."[79] The zombies enact a particularly gruesome killing of a "sell-out"

Black man, Fabulous (Charles Robinson), who permits Morgan to call him nigger and who shines Morgan's shoes.

Sugar is there nearly every step of the way as her zombie army takes on her enemies: "Hey Whitey, you and your punk friends killed my man ... I'm not accusing you, honk, I'm passing sentence and the sentence is death." However, hers is far from an image of a focused, competent leader. Sugar is still very much presented as the "Voodoo sexpot"[80] who tempts and teases her prey while clad in form-fitting, revealing outfits. Sugar's depiction presents the film's adherence to traditional gender roles. Right after her boyfriend dies, Sugar flirts with her ex-boyfriend, a policeman named Valentine (Richard Lawson). The message looms—Sugar cannot be without a man. Sugar suggests sexual availability to friend and foe alike. She even engages in the requisite sexy catfight with another (White) sexpot, Morgan's girlfriend Celeste (Betty Ann Rees). Sugar's portrayal "equivocates any change in the narrative representation of the Black woman"; she has not really usurped power from men.[81] This equivocation is best revealed when Sugar offers her soul to Semedi in return for his services, which he rejects, lustfully proclaiming, "It ain't souls I'm interested in." It is understood that she is to join his harem of "wives."

In *Sugar Hill*, the zombies fulfill their contract, and when it's time for Sugar to pay up with her own body she offers a trade. Semedi, who has been described as sexually ravenous, is offered Celeste. The acceptance of the White woman by Semedi—though he "prefers" Sugar, but Celeste "will have to do"—is likely to be read as political, the apropos punishment for a "protected" White woman. On the other hand, the trading in women is obviously sexist and objectifying; though Celeste's "White slavery" is a play on an important taboo.

Though Enduring Women were becoming scarce in this film cycle, Black women continued to figure prominently in films such as 1974's *Vampira* [a.k.a. Old Vampire] and *The Beast Must Die. Vampira* is a "Blacks in horror" comedy-horror film that presents the story of an "Old Dracula" (David Niven) who, too elderly to hunt for his young victims, gets them by luring them to his castle, which he has opened up to tourists. Dracula's wife, Vampira, is also out of commission, so he transfuses her with the blood of one of his victims to revitalize her. That blood happens to be from a Black woman, which, in Vampira, turns her young and Black—justifying (and exceeding) the mythical "one-drop rule." Vampira (Teresa Graves) is now regarded as sexy, giving unique credence to the mantra "Black is beautiful." As Null observed at the time, "if Black movies have hardly begun to elevate women to real character roles, at least the white-dominated ideas of beauty are gone.[82] Unable to "cure" his wife, whose skin color moves her to speak jive talk, Dracula unhappily joins her with Niven appearing in the film's final frames in blackface.

In the film *The Beast Must Die*, also a "Blacks in horror" film, Marlene Clark plays Caroline, the gorgeous wife of Tom (Calvin Lockhart), a wealthy big game hunter.[83] This elite Black couple, Tom and Caroline, along with their

White assistant Pavel (Anton Diffring), host five White guests at an island estate in the hope of uncovering which among them is a werewolf. Tom is devastated when his beloved Caroline is accidentally infected by one of the guests, who is the real monster. In a heart-wrenching scene, he must kill his wife with a silver bullet so that she does not begin her own murderous werewolf rampage. Though very different films, *Vampira* and *Beast* share common themes of Black women as desirable and worthy, but also stricken with a taint that threatens their men.

J.D.'s Revenge (1976) echoes *Sugar Hill* in that it is similarly about possession and love denied. However, *Revenge* is also an extraordinarily sexist film, raising the ante far and above *Sugar Hill* with a startling, misogynist, anti-feminist subtext that linked the independence and sexual revolution of women with being "uppity."

J.D.'s Revenge tells the story of New Orleans resident Isaac, or "Ike" (Glynn Turman), a young, strait-laced, law school graduate studying for the bar exam. His girlfriend, Christella or "Chris" (Joan Pringle), convinces Ike to take a break from his studies for a double-date night on the town with friends. The group visits a nightclub where a hypnotist is performing. Ike is among several who volunteer to be hypnotized. Something goes wrong while he's "under," and Ike becomes possessed by the angry spirit of a 1940s' gangster J.D. Walker. Walker wants revenge for himself and for his sister Betty Jo (Alice Jubert), for their murder more than three decades earlier back in 1942.

J.D. possesses Ike's body in an attempt to reveal the true circumstances around the murders. As the violent hustler J.D. becomes more dominant in Ike's body, Chris falls victim. Chris is depicted as Isaac's complete equal. She capably quizzes Ike on legal concepts and helps him with his exam prep. She is outspoken, has a network of friends, and it is implied that she has her own money. In one scene, in a gender role reversal, Chris initiates sex while Ike opts out with "Not tonight, I got a lot on my mind tonight." The audience learns that the kindly Ike is viewed as less of a man by his friend Tony (Carl Crudup) because he is so respectful of his girlfriend. When, Ike (possessed by J.D.) slaps Chris around, Ike's buddy Tony praises him for finally being a man:

> I think it's a good thing to go upside a woman's head when she starts handing you lip. I mean, believe it or not, they like that. Eh man, honest to God, you've got to go into your nigger act every once in a while. They gonna push you till you do. They want you to show 'em where the lines are. You know something, man? It's pretty encouraging that you did what you did. As long as I've know you, you always seem to be, you've been sort of repressed … That's fantastic man.

Putting Chris in her place through a beating is particularly important because, the audience comes to learn, she likes and understands football, does not permit Ike to store his smelly sneakers in their apartment, and she is a divorcee who left her husband.

An intriguing plot point is that except for a change in style—wearing a fedora, "conking" his hair, donning a 1940s-style suit—Ike's new brutal masculine performances do not seem out of place in the 1970s (the context for the second wave of the Feminist Movement); rather, they are rewarded. As J.D., Ike is rough and dangerous—traits (certain) women find alluring. Ike picks up an attractive woman in a bar and returns to her place, providing her with "the best fuckin' I've ever had." When the woman's "old man" catches them, J.D. delights in slashing the woman's partner with a straight razor, his hyper-masculine bravado fully on display.

When Chris sees Ike come home drunk, she is angry. J.D./Ike reveals what is wrong with her kind of women (unlike those he is currently finding in bars) by calling her a "bitch" and a "bitch ho" while screaming, "How dare you talk to me like I'm some kind of common sissified nigger wimp." Eventually, Chris is completely silenced when J.D. badly beats and sexually assaults her, thereby putting an end to her uppity-ness. The film, Benshoff observes,

> suggests a man caught between two different constructions of African American maleness when Ike … treats his girlfriend as a pimp might treat his whore. The film points out that J.D.'s style and masculine brutality are still a lingering problem in 1970s Black macho culture.[84]

Moreover, the film communicates through J.D./Ike that Chris' performance of female independence should be rejected. Chris is neither a Final Girl nor an Enduring Woman; her ex-husband comes to her aid and in the end she happily returns to Ike.

It Has Come to This

> I walked through the graveyard like a bolt of thunder.
> Made the tombstones jump and put the dead on the wonder.
> —Rudy Ray Moore[85]

The demise of 1970s "Black horror" was symbolized by a horror-comedy that left some entertained, but many more scratching their heads while speculating whether the inevitable decline of the Blaxploitation genre was coming none to soon. The epitome of the Blaxploitation era, stand-up comedian Rudy Ray Moore, offered the film *Petey Wheatstraw: The Devil's Son-in-Law* (1977). The jaw-dropping film opens with a pregnant Mother Wheatstraw (Rose Williams) laying in a bed inside a shack, in labor, surrounded by midwives dressed as mammies. She is experiencing a difficult labor, and a White male doctor is summoned to assist with the birth. The doctor first delivers a large watermelon and finally (as afterbirth) a fully formed, fighting and profanity-spewing boy about seven years of age. The boy, Petey Wheatstraw (Clifford Roquemore II), arrives to the beating of drums as well as to screams by the doctor of "It's alive! It's alive!," a line borrowed from *Frankenstein*.

The plot of this lowest of low-budget films is fairly indecipherable (a "pimp cane" figures prominently); however, the main narrative thrust is that the adult Petey Wheatstraw (Rudy Ray Moore), a comedian, is killed by rivals. Petey will be given a new lease on life by the Devil, provided that Petey marries the ugliest woman on Earth—the Devil's daughter. Along the way, Moore performs his trademark rhyming and signifying comedy raps.

Petey Wheatstraw was a reflexive look at 1970s films, as Moore appropriated and spoofed their most clichéd aspects of martial arts, exploitation, B movies and dumped them into his films. For example, as a boy, Petey is trained like Caine in the *Kung Fu*[86] television series by a mysterious, elderly martial arts Master. Later, as an adult, Petey would (badly) karate chop his assailants, including "demons" dressed in purple leotards and capes with red horns affixed to their heads. In between fights and other escapades, portly Wheatstraw is also presented as a sex symbol, an insatiable lover with a trove of women. Moore, in keeping with the Blaxploitation themes he perfected in his earlier films (e.g. *Dolemite* [1975]), even dropped in a revenge-against-Whitey storyline as well. For Moore, his film contributions were far from exploitative: "When we wasn't getting kicked in the ass and beat upside the head, then they termed it as 'blaxploitation,' and I think it was extremely crude to us as a people."[87] Thomas Cripps summarized Blaxploitation's end, implicating Moore's film: "Predictably, such 'blaxploitation' movies soon fell from favor and were rivaled by Oriental martial arts movies, a new generation of science fiction monsters, and other arcana."[88] Not surprisingly, the genre could not sustain itself, as the exploitative nature of the films—content, investment, quality—fell from favor. In 1977, the same year *Petey Wheatstraw* was released a historically Black university "opened its spring term film series, not with one of the ephemeral Black heroes like Shaft, but with *The Texas Chainsaw Massacre*."[89]

Conclusion

Though many 1970s horror films were exploitative in so many ways—in budget, in quality, in the treatment of women's bodies, and in the presentation of the underclass—they should not be readily dismissed as lacking relevant discourse. The decades' "Black horror" films and "Blacks in horror" films left audiences with a clear indication of the role and function of race, gender, sexuality, culture, and class in popular culture, as well as how these identity positions may, rightly or wrongly, be reflected upon in the social world. In the films, struggles against those oppressions, and themes of (intra)racial uplift in the face of those oppressions, were in conversation with the rhetoric of non-violence and integration, as well as armed resistance and Black self-reliance, if not supremacy. The films also worked hard to reveal to audiences that for Blacks, the horror (or the monster) was located within Whiteness—Whitey, the system, the Man. Unlike mainstream horror films in which (Final Girl) heroes took on an individual evil (such as an alien with acid for blood) and fought to bring about its demise, Black horror films revealed that the evil enveloping Blackness was enduring.

While "the Black audience had always been a substantial part of the horror crowd," these 1970s films, which specifically hailed Black audiences, encouraged them to look beyond the monsters to identify with messages of Black equality through metaphorical unity (zombie armies) or through the metaphorical bullet (Voodoo potions or the penis).[90] With Black stars in these roles, even if at times exploitative, their presence and performance exploded past horror film treatments of Blacks as spooked, bug-eyed, and shuffling. Blacks of this decade were unbowed.

This period was not always purely reactionary to the kinds of racism and classism Blacks had to endure at the time. *Ganja & Hess*, by way of example, largely excluded Whiteness in an attempt to privilege stories coming out of Blackness. Here, there were no "cardboard" and "oversimplified" characters who make their reputations "by kicking white villains all over the screen."[91] Black horror films which worked to break free of such traditional Blaxploitation tropes found a tepid response among some movie-goers, as film producer Rob Cohen explained: "They want a shark marauding off the coast of a vacation spot or 'the Sting.' If there's one thing an audience doesn't want, it's a message. If there's one thing beyond that, it's a Black message."[92] In short, Blaxploitation-era films were facing a multifaceted quandary of being too culturally and politically Black, not Black enough, or not purely entertaining enough.

Blaxploitation horror films showed fairly homogeneous and confined characters—in class, gender roles, politics, and interactions with Whites. The *Washington Post* predicted the filmic trend would turn to "blacks interacting among themselves, or with whites."[93] Moreover, the newspaper expressed an optimism around the representational treatment of Blacks in which they are "portrayed as complete human beings—good and evil, rich and poor, smart and dumb."[94] Any predictions of more substantive interaction for the coming decade did not pan out. In the 1980s, Blacks become associated with dreadful urban spaces, prompting White flight to the suburbs. Blacks and their horror films were left in the cold as the genre shifted attention more exclusively to White, middle-class fears.

6

WE ALWAYS DIE FIRST— INVISIBILITY, RACIAL RED-LINING, AND SELF-SACRIFICE

1980s

And every night, say a prayer to the patron saint of Black death, Scatman Crothers, who took an axe for that crazy-ass White boy in *The Shining* so that others might follow in his footsteps.

—Harris[1]

During the 1980s the urban world (also termed the inner-city, the 'hood, or the ghetto in pop culture) was depicted in film as being largely inhabited by Blacks and non-White Others, and home to uniquely "Other" problems. The urban setting, writes Nama in *Black Space*, "became political shorthand for discussing a myriad of social ills that disproportionately affected Blacks—such as poverty, crime, drug abuse, high unemployment, and welfare abuse—without focusing on race as the specific source of the problem. Instead, geography or spatial location defined the scope of the problem."[2] Urban spaces were portrayed as places where the schools were poorly equipped (*Lean on Me* [1989]) and where school children behaved with insolence (*Stand and Deliver* [1988]). Urban neighborhoods housed gangs (*Colors* [1988]). These were places where murder and drug distribution ran rampant and unchecked (*Scarface* [1983]), and where criminals ruled over law enforcement (*Robocop* [1987]). They were also presented as places of brutal violence, rife with sexual assaults and slaughter (*Death Wish II* [1982]).

One dominant message coming out of 1980s films was that cities were savage, lawless terrains to which the most irredeemable in our society—the underclass and people of color, two groups often understood to be one and the same— should be consigned. In all, these were images of decaying or "dead" cities,[3] reflecting a post-White flight America, in which Whites "turned their backs upon the old downtown areas and retreated to the suburbs."[4] White flight represented a new variation on racial and economic segregation (e.g. Jim Crow, racial red-lining). Avila explains this process in his essay "Dark City: White Flight and the Urban Science Fiction Film in Postwar America":

> as racialized minorities concentrated in American inner cities during the late 1940s and throughout the 1950s, millions of 'white' Americans took to new suburban communities to preserve their whiteness [with the] collusion of federal policy, local land development strategies, and the popular desire to live in racially exclusive and homogenous neighborhoods.[5]

For many Whites, urban communities were blighted slums breeding a "culture of poverty," while the suburbs held out the promise of a "culture of progress."[6]

While Blacks played a central imagistic role in inciting racial, spatial, and underclass fears, in 1980s horror films the actual participation of Blacks was fairly fleeting or nonexistent. That is, the fear of the Black urban world relied on myth; Blackness became a sort of ghost story symbol or invisible boogeyman. Most notably, Blacks were nowhere to be found in popular horror films set outside of the urban, such as the following:

- *Amityville Horror* (1979), set in a small Suffolk county (NY) village;
- *Friday the 13th* (1980), set in a camp called Crystal Lake;
- *The Evil Dead* (1983), set in rural woods;
- *Halloween* II (1981), set in an Illinois suburb in Haddonfield;
- *Poltergeist* (1982), set in suburban California;
- *Critters* (1986), set in rural Kansas.

This is not to say that Blacks were entirely absent from the big screen. Rather, Blacks played an integral role in what became known as the "buddy" subgenre—a cycle of comedy/drama films that problematically paired Black and White actors in adventure. These films included: *Stir Crazy* (1980), with Richard Pryor and Gene Wilder (who appears briefly in blackface); *48 Hours* (1982), with Eddie Murphy and Nick Nolte; *Beverly Hills Cop I and II* (1984 and 1987), with Eddie Murphy, John Ashton, and Judge Reinhold; *Running Scared* (1986), with Gregory Hines and Billy Crystal; and *Lethal Weapon I and II* (1987 and 1989), with Danny Glover and Mel Gibson.[7] The effect of such couplings was not exactly the racial harmony the films promised; rather, as Guerrero explains, Blacks were "completely isolated from other Blacks or any referent to the Black world. In this situation, what there is of Black culture is embodied in an individual Black star surrounded and appropriated by a White context and narrative for the pleasure of a dominant consumer audience."[8]

These Black–White assemblages aside, a significant number of top films in the 1980s, many with settings outside of the urban, rendered Blacks and Black

culture largely out of sight, as these 20 popular non-horror films illustrate: *E.T.
The Extra-Terrestrial* (1982), *Batman* (1989), *Raiders of the Lost Ark* (1981), *Indiana
Jones and the Temple of Doom* (1984), *Indiana Jones and the Last Crusade* (1989), *Back
to the Future* (1985), *Tootsie* (1982), *Rain Man* (1988), *The Terminator* (1984), *Who
Framed Roger Rabbit?* (1988), *Gremlins* (1984), *Top Gun* (1986), *Amadeus* (1984),
The Breakfast Club (1985), *The Big Chill* (1983), *Ferris Bueller's Day Off* (1986),
Fatal Attraction (1987), *Working Girl* (1988), *On Golden Pond* (1981), and *Nine to
Five* (1980). The result was an affirmative construction of Whiteness through
racial segregation or exclusion. Such omissions were most assuredly a "form of
stereotyping, one that reinforces the idea that Blacks and other non-white groups
are obscure, marginal, and dependent."[9]

Isolation and invisibility were but two of many representational attacks Black
culture endured. The infamous Willie Horton political ad campaign, produced
by Republican candidate George H.W. Bush's camp during the heated 1988
Presidential race against Democratic candidate Michael Dukakis, also served as a
defining backdrop to popular constructions of what happens when Blacks enter
White spaces. The ad's message, as offered by the National Security Political
Action Committee, was not at all dissimilar to the 1980s *Death Wish* films—
without the proper (White) authority figures in power, Black men would come
to rape and murder America's White women. The ad shows two photos—one of
Willie Horton, a Black male, the other of Gov. Dukakis. A voice-over proclaims,
"Bush supports the death penalty for first-degree murders. Dukakis not only
opposes the death penalty, he allowed first-degree murderers to have weekend
passes from prison." This narrative is accompanied by the words "kidnapping,"
"stabbing," and "raping" flashing across the screen. Likewise, the Maryland
Republican Party distributed a letter that read "Dukakis/Willie Horton Team"
and "You, your spouse, your children and your friends can have a visit from
someone like Willie Horton if Mike Dukakis becomes president."[10]

Chocolate Cities and Vanilla Suburbs

"Main Street and Elm Street U.S.A.," writes Crane, "it is on these avenues,
common to all of the public, where terror implacably strikes. The great man's
laboratory, the gothic castle, the ruined mansion, and the pharaoh's sacred tomb
have been dismissed from the screen."[11] While Main and Elm streets were now
"common," horror said that these streets were not accessible to just any old
member of the public. Implicitly, no Blacks (or any racial minorities for that
matter) were allowed. These "Whitopias," as Rich Benjamin, in *Searching for
Whitopia: An Improbable Journey to the Heart of White America*, dubs them[12], pride
themselves on a seemingly ordinariness, friendliness, orderliness, safety, and
comfort. Traits that on their surface seem race- and class-neutral are critical in
distinguishing White from Black, the middle class from lower class, the suburban
from the urban.

Still, horror needed its monsters, and in this decade they infamously came in the form of a host of supernatural suburban White males as the embodiment of evil, taking up a "masochistic aesthetic" through the use of machetes and power tools.[13] If Whites were to survive their stay in the suburbs, they would have to figure out other ways to discern the good neighbor from the monster, as color-coding did not apply. These White monsters had the particular goal of punishing those closest to them: White, non-urban (e.g. suburban or rural) families. White parents were held in contempt for failing to care for their children, leaving their offspring in the care of babysitters or a TV set. White children, whose parents seemingly failed to instill high moral or religious standards, met a particularly gruesome end for engaging in out-of-wedlock sexual activities or substance abuse. For example, in the horror films *Halloween* (1978) and *Halloween II* (1981) Michael "the Shape" Myers (Nick Castle) slashes his way through the village-town of Haddonville. These movies flipped the script on the place where Whites believed they could find a sense of comfort and security. These films said "gotcha" to those who thought White flight away from the urban Black and poor and into the welcoming arms of White, middle-class suburban communities would bring them peace. The *Halloween* films, specifically, proved duplicitous as they played on ideals of racial and class homogeneity, while destroying that very same sense of community by challenging suburbanites' "ability to recognize strangers and predators."[14] More pointedly, these monsters were not coming from outside the suburbs to wreak havoc on middle-class domesticity; rather, Whites saw that "they are us, and we never know when we will act as monsters."[15] Still, perhaps the most deliberate horror "gotcha" came from the comedy-tinged, non-Black horror film *A Nightmare on Elm Street* (1984). Here, inattentive, alcohol-soaked parents discover that their "McMansions" simply gave a murderous pedophile named Fred Krueger (Robert Englund) more space to practice his sadism. Nevertheless, Krueger is likened to a "moral blemish" in an otherwise comfortable suburban community.[16]

Just as Whites in 1980s films were warned away from urban spaces, Blacks received cautions about foisting themselves into suburbia. In the "Blacks in horror" film *Lady in White* (1988), set in 1962 in the "small town" of Willowpoint Falls, "25 miles south west" of "the city," there resides the rare Black family. The family's patriarch is a drunkard school janitor, Harold Williams (Henry Harris), who is falsely accused of the rape and murder of a White girl. Harold is called a "Black son of a bitch" and described by the town's sheriff as "the perfect scapegoat" because "he's Black." It is eventually revealed in the film that Harold was falsely accused, and that a White member of the community was the culprit. Still, the film brought home another message: White small towns are tough on Blacks. Williams is shot and killed by a vigilante who does not believe that he is innocent.

Still, relative invisibility did not mean racial Others were given a wholesale reprieve from their symbolic annihilation. One possible implication of the representational absence could be that audiences were left to ponder: If all of this horror is going on in the suburbs among those we know and who look like us, what might be happening among those racially and culturally different people in the 'hood?

In a few instances, though "Other" races were not actually depicted on screen, horror films did work to cure viewers' curiosity about what goes on among those absent, different-looking strangers. Native Americans bore quite the brunt of symbolic attacks. They were simultaneously portrayed as being (too) spiritual, (too) volatile, and (too) primitive. This tripartite of virtue equivocation was tied to "a field of romantic nostalgia" around symbols of stoicism in the face of massacres, and in the face of displacement from their ancestral homes and land.[17] Native American culture was so excessive that it could not be adequately contained or completely destroyed, forever rising up to haunt White domains and bodies. White suburbanites were horrified whenever they discovered that their housing developments were built upon, and thereby disrupted, "sacred land" in the form of "ancient Indian burial grounds."

Whites were depicted as unwitting interlopers unable to reason or co-exist with the intemperate otherworldly inhabitants. For example, 1979's *Amityville Horror* places a Long Island haunted house atop a long forgotten Native American cemetery. The disturbed dead are relentless in their terror, first with a set of residents who become susceptible to demon possession and who ultimately become the victims of mass murder in the house, and then with the Lutz family, who are driven from the home just weeks after moving in. The audience is asked to mourn over the Lutzes' failed attempt at securing the suburban American dream (they live in their home only 28 days), and the great financial hardship that the whole sad affair has cost them—rather than mourning for any dead Native Americans.[18]

The Shining's (1980) mountaintop Overlook Hotel, too, was built over the graves of Native Americans. In addition, its ground was blood-soaked over a two-year period between 1907 and 1909 by the bodies of Native Americans seeking to preserve their land, as explained in the movie: "The site is supposed to be located on an Indian burial ground. They actually had to repel a few Indian attacks as they were building it." The result of this incursion was similarly deadly—exposure to evil attacks, possession, and murder. The same inattention to Native American hallowed ground is the terror trigger for the suburban housing development in *Poltergeist* (1982). Here, a real estate developer has built a sprawling housing plan atop a cemetery without first relocating the bodies. Hence, those seeking the American dream sans Black people may still find that there are "skeletons in their closets (not to mention their swimming pool)."[19] Like the Lutzes, the audience is encouraged to feel for one particularly beleaguered family whose "Whitopia" dreams come to an abrupt end when they are forced to surrender their prized home to the spirits, swapping it for a cramped motel room.

In the film *Wolfen* (1981), the story is a gentrification tale with a twist. Shape-shifting Native Americans-cum-wolves live and lurk in the dark shadows of a desolate New York city. A White corporate developer wants to reclaim the space, thereby reversing the White flight trend but with the effect of displacing the sorcerous Native Americans—a slight deviation from the well-known colloquialism of "urban renewal–Negro Removal."[20] In the end, many must die before the project is scrapped, and White developers are convinced to stay away. And somehow the Native Americans are presented as "winning" the battle against gentrification and corporatization by being left alone to happily live in the dead city while Whites, it is assumed, drive back to their thriving "vanilla" suburbs.[21]

But what of Blacks' roles in the horror films of this decade? Horror films failed to build a plausible narrative around their suburban presence as had been done with Native Americans. This prohibition stemmed from the fact that horror films had largely confined Black horror to urban locations (e.g. New Orleans, Chicago, New York, L.A.), or outside of that, Africa or the Caribbean. For example, in the "Blacks in horror" film, *Zombie 4: After Death* (1988), Whites have to travel to meet up with Black horrors. In the film, Blacks are confined to a remote island (far from any suburb) where a Voodoo priest has his revenge on White interlopers by letting his zombies feed on them. In short, it was unlikely that zombies and Voodoo could believably find their home on Main or Elm Street.

Black Saviors and Self-Sacrifice

In striking contrast to the nationalistic, revolutionary themes of the 1970s horror films, in the 1980s, if Blacks were tapped at all to make a contribution to the genre, their participation was largely seen in "Blacks in horror" films and marked by their affirmative support of Whites. What little Blacks did offer to horror was not only disheartening, but could be described as a new form of Black exploitation. Tony Williams, in his essay "Trying to Survive on the Darker Side," describes the overall pessimism around the decade's fare:

> The 1980s decade was extremely disappointing for critics impressed by the horror genre's brief 1970s renaissance. While the 1970s saw the emergence of racial works by directors such as … George Romero, the following decade appeared to feature reductive exploitation films such as the *Friday the 13th*, *Halloween*, and *A Nightmare on Elm Street* series—all highly dependent on spectacular special effects and gory bloodbaths of promiscuous (mostly female) teenagers.[22]

So, while horror focused on the White teen-meets-pickax money-shot, Black characters' value was confined to their ability to affect an assimilable air in cross-racial, interpersonal encounters. In the films of the 1980s, Blacks were pressed to enter into support relationships with Whites, and to display a value system of loyalty and trust that was generally unilateral. That is, there was no expectation that the kinds of displays of faithfulness emanating from Blacks would be reciprocated by Whites. More striking, in this decade's horror films, a Black character's constancy to Whites was frequently evidenced by a willingness not only to pitch in, but often to die a horrific death on Whites' behalf—horror's version of the buddy film.[23]

Stanley Kubrick's film *The Shining* (1980) is especially powerful in its two-prong approach to the symbolic annihilation of Blacks. First, *The Shining* represents *the* defining (re)turn toward the self-sacrificing Black character—a character who dies in the course of saving Whiteness. Second, the film invokes the "magical Negro" stereotype, in which a Black character is imbued with supernatural powers, which are used, notably, not for his or her own personal, familial, or community protection or advancement; rather, the powers are used wholly in service to White people.

In *The Shining*, the White Torrance family—father Jack (Jack Nicholson), mother Wendy (Shelley Duvall), and young son Danny (Danny Lloyd)—temporarily relocate to the Overlook Hotel, an isolated Colorado mountain-top resort, which happens to be built over a Native American cemetery. Jack has taken on the job of caretaker of the hotel while it is closed for the winter, and its staff is on winter break. Before heading out for his winter vacation, the hotel's Black cook, Dick Hallorann (Scatman Crothers), spends the day orienting the family to their responsibilities in maintaining the hotel. Before Dick departs for his vacation, however, he reveals to young Danny that he has secret telepathic powers. Dick calls his mental telepathy "shining." In Dick, shining is endearingly folksy. Specifically, shining is an unproblematic condition he inherited from his grandmother, who long ago explained to him that it is a magical gift. Dick readily shines to Danny—offering him ice cream—because he correctly detects that Danny is also telepathic.

Dick is played by then 69-year-old entertainer (singer, dancer, musician, comedian) and former vaudeville performer Scatman Crothers. With the elderly Crothers in this role, Dick presents an amiable and safe figure. As such, the wooing that Dick displays toward Danny is depicted neither as pedophilia nor as otherwise predatory. To be sure there is no mistake, Black women are objectified. In one scene Dick is in his vacation home in Florida. He has adorned his room with two large prints, one of a busty, naked and another of a semi-nude Black woman.[24] Nevertheless, Crothers, who had played helpful roles such as railroad porters, gardeners, waiters, and shoeshine boys in the past, recalls earlier popular culture Black male adult/White child asexual relationships such as that of Huckleberry Finn (Junior Durkin) and Jim (Clarence Muse) in *Huckleberry Finn* (1931) or Virgie (Shirley Temple) and Uncle Billy (Bill "Bojangles" Robinson) in *The Littlest Rebel* (1935). In each of these cases it goes unquestioned why Black men would find satisfaction in the company of White children.

Though shining is portrayed as natural to and accepted in Black families such as Dick's, to Danny's family it is something aberrant, thereby casting shining in the boy as a harmful trait. Danny's shining is dubbed "Tony, the little boy that lives in my mouth" and is viewed as negative. Jack and Wendy have even sought medical help for Danny's condition. Hence, shining and other supernatural events in a Black body and among Black families are not completely unexpected or condemned, but in a (young) White body and among White families, such things are marked as disturbingly out of place.

Central to the film's plot is the reality that Danny's powers are growing stronger and more dangerous the longer he spends in what is revealed to be a haunted hotel. By contrast, Dick is unaffected by the hotel, even as he knows that the hotel is a discontented space due to a bloody ax murder on its premises committed by the previous caretaker. Nevertheless, Dick is not troubled enough by these conspiring presences or "muted echoes"[25] to feel overly endangered: "I ain't scared of nothing here."

In *The Shining*, Danny eventually faces mortal danger while trapped in the blizzard-bound hotel as his evil-possessed, ax-wielding father tries to kill him and his mother Wendy. Danny telepathically calls out to the vacationing Dick for help, and Dick promptly and without hesitation responds by dropping everything to return to Colorado to save the boy. With tremendous, tireless effort, Dick purchases a last minute plane ticket, rents a car, borrows a SnowCat, and drives through a blizzard, in an attempt to get up to the remote hotel. No expense seems to be too great. Undaunted by being alone, by life-threatening temperatures, or by impassable highways, the elderly Dick presses on to make the final push up the mountain to the hotel.

Dick's efforts to come to Danny's aid prove threatening to the hotel, which expresses its great displeasure over Dick's interference through the ghost of the Overlook's former murderous caretaker, Grady (Philip Stone). While Dick has been called the "head cook" by the hotel's manager, Grady diminishes Dick by warning Jack that "the nigger cook" is coming.

Notably and oddly, Dick's entire harrowing experience is shown to be all for naught. He never reaches Danny. Rather, immediately upon Dick's arrival to the hotel—he makes it a few steps through the main door of the hotel, but does not get the snow dusted from his coat and boots—he is quite literally cut down with an ax by Jack. Danny and Wendy make their escape to safety in Dick's SnowCat, while Dick's body is left lying in the hotel lobby in an ever-expanding pool of blood. Certainly, Dick's startling death is the stuff that makes the horror genre what it is; however, as the only character to be slaughtered in real time in the film, Dick's primary function was to serve as magical Negro and sacrificial lamb for the Torrances. For his portrayal, Crothers earned a Saturn Award for Best Supporting Actor.

Poof! More Magical Negroes

The Shining functions to imply that in modern-day America all that remains of the legacy of the wild and primitive African medicine man or the frenzied Voodoo priestess is the subtler magical Negro. The magical Negro, writes Matthew Hughey in his essay "Cinethetic Racism: White Redemption and Black Stereotypes in 'Magical Negro' Films,"

> has become a stock character that often appears as a lower class, uneducated black person who possesses supernatural or magical powers. These powers are used to save and transform disheveled, uncultured, lost, or broken Whites (almost exclusively White men) into competent, successful, and content people within the context of the American myth of redemption and salvation.[26]

This contemporary magical Negro, be it in horror, science fiction, or drama, continues to capture the imagination of Hollywood. For example, in the film *The Green Mile* (1999), set in the 1930s, the Black character John Coffey (Michael Clarke Duncan) is depicted as a dull-witted, magical giant of a man on death row for a crime he did not commit—the rape and murder of two White girls. Coffey cures his executioner's hernia with a touch of the hand, thereby freeing the man of pain and permitting him to restore his sex life. Coffey removes cancer from the prison warden's wife, thereby saving her life. Coffey even dramatically slows the aging process of a mouse. However, Coffey does not use his powers to save himself, and is executed by those he has helped, even though they know he is innocent. In the 2000 film *The Legend of Bagger Vance*, also set in the 1930s, a Black ghost appears (Will Smith) to serve as a caddy to Rannulph Junuh (Matt Damon), a depressed White World War I veteran and former golf star. Vance restores Junuh emotionally, helping him succeed at golf and to get a girlfriend, and then Vance disappears. *Mile* and *Vance* not only feature a very specific role and function of Blackness; they also prize a particular period in American history and race relations—pre-Civil Rights movement.

Heather Hicks speculates on the impetus behind such magic Negro portrayals.[27] She writes that Black characters are given saintly, even magical qualities in a misguided attempt by filmmakers to counter racist stereotypes. However, such characterizations are really for White audiences, in that it takes a saintly Black character to become the moral equivalent of a "normal" White one. More, Hicks observes that there is a fantasy of equality when the downtrodden, dispirited, or those at the bottom of the socioeconomic ladder (e.g. John Coffey) are bestowed with magic to compensate for what they lack. However, magical Negroes have necessary limits, else they become (White) superheroes such as Superman or Captain America.[28]

In the "Blacks in horror" film *Jeepers Creepers* (2001), a Black woman, Jezelle Gay Hartman (played by accomplished stage actress Patricia Belcher), has some psychic ability, and senses danger for two young, White siblings—Patricia (Gina Philips) and Darry Jenner (Justin Long)—who are driving home, through the countryside, for their college spring break. Under her own volition, Jezelle locates the youths to help them survive an encounter with an otherworldly cannibal engaged in the ritualistic eating of humans. Like Dick in *The Shining*, Jezelle stays close to the Jenners, though she is a stranger to the duo, and remains by their side even after she is initially harshly rejected by them as being crazy. Eventually Jezelle places herself face to face with the monster, and falls to her knees in prayer in preparation of self-sacrificial death. However, in an interesting horror twist, Jezelle is spared when the monster consumes Darry instead. Her life spared, Jezelle continues to stand by the Jenners, providing comfort to the surviving sibling, Patricia, acting as a surrogate mother until Patricia's parents arrive to take her home.

Already insightful, "seeing" people who use their powers for good, magical Negroes' goodness is made even more obvious through their self-sacrifice. Their heroism is offered not only without regard for self, but also without regard for their loved ones (who are absent in all of these films). That is, while it is a noble goal to try to maintain Whites' family units, magical Negroes seem to have no families who will mourn and suffer for their deaths.

In the "Blacks in horror" film *Angel Heart* (1987), the character Epiphany Proudfoot (Lisa Bonet) is the rare self-sacrificing Negro with a family member. She is the biracial daughter of a Black, deceased, New Orleans Voodoo practitioner. Her White father disappeared long ago. Epiphany is shown caring for her toddler son, who is no older than two. They seem to have only each other, as together they visit her mother's grave. With no family around, the only other support Epiphany has is a for-hire babysitter—a woman with 14 children of her own who looks after the boy while Epiphany goes about her day, which includes dancing sensuously in a bloody Voodoo ritual or bedding a White, male stranger who has come to New Orleans. Though a highly intuitive "mambo" priestess who controls her followers with fear and punishment, Epiphany is not intuitive enough to realize that she is having (soft-porn) sex with someone who is her kin and who is possessed (the man has taken the soul and body of another). Epiphany experiences a particularly gruesome misogynistic annihilation after sleeping with the man, Harold Angel. Her nude, bloody body is found with her legs spread wide to reveal that she met her death by a "gun in her snatch." Epiphany's son becomes an orphan.

The character Harold Angel (Mickey Rourke) reveals a troubled relationship with Blackness that runs deep throughout the movie. In the opening scenes, he is summoned to 1955 Harlem by the mysterious Louis Cyphre (read: Lucifer) for a meeting. Cyphre (Robert De Niro) meets with Angel in a Black church, seemingly Pentecostal, where Cyphre is welcomed, housed, and protected by parishioners. Hence, the symbiotic and symbolic relationship between Blacks, Black religions, and evil is made clear in the film from the start. Angel's next stop

FIGURE 6.1 Epiphany Proudfoot in Voodoo ritual in *Angel Heart*
           Tri-Star/Photofest

is (of course) New Orleans, where he encounters more Blacks and Black religion—in this case Voodoo. He discovers that Blacks are willing to share their most prized religious secrets with Whites, and that Whites have become particularly adept in wielding Voodoo's black magic. Specifically, they communicate directly with the Devil. In the film, a White man named Johnny Favorite has mastered black magic with a level of expertise that is unrivaled, even by the Blacks who taught it to him, and made a deal with the Devil to sell his soul in return for fame as a singer. When it is time to fulfill his bargain and submit to the Devil, Johnny attempts to renege on the deal by hiding in another man's body.

Angel's sexual encounter-turned-rape of Epiphany puts him one step closer to discovering the truth regarding Johnny's fate—Angel *is* actually Johnny Favorite. Johnny, as Angel, however, suffered from amnesia and had no memory of the body possession. The punishment for Epiphany's (unknown to her) incestuous encounter with her father Johnny/Angel is ultimately far greater than that which Angel experiences for being on the wrong side of Lucifer. Angel's fate is to simply take a slow ride in an antique elevator down to Hell, to join the Devil. If abuses are coming, and it is unclear that they are, no hint is offered as to what they might be.

The Serpent and the Rainbow (1988) features several self-sacrificing Blacks. In this "Blacks in horror" film, a White American anthropologist, Dennis Alan (Bill Pullman), travels to Haiti to take from Voodoo practitioners a powdered drug concoction that turns people into zombies. Dennis plans to acquire the drug for the U.S. pharmaceutical company Bio Corp, who will use it as an anesthetic. As such, this is a film that "repeatedly elaborates the distinction between White Science [American pharmaceuticals] and Black Magic."[29] Those Blacks who work to aid Dennis in his appropriation efforts meet grotesquely violent ends. For example, Dennis enlists the help of a Voodoo priest/nightclub owner, Lucien Celine. It is made clear to Lucien by rogue Haitian law enforcement officials— members of the infamous Tonton Macoute secret police—that Dennis should not be assisted in any way in the theft of the cultural practice/drug. When Lucien fails to stop rendering aid to Dennis, Lucien is sacrificed by being bitten by a venomous scorpion that magically appears in his mouth. It comes as no surprise, then, that Louis Mozart, a poor Haitian who knows how to make the zombie drug, is decapitated because he teaches Dennis how to make the drug and helps him to secret it back to the US. Louis' motivations in helping Dennis are the promise of a small pay out—$1,000—and the hope that Dennis will tell everyone about, and boast on, Louis and his "magic powder." Dennis follows through on neither promise.

Though the backdrop of *The Serpent and the Rainbow* is the rising revolution against the violent, oppressive presidency of Jean-Claude "Baby Doc" Duvalier, no government or police personnel who are opposed to Dennis' efforts think of doing away with him through traditional murderous means such as death by machete or shooting him with a pistol—fates that, in the film, befall Haiti's innocent Black citizenry with swift regularity. Rather, Dennis is closely watched, harassed (he is magically made to dream bad dreams), tortured, before finally being cajoled to fly back to the States. Dennis defiantly returns to Haiti, reuniting with yet another one of his Haitian helpers, Marielle (Cathy Tyson), with whom he has had sex. Marielle wants to stop the corrupt Haitian government, although how she will do so by helping Dennis is not explained. Upon his return, Dennis is zombified and buried alive. He is unearthed by yet another Black helper, Christophe (Conrad Roberts), a zombie who cannot save himself from the suffering. Of course, it is Dennis' nemesis, the cruel chief of police Dargent Peytraud (Zakes Mokae), who meets the worst end. Peytraud, himself, a masterful practitioner of black magic, engages in a variety of supernatural scare tactics to throw Dennis off the trail of acquiring the valuable concoction. However, Dennis gets one last bit of invaluable assistance from the souls of those Blacks Peytraud has killed. Dennis goes head to head with the powerful Peytraud with a success and finality that none before him ever achieved. Dennis acquires the gift of telepathy, and he is able to torture Peytraud with a dramatic genital mutilation before sending him to Hell.

The Changing Cinematic Experience

In the 1970s, socially vibrant, urban, independent theaters such as New York's Elgin, Boston's Orson Welles Cinema, and San Francisco's Pagoda Palace Theater offered "midnight movies" (as did many drive-in theaters across the country). These movies were defined as much by their independent, limited-budget production and counter/oppositional sociopolitical themes as they were by their late-night showing times. The result was a cinematic evolution in which horror films such as *The Rocky Horror Picture Show* (1975), *Eraserhead* (1977), and *Night of the Demons* (1988), as well as non-horror offerings such as *Pink Flamingos* (1972) and *The Harder They Come* (1972), embraced their non-mainstream status and in return rose to become cult-classic favorites among hip, young adult movie-goers. "Here was a movement," writes Heffernan,

> "of exploitation films for art theatres" in [filmmaker] John Waters's phrase. Many art theaters remained open throughout the seventies on the strength of box-office receipts generated by eccentric hybrids like Waters's own *Pink Flamingos* [or] *The Texas Chainsaw Massacre*, which combined grueling visceral horror with eccentric stylistic flourishes and non sequiturs from the art film.[30]

The more successful midnight films saw unusually long runs that lasted, not the few weeks typical of mainstream, studio films, but several months, if not years. For example, the British *The Rocky Horror Show* (1973), despite its failure as a Broadway play, experienced an unprecedented revival for U.S. audiences when it was remade and released in the US as a musical-horror film. Renamed *The Rocky Horror Picture Show*, the film "went midnight" and became a cultural phenomenon as viewing the film repeatedly, as well as performing along with it, often in full costume, became a regular ritual for legions of the movie's fans. In movie houses such as the Oriental Theatre in Milwaukee, Wisconsin and the Clinton Street Theater in Portland, Oregon, the film has been running for decades, while, notably, the Museum Lichtspiele in Munich, Germany, has shown the film daily, without interruption, for 30 years.

The 1980s movie-going experience saw the demise of independent and drive-in theaters, along with the disappearance of the raucous, often pot-smoking midnight movie revelers these businesses thrived on. The end of the cult film/art theater phenomenon in the early 1980s coincided with two trends: "first, the upscaling of the horror and science fiction genre in films such as *Alien*, and second, the success of home video, which put the final nails in the coffin of the drive-in theater, the sub-run grind house, and the art theater."[31] In the stead of small theaters and drive-ins, large chain multiplex theaters (e.g. AMC or Showcase Cinemas) assumed a dominant position. In response, in the early 1980s, "entertainment architecture" companies such as Mesbur and Smith Architects (Canada) emerged offering "substantial expertise in the multiplex cinema design," including "the restoration, renovation, and refurbishment of historic theatres" to incorporate "the latest technologies, including equal sightline stadium seating."[32] The multiplex business plan revolved around presenting mainstream, blockbuster movies on multiple screens. Interestingly, as theaters grew bigger, their offerings became less diverse. The variety of movies once shown in smaller movie houses was sacrificed to provide a greater number of auditorium seats for simultaneous screenings of the same movie.

Working to fill the spatially large and architecturally modernist theaters, horror filmmakers sought to attract a profitable, mass, White young adult market. Youthful stars were cast and youthful themes adopted. Improved special effects technologies enabled grotesquely innovative ways in which to kill young people, which were heavily relied upon while further exploiting the evil-within-White-community fears. These films included special event/date night holiday horror films such as *Prom Night* (1980), *My Bloody Valentine* (1981), and the Christmas-themed *Silent Night, Deadly Night* (1984).

These slasher-splatter horror films were, apart from being extraordinarily grisly, also very White. Audiences were asked if they could discern whether the person behind the Halloween mask or Santa beard was a White friend or a foe.[33] At worst, they were being asked to sort out whether, in viewing these films, they were monsters or monstrous: "either you identify with the slasher—you'd like to have a razor-sharp, foot-long machete in hand as well—or you identify with the worthless victim whose spectacular dismemberment becomes the death you too merit."[34]

Alongside hyper-violent horror films, the horror genre was also being moved into the *very* center of popular culture in exciting ways, from a wholly unlikely source—singer Michael Jackson, the King of Pop.

Michael Jackson as Horror Impresario

Jackson's album *Thriller* (1982) turned Jackson from a pop music star into a musical phenomenon and global cultural icon. Jackson's surge in popularity coincided with the emergence of music video programs (e.g. *Video Concert Hall*) and cable networks (e.g. MTV). The titular single from *Thriller* (written by Rod Temperton) was released in 1983, and pays homage to the horror film genre. Jackson sings about evil, stalking beasts lurking in the dark, and victims with nowhere to run or to hide as they are paralyzed by their own terror. Vincent Price, a horror film icon (e.g. *The Fly* [1958], *The Pit and the Pendulum* [1961], and *The Abominable Dr. Phibes* [1971]) is also featured on the single delivering a "rap" accompanied by staple horror sound effects such as creaking and howling: "Darkness falls across the land/The midnight hour is close at hand/Creatures crawl in search of blood/To terrorize y'awl's neighborhood." The lyrics of *Thriller*, Mercer (31) observes, "evoke allusions and references to the cinematic culture of 'terror' and 'horror' movies … The lyrics weave a little story."[35]

In working to further align the "Thriller" song with the horror film genre Jackson enlisted film director John Landis to direct the *Thriller* music video and special effects technician Rick Baker to create the horror. Landis and Baker also made the cult-classic horror film *An American Werewolf in London* (1981), with a predictable "man becomes monster" storyline that can be forgiven thanks to its special effect feats. Landis' approach to the filming of the man-to-wolf transformation provided film audiences with a graphic revelation, in bright light rather than shadowy view, of how the delicate human body must undergo an extremely painful alteration to become a distinctly, biologically different creature. For Landis' and Baker's efforts, *An American Werewolf* won an Academy Award and a Saturn Award for best make-up, and a Saturn Award for Best Horror Film.[36]

Jackson wanted Landis and Baker to produce a similarly high-quality horror-music video. "Jackson told Landis that he had seen *Werewolf* 'a hundred times' and wanted to turn into a monster. 'That was his quote,' Landis remembers. 'That was what he wanted. He clearly was fascinated by the metamorphosis.'"[37] The result was a 14-minute music video—the first of its kind—at a cost of nearly $1 million.

In the video, Jackson plays a teen named Michael on a date with his "girl" (Ola Ray). He is dressed in 1950s clothing, and driving a 1950s-era convertible, hailing a presumably more innocent time in (White) American history.[38] Jackson runs out of gas in a remote, wooded area. The audience gets a glimpse of a full moon just as Jackson turns to his date and shyly reveals that he is "different" and then proceeds to show the young woman just how unlike "other guys" he is when he turns into a werewolf, in an obvious play on the 1957 horror film *I Was a Teenage Werewolf*. Of course, Jackson's caution about his being "different" can also be read as a triple-entendre speaking to Jackson's transgressive body and sexuality, odd stories that engulfed the pop star (e.g. attempts to buy the "Elephant Man's" bones) and, now, his monstrous state.[39]

As the *Thriller* video progresses, it is revealed to the audience that they have really been watching a movie-within-a movie, as the scene changes to the modern day to show Jackson and his date in a movie theater watching the 1950s couple in a movie. Jackson and his date leave the theater for home; they are suddenly alone and passing a graveyard, at which point Jackson changes into a zombie à la *Night of the Living Dead* (1968). The *Thriller* video presents the mutilated, bloody undead rising from graves. These ghouls join the Jackson zombie (with *Frankenstein* undertones) for what has become one of the most iconic dance sequences in modern media history. The video ends with Jackson striking a wolf-like pose with an endearing smile, thereby leaving an open ending like so many popular horror films of the 1980s.

Landis hoped the music video would bring back the theatrical short; however, CBS records, Jackson's label, responded poorly: "'CBS records told us to go fuck ourselves,' Landis recalls. 'Walter Yetnikoff, that was his exact words, "Go fuck yourself"; that is what he said to me on the phone.'"[40] While the music video did not resurrect the film short, the video did go on to earn Jackson three MTV Video Music Awards for best video, viewer's choice, and choreography.[41] It also set up the direct-to-home-video or "sell-through" market, in which video rental stores were bypassed for sales directly to consumers—Jackson's *Thriller* music video coupled with a behind-the-scenes *Making Michael Jackson's Thriller* sold millions of copies even though both could be seen for free, and quite regularly, on television.

The success and profitability of the home video "paved the way for sell-through videotapes and DVDs, a cornerstone of Hollywood's business model for the last twenty years"[42] and from which the horror genre in particular has greatly benefited. Ironically, White flight also plagued the film industry's urban exhibition outlets, and the home video market worked to provide some relief of the trauma as "suburbanization shifted the locus of American popular culture during the postwar era and emptied downtown movie theaters in cities across the nation."[43] Jackson, Landis, and Baker effectively moved the horror film out of the multiplex, and even away from late-night television and any remaining midnight movie showings, and placed it squarely onto daytime cable television (and later home video viewing). It also courted a demographic as young as 12 years old.[44]

In 1997, Jackson would revisit horror film, this time under the direction of make-up and special effects wizard Stan Winston, who first worked with Jackson on *The Wiz* (1978) and whose claim to fame also includes horror films: *Dr. Black, Mr. Hyde* (1976), *The Thing* (1982), *Aliens* (1986), *Predator* (1987), *Predator 2* (1990), and *Terminator 2: Judgment Day* (1991). With a story conceived by horror fiction author and screenwriter Stephen King, the 40-minute horror film/music video *Ghosts* focuses on the odd "Maestro" who is liked by children, but is misunderstood by adults who want to see him ejected from their community. In a scene shot in black and white (before the video turns to color), the adults, with children in tow, march up to the Maestro's castle with lit torches in hand à la *Frankenstein*. In a seemingly semi-autobiographical tale, Maestro proceeds to transform himself into various demon figures in an effort to scare the adults away, leaving him alone with the children to play in his home. Jackson relied on make-up and special effects to exploit his face—which was already dramatically altered by plastic surgery and by then greatly resembled a skeleton—to cast himself as a fleshless, skeletal demon. Jackson, in a dual role, would also rely on special effects to transform himself into "the Mayor," an intolerant, overweight White man who is particularly opposed to Maestro's presence in the community.

Though *Thriller* and *Ghosts* were on the rather light side of horrifying audiences, they did foreshadow something much more insidious going on inside of the singer himself, specifically his desire for a real-life bodily transmogrification that would eventually render Jackson himself monstrous. The themes of horror and (monstrous) bodily alterations would present themselves repeatedly for Jackson in his video/films *Captain EO* (1986), *Moonwalker* (1988), and *Black and White* (1991).

However, Jackson's real-life metamorphosis was more startling. Though he often denied the extent of his surgeries, the physical evidence is clear: Jackson engaged in an obsessive reconstruction of his facial features (chin, nose, eyes, etc.). He likened himself to Peter Pan, a fantasy character associated with rejuvenation and eternal youth fantasy;[45] however, Jackson's quest to make this fantasy real through cosmetic alteration was far more shocking and provocative than any transformation seen in *Thriller* or *Ghosts*. Skal, in his book *The Monster Show*, sums up the "horror"-able Jackson affair, linking his real, corporeal body to the horror genre:

> Perhaps it wasn't surprising that the star of "Thriller" should be intent on transforming his face into a kind of living skull. From some angles, the bone-white skin, cutaway nose, and tendril-like hair resembled nothing so much as Lon Chaney's Phantom of the Opera. The comparison is apt, because it underscores Jackson's and Chaney's parallel cultural function: the embodiment of a powerful transformation metaphors [sic] for a public basically unsure and fearful about the actual prospects of change in a supposedly classless and mobile society.[46]

As such, Jackson's films are often complicated and nuanced in their mainstreaming of racial subjects. At times, Black monsters are oddly cute (*Thriller*) or function to challenge "Otherings" (*Ghosts*). Jackson's contributions to discourses of Blackness in horror are confounded by his seeming quest for phenotypical whiteness, as well as 1980s mainstream audiences' conservative desire for pop culture imagery sans (racial) commentary of any sort. Kobena Mercer, in "Monster Metaphors: Notes on Michael Jackson's Thriller," describes Jackson's sexual and racial indeterminacy as being a social hieroglyphic—someone who "demands, yet defies decoding."[47]

Mouthy Black Men and Mule Black Women

As its movie poster boasted, the "most controversial film of the year!," *White Dog* (1982) tells the story of a single, young actress, Julie Sawyer (Kristy McNichol), living in the Hollywood hills. She comes upon a stray, large, white German Shepherd and decides to keep it for security and companionship. However, it is soon discovered that the dog has a darker side: it likes to sneak away from Julie's home to kill any Black person it encounters; Whites go untouched. It mauls to death a Black male city worker, and nearly kills a Black actress where Julie works. Assuming the dog was simply trained as an attack dog, Julie takes the dog to an animal training facility—Noah's Ark. There, the dog attacks a Black male groundskeeper. The facility's aged White owner, Mr. Carruthers (Burl Ives), reveals to Julie that she does not just have an attack dog, but a "white dog."[48] It is explained that "white dog" is a colloquialism for dogs programmed to kill Blacks.

The film claims there is a "white dog" history: originally "white dogs" were used to hunt down runaway slaves, and later runaway Black convicts.[49] More recently, "white dogs" are used to attack and kill any Black person that comes along. Carruthers recommends immediate euthanization of Julie's dog. However, a Black animal behaviorist, Keys (Paul Winfield), intervenes, volunteering to make it his very personal mission to try to rehabilitate the dog: "I'm going to make you learn that it is useless to attack Black skin." However, in one particularly violent scene, the dog escapes from Keys' care and ends up stalking a Black man. Pursuing the man into a church, the dog mauls him to death, leaving his body on the altar. Oddly, Keys brings the dog back for more training rather than killing it, despite Julie's and Carruther's pleas to put the dog down before it murders again.

Julie eventually meets the dog's original owner, a (stereotypically) poor, White racist from "the trailer park." The owner confirms he trained the dog to be the "very best" white dog. *White Dog* encourages its audience to despise, as well as to consider anomalous, the dog's previous owner, who is costumed to look as though he just emerged from 1930s rural Mississippi, complete with Southern drawl. The film attempts to introduce provocative debates on racism: Is it nature or nurture? Should even racists be viewed as salvageable members of society? However, it fails to rise to a greater discursive challenge—to question the more subtle, post-Jim Crow racial quandaries that plague American society. As Keys continues to insist on trying to rehabilitate the dog, attempting to turn it back into "Dr. Jekyll," his ideology of assimilation is coded as heroic as he continues

FIGURE 6.2 *White Dog*
Paramount Pictures/Photofest

to strive for reconciliation with the dog. As such, the dog and his Black supporter serve as a metaphor for hope in improving race relations, but that hope comes at the great expense of Blackness. In some ways, Keys joins Dick Hallorran, and Jezelle, sacrificing his safety (and others') on behalf of Whiteness.

The film ends on a disturbing note. Though the dog has done its best to single-handedly wipe Blacks out of California, Keys has forced the dog to tolerate Black skin. In the film's final scenes, the dog turns on the White Mr. Carruthers. Only then does Keys conclude the dog is absolutely not salvageable and shoots it.

From the start, *White Dog* was awash in controversy. The NAACP objected to the movie even before filming began,[50] and during filming the organization pressed for script changes.[51] The *Village Voice* reported:

> at the time the film was being made, amid an awareness of the need for strong black images, Ku Klux Klan activity was on the rise. In this climate, the N.A.A.C.P. warned Paramount that the film, in which three Blacks are viciously attacked by the "white dog," could be a dangerous incitement to racism.[52]

Once the film was completed, Paramount Pictures, producers of the film, shelved *White Dog*, opting not to release it in the US. Paramount has claimed *White Dog* did not test well in Detroit.[53] Conversely, its filmmakers have claimed the studio wanted a film more like *Jaws*, but with paws—something the more cerebral *White Dog* was not.[54] It was not until 1991 that the film saw limited release in the US largely as part of short-run film festivals.[55]

John Carpenter's *The Thing* (1982) presented audiences with an unlikely horror move anti-hero—a scrappy, fiercely independent Black man who (presumably) survives the monster. In the "Blacks in horror" film a group of researchers housed in a remote Antarctic science station mistakenly admit a recently thawed alien into their camp. The alien has the single goal of survival at the expense of other living things. "The thing" not only has the ability to assume the appearance of any evolved living species (human, dog, other alien life forms, etc.), but can also fully assimilate that which it has consumed, taking on its behaviors and memories. The film is effective, observes Guerrero, because of its "technological ability to construct the monster not as a humanoid vegetable of 1950s vintage but rather as a much more potent and pathological xenomorph, an alien being that has the power to invade, absorb, and imitate to the finest detail any creature it comes in contact with."[56]

As members of the all-male camp begin to perish at the hands of the doppelgänger monster, they become consumed by fear and paranoia (of each other). However, two men are tough under fire. The first is MacReady (Kurt Russell), a White helicopter pilot whose reasoning and quick action move him into a role of leadership. The second man who is brave and focused is Childs (Keith David), a mechanic, and one of two Blacks in the group. Unlike MacReady, who is cerebral and steady, Childs appears to be a mistrustful hot-head. As the body count and tensions rise, the group decides they need a leader to organize them in the fight for their lives. Childs volunteers himself as leader, and automatically reaches for the weaponry that comes with the rank. However, Childs' attempt to assume power is summarily rejected by MacReady—"It should be somebody a little more even-tempered, Childs"—and the group agrees.

Doherty reads the stranded group of men as "angry, unpleasant, and self-interested individuals, as chilly as the stark Antarctic landscape they inhabit. That men could live like this in close quarters—in total isolation, depending on each other for survival and succor—and not develop a fraternal bond defies social reality and dramatic logic."[57] However, there is another reading of the group which can explain why and how they are "unpleasant" rather than fraternal. It is an interpretation which accounts for power relationships along class, education, and racial difference lines. The camp is predominately White. Among the group there are obvious social hierarchies. The bulk of the group is made up of the educated, skilled, and trained—doctors, research scientists (biologists, geologists, meteorologists), and technicians such as pilots—all of whom are White. A minority of Whites are "lesser" in status, serving in roles such as radio operator, dog handler, and mechanic. The two Blacks, Nauls (T.K. Carter), a cook, and Childs, a mechanic, do not "rank," so to speak. In one scene, Nauls is asked by a resting, injured White crew member to turn down his music. Nauls, who is working in the kitchen, attempts to enact a small measure of comeuppance by defiantly ignoring the order. Similarly, Childs works to exert some power by challenging the leadership power MacReady wields, as well as questioning whther MacReady may be a "thing." In no way does Childs present a self-sacrificing or scared-Negro performance.

The narrative climax builds when Childs leaves the camp, disappearing into the harsh elements. MacReady, who was also out of sight for a period, and possibly assimilated, dynamites the camp. Such an act of destruction is a horror staple as characters realize that "the house or tunnel may at first seem a safe haven, but the walls that promise to keep the killer out quickly become, once the killer penetrates them, the walls that hold the victim in."[58]

The Thing presents a surprise ending. MacReady readies himself to die in the freezing elements as the lone survivor. If the alien is not in his body, without the camp to provide it shelter, the alien will refreeze. If the alien is in his body, MacReady will freeze to death along with the alien that is in him. However, just as MacReady is settling on his fate, Childs suddenly reappears. MacReady and Childs are unsure if either or neither one of them is the alien. The film concludes with them eyeing each other skeptically, but also establishing a friendship—as they are now equals. They share a bottle of booze as they wait to see what will happen next. *The Thing*, then, presents a rather open-ended conclusion in which the monster's and the men's fate is unknown. It is this narrative openness, writes Hutchings, that may be seen as "expressing an ambivalence about, or even a critique of, dominant social values."[59] Could such an ending where monster, Black man, and White man may survive be a critique of dominant values about power, or present a racial ambivalence? Guerrero pessimistically thinks not:

> as the camera frames the survivors in medium close reverse shots of mutual suspicion, one can discern that the breath of the white man is heavily fogged in the Antarctic air, whereas the black man's is not. The implication is subtle but clear: The Thing lives on and, interestingly enough, its carrier is yet another socially marginalized form, the black male.[60]

Whether Guerrero is on to something about who is the thing is not as material as the fact that Childs is part of that very discussion in the first place. He defies the stereotypical buddy, self-sacrificing, and Blacks-always-die-first roles. Childs' character, who stares down MacReady like Ben of *Night of the Living Dead* does with Harry, may be read as the survival triumph that Ben of *Night* was denied. More, Childs is not working in support of Whiteness, as seen in *The Serpent and the Rainbow*. Childs could be read as headstrong and even unlikable—either is usually worthy of the death penalty for a Black man in horror film. His heroism and his flaws are what they are—they are "real." He also need not carry the burdensome expectations of hierarchies all alone. Indeed, the "apocalyptic dimension"[61] of *The Thing* allows the monster to take up some of that burden, as it represented a new interloping Other entering a society.

Black women did not enjoy much in the way of inclusion in the genre during this horror cycle. A notable exception was the "Blacks in horror" film *Vamp* (1986), starring entertainer/model/singer Grace Jones. The film capitalized on Jones' striking look—a 5 foot 10, lithe, androgynous figure in haute couture— while casting her as the vampire Katrina, a strip club owner. The downtown club, the Afterdark, is in a desolate, trash-strewn part of the dead inner-city Los Angeles, removed from the more vibrant city life that surrounds it. The club serves as a cover for Katrina's nightly vampiric hunts. Her minions bring Katrina men (though she is "bi-vampiric" and will happily take a woman) to feed on. Trouble ensues when three college students, Keith (Chris Makepeace), A.J. (Robert Rusler), and Duncan (Gedde Watanabe), whose non-urban campus is "200 miles from civilization," drive to the Afterdark with the goal of bringing some strippers back to their university for a fraternity party. A.J. is fed on by Katrina. Keith (who is White), Duncan (who is Asian), and "Amaretto" (Dedee Pfeiffer) a young, White woman whom they rescue from the club, work to survive until dawn. Notably, of the heroes, only Duncan, the Asian male, dies, as he is turned into a vampire and then destroyed by fire. Even A.J., Katrina's victim, unexpectedly lives on, but as a vampire who happily resigns himself to living as a night creature. Keith and Amaretto kill Katrina and walk off into the rising sun, enjoying their day.

Katrina is simultaneously beautiful and horribly grotesque, cruelly deadly, and sexy. She is cast as the exotic as she is surrounded by symbols which connote a foreign Otherness—her clothes, crypt, and other accoutrements all hail Africa. Her body is painted with emblems resembling hieroglyphics. Katrina conforms to the exotic, literally; although she is the club's owner, and vampire leader, she also performs as an exotic dancer, putting on a highly sexualized dance routine where she affects a sex act with a prop chair. Katrina is, in fact, more sex-obsessed than blood-lusting. Notably, there is little else to say about Katrina, as she says so little in the film. Katrina is silent, except for making suckling sounds and moaning, grunting and hissing wickedly. Hudson sums up the function of Katrina succinctly: "She is associated with hypersexuality and violence. Her agency is portrayed as animalistic: she grunts and howls as she licks A.J.'s body … Because Vamp's protagonists are white, Jones stands out as the (muted or silenced) cultural other."[62]

Katrina's lack of speech, perhaps, adds to the allure of her monstrosity, but also limits it. Katrina's absent dialogue coupled with the focus on her body means that her role is singularly as eye candy. There is little else to her.

FIGURE 6.3 The silent but deadly Katrina in *Vamp*
New World Pictures/Photofest

Conclusion

The monsters of the 1980s generally worked against type. They were not racialized as Blacks, as seen in films such as *King Kong* or *Creature from the Black Lagoon*. Instead, the monsters of the 1980s were White, male, and suburban. As such, in White suburban horror films, "race [became] a structuring absence in the milieu of the contemporary horror film where monsters, victims, and heroes are predominately White, a racially unmarked category."[63] Monsters of the 1980s had access to resources such as Santa costumes or miner's gear, they drove cars, and made their own weapons. These White "monsters whose faces come from a random assortment of high school yearbook, driver's licenses, and bathroom mirrors" could move about largely undetected as their evilness was not immediately identifiable due to their lack of color-coding.[64] If they did not hail their victims, for example, by inserting themselves into dreams, the monsters could have been largely invisible because they fit in so well.

Blacks were not so lucky. They were stuck on islands or left behind in dead cities. Black characters saw imagistic recuperation only if they became the symbol of a unilateral, cross-racial devotion. While there was no exchange of kindness coming their way from the Whites they sought to help, Blacks' reward was that they went to their deaths facilitating the continuation of Whiteness. Surely, that was sufficient to get them past the pearly gates, and keep them out of Hell. It would have to be this kind of self-sacrifice for Blacks (or super-duper magical mystical Negroes, as filmmaker Spike Lee called them),[65] as even their own magic could not be used for self-salvation.

Some scholars reflect upon the horror genre of this period as seeming to understand "the Other as a scapegoat" thereby refusing "to see the monster as an aberration to be put down to secure bourgeois normality."[66] But, such a conclusion cannot be reached in the context of the treatment of "Blacks in horror" or the absence of "Black horror." James Snead argues that omission, or exclusion, is the most common form of racial stereotyping, but also the most difficult to identify because its manifestation is absence itself.[67] It was the Native American Other indeed that became a scapegoat for evil, and the entire decade was a commentary on how to re-secure White bourgeois normality. One way, for sure, was to stay away from burial grounds or down-town urban areas.

If Michael Jackson had not inserted a self-deprecating quip about his identity in *Thriller*, male heterosexuality would have remained an unexamined and pre-sumed norm. It was women like sexy, silent Katrina who were to be looked at, but not heard from, who are thought to be "a problem, a source of anxiety, of obsessive enquiry" while men are not.[68]

However, while Black and White communities occupied a "never the twain shall meet" existence in the 1980s, things begin to change dramatically in the next decade—the 1990s—as the plight of the urban world would take center stage. The Blacks who were left behind would finally be featured in rather serious tales of moral redemption—with Black women, in some cases, acting as very vocal and powerful saviors.

7

BLACK IS BACK! RETRIBUTION AND THE URBAN TERRAIN

1990s

> But is not every square inch of our cities the scene of a crime? Every passer-by
> a culprit?
>
> —Benjamin (256)[1]

The horror film genre celebrated its first century in high, cinematic style by
offering what can only be described as "prestige" horror films.[2] *The Silence of
the Lambs* (1991), directed by Jonathan Demme, took its horror seriously,
enlisting Academy Award winner Jodie Foster and nominee Anthony Hopkins to
deliver nauseating, psychological chills. Respecting the genre paid off, with *Lambs*
going on to earn a whopping five Oscars—Best Actor, Best Actress, Best Director,
Best Picture, and Best Writing. The film set the stage for an exciting, horror-filled
decade. Neil Jordan's *Interview with a Vampire: The Vampire Chronicles* (1994) brought
sexy back to horror with a matinee idol triple-threat through Antonio Banderas,
Tom Cruise, and Brad Pitt. That strategy worked as well, securing the film two
Oscar nominations, and over a dozen other cinema awards. As Abbott notes, the
1990s represented America's love affair with horror, with Hollywood putting
some serious star power and big budgets behind their horror film efforts.[3] Oscar
winner Francis Ford Coppola, of *The Godfather* trilogy fame (1972, 1974, 1990),
took on the task of directing *Dracula* (1992). Actor Jack Nicholson, the winner
of two Oscars and the star of the horror film *The Shining* (1980), returned to
horror in *Wolf* (1994). Likewise, actor Robert De Niro, also a double Oscar
winner (*The Godfather, Part II* [1974]; *Raging Bull* [1980]) and star of the horror
film *Angel Heart* (1987), revisited the genre to star as the Creature in *Frankenstein*
(1994). There were more films—many, many more—in the 1990s, such as
the action/monster blockbuster movie *The Mummy* (1999) and the haunting,

desperately sad *The Sixth Sense* (1999). And then there was the surprise hit of the decade, *The Blair Witch Project* (1999), made for less than $100,000 but driven to box office gold (to the tune of over $130 million in its first few weeks of release) by drumming up internet buzz. Horror had become so sizzling hot that, in 2004 while riding the wave of popularity generated by 1999's *The Mummy* and *The Mummy Returns* (2001), Universal Studios Hollywood theme park even introduced its rollercoaster, Revenge of the Mummy—the Ride.[4]

Black participation in these prestige horror films was notably limited, begging the question, what did the horror genre mean for Blacks in the 1990s? The good news was that "Black horror" was back with a vengeance (pun intended) in the decade, with a force that had not been seen since the 1970s Blaxploitation-era horror cycle. One stand-out film, *Def by Temptation* (1990), was reminiscent of Spencer Williams' 1940s religious-horror films *The Blood of Jesus* (1941) and *Go Down, Death* (1944), breathing new, scary life into morality messages. Likewise, "Black horror" films such as *Tales from the Hood* (1995) updated the Black Power message offered in films such as *Sugar Hill* (1974), to address the wave of gang and drug violence plaguing some Black communities. More importantly, finally, in the 1990s there was plain ole "Black horror" monster movies, such as *The Embalmer* (1996), in which Blacks got to slash and scream, live and die just like anybody else featured in the genre.

There were few so-called prestige films in "Black horror," but if anyone was going to be behind such a project it would be Oprah Winfrey, with *Beloved* (1998). Otherwise, "Black horror" was lucky to have any financing at all (e.g. *Bugged* [1997]). Fortunately, or perhaps not, given their wavering quality, countless "Black horror" films were made, fueled by the exploding home video market. In short, while "Black horror" was not racking up awards or setting box office records, it was making inroads by featuring Blacks in substantive roles, not just bit parts, as evidenced in *Vampire in Brooklyn* (1995).

"Blacks in horror" films, likewise, were abundant. *Candyman* (1992) played on old stereotypes by again placing a blond beauty in peril at the hands of a Black boogeyman. Notably, "Blacks in horror" films also introduced the Black superhero, with Blade and Spawn, men driven to revenge after White villains destroy their lives.

There were red threads running through many of the "Black horror" and "Blacks in horror" films. One unifying theme of the 1990s was that the urban, specifically the Black inner-city, was deadly real estate. In several "Black horror" films, the inner-city was depicted as dangerous and troubled, but worth fighting for and cleaning up (e.g. *Urban Menace* [1999]). By contrast, the "Blacks in horror" film *Predator 2* (1990) depicted the urban much as 1920s and 1930s movies represented the jungles of Africa—as bloodthirsty. The only difference between the jungle and the city was that Black American city dwellers were slightly more clothed than African natives, and their weapon of choice was a gun instead of spears. Still, Black was back, busting the modern horror genre wide open.

Yielding to Temptation

The 1990s opened with *Def by Temptation* (1990), an earnest, independently produced "Black horror" film that closely resembled the work of Spencer Williams' *The Blood of Jesus* (1941). Distributed by Troma Entertainment, infamously known for their large catalogue of cheesy, low-budget exploitation and horror films such as *The Toxic Avenger* (1984) and *Killer Condom* (1996), *Temptation* stood out for its quality, and was hailed by Troma's President Lloyd Kaufman as the "best" in the Troma collection.[5] Like *Blood*, *Temptation* was stymied by budget, and like *Blood*, *Temptation* made up for it through imagination and highly stylized sequences.

Temptation was written, directed, and produced by the Black actor James Bond III, a first-time director, who also stars in the film. It presents a talented Black cast, with Samuel L. Jackson, Kadeem Hardison, Bill Nunn, and Bond (all of whom had appeared together in Spike Lee's 1988 *School Daze*), and boasts cameo appearances by singer/theater performer/TV actress Melba Moore and jazz saxophonist Najee. The film serves as noted television and film producer, writer, actor, and director Nelson George's first foray into production. Additionally, award-winning cinematographer and director Ernest K. Dickerson (*Dexter*, seasons 2008 and 2009; *Day of the Dead*, 1985; *Malcolm X*, 1992; *The Wire*, seasons 2004–2006) serves as cinematographer.

The film's focus is 20-year-old Joel (Bond III), a seminary student, visiting his slightly older, actor brother "K" (Kadeem Hardison) in Brooklyn. This is Joel's first trip to New York as he travels from a small town in North Carolina. He leaves behind, his "Grandma" (Minnie Gentry), who raised him after his parents' untimely death in a car accident. The story centers on Joel's attempts to be certain of his decision to follow in his father's footsteps by becoming a minister. Brooklyn, as a Northern big city, is depicted as home to a number of corrupting influences—sexual escapades, infidelity, booze, and in one dramatic scene even television, literally, becomes deadly. By contrast, the small-town South is depicted as a place out of which righteous wholesomeness radiates. The South is "down home," the Black utopian fantasy of nurturance, piety, and history. Southerners meet in churches, not bars. Southern women wear crosses, not heavy make-up. *Temptation* presents what Reid calls a "regional moralistic dualism," in that Southern culture is akin to decent, forthright sensibilities and in direct opposition to the North.[6]

In the film, a demon spirit named Temptation (Cynthia Bond) is, according to the film, an "it" who uses sexuality to hold morality hostage. The spirit, over the centuries, has been incarnated into fleshly form, seducing sinners and declaring a particular victory when a true innocent—such as a God-fearing minister—succumbs to temptation. Temptation takes on a female form in the film, and, reminiscent of the film *Abby* (1974), preys upon men she picks up, or who pick her up, killing them during sex. The black widow's victims represent a specific, significant purported sin, and, hence, a rather socially conservative view. There is the man who encourages one of his girlfriends to get an abortion. There is also an adulterous bar patron who removes his wedding ring before picking up Temptation. Here, after sex, Temptation taunts the man: "Honey, I've given you something there's no cure for. It's going to grow and grow until it consumes you." The man's response about the beautiful Temptation looking clean—"It don't look like you got anything"—is an obvious warning to the audience about unprotected sex. The man, presumably infected with a sexually transmitted disease, begins to deteriorate immediately, making his sin visible to his wife, who, in response to his infidelity, shoots him. However, the film reserves its most graphic violence (punishment) for a gay man. He is lured by Temptation, with her encouraging him to try her out just once because "a woman, it's much better." In Temptation's bedroom, as the man readies himself for what he believes is consensual sex, she appears malicious rather than seductive as she was with her other male victims. When the man asks if he has done something wrong, she scornfully replies, "Yes," before violently raping him. Here, Temptation becomes an "it" inserting an unseen object or body part into the man's rectum, with him asking "Where'd *that* come from?" before screaming for Temptation to stop and take it out. He bears the full brunt of her anger, with Temptation's growls drowning out the man's screams as she penetrates and slashes him, leaving her bedroom soaked in his blood. The most ferocious scene in the film, it is a startling depiction of anti-gay violence aligning with, and giving tacit approval for, the real-life violence gays and lesbians experience. For example, a 1989 report, issued one year before *Temptation*, revealed that 5 percent of gay men and 10 percent of lesbians polled reported being the victim of anti-gay violence, while 47 percent of all gays polled reported some form of (non-violent) discrimination based on their sexual orientation.[7]

Eventually, Temptation sets her sights on Joel, who is depicted as clearly out of place in New York, in both dress and mannerisms. K, who is "sharp as a tack," sports the latest in urban wear—expensive sweat suits and sneakers. His talk is hip and peppered with slang and profanity. However, Joel arrives in khakis, a button-down collar shirt, and "ugly brown" loafers. He is refined in his speech, and unschooled in colloquialisms, responding, "Fornication is a sin" when asked by K if he would "jump in them draws" if he met an attractive woman. Joel, from his "small town," where he proverbially "swats flies and milks cows and shit" has to be given a primer in dress, and urban vernacular.[8] K grows suspicious of Temptation and with the help of an undercover federal agent, Dougy (Bill Nunn), who investigates paranormal crimes, tries to kill Temptation.

FIGURE 7.1 Joel and K in *Def by Temptation*
Troma Films/Photofest

Temptation's story turns on the heroism of a woman. K and Dougy are killed, leaving Joel vulnerable. Suddenly Grandma arrives on the scene to save her grandson. Armed with Joel's bible (which he left behind at home) and a wooden cross, Grandma kicks down Temptation's door, ready to engage in some spiritual warfare by shoring up Joel with a bit of preaching. Together Grandma and Joel fight Temptation. Grandma embodies a kind of womanist theology at work—a concern for the Black community and its salvation as a whole—while showing the "resiliency of women-centered family networks and their willingness to take responsibility for Black children."[9] *Temptation* holds on to and celebrates the notion of a grandmother or surrogate kinfolk stepping in, even as such community connectedness is increasingly elusive.

The portrayal of this kind of mother figure evidences a significant departure from non-Black horror films. The "mother-as-devouring-and-poisonous figure" is anomalous in "Black horror," with Black women, if depicted, generally revered.[10] In "Black horror," the central narrative does not regularly focus on Black mothers producing "bad seeds," or "psychos," nor does it twist religion with abusive cruelty to give rise to supernatural, monstrous children (e.g. *Carrie* [1976]).

In the film's climax Joel chooses God, proclaiming, "Demon, I rebuke you!" Thanks to the cross Grandma brought along, Joel destroys Temptation by holding it up to her, revealing her true grotesque demonic form before it explodes. Joel and Grandma, then, represent family and faith restored.

The film ends on a cautionary note as the dead K and Dougy have been resurrected as evil and are now luring women. However, back on the straight and narrow, Joel assures viewers that he is ready to fight for righteousness. As such, the film asserts, "the only answer to urban strife and decadence is Jesus."[11]

Temptation was hailed in the *Washington Post* as being "light-years ahead of *Blacula*," possessing "depth and emotional detail generally absent from such films," and avoiding some of the stereotypes too often offered "by the White film establishment."[12] The film was also cited for being low budget. However, if the film is evaluated outside of Hollywood frameworks (as Troma's President did), it cannot be simply dismissed as a B movie. Rather, as the *Post* review reveals, this is a Black film with unique narrative conventions, conventions that should not be "glossed over as technical and artistic liabilities."[13] Instead, it contributes to a Black filmmaking tradition that does not work to replicate the sensibilities or aesthetic leanings, or, in the case of horror, special effects obsessions, of Hollywood.

Temptation joined two other eerie Black dramatic films, *To Sleep with Anger* (1990) and *Eve's Bayou* (1997), thereby making the 1990s a decade for focused attention on Black families and culture, particularly those outside of the 'hood. *Anger*, directed by the acclaimed Black director Charles Burnett, is horror-inspired, focusing on an evil trickster of a man, Harry (Danny Glover), who has entered the house of a God-fearing family in a Black middle-class Los Angeles neighborhood. Harry brings with him a range of superstitious rituals (tossing pinches of salt to ward off bad luck) and folkways (folk medicine, charms) from "home"—the South—that seemingly no longer apply in the Northern Christian home, thereby "stirring tensions between the latent values of the rural South and those of contemporary Black urban culture."[14] After Harry falls victim to one of his superstitions and dies, the family shakes free of his evil and avoids killing each other. The equally haunting dramatic film *Eve's Bayou* (1997), directed by the award-winning, Black, female director Kasi Lemmons, places Black folk religion as central to her narrative. Set in a small town in Louisiana in the 1960s, the film tells the story of the Baptiste family, descendants of a White slave owner and his Black slave. The family is negotiating a series of traumas. The family includes the young Eve (Jurnee Smollett), who, like her aunt Mozelle (Debbie Morgan), has the gift of "sight." As a professional "psychic counselor," Mozelle prays to Jesus before "seeing" on behalf of her clients. However, this is not Voodoo and Mozelle denies knowing how to perform Voodoo, that is, until a woman desperate for help leaves Mozelle with no other option than to apply its power. Likewise, there is a conjure woman, Elzora (Diahann Carroll), whose power is ambiguous, but is nevertheless believed in, fueled by traditional belief systems and understandings of ancient Black religious folkways. *Bayou* becomes a "good Black film" as it demonstrates "expert and intimate knowledge of the Black experience."[15]

Reinventing the Black Urban Image

White folks, flee!
Still—here's me!
White folks, fly!
Here am I!

—Langston Hughes[16]

Horror and science fiction films such as *War of the Worlds* (1953) and *Them!* (1954) assured White suburbanites that they made the right decision in rejecting urban life as Martians and giant ants—"spectacular representations of the alien Other and its violent onslaught"—wrecked cities.[17] But horror was all about fear and chaos through disruption, and over the years the genre brought terror to these purportedly idyllic enclaves by showing that White monsters (no Blacks allowed!) could move in, too.

With monsters such as Freddy Krueger and Michael Myers busy pureeing White suburbanites, "Black horror" film took advantage of the representational gap left when White horror fled to the suburbs, as well. These urban-based horror movies presented narratives that were Black-centered, that is, drawing on Black folklore, histories, and culture. The aesthetic was Black, with expressions of style, music, language, and overall cadence—culturally specific references and insider talk—speaking to Blackness, as well. The films brought a social realism, revealing that what was most threatening to urban Blacks, the stuff that haunted them while awake and in their dreams, was lingering racism, socioeconomic disparities, health crises, and specific forms of criminality, such as gun and gang violence, rogue cops.

Blacks were depicted not only as urbanites, but also as living in the inner-city, which was not to be confused with cities' downtowns, which were still home to businesses. Rather, Blacks were located in the desolate, ghetto core of the city, quite the opposite of the suburbs or other nonurban places (e.g. the rural). The inner-city became tied to a racialized and lower socioeconomic image, with Blacks being shown as poor or participating in illegal, underground economies such as drug sales. Only the violent, dangerous, and depraved thrived in the inner-city, while the innocent, those who could not get out, were held hostage.

There were also moves in horror film to recast how Black neighborhoods were portrayed. They were not always merely inner-cities or, as they had been described in the 1970s, "the ghetto." Now, "the 'hood" was the moniker, with the 'hood in some cases accommodating the spatial image of the ghetto, while also allowing "greater flexibility ... to describe and delineate locality—literally, one's neighborhood and the space to which one relates as a local home environment."[18] The 'hood, then, was also a place that had real meaning as it pertained to identity construction and understandings of community. For example, it was a place where Blacks were "real," authentically Black. While some

Blacks "got out" through, for example, work or education opportunities, sell-out Blacks were those who turned their backs to their relationships with, and memories of, the 'hood. While the 'hood had a difficult reputation, it was still home and viewed as having much to offer, including making seminal contributions to all facets of Black culture. For this cultural and rhetorical freedom, the hip-hop generation can be specifically thanked for reminding Blacks that relationships with one's communities are deeply profound and complex, and not reducible to hackneyed conventions.

Fighting for the 'Hood

Black director Rusty Cundieff's "Black horror" film *Tales from the Hood* (1995) was not quite Hollywood, but it did have impressive backing from Spike Lee's production company, 40 Acres and a Mule. The film borrowed from the *Tales from the Crypt* 1950s comic book stories, film (1972), and HBO television series (1989–1996), in which short, often comical horror vignettes are presented that show how someone met their untimely death. *Hood* worked to signal it was different from *Crypt* by focusing on Black stories and presenting its version of the Crypt Keeper, the *Crypt* narrator and mascot (a decomposing skeleton). *Hood* offered a black skeleton with a bandana tied, gang-style, around its head, while wearing dark sunglasses, and with a gun in its hand. *Hood* presents four vignettes, introduced by a spooky funeral home director, Mr. Simms (Clarence Williams III), who is also charged with revealing the story behind the deaths of those in his parlor. In the film, his audience is three young drug-dealing gang members.

In the first story, a distinguished Black activist, Martin Moorehouse (Tom Wright), who is trying to rid the 'hood of racist, rogue White police officers, is murdered by three cops. Among the trio is a virulent racist named "Strom," a likely reference to segregationist Strom Thurmond, Governor of South Carolina (1947–1951) and U.S. Senator (1954–2003), who infamously proclaimed in 1948, "And I want to tell you, ladies and gentlemen, that there's not enough troops in the Army to force the Southern people to break down segregation and admit the nigger race into our theatres, into our swimming pools, into our homes and into our churches."[19] Thurmond also opposed the Civil Rights Act of 1957. The officers kill Moorehouse and plant drugs on him, thereby ruining his reputation as well. The entire affair is witnessed by a Black rookie cop, Clarence (Anthony Griffith), who fails to intervene. Maddened by the guilt, Clarence quits the force and becomes a drunk. On the one-year anniversary of the murder, Moorehouse's ghost exacts a series of gruesome acts of deadly revenge on the cops. However, Moorehouse reserves his express contempt for Clarence, demanding, "Where were you when I needed you, *Brother*?" In the second vignette, a child named Walter (Brandon Hammond) is the victim of physical abuse by his mother's boyfriend, whom he calls Monster (David Alan Grier).

The horror twist is that when Walter draws Monster (as a green beast) on pieces of paper, he can tear the drawings, injuring the man. Walter eventually burns the picture of Monster, thereby burning up his abuser. The story features a caring, involved teacher, Richard (Rusty Cundieff), who works to help the boy. Richard is hailed as the kind of person that Black communities need.

The third story focuses on a White Southern politician, Duke Metger (Corbin Bernsen), a name that recalls Tom Metzger, the founder of the White Aryan Resistance, and David Duke, a member of the Ku Klux Klan and a politician. Metger is depicted as running for office on a no affirmative action, no reparations platform, supported by a "White Hands" commercial featuring a White man's hands crumpling up a rejection letter after losing out on an employment opportunity because of racial quotas. Here, the film reproduces the real 1990 controversial "Hands" political ad supporting the candidacy of North Carolina Senator Jesse Helms.[20] In the film, Metger hires a Black image-manager who tells racist jokes, and is promptly killed in what appears to be an accidental fall down the stairs in Metger's home. Metger has purchased the plantation home where a slave massacre occurred nearly 200 years earlier. Not long after the murders, a Black Voodooist, Miss Cobb (Christina Cundieff), buys the property, seeking to put the souls of the slaves to rest by placing their spirits into dolls. The home becomes a tribute to the slaves, and after Miss Cobb's death it remains untouched until Metger buys it against the wishes of the Black community. The dolls and Metger battle, with Metger meeting his death at the hands of the dolls while questioning why he should be their target since he was not the one actually responsible for their enslavement and deaths. The failure to understand the lingering effects of slavery on the Black community is a theme that would be more deeply explored in the film Beloved (discussed on pp. 183–186), in which the audience is prompted to consider whether Blacks have really secured their psychic freedom and whether those who were not direct participants in the slave trade, but benefit from its legacy, are still culpable.

The final vignette brings the film full circle as the young men, with whom the funeral director is talking, hear the story of someone they killed. They learn that after a shootout with a rival named Jerome (Lamont Bentley), Jerome enters a liminal stage between life and death, and is given the opportunity to modify his gangster behavior under the supervision of a scientist, Dr. Cushing (Rosalind Cash). Jerome is delivered in chains and caged next to a White supremacist who thanks him for killing "niggers," telling Jerome, "You cool with me." Jerome is shown a series of images aligning gang violence with Klan terrorism. The film also invokes religious metaphors linking Jerome to Cain, a man who killed his brother, by asking Jerome, "How many Brothers have you slain?" Interestingly, Jerome is being attended to by women dressed in dominatrix-stripper nurse's costumes, women whom Jerome ogles. Presumably, the women function to dispel any notions that Jerome's heterosexual masculinity is being compromised at the hands of a female scientist who has all but stripped him bare of both his clothes and his emotions. Finally, Cushing demands that Jerome take personal responsibility for his actions, explaining that he cannot blame his parents, teachers, or the world for his aberrant behaviors. Jerome fails to accept change, and dies. It is revealed to the three young men in the funeral parlor that they too died in a revenge killing carried out by Jerome's friend Crazy K. All are in Hell with the Devil, who turns out to be the funeral director.

The film was a far from subtle commentary on Black unity and commitment. While *Temptation* identified a range of sins, for *Hood* there was only one principle sin—selling out—which was punishable by death. Those who sold out Blacks were depicted as a triumvirate of monsters in *Hood*: the White racist, the Black enabler of White racism, and the sell out who in some way or another abused Blacks or Black communities. In contrast, notably, it is the Voodoo woman who stands as a heroic agent of justice.[21] *Hood*, then, also had a message for the horror genre—selling out Black religion would no longer be tolerated either.

Temptation and *Hood* are post-Civil Rights era, social problems films which simultaneously casts Black communities as full of dangerous pitfalls but also enormous pride and talent. For Denzin, films such as these located the responsibility for the 'hood's problems "with the media, the police, and other apparatuses of the state. These films make these structures at least partially responsible."[22] Indeed, such films claim that Blacks' problems are externally inflicted, such as drugs and guns being delivered into the Black communities, or poverty as a result of misguided economic policies. The films caution that though Black communities are victimized by these phenomena, Blacks do not have to succumb.

The films of this decade also present the idea that those most susceptible to the dangers found in the 'hood are Black youth, specifically those invested in gangsta rap culture. The films evidenced a concern over the glamorization of the Black "gangsta" lifestyle as the real and imaged violence associated with it dominated headlines in the 1990s. For example, the explosive, phenomenally popular members of NWA, or Niggaz With Attitude, introduced themselves as a "gang," not a rap "group," dressed in their "gang" colors of black and silver, and talked about kicking off violence in the 'hood, all as part of their image-making.[23] The films revealed the profound concern among some Blacks over the blurring of mythical and real-life violence with Blacks targeting each other. For example, in 1991, rapper Dr. Dre threw another rapper, Dee Barnes, through a door. In between 1992 and 1995, "thug life" rapper Tupac was associated with a string of crimes, including sexually assaulting a woman, and was jailed for it in 1995. Suge Knight, co-founder of "Death Row" records, was jailed, and later present for the drive-by shooting death of Tupac in 1996. In 1997, New York gangsta rapper Biggie Smalls was gunned down as well. The decade ended with Puff Daddy of Bad Boy records being arrested twice, once for assault and a second time for a shooting in a nightclub.

Tales from the Hood attempted to fight back against such gangsta culture with more traditional forms of folkloric storytelling, while rewriting the most common plots of horror films, linking them to bigotry and inequality: "zombie movies and police brutality; monster movies and domestic violence; ancient curse movies and White supremacy accompanied by co-option; mad scientist movies and gang violence as self-hatred"—it was an innovative way to get young people's attention.[24] More, *Hood* popularized a trend in presenting Blackness-centered, cautionary tales in short story, anthology style. For example, *Street Tales of Terror* (2004) featured three blood-drenched stories warning against violence against or by women, while *Urban Evil: A Trilogy of Fear* (2005) showed how the 'hood "had gone to hell," and '*Hood of Horror* (2006) similarly worked to explain why "it *ain't* all good in the 'hood."

The *Crypt* franchise, the inspiration for *Tales from the Hood*, even featured Blacks in *Tales from the Crypt: Demon Knight* (1995), directed by Ernest Dickerson. In the film, a Black woman, Jeryline (Jada Pinkett), rises to hero status to keep an ancient, powerful relic filled with the blood of Jesus out of the hands of the Devil. Jeryline, a thief, from Wormwood, New Mexico, survives a night of demon attacks; in no small measure with the help of Irene (C.C.H. Pounder), a self-sacrificing Black woman. Jeryline is chosen to carry on as a guardian angel because she is much like Sirach, a thief present on the night of Jesus' crucifixion who first stole the relic but upon discovering its power (to keep the Devil at bay) ended up protecting it. In the film, one of the demons seeking the artifact changes appearance to fit the context in which he is hunting. For example, when the demon arrives in New Mexico, it appears as a White male and dressed as a cowboy. As Jeryline leaves New Mexico by bus to begin her journey of dodging demons, her demon appears, and is a young Black man. The film leaves its audience to guess where the two Black warriors will go to try to blend in.

You Don't Always Get What You Pay For

Certainly money is not everything, but in film, box office sales are incredibly important and horror films featuring Blacks were attracting audiences. *Demon Knight* opened on 1,729 screens and earned $10,019,555 in its opening weekend.[25] While *Temptation*'s exact budget is unknown, and it earned a mere $54,582 in an initial, limited 11-theater release, *Temptation* received some important critical kudos, eventually earned $2,218,579 (not bad for an indie film with no theater play), and is a popular commodity for Troma.[26] By contrast, the "Black horror," comedy-tinged film *Vampire in Brooklyn* (1995) boasted a budget in excess of $14 million, was released in over 2,000 theaters, earning $7,045,379 in its opening weekend, and was panned, with Roger Ebert of the *Chicago Sun-Times* succinctly summarizing the reviews by describing the film as a "disorganized mess."[27] This in spite of the film's (White) veteran horror film director Wes Craven, who made several horror films which focus on Black characters.

For example, Craven directed *Swamp Thing* (1982), which featured a Black boy, Jude (Reggie Batts), as a reluctant helper (with a subtle, deadpan wit) to the film's co-star Alice (Adrienne Barbeau) after Alice is accidentally caught up in a murder plot. The director would again feature a Black boy, "Fool" (Brandon Adams), as savior, in the "Blacks in horror" film *The People Under the Stairs* (1991, discussed on pp. 191–193). Craven also directed the "Blacks in horror" film *The Serpent and the Rainbow* (1988, discussion on pp. 155–156), about Black Haitians, Voodoo, and the White people who want to appropriate its power of zombification.

Vampire was largely a Black affair, starring Black comedian/actor Eddie Murphy, written by members of the Murphy clan—Eddie, Charles, and Vernon Lynch, and co-produced by Ray Murphy, Jr. The film had a predominately Black cast, with Eddie Murphy even sporting some whiteface to portray a White character. The film updated *Blacula* (1972), sharing themes of a lost love and a Black vampire wreaking havoc on a Black urban community. While *Blacula* was inspired by the wave of interest in Black nationalism and connection with the African "motherland," *Vampire* absented itself from Black political movements, opting to signal its connection to Black culture through its inner-city location.

Vampire stars Murphy as Maximillian, or "Max," a "nosferatu" who is in search of "the last of his kind," a female vampire and police officer, Rita (Angela Bassett), who does not know she is "mixed-race," half-human, half-vampire. Max travels the world looking for Rita, finding her in Brooklyn, where he hopes to draw her into vampirism, and ultimately to him.

Vampire did little to challenge the notion that the urban, specifically a Black neighborhood in Brooklyn, is a dreadful place. Black Brooklyn is filthy, covered in graffiti and littered with trash. It is a slum in which gambling (numbers-running) and Italian-led gangland murders are not uncommon. The police have more than their share of crimes, and it takes several days for them to discover one of Max's victims, hanging Christ-on-the-cross-like from a bridge tower. In fact, inner-city Brooklyn is depicted as so deplorable that Max is forced to cast spells to create the illusion of a livable space for himself, thereby camouflaging the dismal, dark conditions of its tenements.

Like so many "Black horror" films, the *Vampire* narrative rises and falls on the actions of a Black woman, and this time it is Rita (Angela Bassett). In this film, Rita is a tough, resourceful cop, whose vulnerability is represented through a new twist on the tragic mulatto stereotype. Rita is a moody, sorrow-filled soul, torn between two racial worlds—the human race and the vampire "race." Already teetering emotionally, Rita is pushed further into madness by way of a love triangle forcing her to choose between her human work partner, the obviously named Justice (Allen Payne), and Max. Caught between abject boundaries of insanity and (love and vampiric) possession, Rita must figure out how to cleanse and restore herself. She fights through her abjection, first by choosing to belong to only the vampire world, hoping to rid herself of her human side, thereby bringing stability.

When Rita's racial quandary is momentarily resolved, the film turns against a White woman. In a brief scene, a monied, selfish woman (Jerry Hall), during a walk through the park, complains to a companion that her Cuban maid's sick young son is a nuisance. When Rita and Max appear, ready to feed, in a comic scene the panicked woman scrambles to explain that she is actually sympathetic to the plight of downtrodden Blacks who are victims of a racist system. The scene, though seemingly no more than a bit of comic reprieve, is important when one considers the history of Black man/monster and White female/victim dynamics in horror. Hutchings notes that while the victim is a caricature, the attack is violent all the same.[28] For Hutchings, though this is horror, the attack is a disturbing because it comes from a Black man. Its irony and comic inflections are insufficient. However, the scene also supports another key function, to secure a bit of retribution for all of those horror movies before (and since) in which White womanhood is so prized. Max's violent attack (against the nameless White woman) is a highly politicized moment of comeuppance, for example, for the nameless coachman in *I Walked with a Zombie* (1943) who silently endures a White woman's patronizing dismissals of the brutalities of slavery. Indeed, Max is a monster, but with Rita, his real lady-on-a-pedestal, present for the attack, he reminds the viewer that White women are not really as special (to Black men) as horror makes them out to be. In fact, the vast majority of Max's victims in the film are, in an interesting racial reversal, (nameless or uncredited) Whites, and their deaths largely inconsequential.

In the end, Justice arrives to play savior and, like Joel in *Temptation*, is beaten back by the monster. Rita rejects vampirism and, by donning a necklace with a cross, embraces Christian Godliness. She is the one who destroys Max, thereby saving Justice as well as herself. Together, as a couple and as police partners, Rita and Justice are just the right-living team Brooklyn needs as a new vampire is created to terrorize the inner-city.

Straight Urban Horror, No Chaser

S. Torriano Berry is a professor of film studies at Howard University in Washington, D.C. His published scholarship focuses on Black film across all genres. He has a special relationship to horror as he has spent the last decade researching and restoring the circa 1930s films of James and Eloyce Gist, which include the "Black horror" film *Hellbound Train*. He worked as cinematographer on the "Black horror" Troma film *Bugged* (1997). In the film, Black scientists (rarely seen since Dr. Jackson in *Son of Ingagi* [1940] and Dr. Pride in *Dr. Black, Mr. Hyde* [1976]) invent a formula to create a superhuman, which accidentally finds its way into a supply of bug spray. The formula transforms bugs and an all-Black, male crew of rather intelligent exterminators, dressed in uniforms sporting patches of kente cloth, into monsters. Most notably (for the purpose at hand here), Berry wrote, directed, and produced the independent "Black horror" film

The Embalmer (1996). *Embalmer* is plain ole bloody horror in which Zach (Dexter Tennie), a funeral home operator, in a fit of rage, slaughters his doting wife and children. Crazy with guilt, Zach stalks and preys on his community to secure the necessary body parts he needs to put his family back together and reanimate them (which he successfully does). The mortician gets unexpected help from his latest target, Chiffon (Jennifer Kelly), who, in a pact with this Devil, delivers the man two victims—a couple—so that she may live.

The Embalmer, though low in budget and targeting the home video market, is not at all dissimilar from horror (franchise) movies such as *Halloween*, with Michael Myers, or *A Nightmare on Elm Street*, with its Freddy Krueger, in which the monsters troll their neighborhood in search of their next victim. *Embalmer* is far from an A-list movie, and does not have the same quality cast as *Temptation*, but it is important in that it put Blacks at the center of a routine horror story. The film's star, Chiffon, is a bit like *Halloween*'s Laurie Strode in that she enjoys the company of her friends and they hers, she is an orphan, and there is a mad man stalking her. More, like Laurie, Chiffon is a resourceful, quick-thinking "Final Girl" who takes on the monster, using her wits rather than knives, and assures her own survival. She allows the scientist to bring an end to his hunt for victims by delivering the last two bodies that he needs in the form of her abusive adoptive parents. More, with her parents attempting to adopt a new child to abuse, Chiffon is a hero, protecting her community from predators. As such, Chiffon also becomes an Enduring Woman; understanding that monsters can assume any form, she turns resilient, helping one monster to eliminate two. The community that Chiffon ultimately protects, Washington, D.C., is presented quite differently from other depictions of D.C.'s Black neighborhoods. This Black D.C. is home to gorgeous architecture, clean streets, and homeowners. The funeral home, which is in disrepair, stands out as an eyesore. The home is so anomalous that an explanation is explicitly offered in the film as to why it has not yet been demolished, thereby restoring the wholeness of the neighborhood—it was part of the underground railroad and it holds historical significance. Importantly, the funeral home itself is noteworthy for its absence of squatters or criminals, or trash and graffiti blighting its interior. This is a dramatically different representation of abandoned property to that presented in films such as *Vampire* and *Candyman*, which depict such structures as filthy and squalid, hence implicating the surrounding neighborhood as enabling urban blight.

Home Is Where the Heart Is: Out of the Urban

Spirit Lost (1997), like *Embalmer*, was no blockbuster. However, it was the rare horror film that was nearly an all-female affair. *Spirit Lost* is based on a book of the same title by Nancy Thayer. In the book, wife and husband Willy and John leave the bustling life of Boston to live quietly in an old home in Nantucket. Their peace is disturbed when a sexy female ghost seduces John. The screenplay was written by Joyce Lewis, who changed the New England location to Catch Hook Island, presumably much farther south. The independent straight-to-video "Black horror" film was directed by Neema Barnette, the rare (Black) female horror film director, who has an extensive television-directing portfolio. *Spirit* is interesting in that it moves "Black horror" out of the urban to the seaside while recuperating out-of-the-Caribbean Voodoo myths. In the film, Willy (Regina Taylor) desperately wants a baby but is unable to get pregnant until she and her husband John (Leon) arrive at the peaceful, racially diverse Catch Hook Island. There, Willy encounters a range of helpful women—a White antique shop owner, her Black customers, a White doctor, and Vera (Juanita Jennings), a Black Jamaican who immediately senses Willy and John's house is haunted and talks to the ghost in it. *Spirit* is a love story about a slave, Arabella (Cynda Williams), who 200 years earlier was won in a poker game by a slave trader and sea captain, John Wright (Christopher Northrup). Wright promises to marry Arabella, even building her the house that Willy and John, generations later, move into. However, Wright leaves Arabella to "marry a proper English woman." Heartbroken, Arabella haunts the home waiting for her John to return. She terrorizes Willy, causing her to lose their baby, and, confusing Willy's John for her own, seduces him while driving him insane. Most interesting, Arabella is sent to her (peaceful) death by Vera and two helpers performing a Black religious ceremony. Vera fights her way into the house along with two priestesses[29] who want to remove the "lost soul." The women present themselves as pure in their motives and in their religiosity, even dressing in white and covering their hair in a white head wrap. The three perform a ritual (to the soundtrack of a single, steady drumbeat), cleansing John by rubbing salt on his hands and splashing blessed water over him; they then blow tobacco smoke into the air to see Arabella. Finally, they assemble an altar with clean water and white candles at its center, praying over it. Arabella disappears. It is Black religion that saves this Black couple.

The Midas Touch

"Black horror" took on epic proportions when, in 1998, the genre was touched by Oprah Winfrey with her film *Beloved*. The rare "Black horror" film with a Black literary origin, *Beloved*, was based on a novel by Nobel and Pulitzer Prize winner Toni Morrison. The film's screenplay was written by the Black actress Akosua Busia, and co-produced by Winfrey's Harpo Films. The film featured a predominantly Black, award-winning, all-star cast lead by Winfrey herself. Its director was Jonathan Demme, a White director, who won an Oscar for his horror film *The Silence of the Lambs* (1991). Together, *Vampire in Brooklyn* and *Beloved* serve to remind one of the cultural contributions a film can make to discussions of Blackness, even if it is not entirely made by Blacks. Both films have White directors, but are "Black horror" films in their attention to Blackness. As Yearwood observes, there is no hard and fast rule on the tacit feel of a Black film, just that Black audiences are able to discern the difference.³⁰ In *Beloved*, the wicked she-ghost turns out to be the victim. The killer turns out to be a protector. The pedophile turns out to be a casuality of the ghost and the committed lover of the killer. And the real evil turns out to be slavery. Scott writes, "the narrative of the story (with its hauntings, its living dead, its air of mystery, its sickening violence, and its exorcism) is itself horrific enough to substantiate its connection to the horror genre."³¹ The whole thing plays out in a house in which things (and even a dog) fly around, crash and break. But as Anissa J. Wardi notes, *Beloved* was not supposed to be a nineteenth century *Poltergeist*. Indeed, the translation of the novel to the big screen, in the hands of a horror-film director, "reduced the complexity of the text, creating in its stead nothing short of spectacle."³²

The film opens in 1865, the year slavery is abolished through the 13th amendment to the U.S. Constitution, in the modest home of Sethe (Oprah Winfrey), on the outskirts of Cincinnati, Ohio. In the home live Sethe as well as her mother-in-law, Baby Suggs/Grandma Baby (Beah Richards), an elderly bedridden woman, who is living in the home and who has turned the home over to Sethe. Sethe has three children, a young daughter, Denver (Kimberly Elise), and two teen-aged sons, Howard (Emil Pinnock) and Buglar (Calen Johnson). A ghost is laying waste to everything it can get its hands on. Howard and Buglar flee the home, never to return. The film moves eight years ahead, with Baby Suggs dead and Denver a young woman. An old friend, Paul D (Danny Glover) arrives to reacquaint himself with Sethe and they become lovers. The two share a gruesome history of being enslaved on a Kentucky plantation called Sweet Home, owned by a sadistic slave owner called Schoolteacher (Jude Ciccolella).

In response to the arrival of Paul D (who immediately understands the home to be haunted) the unseen apparition takes on physical human form, arriving as Beloved (Thandi Newton) to compete for the attention and affections of Sethe. Beloved is an infant in a young woman's body. Beloved can barely speak, opting to growl until she is taught how to mumble a few words. She drools, bobs her head, and staggers about on legs she has just discovered. Her newness is marked by the soft, delicate skin on her (unused) feet. She knows no modesty. The longer Beloved stays, the deeper Sethe falls into madness in an obsessive preoc-cupation over Beloved that neither Paul D nor her daughter Denver can drag her out of. The ghost is equally obsessive about Sethe, and works to alienate her from those who love her. Beloved tempts Paul D, and he succumbs, having sex with her. Not long after, Paul D leaves Sethe's home. As Beloved uses up all of the love and resources Sethe has, the young Denver is left to her own devices and seeks work to support herself and her family by leaving home and securing work in the city.

The plot centers on Beloved's identity, and why she has come to haunt Sethe. Their connection is revealed during a flashback. While a slave and advanced in pregnancy, Sethe was raped by her enslaver and his sons. She and her husband Halle (Hill Harper) plot their escape from Sweet Home, aiming for the home of his mother Baby Suggs, an elderly freed slave. They send their children ahead, but Halle is unable to get away, leaving Seth to seek out freedom without him. Not long after she arrives at Baby Suggs, slave catchers arrive to reclaim Sethe and her children. Rather than see them returned to such brutality, she decides to take her children's lives. Sethe is able to cut the throat of her baby, Beloved, before being stopped. At the sight of her with the infant and an old hacksaw, the slave catchers leave her, believing Sethe is too insane to take back. Beloved, then, is the physical manifestation of conjoined cruelties: the first is Sethe's act, for which Beloved returns to portray Sethe's guilt; the second, the cruelty of slavery which led to the infanticide in the first place. *Beloved* asks who is to carry the responsibility and memory of the cruel institution.

Ellen Scott, in her essay *The Horrors of Remembrance*, observes that the film recovers a narrative of emotional, physical, and political pain that is effectively erased in most other popular treatments of slavery:

> *Beloved* begins to enunciate a profound and difficult question, one repressed by traditional representations of slavery and one which is

FIGURE 7.2 Sethe and Beloved in *Beloved*
Touchstone Pictures/Photofest

particularly important to African Americans in the post–Civil Rights, post–Black power era: what (moment, place, feeling) defines freedom for African Americans?[33]

The film challenges its audience to consider what it means to declare the legacy of slavery as having come to an end, particularly if one can claim historical distance from holding slaves. *Beloved* shows that the destruction (end) of the monster that is slavery does not mean freedom, or, as Scott argues, healing. *Beloved*'s real contribution, given the history of the horror genre, is its poignant attention to the effects of slavery. Horror had long been built on colonial fantasies of Black servitude in which Whites were simply, heroically negotiating their White man's burden, dragging Blacks along into civilization. Because horror obsessively focused on Voodoo and other out-of-Africa/Caribbean "savage" rituals threatening European and American Whites, the films invoked a distorted history of slavery while glossing over its effects. More, by adding the myth of zombism, slavery was denied, replaced with wishes of unthinking, silent, obedient automatons who labor tirelessly. *Beloved* put the brakes on such delusions, forcing horror audiences to see if they could stand real atrocities while restoring Black history.

The film reaches its climax when, as Sethe slips deeper into a mental breakdown, a large group of women—"the Thirty Women," as they are called in the film's credits—arrive at her home, Bibles and crosses in hand, to pray over her. They are there on behalf of Denver, who is breaking down under the weight of her home life. The women become Denver's extended family, feeding her and helping her find work, hence a community of kin stepping in to help. The film does not stray from invoking the power of kinship as well as a prayer circle, notably led by women. In *Temptation*, it was only Joel and Grandma united in prayer, and *Spirit* brought in three priestesses. *Beloved* called upon 30. Praying and singing, the women hold their ground even as Beloved emerges from the home, in the bright light of day and in full view of the gathering crowd, completely nude and very pregnant. Her immodesty and oozing appearance (she is both sweaty from the heat and drooling) are met with shock, moving the women to pray harder. Beloved disappears under the pressure of prayer as well as at the psychological moment in which Sethe comes to the realization that she took the hacksaw to the wrong person—she should have tried to take out the slave catchers, not her baby.

This final view of Beloved, the revealing of her body, the presentation of her pubic hair, coupled with earlier views of her vomiting, soiling her bed, and her animalistic hunger, makes Beloved not just monstrous but an exotic, grotesque, freak.[34] The trouble here is that in the novel Morrison does not write Beloved as monster or freak but as a metaphor for history, memory, and trauma. Morrison's story is neither horror nor spectacle.

They're Baaaack! Monsters in the 'Hood

Predator 2 (1990), a "Blacks in horror," film did double damage, casting the inner-city as a despicable, crime-ridden, hyper-violent place, while also resurrecting old stereotypes of Black terrains as savage lands, places one enters to hunt, kill, and conquer. In this bloody "coming of age tale," the monster Predator is tasked by his elders with proving himself an undefeatable, intergalactic warrior by laying waste to the toughest, most loathsome creatures in the cosmos.[35] In the film, the Predator locates his challenge on Earth, in a hyper-violent Jamaican drug "posse" who emerge from their disgusting inner-city alleys to run wild through steamy Los Angeles. It is explained in the film that the Predator is indeed on safari; his prey is described in animal terms: "Lions, and tigers, and bears, oh my!" The film's strategy is, first, to reveal how brutal the posse is, to show that they are the right kind of challenging sport for the Predator. In the first glimpse of the posse, the Jamaican's have the upper hand over their rivals, the Colombians. The Colombian leader is seen hanging upside down by his ankles from the ceiling of his apartment. With him stripped of his clothing, the Jamaican posse is preparing to skin him alive. Though the posse appear to be the toughest things going, the film adds to their dreadful mystique that they also practice a wicked form of Voodoo, thereby making them appear all the more outside the bounds of civility. This scene of the warring posses exploits foreignness, as the men have thick accents as if newly arrived from their countries to wreak havoc in the US. The confrontation turns blood-drenched when a third, otherworldly illegal immigrant (alien) arrives; his accent is a growl. The Jamaicans and the Predator are depicted as mirror images of each other. Both are armed with knives and firearms, both hang their prey upside down to skin them, and both have the same appearance, sporting ropes of dreadlocked hair. Clearly, they are made to battle.

Eventually the Predator engages in a showdown with the posse's fearsome leader, King Willie (Calvin Lockhart), and the two are again aligned imagistically from their hair, to their spears, and even to their accessories of bones. The two monsters meet in the deepest, most isolated regions of the inner-city in a dank, dark, garbage-strewn alley. Though the Predator kills throughout the movie, it is the death of the Jamaican leader, in his own territory, that works to evidence the Predator's power. In a single, quick move, the Predator reaches inside of the leader's body, ripping his spine and head from the body. The result is a gruesome trophy—the head of the leader, with his face frozen in a horrifying scream, dangling from his exposed spine. Hence, the Predator has conquered Willie's 'hood.

Notably, *Predator 2* stars Black actor Danny Glover as the resourceful, though hotheaded cop Lt. Mike Harrigan. Harrigan is introduced by way of his personnel file that lists dozens of police brutality complaints. He is the rogue cop that, in other films, is depicted as a terror to the inner-city. In this film, he is heroic for his policing tactics. This film, then, becomes a three-way battle between Black drug lords, a Black cop, and an alien who resembles Blacks. Harrigan pursues the monster relentlessly, and with the inner-city as his (literal) stomping ground, he is able to maneuver capably over its terrain. Harrigan proves to be the Predator's biggest challenge and the film ends with the monster meeting its demise at his hands. The film's final scenes are to be seen as mildly comical, but function to be racially painful. As the aliens take off in their ships, Harrigan is covered in the soot of their exhaust, whitening him. His white-skin/wide-eyed appearance recalls Earnest "Sammy Sunshine" Morrison in *Haunted Spooks* (1920), with the spooked child dipped in flour.

Candyman, Candyman, Candyman, Candyman, Candyman

> What does it mean when the genre violates conventions by locating violence in the city where it is most expected, and furthermore plays openly on prevailing cultural anxieties by marking the monster as a racial Other?
>
> —Pinedo (112–113)[36]

The 1992 Bernard Rose "Blacks in horror" film (Clive Barker's) *Candyman* continues to exploit fears of the inner-city, making a fearsome housing project home to gang violence, filth, and a most violent monster.[37] The film centers on Daniel "Candyman" Robitaille, the son of a former slave. Robitaille's father made his fortune after inventing a device enabling the mass production of shoes. As a result, Robitaille attended the best schools, where he learned to become an accomplished artist. Robitaille is sophisticated, elegant, educated, and cultured. In 1890, he is commissioned by a wealthy White Illinois landowner to paint his daughter's portrait. The two fall in love, and she becomes pregnant. Outraged at the interracial love affair, the woman's father mounts a lynch party, whose members pursue Robitaille. Catching him, they exact the most gruesome of tortures. They saw off his right hand with a rusty saw blade. Stripped naked, his body is smeared with honey from a nearby honeycomb, and Robitaille is then stung to death by hundreds of angry bees. He is then burned and his ashes scattered over what is the modern location of the Cabrini-Green housing project. A century later, the Candyman story rises to mythic proportions, particularly among Blacks, and spawns a popular urban legend: peering into a mirror while calling the name Candyman five times will summon Robitaille as the vengeful Candyman monster who will rip you with his hook of a hand from groin to gullet. Graduate students Helen (Virginia Madsen), a White woman, and her friend Bernadette (Kasi Lemmons), a Black woman, are researching urban legends, and make (or safari) their way to Cabrini-Green to investigate rumors that the monster holds the housing project hostage. Their visit to the complex sets the racial tone of the film. Cabrini is overrun with gang violence. Bernadette is petrified as they enter the towering apartment complex, which is controlled by

Black male gang members, and is strewn with filth—from litter to feces, as well as being covered in graffiti. Helen is confident, guiding Bernadette by the hand through the project's maze in search of the information she needs. They encounter the rare Black woman in the building, Anne-Marie (Vanessa Williams), a young single parent with a newborn and a large guard dog. Anne-Marie repeatedly refers to Helen and Bernadette, who is Black, as "White folks" while accusing them of snooping around a Black space they presume is deficient and worthy of yet another exploitative story. The two women are Whitened through class positioning and education level by Anne-Marie, who views such status as the root of Black exploitation.

Here, the film addresses the kinds of racisms Blacks experience head on. It makes clear that Robitaille was lynched out of racism. Through Cabrini residents call for police protection, the film makes explicit that when Helen returns to the project alone and is (of course) attacked, the police rush to her rescue, because she is White. It even notes that Helen lives in a building that is Cabrini's twin, but on the wealthy side of town, and her spendy condo apartments merited the construction of a highway to separate them from Cabrini. To re-conjoin the two locations, Helen's city and Anne-Marie's inner-city, *Candyman* turns to the "ever-elastic paradigm of the detective story, with its gumshoe on the prowl, here rooting out the clues contained in [inner-]city lore."[38] The problem remains, however, that both locations are talked about and viewed in the film through a lens of Whiteness.

Though Helen's questions about whether Candyman is real challenge his myth and, hence, his fearful control, he does not kill her (even as she calls his name five times, summoning him). Rather, he punishes Blacks, first by beheading Anne-Marie's dog, and then by kidnapping her infant son, Anthony (Lanesha Martin/Latesha Martin). As for Helen, he courts her, hypnotizing her, asking her to join him—"be my victim"—he loves her. As Helen continues to disrupt Candyman's world, he continues to give Helen a pass. There are many other Whites to whom Candyman gives a pass to as well. He does not enter Helen's building to, for example, take out his beloved Helen's cheating husband, Trevor (Xander Berkeley). Rather, he breaks in to kill the visiting Bernadette and leaves. Even the location of his actual murder (not where his ashes were blown to) is well within reach. Still, Candyman is not looking for real revenge, he is looking for love … but not from Black women. He only wants to kill them.

Candyman is to be viewed as a tragic, wounded monster, perhaps *Frankenstein*-esque in that he was created, made by folks far more terrible than he is. However, the film strays from the monster-with-a-heart-of-gold theme by playing on fears of the big Black boogeyman coming in and taking away a White woman. The film's producer, Alan Poul, acknowledges the filmmakers "were using a very loaded imagery," such as that seen in *The Birth of a Nation*, by showing a Black monster trying hard to seduce a White woman, even as they worked hard

FIGURE 7.3 Candyman invites, "be my victim," in *Candyman*
Tri-Star/Photofest

not to "exploit the same kinds of stereotype views."[39] Candyman is not the monster to fall in love with. He is no charming vampire. Indeed, when Candyman and Helen (who is only partially conscious) finally have a consummating kiss, the moment of miscegenation is punished as "bees stream from his mouth. Thus ... horror operates here to undermine the acceptability of interracial romance."[40]

In the end, this is a movie about celebrating White womanhood. Helen rejects Candyman's love and vengefully Candyman is prepared to add another Black victim to his belt—the infant Anthony, burning him alive in a garbage heap. But Helen saves the boy, sacrificing her life to do so. While Helen is blamed for the deaths, the Black community is depicted as knowing better. At Helen's funeral, attended by five Whites, including Trevor and his new girlfriend and a professor who antagonized Helen, there is little mourning until a large procession of Blacks, led by Anne-Marie, parade in from Cabrini. They have found Candyman's hook and bury it with Helen, while mourning her death. In the end, Candyman disappears along with the history of racism he brings. It is all about Helen as she becomes monstrous. As a White woman she can do what

Candyman would not: terrorize those on the other side of the tracks. She is a woman scorned, exacting her revenge on Trevor.[41]

The 'Hood Comes to the Suburbs

The People Under the Stairs (1991) was the rare horror film of this period in which the 'hood and the suburbs stood in confrontation against each other ... with the 'hood proving victorious—though at great cost. In this Wes Craven "Blacks in horror," film a wealthy, White suburban couple, "Mom" and "Dad" (Wendi Robie and Everett McGill), are slumlords living in a cavernous mansion home packed with money and other loot (e.g. trunks of gold coins and silver). Three Black thieves intrude on Mom and Dad's suburban home, a location marked by their ability to "smell" but not see "the ghetto from here." There is Spenser (Jeremy Roberts), a White man and career thief, Leroy (Ving Rhames), a Black man, who is a thief as well as a pimp, and the unfortunately named Black boy "Fool" (Brandon Adams), whose sister, a tarot card reader/prostitute, is being pimped by Leroy. For the men, the goal is simple robbery. Fool's motivation is Robin Hood altruism. He hopes to rob from the rich to give to his poor sister, her babies, and his cancer-stricken mother who can't afford medical care *and* is facing eviction from their decrepit slum apartment (owned by Mom and Dad). Fool and his family happen to be standing in the way of Mom and Dad turning their building into luxury condos.

Mom and Dad, living as husband and wife, are actually in an incestuous relationship; they are brother and sister. While the 'hood is depicted as home to the criminal element and the poor, the suburbs are shown as being the ideal place for providing cover to the truly grotesque and wicked. Piling on to their sexual deviance, the pair are depicted as sadomasochists, and it is implied that Dad molests little girls. More, the couple have abducted dozens of White children in their search for the perfect child. When a child disappoints the pair, they invoke a hear, see, or speak no evil rule by cutting out the child's tongue, eyes, or ears, feeding the parts to the family's dog. They then discard the children, filthy and starving, into the basement, hence "the people under the stairs." The couple, then, represent a bundle of horrible taboos: (1) food (forced cannibalism); (2) death (they murder the two thieves); and (3) incest (among themselves and with their "daughters").[42] Central to the narrative of their taboos is that these are horrors easily hidden behind wealth and Whiteness; two positions of power which mean one would seldom be suspected of, or can get a pass for, evil.

After the men are killed in booby-traps while trying to rob the home, Fool becomes trapped inside. He discovers an abducted White girl, Alice (A.J. Langer), who helps him hide from the couple, and in return he becomes focused on saving her. Mom and Dad's concern is that a Black man has entered their lair—a "filthy" boy who might defile a white girl—he does not, but he is guilty of entering the boudoir and for that Dad announces, "It won't be his ear I cut off!" After several dramatic brushes with death, Fool gets away from the house but is forced to leave Alice behind. Fool phones the police to save the girl, but the officers, glancing around, judge the neighborhood, the home, and Mom and Dad as symbols of normalcy. As such, the movie highlights that White deficiency, because it is not expected, is difficult to see and never presumed.

Jeffrey Dahmer: Serial Killer, Zombie Maker, Presumed Safe White Man

The People Under the Stairs, released in theaters four months after the July 1991 arrest of serial killer Jeffrey Dahmer, anticipated the kinds of social passes Whites receive. Dahmer lived and hunted for his victims in a Milwaukee, Wisconsin inner-city neighborhood, home to a diverse, lower socioeconomic community of non-Whites (e.g. Blacks and Laotians). Two Black women spotted their 14-year-old neighbor Konerak Sinthasomphone drugged, beaten, and nude, staggering in the street. The women phoned police, who arrived on the scene just as Dahmer, already a convicted sex offender, arrived on the scene to reclaim the boy. Dahmer, a White male, was reported as presenting himself calmly and rationally to the White officers. He explained that Konerak was really his young adult lover and that they had quarreled, and Dahmer was there to take his boyfriend home. The women protested the story and even tried to prevent Dahmer from retaking the boy. The officers reported that the women somehow just did not seem credible, and personally escorted Sinthasomphone back to Dahmer's home. They failed to check Dahmer's identification, which would have revealed his violent past, and, importantly, dismissed the odor of rotting bodies coming from his apartment. Dahmer himself, after all, appeared so respectable. After the police left, Dahmer killed, dismembered, and partially consumed the boy—making him one of at least 17 known victims. The women's follow-up calls to police about the boy, who was soon after reported missing by his family, were brusquely dismissed, and their calls to the FBI ignored. Later, the scenario was repeated when a Black man, Tracy Edwards, fought off and escaped Dahmer while the killer was trying to handcuff him. Battered and with cuffs dangling from his wrist, Edwards flagged down authorities, leading them back to Dahmer's apartment. Again, Dahmer presented himself respectably and the police prepared to leave, when Edwards pointed out to the officers pictures of real, mutilated bodies strewn about Dahmer's apartment as well as the knife Dahmer threatened him with. And then there were the body parts on display and in the fridge … and of course the smell.[43] A successful lawsuit filed against the city by Sinthasomphone's family argued that police had to go to great racist and homophobic lengths to fail to see Dahmer as the monster that he was. As for Dahmer, he explained that he was taking the men, drugging and raping them, before drilling holes into their frontal lobes and pouring in chemicals to create silent, zombie (sex) slaves. When his victims died, he would variously keep their body parts around, engage in necrophilia, or eat them. His escapades were later turned into a novel called *Zombie* by Joyce Oates.[44]

The People Under the Stairs aligned with the real-life case of Dahmer in revealing White privilege, Black oppression, and a range of taboos. The film also offered the reminder that children could be victimized and that they could not always be protected. "No longer," writes Crane, "would the young be treated delicately, snatched out to safety by loving arms before something awful could transpire ... The guiltless child in peril offered a grim lesson: relative innocence is no blessing. The pure will inadvertently suffer along with those who might seem more deserving of punishment."[45] While "bad seeds," over-sexed teens, and demon-possessed girls had a terrible time in non-Black horror, "Black horror" films tended to avoid the regular destruction of its innocent youth. This film takes the middle ground; when the police fail to act, Fool turns heroic savior, breaking into the home again, alone, to do battle with Mom and Dad and to save Alice. He also ends up freeing the remaining surviving children and putting the hidden, ill-gotten wealth into the hands of his community.

Black Urban Superheroes: Emotional Wrecks

Spawn's (1997) Al Simmons (Michael Jai White), a Black military assassin, would seek the protective cover of the inner-city after he is killed and resurrected as Hell Spawn, or Spawn for short. Based on the popular Todd McFarlane comic book of the same title, *Spawn* tells the story of Simmons, a Marine and deadly mercenary working for a covert government agency. Jason Wynn (Martin Sheen), Simmons' boss, has made a pact with the Devil, and on the Devil's request Wynn kills Simmons, burning him alive. The Devil wants Simmons to lead an army of wicked souls to take over Heaven for the start of Armageddon. Promptly sent to Hell, Simmons becomes Spawn and is invited to make his own Faustian deal: he can return to Earth, and even see his wife and child, if he leads Hell's Army.

Spawn is much like Candyman, returning to Earth desperate for those he loved and who once loved him. However, he discovers that a true reunion with his suburban family is impossible. In his first attempt to connect with his family, he appears outside of their cheery, white picket-fenced home. However, Spawn is now an overly blackened body and his burned, monstrous appearance makes it impossible for him to move about the neighborhood. Observing his former home from a thicket of bushes in the backyard, Spawn discovers that five years have passed and his Black wife, Wanda (Theresa Randle), has remarried, taking as her husband his White best friend, Terry (D.B. Sweeney). Their suburban family life comes to represent happiness, an absence of class and race divides, and a lack of hostility. Indeed, Terry is not a warrior, but forthright advisor. Spawn is unhappy, destitute, and enveloped in evil and violence. Hence, Spawn retreats from the suburbs, seeking refuge deep inside the inner-city's filthy, forgotten back alleys—"Rat City." He lives miserably, much like Candyman, among the drunken homeless, those suffering from mental illness, rats, and seeping garbage. In the end, Spawn is able to save his family, his old friend Terry, and Earth, by keeping the Devil at bay. Though Spawn's true identity is made known to his loved ones and he has saved the world, he still cannot dwell in their world. The inner-city is where his kind are segregated and invisible.[46]

Urban Day Walker

Blade (1998), a "Blacks in horror" film based on the Marvel Comics character of the same name, like *Vampire in Brooklyn*, took up the tragic mulatto theme, but by tripling the threat: half-human, half-vampire, not quite Black. The Black vampire, Blade (Wesley Snipes), is a brooding, vengeful vampire seeking retribution against the race of monsters who made him. In the film, through flashback, it is revealed that Blade's mother, Vanessa (Sanaa Lathan), was attacked and bitten by a vampire while pregnant with Blade. Though not directly bitten, Blade was infected with vampirism in utero. He was delivered from his dying mother, emerging half-human, half-vampire, making him a one-of-a-kind specimen. He is a "day walker," or immune to the destroying power of the sun, and garlic does not affect him. He is powerfully strong, filled with hate for his vampire kind, and constantly at war with his thirst for blood.

In the film, in the present day some 30 years later, in what is to be a particularly heart-wrenching scene for Blade, he discovers his odd, parentless life—seemingly Vanessa was to be a single parent—was a lie. Vanessa did not fully die during his birth but returned as a vampire, choosing to pursue a life among vampires rather than with her son. More, not only is the man she is coupled up with, Deacon Frost (Stephen Dorff), a (very) White man and Blade's principal adversary, but it is Frost who cruelly, mockingly reveals the secret behind Blade's identity—Frost is, in essence, Blade's White "father," having been the one who turned him vampiric, thereby replacing Blade's unseen Black father.

Though Blade is an adult, the film asks that audience grieve for this motherless child, an unnatural infant who becomes a sympathetic victim as a result of a denial of parental love and authority, and whose "special powers are justifiably provoked," while his rage becomes understood.[47] Blade quickly moves from callous killer, to anti-hero, to superhero when his history becomes part of his motivations. Vanessa, not Blade, is depicted as the one who is truly mixed up and monstrous. An ageless, beautiful woman about Blade's age, she caresses her son seductively, her lips brushing against his as she sets him up for death. She again sacrifices her son for Frost. When Blade survives and kills his mother, she is made to suffer for her monstrosity and his racial tragedies.

Through the film *Blade* comes the rare depiction of the poisonous, consuming Black mother. However, Blade finds her replacement in Whistler (Kris Kristofferson), his White surrogate father, with whom he fights side-by-side in a war against vampires. Perhaps the relationship between Blade and Whistler "suggest[s] a servile relation to White paternalism"; however, the film does not exploit such a connection in ways that the genre has in the past, through, for example, the loyal sidekick/servant.[48] Rather, the film depicts a complex relationship of mutual friendship and love, first born out of tragedy and goals of revenge (Whistler's family was killed by vampires), ultimately evolving into years of isolated life together.

Blade denies any further exploration into the men's years of professional and domestic partnership, opting to color Blade with traditional hypersexual, hypermasculine stereotypes. For example, Blade is brought back from the brink of death by Dr. Karen Jenson (N'Bushe Wright)—a Black, female hematologist, who must allow Blade to suck her blood if he is to survive. The scene of Blade "taking" Jenson is a violent, extraordinarily erotic display as Blade becomes engorged, and when fulfilled produces a reverberating, orgasmic yell.

Blade, like *Vampire in Brooklyn*'s Max, has no such encounter with men. Max turns men by dropping a bit of blood onto their tongues, with the film explicitly noting that he "ain't got to pull that Blacula shit." While Max does turn his victims, turning them into ghouls, he does not do so Blacula-style with a bite to a man's neck or any other body part. Max reserves that kind of close encounter only for women, as does Blade. Blade and Max function to remind the viewer of the "lasciviousness of female sexual desire," as well as of their ability, as purportedly only men can, to fulfill that desire while conflating "sexuality and apocalypse."[49] However, such a conflation is not confined to the vampire, as male monsters (e.g. Candyman) are frequently masculinized by promising women a sexual encounter so out of this world it sends them to the afterlife—the ultimate rough sex/rape, sadomasochistic fantasy.

In the end, Blade, like Spawn, would keep a watchful eye over the human race, not letting the monsters win. Together they are the über-police; the kind of social regulators one could expect to patrol hostile environments. Hell demons and vampires are not the purview of typical saviors; rather, they are a job for monsters, willing to police their own kind. The two superheroes gave new meaning to Black-on-black (evil) crime. In the case of *Blade*, the portrayal was extraordinarily popular. *Blade* was ranked #1 in its opening weekend, earning $17,073,856 and going on to earn over $70 million domestically. The film would spawn two more films.[50]

Conclusion: Horror Is the New Black

After 100 years of uneven participation in the horror genre, Black was back in the 1990s, playing a central role in producing its chills and thrills. Black was everywhere—in "Black horror" and "Blacks in horror" films, in independent films and Hollywood films, in high-budget blockbuster features and low-budget straight-to-video efforts. Black characters such as Blade and Spawn were "superhero" monsters, ripped from the pages of comic books and turned into lucrative franchises. Black evil corrupting White women was seen before, but in *Candyman* audiences were actually asked to side with the monster, rooting for the beast to enter the boudoir and convince a White woman to be his victim. It did not seem to matter that Candyman suffered as a result of sleeping with a White woman in the first place.[51] Importantly, Blacks not only did not die first in horror, often they did not die at all or they did the killing.

Blacks stormed the suburbs and (White) monsters wandered back into the urban as well. In 1995, the film franchise *Children of the Corn* left rural Nebraska's farmland, and took up residence in Chicago. In *Children of the Corn III: Urban Harvest*, the kids and their scythes laid ruin to those hanging around an abandoned inner-city industrial park. The corn worshiping kids should not be conflated with those Whites who made their way back out of the suburbs. Rather, these kids are rural Whites, the "disregarded"[52] or lowest classes, presenting a wholly aberrant, monstrous clan or family located in the Black-free countryside.

Likewise, the inner-city would virtually resurrect the *Leprechaun* film series, with the mythical Irish monster in *Leprechaun in the Hood* (2000) looking for his charmed flute in the 'hood among gun-toting wannabe rappers, which he destroys in a most gruesome way. The whole thing went so well that the Leprechaun returned for *Leprechaun: Back 2 tha Hood* (2003) to smoke weed and snatch gold teeth.

Overall, Black participation in the 1990 horror cycle was increasingly ubiquitous. The horror genre itself was showing signs of turning stale, such as the coming trend of rehashing films (e.g. *Night of the Living Dead* [1968], *Night of the Living Dead* [1990], *Night of the Living Dead 3D* [2006]). For Blacks, the horror genre was still fresh. Market and technological changes opened up new spaces for representational intervention. The straight-to-video market gave rise to the habitual viewer—one who would rent a stack of movies at a time, some specifically desired, most randomly selected. Horror was again faced with the proposition of meeting the need, and in a repeat of the 1940s and 1970s all manner of "Black horror" went into quick, cheap production. The films were not all new, as the video industry was looting entire back catalogs, shoehorning hundreds of films into the bursting market.[53] There would be much for audiences to choose from as access to digital technologies (from cameras to software) made filmmaking—albeit presenting a wide range in skill and quality—accessible in ways unimagined just a few years earlier.

The crush of films, offered by professionals and up-and-comers alike, means that with the arrival of the twenty-first century, no longer can one easily list the films Blacks appear in. Still racial and spatial divides remain. Keeping Blacks largely confined to the 'hood meant that horror presented a Black aesthetic to match. Horror and hip hop have become intrinsically intertwined, and thanks to the likes of rapper Snoop Dogg and his many contributions to horror films the genre reflects that cultural influence. Today the horror titles do their best to signal their relationship to hip hop, often by disrupting traditional spelling to reflect hip hop's style of deconstructive language: *Zombiez* (2005), *Vampiyaz* (2004), *Bloodz v. Wolvez* (2006), *Kracker Jack'd* (2003).

"Black horror," which is now so prevalent, is not without its serious flaws. There is plenty of exploitative garbage, and films such as *Chop Shop* (2007), with its half-dozen vile scenes of rape against the same woman (and with no real plot purpose), show that the films are not always revolutionary and are susceptible to the same problems which could plague any other film.

One can only wait and see if Blacks' participation in horror will continue to thrive, and evolve, or devolve and possibly self-destruct.

CONCLUSION

Catching Some Zzzzzs—Blackz and Horror in the Twenty-First Century

They claim we're products from the bottom of hell 'cause the Black is back and it's bound to sell.

—Public Enemy[1]

The twentieth century ended on a high note for horror. The Academy Awards, which did not typically recognize the importance of such films, centered attention on the genre when movies such as *The Sixth Sense* (1999) earned six Academy Award nominations and when *The Silence of the Lambs* (1991) actually swept the top awards, including the Best Picture Academy Award. All eyes were on the genre. An obvious question followed: what new heights would the genre reach? For example, could Academy Award winner Halle Berry bring her star power to horror with the "Blacks in horror" film *Gothika* (2003), about a woman and a ghost teaming up to expose sexual sadists murdering young girls? Or, in the tradition of *The Blair Witch Project* (1999), could the "Blacks in horror" film *Snakes on a Plane* (2006), starring Samuel L. Jackson, drum up enough internet buzz to make it a break-out hit?[2] Thus far, the twenty-first century is providing a fairly clear answer about its next move: the horror genre is not reaching for the new; instead it is digging back through past horror catalogues to present old horror warmed over. Rather than continue the trend of innovation, new millennium filmmakers are in remake mode. For example, John Carpenter's horror classic *Halloween* (1978) has been "reimagined" into Rob Zombie's *Halloween* (2007). Other horror films have not even received the reimagining treatment; they have simply been remade: 1972's *The Last House on the Left* was remade in 2009, 1974's *The Texas Chainsaw Massacre* was remade in 2003, 1976's *The Omen* was remade in 2006, 1978's *Dawn of the Dead* was remade in 2004, and 1977's *The Hills*

Have Eyes was remade in 2006.[3] Critics are complaining of a "horror glut" (for example, 39 horror films were in production in 2007) as film studios are rapidly churning out rehashed horror.[4]

While all film genres are prone to some measure of duplication, in horror the practice seems to be "a more pronounced and extreme feature than it is elsewhere."[5] Film studios have long asserted that there is a method behind the madness. Those who were just old enough to see the original horror films are now in their forties and fifties, and generally too mature for new fright fare. According to Fischoff et al., audiences 25 years and younger appreciate violence and special effects-heavy, plot-light fare. Older audiences tend to remain in an "aesthetic time capsule," evidencing a preference for their earlier cinema experiences.[6] In short, the remakes are for the next generation of film-goers. Simply re-releasing original, classic horror films cannot cut it, as this new generation, has grown up on a healthy, modern diet of violent media.[7] The coming cycle of horror films have to negotiate three issues—targeting a youth market, performing in a media market in which violence is already ubiquitous, and competing with the popularity of (violent) video games. Horror makers have responded to this trend by testing early cuts of their coming movies on pre-teens. For example, parts of the horror film *I Know What You Did Last Summer* (1997) were tested on children as young as nine.[8] However, out of this research by filmmakers comes an important understanding: horror must step up its game to compete with the "hyper-real violence"[9] horror-themed video games such as *Resident Evil* (1996) and *Bioshock* (2007) offer to young people (albeit purportedly off limits to children). The horror film genre has responded by: (1) skewing to young people; (2) adopting video games' aesthetic (first-person shooter vantage points, computer generated effects, and a frenetic feel); and (3) in addition to rehashing the old, its new horror fare mines video game products (e.g. *House of the Dead* [2003]; *BloodRayne* [2006]).

A Final Lesson on Blacks and Horror Films

This review of the last century of horror has worked to chart Blacks' contributions to the horror genre. It has shown Blacks' overall resiliency in staking a participatory claim either in front of or behind the camera. Blacks' participation has been, and continues to be, about more than cultural commodification; rather, it has been posited here that Blacks' involvement in the genre is an interesting study in social ideas and cultural values, re-inscription into or resistance against dominant ideologies, and negotiations of representation—such as how to display Black culture and bodies, be it by way of realism or spectacle.

In the twenty-first century, Blacks have come to terms with the changing market as well. Like the horror genre as a whole, films featuring Blacks (though not necessarily written, directed, or produced by Blacks) are skewing to young people, purposefully hailing youth of all stripes of the hip-hop generation by saturating its horror with rappers and rap music through "Black horror" films. For example, *Urban Menace* (1999), about a ghost killing off criminals preying on the inner-city, features rappers Snoop Dogg, Big Pun, Ice-T, and Fat Joe. In a bit of self-reflexivity, acknowledging its low quality, the DVD release permits viewers to skip the film and simply listen to Ice-T rap. *Da Hip Hop Witch* (2000)—a *Blair Witch Project* (1999) in the 'hood—ups the rapper quotient by featuring a whopping 24 rappers, including Eminem, Charli Baltimore, Professor X, Ja Rule, Pras, Vanilla Ice, Rah Digga, and Mobb Deep. Over 100 hip-hop inspired "Black horror" films were released in the first decade of the twenty-first century alone.[10] To make clear their connection to hip hop, the films disrupt traditional spelling, adopting hip hop's postmodern, deconstructive language, often adding "z" to film titles: *Cryptz* (2002), *Vampz* (2004), *Vampiyaz* (2004), *Zombiez* (2005), *Bloodz v. Wolvez* (2006). Thanks in great part to the straight-to-DVD market, which makes the production and distribution of films accessible to just about anyone with access to digital equipment, first-timers, such as H.M. Coakley with *Holla* (2006), and the well established, such as Eriq LaSalle with *Crazy as Hell* (2002), are making "Black horror" films. Simply, "Black horror" has learned some important lessons about how to survive by carving out a popular and profitable niche coupling youth, hip hop, and the home video market.

Tales from Hip Hop

The 1980s marked a surge in the development of the rap music genre. Rap styles were becoming increasingly diverse, from the radio-friendly, disco-inspired Sugar Hill Gang and the machismo-based lyrics of LL Cool J, to the political pronouncements of Grandmaster Flash and the Furious Five and the gangsta preachings of Ice-T. In the midst of this flurry of music activity, horror is present, and the two popular culture forms easily sync. In 1988, the rap duo DJ Jazzy Jeff (Jeff Townes) and the Fresh Prince (Will Smith) released their album *He's the DJ, I'm the Rapper*, featuring the song "Nightmare on My Street." The album's debut happened to coincide with the release of *A Nightmare on Elm Street 4: The Dream Master*, with the song, performed by the Fresh Prince, serving as an unofficial tribute to the popularity of the film franchise:[11]

> I walked in the house, the Big Bad Fresh Prince/But Freddy killed all that noise real quick/He grabbed me by my neck and said, "Here's what we'll do. We gotta lotta work here, me and you. The souls of your friends you and I will claim. You've got the body and I've got the brain."

The song, co-written by Will Smith, anticipated Smith's eventual move into horror as a new Black (super)hero for the twenty-first century. Smith's arrival marks a dramatic departure from tragic, disaffected Black horror superheroes, such as Spawn and Blade, in battle with otherworldly, other-racial creatures.[12]

Spawn and Blade are monstrous in their own right; essentially anti-heros warring with their own aberrant kind. Smith rode in on a different kind of horse, playing Black male savior, purging the world of all manner of alien invasion. In the science fiction films *Independence Day* (1996) and *Men in Black I* and *II* (1997, 2002), Smith's iconic status is on display as he portrays a clean-cut (notwithstanding his stripper fiancé in *Independence Day*), good-looking, affable, and quick-witted monster slayer. Smith's presence works to disrupt (though not fully expel) horror's obsessive insistence on linking alien menace to Blackness, real or metaphorical, as seen from *Creature from the Black Lagoon* (1954) to *Predator 2* (1990). His mega-stardom and race have been "made to play nice together," leading to claims that Smith transcends race.[13] Presumably, his monsters—stinky octopi and giant bugs—transcend race as well.

Smith's turn in the "Blacks in horror" film *I Am Legend* (2007) represents, in some ways, absolutely nothing, neither progression nor regression for Blacks in horror. The film is based on the 1954 Richard Matheson novel *I Am Legend*, about the last human in a world of vampires. The novel has been the basis of several movies, including Smith's *Legend*.[14] For example, *Last Man on Earth* (1964) stars Vincent Price as Dr. Robert Morgan, who is immune to the vampire plague. The film depicts heart-wrenching, grey solitude as Morgan watches his family and the world around him die. Though he discovers a cure in his own blood, in the film's tragic ending Morgan represents an unwanted minority in a vampire-dominated world, resulting in his extermination—he is killed by vampires on a church altar in a Christ-on-the-cross pose. In *Omega Man* (1971) Charlton Heston portrays Robert Neville, whose maddening solitude is suddenly interrupted when he discovers there are a few other survivors of a plague that has turned the world's population into sun-averse mutants. Neville becomes romantically involved with a Black woman, Lisa (Rosalind Cash), who eventually succumbs to the plague, betraying him to the mutants. Neville is killed, his body, too, falling into a crucifixion-of-Christ pose. Like Morgan, Neville's blood is the antidote to the plague. Just before his execution, Neville delivers salvation, as he is able to harvest his blood and put it into the hands of untainted humans who will begin the process of restoring humanity.

In Smith's *I Am Legend*, he also portrays Dr. Robert Neville, who is a desperately lonely survivor of a plague which has produced bloodthirsty monsters. His solitude is disrupted by a female monster that he has captured to study, as well as by an uninfected woman and child who are seeking an outpost of other survivors. However, Smith's Neville is denied the racial commentary afforded Price's Morgan or Heston's Neville, as well as the "blood of Jesus" salvation iconography they each shared. Notably, Smith's Neville does not draw the cure for humankind from his veins—from his Black blood. Rather, the cure comes from the monster's blood after he has injected her with a serum of his blood and chemicals. Salvation is a soup of the natural, the tainted, and the chemical. He is even denied his Christ pose, as he is blown up in a fireball instead.

Here Smith's stardom, action star persona, and race are indeed made to play nice at the expense of the deeper meanings previous portrayals and the original novel made available. Though the audience knows something about Smith's Neville—the audience sees his wife and daughter before the tragedy, he likes bacon, he loves Bob Marley's music—he is socio-cultural window-glass. That is, there is not much complexity to him. He can be appropriately contrasted to *Night of the Living Dead*'s (1968) Ben (Duane Jones), who the audience is told virtually nothing about. Though Ben's Blackness is never mentioned, Ben is still a complex, meaningful symbol of race histories and relationships as he, the only Black man, works to survive attacking zombies and attacking Whites—both equally bloodthirsty. The comparison between the two representations—Neville and Ben—is not a forced one. Rather, director George Romero's *Night of the Living Dead* was inspired by Matheson's novel, from which Romero borrowed the shuffling undead reaching through boarded up windows to get at the final human, as well as a dying child, burning victims in a pyre, and the death of the story's protagonist.[15] Similarly, in a send-up of *Night of the Living Dead* (1968) and *Day of the Dead* (1985), the straight-to-DVD film *Day X* (2006) places Frank (Ken Edwards) in an abandoned steel mill when a zombification virus is accidently released. He is the only Black man, and assumes control of 10 Whites (a few of them hostile) who have wandered in for protection. The film's tension carries a racial overtone, which is addressed head on during a brief deadpan comic comment in this otherwise deadly serious movie: "You ever see that movie with that Black guy in that house?" Add to this overt racialization Riddick of 2000's *Pitch Black*, who is racially "outed" as Black with the sardonic line that he will ride as a prisoner "all back-of-the-bus." However, Smith as Neville is not afforded such commentary even as he is enveloped in national, if not global trauma, as a military officer presumably shifting his attention from war (e.g. Afghanistan) to plague, and who is left to come to terms with his America, symbolized by a post 9/11 New York, now absent political, cultural, or value-system (e.g. is killing the monsters murder?) uncertainties.

The Darker Side of Hip Hop

> For every metropolis there is a necropolis
>
> —Adam Simon, producer, *Bones*[16]

If one is looking for sociopolitical reflection, hip-hop infused horror rarely disappoints, hitting audiences over the head like a sledgehammer with tales of morality and social responsibility. The rapper Snoop Dogg has taken the lead with, to date, three morality-horror features. The straight-to-video *Urban Menace* (1999) showcases Snoop in the starring role of someone lamenting the violence permeating his community by, ironically, killing as many gangsters as he can. Snoop's next film *Bones* (2001) boasted a moderate budget of $16 million, the backing of New Line Cinema, and the accomplished director Ernest Dickerson.[17] In the film, Jimmy Bones (Snoop Dogg) is a 1970s living legend "gentleman gangster" numbers runner who is respected by members of his Black community.[18] His 'hood is thriving until hard drugs are introduced. Refusing to join up with other drug dealers, Jimmy is killed. The dealers plunge knives into his body, reminiscent of Christ being nailed to the Cross. Jimmy becomes a folk legend, remembered over the years, only to return two decades later as a vengeful, violent ghost. He exacts bloody revenge on those who killed him, contributed to the demise of the 'hood, and who continue to deprive the 'hood of its buoyancy, leaving it derelict under a plague of drugs. Until Jimmy's return, drugs have become an "uncontrollable capitalism" untouched by corrupt law enforcement, and unseen civic leaders and community activists. Only something out of the gangster culture, evolved into an angry spirit, can rein the terror in.[19]

In a move of intertexuality, *Bones* features Pam Grier as Jimmy's girlfriend Pearl, depicting them as a couple at the height of his power in 1979. Here Grier is to be imagined as her 1970s Blaxploitation iconic characters Coffy, Foxy, or Sheba, the buxom bad-bitch who provided rape money-shots to people like Snoop, who claims to have grown up on her films. Her presence cannot be separated from Snoop's frequent appearance in his music videos and at award ceremonies costumed in 1970s pimp-style attire, complete with a "pimp cup" and accompanied by Don "Magic" Juan, a Chicago pimp featured in the documentary films *Pimps Up, Hos Down* (1999) and *American Pimp* (1999). Grier's inclusion then is a misogynistic fantasy of prostitution and rape. Denzin asserts that it would be inappropriate to interpret such sexism as the purview of only Black youth culture. Instead, these troubling gender practices are implicated in a White supremacy which casts Black men as dope dealers and pimps, and women as ho's.[20] Less developed is modern-day Pearl, 20 years after Jimmy's death. She is now a seer, connecting with Jimmy in the spirit world. However, the film does not link the older Pearl with the likes of her character Lisa of *Scream, Blacula, Scream* (1973), who avoids eroticism with the vampire Blacula, and uses her seer/Voodoo powers like a superhero to save her Black community. On the whole, Snoop's horror tale plays nostalgic for a life before drive-bys and crack when gangsters were smooth, and their business was dealing in women.

Despite its budget and star power, including a Snoop Dogg soundtrack CD which placed 39 on the Billboard 200 in October 2001, *Bones* is a prime example of how "Black horror" still struggles to gain a foothold in Hollywood. Earning just over $7 million gross, director Ernest Dickerson is skeptical of the industry's commitment to Black filmmaking:

> So yeah, I sometimes really think that there's an element that really does not want African Americans to gain a significant foothold in making films, deciding what films are made, stretching the genre and stretching what

Black films can do. ... *Bones* got great reviews from *The New York Times*, *The L.A. Times* and *Variety*, but the studio refused to capitalize on those good reviews. The common industry practice is to put blurbs from good reviews in the ads, but they refused to do that and they spent one-third of what everybody else was spending to advertise the movie. So the movie came out and had a great soundtrack that never got to the radio stations. How are you going to turn down a Snoop Dogg album?[21]

Snoop would continue to preach, appropriating *Tales from the Crypt* (1972) and Rusty Condieff's "Black horror" film *Tales from the Hood* (1995) to offer *Snoop Dogg's Hood of Horror* (2006), in which Snoop appears as the "Crib Keeper" sending souls to Hell.[22] *Hood* is an anthology, presenting three vignettes about cleansing the 'hood of gang graffiti, slumlords, and killer rappers who forget where they have come from.

The link between horror and hip hop continues with horrorcore, a music subgenre of rap deeply influenced by horror, featuring stories of zombies and cannibalism, with performers, at times, appearing in gory costumes. Horrorcore's roots are debated, with some pointing to the rap group the Geto Boys serving as inspiration for the form, with their 1991 album *We Can't Be Stopped* featuring two horror inspired songs: "My Mind Is Playing Tricks on Me," about a Halloween-inspired nightmare, and "Chuckie," a song featuring a character who professes to "eat a dog's brain," inspired by the *Chucky* horror film franchise. Others point to rap artists Prince Paul of Stetsasonic and RZA of the Wu-Tang

FIGURE C1 Snoop in *Hood of Horror*
Arclight Films/Photofest

Clan as its innovators when they formed the group Gravediggaz, releasing their 1994 debut album *6 Feet Deep*. The album has been described as a "morbid, campy and complete commercial flop."[23] However, horrorcore's yardstick is not mainstream, commercial reception, but the underground and the fringe. Since Gravediggaz efforts, artists such as the Insane Clown Posse, D12, and Eminem—all from Detroit—have been credited with keeping horrorcore (occasionally) before the mainstream. Their work includes the Insane Clown Posse's annual Gathering the Juggalos festival, as well as D12 and Eminem's occasional dark, horror lyrics. Brotha Lynch Hung, a rapper from Sacramento, who claims he is the founder of horrorcore, was one of the first rappers to star in his own "Black horror" horrorcore film, *Now Eat: The Movie* (2000). The movie features Lynch's grisly lyrics: "I don't wanna brag/Fuck Jeffery Dahmer he's a mothafuck'n fag/ I got nigga nuts and guts in a bag, draggin them to the pad."[24] The film's plot focuses on his and his rapper friends' propensity to dine on their rivals, after sprinkling meat tenderizer on them. Horrorcore, which gets limited radio play due to its profoundly violent, sexist, homophobic, and pro-suicide content, continues to have an underground following, with the Detroit-metro area playing host to the subculture. For example, on September 12, 2009, the Strictly for the Wicked horrorcore music festival was held in Southgate, MI, hosted by Serial Killin Records. Largely promoted through the internet, the "all ages" festival featured approximately 25 acts and attracted approximately 250 people. Horrorcore received unexpected attention in the mainstream press when a horrorcore rapper, 20-year-old Richard "Syko Sam" McCroskey, bludgeoned four people to death in their homes after attending the Strictly for the Wicked festival. The link between the violence of horrorcore and the murders was made explicit by Mario "Mars" Delgado, a horrorcore rapper:

> the point is to constantly push the envelope and shock and offend people … It's marketing—it's so shocking and in your face that kids want it, they need it. … If your kids are into stuff like this, you need to sit down and talk to them, and say, "Are you Ok?" … It's a cry for help most parents don't pick up on.[25]

"Black Horror": It's Not For Theaters Anymore

There was a time in the history of the horror genre when an accounting of "Black horror" films could be easily achieved. In some decades, be it "Blacks in horror" films or "Black horror" films, Black images were few and far between. However, the presence of Blacks in the genre experienced an explosion in great part due to the straight-to-video market, a means of distributing movies either with studio support or independently, for purchase and/or rental by consumers. In the 1980s the emerging video market was marred by a reputation for being the dumping ground of only sub-par films. It is now a viable route to produce films that cost significantly less than a theatrical film, thereby permitting a film to be shot on a small budget but with potentially greater profit earnings. Even the major studios have quickly realized that there are tremendous profits to be made in the video market by introducing straight-to-video franchises, as Lions Gate has, with their "Barbie" films, with more than 15 (and counting) in its series. It is not simply the "kidvid" market that has latched on to direct to video. Horror sequels have also found a place in the video market. For example, *Candyman 3: Day of the Dead* (1999) was a video release. *Candyman 3* represents those films which do not merit the investment of a full theatrical push, which can cost upwards of $35 million for prints and advertising.[26] Placing a movie franchise in video has proven to be good business:

> [Film distributor] Mike Elliott saw the celluloid disaster [*Turbulence*, 1997] and thought one thing: *Turbulence 2* (1999). A low-budget sequel wherein a "fear of flying" class goes for the ride of their lives. And then, improbably but inevitably, *Turbulence 3* (2001), featuring a heavy-metal band in concert aboard a 747. And here was the surprise ending: The sequels made money. Good money, actually. … with *Turbulence 2* reaping $10 million in rentals on a $4 million investment.[27]

Even cable television has gotten in on the video action. For example, Showtime Entertainment took its low-budget horror shorts directed by some of the biggest names in the genre—John Carpenter, Tobe Hooper, John Landis, and Ernest Dickerson—to the DVD market. Likewise, the Syfy television network regularly releases its self-produced horror movies to video. Netflicks and the RedBox are seeking out and distributing independent films. Still other filmmakers are selling DVDs directly online, providing teasers through a variety of internet formats (e.g. personal webpage video sites such as YouTube.com).[28] Doug Schwab, a former buyer for Blockbuster and now founder and President of Maverick Entertainment Group, reports he pressed the major studios beginning in the early 1990s to offer more "urban product," from horror to gospel, because such fare is in great demand. Today, through Maverick, Schwab scours "film schools, small production houses, and independent movie makers" for films.[29] One find was Amir Valinia, director of *Dream House* (2006), about a Black couple who sort out the mystery behind their newly purchased, unexpectedly haunted home. Valinia continues to press the boundaries of low-budget, high-quality filmmaking, being the first to film a music video, for rapper Paul Wall, with iPhones.[30]

"Black Horror" Goes Green: Recycling Lots of Horror Stories

Schwab of Maverick Entertainment is correct that the "urban" video market—from dance-themed movies to religious plays to rapper zombie hunters (e.g. rapper Big Daddy Kane in *Dead Heist* [2007])—is thriving. "Black horror" in particular is providing hundreds of titles, delivering something for everyone, even as "Black horror" is not immune to its own rehashing of popular horror themes. The 'hood, as a place that should be protected from exploitation, is a mainstay in "Black horror" films. For example, *Hood Rat* (2001) takes up the theme by presenting residents of a tenement doing battle against their slumlord. This rat-movie, a sort of Willard-in-the-inner-city, offers lessons about cleaning up the 'hood and advocating for the underclass. Two "Blacks in horror" films, *Leprechaun in the Hood* (2000) and *Leprechaun: Back 2 tha Hood* (2003), did nothing for the image of the inner-city. These *Leprechaun* films join other films, such as *Predator 2* (1990), in which monsters storm the urban to tear into Blacks while also exposing the inner-city as a place that even makes evil do a double-take at its neglect. The two films send the damaging message that the only thing to do with the deficient denizens of the inner-city is to kill them, since they are already tearing up their homes, smoking weed, selling dope, and hoping to be, at best, gun-toting gangsta rappers, thereby further victimizing their own communities. The films managed to cast the Leprechaun as the sensible one among fools. The setting, coupled with hip-hop themes, worked to revive the *Leprechaun* series through the straight-to-DVD market.

The film *This Evil One* (2005) follows *Candyman* (1992), revisiting "Chicago's most dangerous neighborhood," and includes a monster abducting children to strike back at a community. In the film, a Black community that is weary of "perverts preying on our people" is terrorized by a White boogeyman from the year 1896 with a Candyman-esque passion for kidnapping Black children to reassert his mythical status. *Bloodz vs. Wolvez* (2006) borrows the monster wars of *Underworld* (2003), recasting the clash as a Black-on-Black, New York City turf-war battle between the sophisticated Bloodz vampires, who own downtown real estate and financial institutions, and the crude werewolves or "Wolvez," who control and terrorize uptown's ghettos with muggings. The film *Killjoy* (2000), featuring a Michael Jackson-esque avenging clown, borrows from the campy 1988 *Killer Klowns from Outer Space*, in which murderous clowns and ice cream trucks figure prominently.

There are also a wealth of simple-plot, low-budget films in which Black monsters prey on the 'hood absent a significant message about the violence being played out (literally) in its streets and abandoned, derelict warehouses. The "Black horror" film *Holla* is novel, rejecting the 'hood as a setting in favor of a rural cabin. Here, hapless urbanites fall victim to a butcher knife-wielding woman who has escaped from a mental hospital. Interestingly, the film nearly failed to materialize, as its writer/director H.M. Coakley explains, "no one could understand what we were trying to do." As a result, the film's already modest $3 million budget plummeted to $10,000 before an investor came in at the last minute with an additional $140,000—still meager by filmmaking standards.[31]

Ladies First

"Black horror" frequently brings with it powerful sociopolitical messages for Black communities. *Street Tales of Terror* (2004) is an award-winning horror anthology in the same vein as *Tales from the Hood* (1995) or *Snoop Dogg's Hood of Horror* (2006) sans the humor.[32] It presents a trilogy of women-centered cautionary morality tales such as "The Clinic," in which Jalissa (Nicole Ford) is contemplating her second abortion. She is terrorized by a bloody creature in her dreams which, of course, turns out to be her first aborted fetus (at the age it would be had it lived). Here, the film ends with Jalissa receiving pre-natal information, her fetus intact. Perhaps "The Clinic" is a pro-life, fundamentalist message and/or it is a message about keeping the Black community intact by aligning Black children with purity, hope, and promise for Black communities and cultures. Sobchack elaborates, "the baby has been culturally produced as a figure of poignant sweetness—helpless, vulnerable, and dependent," not yet corrupted, while assuring the inscription of new social experiences and enacting new, promising histories.[33] What is clear is that "The Clinic" like much of "Black horror" resists the *Rosemary's Baby* (1968) impulse in which "the womb [is] the new graveyard," as childbearing is not typically associated with the monstrous or demonic.[34] In the anthology's "The Reckoning" a well-behaved little girl, Jessica (Tenia Yarbrough), is teased and bullied before being drowned in a swimming pool by three of her classmates. On her twentieth birthday, Jessica's ghost returns and she and her mother, Mama (Shirley Whitmore), get their revenge on the now young women who killed her. Here, the monstrous Black mother is depicted, but the audience is asked to understand her madness turned to evil as she is consumed by unbearable grief. It is explained that Jessica was killed on the same day Mama buried her young nephew. Hence, Mama strikes back against lost innocence and promise. Finally, in "Graduation Night," Bernice (Mykei Gray), a strait-laced college student, is raped by a star athlete at a party as her fellow co-eds fail to intervene. In the aftermath of the rape, upon discovering she is pregnant and expelled from school because of code-of-conduct (hence, blaming the victim) violations, Bernice hangs herself, and as a ghost exacts bloody revenge. Here, put on display is the difficulty rape victims face when attempting to report the crime, as well as a "lesser" victim fighting back against a "star" perpetrator.

In "Black horror" films women are not merely victims. Rather, they continue to thrive as conquering heroes, capably battling zombies or, rather, "zombiez," as Josephine (Jenicia Garcia) does in *Zombiez* (2005), taking on cannibal monsters and sexist co-workers. Josephine recalls the toughness of Sugar from *Sugar Hill* (1974) and the resourcefulness of Lisa in *Scream, Blacula, Scream* (1973), as well as Grandma in *Def by Temptation* (1990), as she fights off evil. Laudably, "Blacks in horror" films also feature Black females. *Alien vs. Predator* (2004) presents a dramatic departure from previous *Predator* films, which located violence in the

South African jungle or the L.A. inner-city, with men serving as saviors. In *AVP*, the battle is moved to the Antarctic Ocean, providing an opportunity for Alexa Woods (Sanaa Lathan), an intellectually sophisticated, expertly trained archeologist/scientist, to save the world from the Alien. Notably, Alexa pairs up with a Predator ("the enemy of my enemy is my friend"). The two function as a striking team, with Alexa even agreeing to allow the Predator to brand her.[35] The "Blacks in horror" film *Queen of the Damned's* (2002) vampire Akasha, portrayed by hip-hop songstress Aaliyah, is not a hero, but the love interest for the White vampire Lestat (who, oddly, is the lead singer of a rock band).

By contrast, the nearly identical "Black horror" films *Cryptz* (2002) and *Vampz* (2004), which even share co-star Rick Irvin as a vampire victim, provide unfortunate misogynistic imagistic abuses of women. Certainly horror is not the genre to carry the flag of so-called political correctness; however, these films do quite a bit of damage to understandings of Black womanhood. Both films invite a primarily male gaze upon, in the case of *Cryptz*, female stripper vampires working a stripper pole, topless, for a very long time before getting on with the business of sucking the blood of their victims. The vampires are denied the seduction of Dracula as their male victims belittle the women and make sexist comments even as the women send them to their (un)death. Of course, the women are eventually

FIGURE C2 Alexa Woods and the alien monster in *AVP*
20th Century-Fox/Photofest

vanquished, with their stripper outfits permitting a better view of stakes, driven into them by a group of men, impaling their breasts before reaching their hearts. *Vampz* builds on this woman-as-sex-object vision by providing scenes of the vampire women kissing and having sex with each other. However, this is not inscribed as a feminist moment; rather, it is a sort of lesbian chic spicing up the film. In both films, the men unfailingly boast of their sexual prowess, more so in the face of the lesbian "make-out" scenes in which the women gaze at the men teasingly while in an embrace. There is no question that these women will die as they still attempt to usurp men's power by attacking and engaging in sexual conquests with women.[36] The scenes fail by presenting lesbianism as a perform-ance for the male audience—both those who are in the vampires' den watching the action as well as those watching on the screen.

Something New

The horror genre is not entirely derivative. *Kracker Jack'd* (2003) is a comedic slasher movie in which rowdy, uncouth Black male students savagely beat a White male student who has completely appropriated a narrow definition of Black hip-hop style, including calling Blacks "nigger." This "Black horror" film makes it clear that only Blacks can deploy the word "nigger," which they do voluminously. In, *Jack'd*, as the students begin to meet their fate, the "White boy" is suspected. However, the film presents a significant narrative twist in that the killer is actually LaShawn (Mark Anthony Riveria), a Black, smart student mockingly nicknamed Carlton (as in the nerdy Carlton from TV sitcom *The Fresh Prince of Bel-Air*).[37] LaShawn, in explaining why he committed the murders, snaps: "Brother can't be light-skinned and educated without some bling bling, ghetto-assed, West Side, dick grabbin' motherfucker talkin' that high yellow house nigger bullshit."

Three equally novel horror films share a medical theme. In the "Black horror" film *Crazy as Hell* (2002), Man (Eriq LaSalle) a mysterious, self-assured, charming patient in a mental hospital, believes himself to be Satan, and with the arrival of a cocky doctor, Dr. Ty Adams (Michael Beach), Man works to teach him a thing or two about humility. However, Man is a trickster, a real-life Devil, forcing Dr. Adams to confront his failures, or what Fulmer describes as the "the limits of amorality."[38] These failures include his dogged insistence that he is infallible as a doctor.[39] Unwilling to listen, Dr. Adams is implicated in the suicide of a patient, and fails to come to terms with the death of his young daughter, which he could have prevented. Dr. Adams is confronted by demons which include Satan, who shape-shifts into his true form, a White man, Delazo (Ronny Cox), who presented himself as the kindly hospital administrator. It is Delazo who welcomes Dr. Adams to Hell. The "Blacks in horror" film *Sublime* (2007) presents a White man, George (Tom Cavanaugh), who goes into the hospital for a routine procedure, but emerges from anesthesia semi-comatose and the victim of several amputations. His nurse, a White woman, is a seductress challenging his faithfulness to his wife. His orderly, Mandingo (Lawrence Hilton-Jacobs), is a Black man who figures prominently in George's life in the hospital. Mandingo is a sadist who torments George, climbing on top of him in his bed, taunting and berating him before using pruning shears to chop away at George's already damaged body. *Sublime* is about stereotypes and fears as the man discovers he is trapped in unconsciousness and his mind has manifested his latent sexisms and racisms into stereotypical figures which torment him. Finally, the award-winning *The Final Patient* (2005) presents innovative casting depicting septuagenarian actor Bill Cobbs in the role of Dr. Green, a retired country doctor/researcher who has found the fountain of youth in rattlesnake venom and herbs from China.[40] Exposed as extraordinarily powerful when he lifts a tractor off a child involved in an accident, Green's secret becomes the target of thieves. The poachers meet their deaths in Green's farmhouse, at the hands of Green's hidden, but equally powerful wife, who is partly transformed by the snake venom into a monster who kills everyone.

Zombies for Obama: Black Horror Forever

> I Could Never Be Barackula.
>
> —*Barackula: The Musical*[41]

A man, out of an "exotic" land, is one part charming and one part mysteriously powerful. He is a mesmerizer turning people into automatons—duping even the smartest and strongest into doing his bidding. In 1932's *White Zombie*, the threat was Murder Legendre, who, tainted by Haiti, exploited its Voodoo power to create a legion of mindless, inexhaustible laborers working on his behalf. Today, seemingly, it's Barack Obama, hailing from exotic Hawaii, or Indonesia or, generically, "Africa," who, according to Klein and Elliott in *The Manchurian President: Barack Obama's Ties to Communists, Socialists and Other Anti-American Extremists*, is "eloquent, winsome and charismatic," "the most powerful man in the world," and importantly, "HE ISN'T WHAT HE SEEMS."[42] Purportedly, Obama is wielding seductive power over the US' most precious commodity, the iPod generation. Jason Mattera, in his book *Obama Zombies: How the Liberal Machine Brainwashed My Generation*, casts young adults under 30 years of age as monstrous disappointments—zombies—for the cause of freedom in America, as they toil to propagate Obama's message of hope and change as if "iPods would drop from heaven."[43] Obama and his campaign managers, particularly his digital technologies coordinating team (e.g. those providing material for Facebook, MySpace, Twitter, and YouTube.com), are, in essence, the twenty-first century equivalent of Murder Legendre as they continue to dupe masses of young people, getting them to focus on the whole shininess of it all as if Obama is a hypnotist. Klein and Elliott and Mattera are far from the first people to link

Obama to horror. There is the rather scary Obama vampire Halloween mask.[44] Add to that Firas Alkhateeb's Photoshopped, widely distributed picture of Obama as the Joker from *The Dark Knight* (2008). The *New York Post* cartoonist Sean Delonas even linked Obama to a rampaging chimpanzee that was shot down, King Kong-style, in Connecticut, by police. The police loom over the body of a blood-soaked monkey with two bullet holes in its chest, concluding, "They'll have to find someone else to write the next stimulus bill."[45] Horror's next theme, which is already upon audiences thanks to the sci-fi and action genres, is one of a Black President at the helm as the US (and, hence, the world) face annihilation, as the following have already depicted: *The Fifth Element* (1997), *Deep Impact* (1998), TV's *24* (Fox, 2001–2010), and *2012* (2009). Fortunately, there is always a White savior (with Bruce Willis saving the world twice for his President) coming to the rescue. Only *Bubba Hotep*'s (2002) John F. Kennedy in the body of a Black man (Ossie Davis) did not allow aliens, meteors, terrorists, or a Mayan-predicted apocalypse to jeopardize the stability of the world.

Horror Veterans Speak! Miguel Nunez, Terry Alexander, Ken Foree

Horror stars Miguel Nunez (*Return of the Living Dead* [1985]), Terry Alexander (*Day of the Dead* [1985]), and Ken Foree (*Dawn of the Dead* [1978]) all have (independently) invoked Obama as an inspiration, even for the horror genre.[46] Nunez sees horror, specifically "Black horror," as just beginning to come into its own among Black audiences. The challenge for horror is to ably compete with (more universally audience-friendly) comedy films and TV sitcoms, which, he believes, continues to be the favored genre among Black audiences, in particular. However, Nunez sees opportunities for the genre to diversify, with young people in particular becoming more used to "seeing each other"; for example mingling at (for now) predominantly White horror fan events such as horror film festivals and conventions. This possibility for improved communication among races is inspired, in great part, by the election of Obama, which has given Nunez "hope" and revealed that "anything's possible" in Blacks' participation in arenas seemingly limited or off-limits. Alexander similarly identified horror and comedy as being in competition for the attentions of Black audiences. However, he argues that George Romero leveled horror's playing field among Black horror audiences—about whom woefully little is known—by "opening the door for Black characters." Alexander is mindful of firsts, as the star of TV's soap opera *As the World Turns*, featuring the genre's first Black family. Since Romero, the genre is wide open for Black participation, with rappers-turned-actors leading the way in broadening the genre's reach. For Alexander, horror's evolution has brought significant change over the old "buddy film" approach in which the Black sidekick is killed off with Whites going on to avenge the sidekick's death while saving the world. Here again, Obama becomes important, as his presence represents hope—reminding actors and filmmakers alike that "we can all be President" either metaphorically or, as the election has proven, in real life. According to S. Craig Watkins, in his book *Representing: Hip Hop Culture and the Production of Black Cinema*, "dominant groups struggle vigorously to maintain control over the same ideological and political landscapes for which subordinate populations struggle"; therefore, Obama's election should challenge image-makers to confront twenty-first century realities in which Blacks can be seen inhabiting a range of social and ideological positions.[47] Foree, like Alexander, views the Romero films as still "paving the way for other Black actors in horror," and like Nunez sees Black fandom around horror—such as attending horror conventions—as a site where inclusion and participation can be improved upon. However, while Blacks have not yet fully embraced horror fan communities, according to Foree they have gone full tilt into contributing to the horror genre, finding "inspiration and money through straight to video" opportunities. Here again, according to Foree, Obama is a symbol, offering a seminal message that Hollywood ... everyone ... can learn from— "Inclusion! INCLUSION!!!"[48]

Black Tales of Horror: The End

Horror, for Blacks, continues to be a study in racism, exoticism, and neocolonialism in which Black Americans are portrayed as outside of Western images of enlightenment, while being subordinated to a system of primitive images— political, economic, cultural, religious, and social. Horror films come out of the imaginations of a diverse cadre of image-makers. One thing that is clear is how difficult it is to create representations that break free from the steady diet of confining depictions image-makers have already been fed. Horror continues to propagate an "us," "them," and "us versus them" understanding of race relationships in which cross-cultural communication is displayed as difficult to negotiate head on. As a result, horror is, at times, overly segregated or too much of just "us." Non-Black horror has been particularly difficult on this point, uncomfortably excluding Blacks, and all manner of gender, sexuality, and racial diversity. The response to such exclusion has been the production of still more "us" horror films. "Black horror," for example, was born, in part, out of exclusion. Horror has also taken up the tact of color-blind-ish casting, assembling a multi-cultural, "one of each," crew of young horror victims. *The Descent* (2005) and *Dracula 2000* (2000) asked audiences to see, but not make a big deal of, race or racial cultural investments. Such erasure is an unsatisfying approach as well, at least for those who do not view identity and cultural invisibility as a viable solution to inclusiveness. Still, the current narrative on race swirls around the unsustainability of race and the "post-racial." Declarations of "race ends here" (Gilroy) are bolstered by claims of internal sameness, superficial external differences, and the cumbersome work of trying to maintain what Louis calls a "raciology" in a world that also embraces anti-racism.[49] However, "Black horror" and color-blind horror do not represent a stalemate. It is worth giving continued careful consideration to privileged racial identities and racially coded cultural practices, styles, and aesthetics while dismantling racial hierarchies. Importantly, racially coded productions can serve a target audience, while not precluding other audiences sharing in the experience.[50]

It is advocated here that "Black horror" (or "gay horror," "Latino horror," "religious horror," or "urban horror" …) has an important place in the genre. Out of the culturally specific come some of the most compelling takes on common themes as well as new innovations—filmmakers Oscar Micheaux and Eloyce Gist are prime examples of such contributions. Morality tales in horror are common; the spiritual turn such tales take, as seen in *Go Down, Death* (1944) or *Def by Temptation* (1990), is novel. Nollywood ("Nigerian Hollywood"), with its horror films based on occult, supernatural aspects of religion (e.g. Devil possession) mixed with healthy doses of real church service, singing, sickening special effects, and messages about alienation from one's communities, is beginning to unite with Black American horror—an interesting morality-tale boom is likely on the horizon. Blacks bring unique interpretations of the vampire and the boogeyman as symbols of racism (e.g. *Blacula* and *Candyman*) and they have harnessed the werewolf, controlling its moon-cycle changes while making it a warrior engaged in class warfare (e.g. *Bloodz vs. Wolvez*). The Final Girl, laying waste to her insane older brother or to aliens with acid for blood, revolutionized horror. However, the introduction of a Black Enduring Woman, whose fight does not end with the demise of the monster, remains a similarly important political and feminist symbol. Blacks even prove to be unique zombies, refusing to fulfill a neo-slavery fantasy. In nearly every horror movie the zombies get a cop, as if still avenging Ben's (*Night of the Living Dead*) death.

In the past, Blacks have been the source of "the funny" in comedy-horror, putting on full display their incredible talents of being simultaneously petrified and hilarious. Unfortunately, the performances were at the expense of Blacks' humanity. Today, "Black horror" says that Blacks no longer need to be assigned "saintlike goodness to counteract the racism … automatically direct[ed] toward a Black character on screen." The loyal, saintly, or hilariously harmless Black need not be the equivalent of a "normal" White character.[51] The Wayans' *Scary Movie* (2001), which has grossed an incredible $157,019,771 domestically and $278,019,771 worldwide, turned the joke back on horror.[52] The movie, and its sequels, includes spoofs of horror's clichéd treatment of Blacks, thus exposing such practices. By turning the lens back on itself, Blacks have worked to subvert such treatments through their own comedy.[53]

Brought together, the story of Blacks in horror is a compelling history and contemporary examination of the understandings of Black people, as displayed through a popular culture form, over the last century. There are plenty of lessons here about stereotypes and oppressions—particularly as they pertain to depictions of the continent of Africa, natives, and Voodoo. However, this is also a tutorial in subversion—yes, the servants did ridicule their White master (so what if he was German) in *Revenge of the Zombies* (1943). This history also reveals a rise of consciousness and resistance, with the likes of actors Clarence Muse and Spencer Williams saying, "No more" to Hollywood's stereotypes.[54] Films such as 2005's the *Skeleton Key* and even Disney's *The Princess and the Frog* (2009) continue to associate Voodoo (and other Black religions) with a dark wickedness. However, as early as 1934, with *Drums o' Voodoo*, and over the decades with *Scream, Blacula, Scream* (1973) and *Tales from the Hood* (1995), the struggle to reclaim Voodoo is ever-present. The inner-city or 'hood remains a contradictory presence in horror, both celebrated and reviled; however, increasingly, Blacks are being depicted outside of its confines. While Blacks have made it out of the 'hood and into, for example, the suburbs and the rural, their brush with places beyond, such as outer or alternative spaces, have been less frequent and, as Janell Hobson would describe it, "digitally primitive." These new primitives are not yet fully able, or willing, to exploit technology, from *Alien*'s (1979) Parker (Yaphet Kotto) and *Dracula 3000*'s (2004) Humvee (Tiny Lister), space travelers who simply want to pummel, to *Strange Day*'s (1995) Lornette, who is a space craft piloting technophobe.[55]

This is also an accounting of financial hardship that continues to plague Black filmmakers. Charles Burnett laments industry practices which fail to promote Black films, such as studios who will buy a Sundance film, only to warehouse it, or who renege on promises of promotion, failing to even purchase $50 newspaper ads.[56] Indeed, director H.M. Coakley screened his film *Holla* (2006) for free for eight weeks before it was placed in two theaters in Atlanta and Houston for one night December 1, 2006. After that, the film's distributor, Lions Gate, marketed *Holla* as straight to DVD.[57] Finally, much of horror's history has been about the removal of Blacks from the genre. Blacks have been rendered invisible by way of Whites in blackface, through a deprecation of Black culture without (and absent a contradictory response), or by way of wholesale exclusion. However, the substantive point to take away is that today "Black horror" is rather progressive, showering the genre with everything from intellectual exterminators, to (helpful) conjure women, to cannibal rappers. It has been said before, and it is worth saying again here … Black is back.

A Very Brief Word from Your Author

This book was hard, enjoyable work. I very much appreciate the smart questions I get as they pertain to Blacks and media. Almost without fail, I am also asked if, having done this research, I have identified my favorite horror films. This is a ridiculously tough question for me. However, I will try to identify my top films. So, here they are in no particular order: *J.D.'s Revenge* (1976), *Night of the Living Dead* (1968), *Def by Temptation* (1990), *Sugar Hill* (1974), *Blood of Jesus* (1941), *Dawn of the Dead* (1978), *Chloe, Love Is Calling You* (1934), *Abby* (1974), *Candyman* (1992), *Lucky Ghost* (1942), and *Son of Ingagi* (1940).

NOTES

Preface

1 Worland, Rick. *The Horror Film: An Introduction*. Malden, MA: Blackwell, 2007. xi. Print.
2 Worland (xi).
3 He operates a special effects school, "Tom Savini's Special Make-up Effects Program," and a digital film school, "Tom Savini's Digital Film Production Program."
4 *White Boyz*. Dir. Marc Levin. Perf. Danny Hoch. Fox Search Light, 2004. DVD.
5 Heffernan, Kevin. *Ghouls, Gimmicks, and Gold: Horror Films and the American Movie Business, 1953–1968*. Durham, NC: Duke University Press, 2004. 204. Print.
6 Johnson, Ben. "Some Say Police Dog Is Racist." *New Pittsburgh Courier*, May 14, 2003: A1. Print.
7 Machosky, Michael. "Seeking the Paranormal." *Pittsburgh Tribune Review*. October 18, 2005. Pittsburgh Tribune. Web. August 2, 2010. www.pittsburghlive.com/x/pittsburghtrib/s_385041.html.
8 Crane, Jonathan. *Terror and Everyday Life*. Thousand Oaks, CA: Sage Publications, 1994. Print.
9 Hutchings, Peter. *The Horror Film*. London: Pearson, 2004. 83. Print.

Introduction

1 Kozol, Wendy. "Relocating Citizenship in Photographs of Japanese Americans during World War II." *Haunting Violations: Feminist Criticism and the Crisis of the 'Real.'* Eds. Wendy Hesford and Wendy Kozol. Champaign: University of Illinois Press, 2001. 235. Print.
2 Taken from the report title *Window Dressing on the Set: Women and Minorities*. Commission on Civil Rights," Washington, D.C.
3 http://www.noiredigerati.com/.
4 Penzler, Otto. *Black Noir: Mystery, Crime, and Suspense Fiction by African-American Writers*. New York: Pegasus, 2009. Print.

5 netnoir.com.
6 Reid, Mark A. *Black Lenses, Black Voices: African American Film Now*. Lanham, MD: Rowman & Littlefield, 2005. 61. Print.
7 King, Stephen. "Acceptance Speech: The 2003 National Book Award for Distinguished Contribution to American Letters." *On Writing Horror*. Ed. Mort Castle. Revised ed. Cincinnati, OH: Writer's Digest Books, 2007. 10. Print.
8 Hutchings, Peter. *The Horror Film*. London: Pearson, 2004. 115. Print.
9 Clover, Carol J. *Men, Women, and Chainsaws: Gender in the Modern Horror Film*. Princeton, NJ: Princeton University Press, 1992. 229. Print.
10 Crane, Jonathan. *Terror and Everyday Life*. Thousand Oaks, CA: Sage Publications, 1994. 23. Print.
11 Brown, Sterling A. *The Negro in American Fiction*. New York: Atheneum, 1933/1972. Print.
12 Clark, Cedric. "Television and Social Controls: Some Observations on the Portrayals of Ethnic Minorities." *Television Quarterly* 8 (1969): 18–22. Print.
13 Nelson, Angela. "From Beulah to the Fresh Prince of Bel-Air: A Brief History of Black Stereotypes in Television Comedy." Unpublished manuscript, 1991.
14 Coleman, Robin Means. *African American Viewers and the Black Situation Comedy: Situating Racial Humor*. New York: Garland, 2000. Print.
15 Hutchings (7, 9).
16 Vares, Tina. "Framing 'Killer Women' in Films: Audience Use of Genre." *Feminist Media Studies* 2.2 (2002): 213. Print.
17 Aristotle (350 BCE). [Trans. S. H. Butcher.] *Poetics*.
18 Gateward, Frances. "Daywalkin' Night Stalkin' Bloodsuckas: Black Vampires in Contemporary Film." *Genders OnLine Journal* 40 (2004): 3. Web. June 20, 2005. http://www.genders.org/g40/g40_gateward.html.
19 See: Cripps, Thomas. *Black Film as Genre*. Bloomington: Indiana University Press, 1978. Print.
20 Leonard, David J. *Screens Fade to Black: Contemporary African American Cinema*. Westport, CT: Praeger, 2006. 3. Print.
21 Phillips, Kendall R. *Projected Fears: Horror Films and American Culture*. Westport, CT: Praeger, 2005. Print.
22 Pinedo, Isabel Cristina. *Recreational Terror: Women and the Pleasure of Horror Film Viewing*. Albany, NY: SUNY Press, 1997. Print.
23 Hutchings (76).
24 Crane (vi).
25 Crane (4).
26 Pinedo (7).
27 Grant, Barry Keith. "Introduction." *The Dread of Difference: Gender and the Horror Film*. Ed. Barry Keith Grant. Austin: University of Texas Press, 1996. 2. Print.
28 Pinedo (111).
29 See: Gonder, Patrick. "Race, Gender and Terror: The Primitive in 1950s Horror Films." *Genders OnLine Journal* 40 (2004): n.p. Web. January 19, 2006. http://www.genders.org/g40/g40_gondor.html.
30 Cripps (*Genre* 11).
31 Yearwood, Gladstone L. *Black Film as a Signifying Practice: Cinema, Narration and the African-American Aesthetic Tradition*. Trenton, NJ: Africa World Press, Inc., 2000. 119, 121. Print.
32 Williams, Tony. "Trying to Survive on the Darker Side: 1980s Family Horror." *The Dread of Difference: Gender and the Horror Film*. Ed. Barry Keith Grant. Austin: University of Texas Press, 1996. 173. Print.
33 Guerrero, Edward. *Framing Blackness: The African American Image in Film*. Philadelphia, PA: Temple University Press, 1993. Print.

34 Grant (8).
35 Du Bois, W.E.B. *Darkwater: Voices From Within the Veil.* New York: Harcourt, Brace, and Howe, 1920. vii. Print.
36 Du Bois, W.E.B. *The Souls of Black Folks.* New York: NAL Penguin, 1903/1969. 45. Print.
37 Cripps, Thomas. *Slow Fade to Black: The Negro in American Film, 1900–1942.* New York: Oxford University Press, 1993. Print.
38 See: Hill Collins, Patricia. *Black Feminist Thought.* New York: Routledge, 2009. Print; hooks, bell. *Reel to Real: Race, Sex, and Class at the Movies.* New York: Routledge, 1996. Print.
39 Clover, Carol J. "Her Body, Himself: Gender in the Slasher Film." *The Dread of Difference: Gender and the Horror Film.* Ed. Barry Keith Grant. Austin: University of Texas Press, 1996. Print.
40 Pinedo.
41 Zimmerman, Bonnie. "*Daughters of Darkness*: The Lesbian Vampire on Film." *The Dread of Difference: Gender and the Horror Film.* Ed. Barry Keith Grant. Austin: University of Texas Press, 1996. 382. Print.
42 See: Winokur, Mark. "Technologies of Race: Special Effects, Fetish, Film and the Fifteenth Century." *Genders OnLine Journal* 40 (2004). Web. January 20, 2006. http:// www.genders.org/g40/g40_winokur.html.

1 The Birth of the Black Boogeyman: Pre-1930s

1 Lively, Adam. *Masks: Blackness, Race, and the Imagination.* New York: Oxford University Press, 1998. 14. Print.
2 Blacks and women have been largely excluded from the story of film's invention and development.
3 Jones, Alan. *The Rough Guide to Horror Movies.* London: Rough Guides, 2005. 13. Print.
4 Zoetrope technology moved static images of an activity, sequentially arranged, at such a rapid speed that the images appeared to move. For example, stills of a galloping horse could be cycled at such a speed as to make it appear that the horse in the images was moving. A "magic lantern" was the predecessor to the modern film projector.
5 Warner Bros. issued the film *Don Juan* with a music soundtrack. However, in 1894 WKL Dickson with Edison Manufacturing Company attempted to sync sound. In the non-commercial, experimental film Dickson is seen and heard playing the violin for a few seconds while two men waltz together to his music. *Edison: The Invention of the Movies.* Disc 2. Prod. Brent Wood. Kino on Video, 2005. DVD.
6 *The Jazz Singer* (1928) was the breakthrough "talkie" for America. It was a silent film, but also included some singing and dialogue. It also featured Whites in blackface.
7 The language of "horror film" was not yet part of the American lexicon. That would not happen until the 1930s with such Universal Studios films as *Dracula.* Instead, horror films were described as "chillers," "shockers," "thrillers," and "frightening." But these adjectives advertised emotional response; they did not hail a genre association.
8 Noble, Peter. *The Negro in Films.* New York: Arno Press & The New York Times, 1970. 27. Print.
9 Butters, Jr., Gerald R. *Black Manhood on the Silent Screen.* Lawrence: University of Kansas Press, 2002. 34. Print.
10 Butters (20).
11 Butters (20).
12 Jones, G. William. *Black Cinema Treasures: Lost and Found.* Denton: University of North Texas Press, 1991. 14–15. Print.

13 Butters (32).

14 Musser, Charles. *Before the Nickelodeon: Edwin S. Porter and the Edison Manufacturing Company.* Berkeley: University of California Press, 1991. 530. Print.

15 Butters (22).

16 Richards, Larry. *African American Films through 1959: A Comprehensive, Illustrated Filmography.* Jefferson, NC: McFarland & Company, Inc. Publishers, 1998. 90. Print.

17 Cripps, Thomas. *Slow Fade to Black: The Negro in American Film, 1900–1942.* New York: Oxford University Press, 1993. 135. Print.

18 Butters (31).

19 Stewart, Jacqueline Najuma. *Migrating to the Movies: Cinema and Black Urban Modernity.* Berkeley: University of California Press, 2005. See: 4–43. Print.

20 Quoted by Richards, Larry (177).

21 Leab, Daniel J. *From Sambo to Superspade: The Black Experience in Motion Pictures.* Boston, MA: Houghton Mifflin Company, 1975. 13. Print.

22 Fanon, Frantz. *Black Skin, White Masks.* London: Pluto Press, 1986. 93. Print.

23 Leab (*From Sambo* 26).

24 Robinson, Cedric J. *Forgeries of Memory & Meaning: Blacks & the Regimes of Race in American Theater & Film before World War II.* Chapel Hill: University of North Carolina Press, 2007. 108. Print.

25 Snead, James. *White Screens, Black Images: Hollywood from the Dark Side.* New York: Routledge, 1994. 39. Print.

26 Guerrero, Edward *Framing Blackness: The African American Image in Film.* Philadelphia, PA: Temple University Press, 1993. 17. Print.

27 Butters (71, emphasis mine).

28 Carter, Everett. "Cultural History Written with Lightening: The Significance of the Birth of a Nation (1915)." *Hollywood as Historian: American Film in a Cultural Context.* Ed. Peter C. Rollins. Lexington: University of Kentucky Press, 1998. 304. Print.

29 Bogle, Donald. *Toms, Coons, Mulattoes, Mammies, & Bucks.* New York: The Continuum Publishing Company, 1993. 13–14. Print.

30 Bogle (*Toms, Coons* 13–14).

31 Guerrero (*Framing Blackness* 13).

32 Snead (41).

33 Carter (vii).

34 Cripps, Thomas. *Black Film as Genre.* Bloomington: Indiana University Press, 1978. 22. Print.

35 Noble (43).

36 Cripps (*Slow Fade* 64).

37 Clover, Carol J. *Men, Women, and Chainsaws: Gender in the Modern Horror Film.* Princeton, NJ: Princeton University Press, 1992. 34. Print.

38 The Whales 1931 Universal *Frankenstein* is considered the classic, seminal film. An earlier, 1910 short, at 16 minutes, directed by J. Searle Dawley through Edison Studios, precedes this effort, and may be the first film adaptation of the Mary Shelley (1818) *Frankenstein* novel.

39 Crane, Jonathan. *Terror and Everyday Life.* Thousand Oaks, CA: Sage Publications, 1994. 91. Print.

40 Crane (72–73).

41 Pinedo, Isabel Cristina. *Recreational Terror: Women and the Pleasure of Horror Film Viewing.* Albany, New York: SUNY Press, 1997. 54. Print.

42 Pinedo (55).

43 Butters (73).

44 Williams, Linda. "When the Woman Looks." *The Dread of Difference: Gender and the Horror Film.* Ed. Barry Keith Grant. Austin: University of Texas Press, 1996. 20. Print.

45 Goldberg, D.J. *Discontented America: The United States in the 1920s.* Baltimore, MD: Johns Hopkins University Press, 1999. 117. Print.

46 Southern Poverty Law Center. 2010. Southern Poverty Law Center. http://www. splcenter.org/. Web June 8, 2009. Also see: Stokes, M. *D.W. Griffith's the Birth of a Nation: A History of the most Controversial Film of All Time.* New York: Oxford University Press, 2007. 9. Print.

47 Bogle (*Toms, Coons* 13–14).

48 Cripps (*Genre* 15).

49 In the film, the woman, Sylvia, is mixed race (Black and White) and adopted by and raised in a Black family. She is to be read as Black.

50 Richards (152).

51 Butters (105).

52 Butters (105).

53 Butters (xvi).

54 Bowser, P., and L. Spence. *Writing Himself into History: Oscar Micheaux, His Silent Films, and His Audiences.* New Brunswick, NJ: Rutgers University Press, 2000. 115. Print.

55 "Carey Theater, *The Crimson Skull.*" *Afro-American*, May 19, 1922: 4. Print.

56 Many of Ebony's films, like most films of from the 1800s and early 1900s, are lost.

57 Bowser and Spence (92).

58 "Ebony Films" [Letter to the Editor]. *Chicago Defender*, July 1, 1916 (4).

59 Bowser and Spence (92).

60 Bowser and Spence (10).

61 Bowser and Spence (10).

62 Davis, T. "Foreword." *Writing Himself into History: Oscar Micheaux, His Silent Films, and His Audiences.* Eds. Pearl Bowser and Louise Spence. New Brunswick, NJ: Rutgers University Press, 2000. ix. Print.

63 Bowser and Spence (16).

64 Bowser and Spence (16).

65 Bowser and Spence (17).

66 Bowser and Spence (17 144).

67 Some movie posters for *A Son of Satan* misprint the story's title as "Tolson's," rather than "Tolston's." There may have also been occasions in which *A Son of Satan* was marketed under the alternate title *The Ghost of Tolston's Manor*, thereby leading to some confusion as to whether these were two distinct films. Credible scholarship, such as that produced by Pearl Bowser, Louise Spence, Jane Gaines, and Charles Musser, leads to the conclusion that *A Son of Satan* is the film, and *The Ghost of Tolston's Manor* is the story.

68 Regester, Charlene. "The African-American Press and Race Movies, 1909–1929." *Oscar Micheaux & His Circle: African-American Filmmaking and Race Cinema of the Silent Era.* Eds. Pearl Bowser, Jane Gaines, and Charles Musser. Bloomington and Indianapolis: Indiana University Press: 2001. 47. Print.

69 Musser, Charles, Corey K. Creekmur, Pearl Bowser, J. Ronald Green, Charlene Regester, and Louise Spence. "Appendix B: An Oscar Micheaux Filmography: From the Silents Through His Transition to Sound, 1919–1931." *Oscar Micheaux & His Circle: African-American Filmmaking and Race Cinema of the Silent Era.* Eds. Pearl Bowser, Jane Gaines, and Charles Musser. Bloomington and Indianapolis: Indiana University Press, 2001. 252. Print.

70 Butters (139).

71 Musser, Creekmur, Bowser, Green, Regester, and Spence (251).

72 Musser, Creekmur, Bowser, Green, Regester, and Spence (256).

73 According to Zora Hurston, hoodoo is an African-Americanism for the West African term "juju." Conjuring, a kind of folk magic, through the use of roots and/or the

mixture of herbs is part of the tradition, as is engaged prayer. See: Hurston, Zora. "Hoodoo in America." *Journal of American Folklore* 44 (October–December 1931): 174. 317–417. Print.

74 Musser, Creekmur, Bowser, Green, Regester, and Spence (260–261).

75 Musser, Creekmur, Bowser, Green, Regester, and Spence (261).

76 Du Bois, W.E.B. *The Souls of Black Folks.* New York: NAL Penguin, 1903/1969. 45. Print.

77 Nesteby, James R. *Black Images in American Films, 1896–1954.* Lanham, MD: University Press of America, 1982. 79. Print.

2 Jungle Fever—A Horror Romance: 1930s

1 O'Reilly, Bill. "Inside Edition." *Haiti's Bad Press.* Ed. Robert Lawless. Rochester, VT: Schenkman Books, 1992. 20. Print.

2 Golden, Nathan D. *Brief History and Statistics of the American Motion Picture Industry.* Washington, DC: GPO, August 14, 1936. Print.

3 Hutchings, Peter. *The Horror Film.* London: Pearson, 2004. pp. vi, 3. Print.

4 When *Dracula* (1931) proved popular, it is reported that Universal Studios announced it was going to make "another horror film," marking the first time the term "horror film" was used. See: Jones, Alan. *The Rough Guide to Horror Movies.* New York: Rough Guides, 2005, p. 21. Print.

5 According to a report for the *Pittsburgh Courier*, in 1934 when Universal Studios premiered the interracial relations-themed drama *Imitation of Life*, starring Black actress Louise Beavers, the studio refused to provide press passes to Black reporters as was the common practice for such race films. The paper proclaimed Universal's message was "the Black press means nothing to us." See: "Race Press Ignored by Big Film Interests: Louise Beavers 'On Spot.'" *Pittsburgh Courier*, December 15, 1934: A9. Print.

6 Roosevelt, Theodore. *African Game Trails: An Account of the African Wanderings of an American Hunter-Naturalist.* New York: Charles Schribner's Sons, 1910. 280. Print.

7 Hendricks, Bill and Howard Waugh. *The Encyclopedia of Exploitation.* New York: Showmen's Trade Review, 1937. 138. Print.

8 Hill Collins, Patricia. *Black Sexual Politics: African Americans, Gender, and the New Racism.* New York: Routledge, 2004. 27, 29. Print.

9 Erish, Andrew. "Illegitimate Dad of 'Kong.'" *Los Angeles Times*, January 8, 2006. Web. June 20, 2010. http://articles.latimes.com/2006/jan/08/entertainment/ca-ingagi8. One of the Depression's highest-grossing films was an outrageous fabrication, a scandalous and suggestive gorilla epic that set box office records across the country.

10 Berenstein, Rhona J. "White Heroines and Hearts of Darkness: Race, Gender and Disguise in 1930s Jungle Films." *Film History* 6 (1994): 316. Print.

11 Berenstein (317).

12 Berenstein (318).

13 *Ingagi* was just one of the hoaxes played against movie-goers and at Blacks' expense at the time. In March of 1930, a Black actor, Firpo Jacko, filed suit against "Dr." Daniel Davenport, a White filmmaker and purported African explorer, for unpaid wages. In the case, Jacko asserted that the "documentary" film *Jango* (1929), set in the Congo, was a hoax and that the "real cannibals" brought back to tour the United States to promote the film were really from Harlem. The lawsuit revealed that *Jango* was not filmed in the Congo, but in the Bronx, New York, and that Jacko the cannibal— who screamed "uga-uga-googie, woogie" at audiences, was really Jacko the janitor from Harlem. The suit also challenged the assertion that Davenport had ever been to Africa. Jacko's key witness was his landlord, Mrs. Montgomery, who was called to

offer evidence that Jacko could not be a cannibal because he attends "church every Sunday." Jacko was awarded his $700 back pay. See: "'Jango' Filmed in Wilds' of Bronx, 'Cannibal' Says." *Pittsburgh Press*, March 9, 1930: 15 News-Section-Editorial. Print. "Wild Cannibal Turns Out to Be Ex-Janitor: Salary Suit Reveals Harlem as Scene of Fake Movie." *Chicago Defender*, March 15, 1930: 3. Print.

14 Erish.

15 Everett, Anna. *Returning the Gaze: A Genealogy of Black Film Criticism, 1909–1949*. Durham, NC: Duke University Press, 2001. 243–244. Print.

16 "Ingagi Review Summary." *New York Times*. NYTimes.com. Web. June 18, 2010. This was Congo's one and only picture.

17 Erish; Erb, Cynthia. *Tracking King Kong: A Hollywood Icon in World Cinema*, 2nd ed. Detroit, MI: Wayne State University Press, 2009, for discussions on copyright infringement concerns around ape films.

18 Snead, James. *White Screens, Black Images: Hollywood from the Dark Side*. New York: Routledge: 1994. 8. Print.

19 Native, jungle, or Voodoo drums were not tinny but deeply resounding. It was the "frightening" bass that became associated with Blackness. The bass and Blacks in popular culture have a long tradition dating back at least to 1887 in Verdi's *Othello*, when the conductor specifies in the orchestral score that only those string basses with the low E string be heard in scenes with the Moor. See: Andre, Naomi. "Race and Opera." University of Michigan. March 2009. Presentation.

20 Snead (17).

21 Bogle, Donald. *Bright Boulevards, Bold Dreams: The Story of Black Hollywood*. New York: Ballantine One World, 2005. 62. Print.

22 Rony, Fatimah Tobing. *The Third Eye: Race, Cinema, and Ethnographic Spectacle*. Durham, NC: Duke University Press, 1996. 177. Print.

23 Etta McDaniel plays the silent, nonplussed ape-bride. She is one of an implied string of many who will be needed to placate Kong. See: *King Kong*. Dir. Doran Cox. Perf. Fay Wray, Robert Armstrong, Bruce Cabot. RKO Radio Pictures Inc. 1933. Film.

24 Greenberg, Harvey Roy. "*King Kong*: The Beast in the Boudoir—Or, 'You Can't Marry that Girl, You're a Gorilla!'" *The Dread of Difference: Gender and the Horror Film*. Ed. Barry Keith Grant. Austin: University of Texas Press, 1996. 344. Print.

25 Greenberg (340).

26 Humphries notes that parallels have been drawn between Kong's (unseen) phallus and the very phallic-like image of the big black bolt, which secures the massive door that contains the ape. See Humphries, Reynold. *The Hollywood Horror Film 1931–1941: Madness in a Social Landscape*. Lanham, MD: The Scarecrow Press, 2006. 82. Print.

27 Sontag, Susan. "The Imagination of Disaster." *Commentary* (October 1965): 44. Print.

28 Greenberg (338).

29 Skal, David J. *The Monster Show: A Cultural History of Horror*. Revised ed. New York: Faber and Faber, Inc., 2001. 175. Print.

30 Young, Elizabeth. "Here Comes the Bride: Wedding Gender and Race in *Bride of Frankenstein*." *The Dread of Difference: Gender and the Horror Film*. Barry Keith Grant. Austin: University of Texas Press: 1996. 325. Print.

31 Tyler, Bruce M. "Racial Imagery in *King Kong*." *King Kong Cometh!: The Evolution of the Great Ape*. Ed. Paula A. Woods London: Plexus Publishing, 2005. 175. Print.

32 *Behind the Planet of the Apes*. Dirs. David Comtois and Kevin Burns. Perf. Roddy McDowell. Image Entertainment, 1998. Film.

33 *Behind the Planet of the Apes*. Dirs. David Comtois and Kevin Burns. Perf. Roddy McDowell. Image Entertainment, 1998. Film

34 Greene, Eric. *Planet of the Apes as American Myth: Race and Politics in the Films and Television Series*. Jefferson, NC: McFarland & Co., Inc., 1996. 84. Print.

35 Hurston, Zora Neale. *Tell My Horse*. New York: Harper Perennial, 1938/1990. 179. Print.

36 "Haiti Country Profile." *BBC*. BBC. 2010. Web. August 11, 2010. http://news.bbc.co.uk/2/hi/americas/country_profiles/1202772.stm.

37 "Living Vodou." *Speaking of Faith with Krista Tippett*. American Public Media. June 28, 2007. Radio.

38 Thomson, Ian. "The Black Spartacus." *Guardian News and Media*. January 31, 2004. Web. June 23, 2010. Guardian.co.uk. Thomson adds: "Most historians agree that Haiti's slaves first rose up in rebellion under a Jamaican Voodoo priest named Boukman. On the night of August 15, 1791, Boukman called on the spirits of ancestral Africa to punish the plantocracy. L'Ouverture was said to have taken part in this ceremony and within six weeks the island's rebel slave armies had begun their 12-year struggle for freedom; that night, a thousand French whites were reportedly massacred and their plantations set ablaze." See also: Steward, Theophilus Gould. *The Haitian Revolution, 1791 to 1804: Or, Side Lights on the French Revolution*, 2nd ed. New York: Thomas Y. Crowell Publishers, 1914. Print. Steward, a historian, AME minister, and Chaplain in the U.S. Army writes of Boukman, L'Ouverture, and others meeting under "the veil of pretended Voodou ceremonies" to organize the revolution. The role of Vodou in the uprising may have taken on mythic qualities over the years; however, it is agreed upon that Boukman, born in Jamaica, was a Vodou Priest.

39 Gelder, Ken. "Postcolonial Voodoo." *Postcolonial Studies* 3 (2000): 95-96. Print.

40 Lawless Robert. *Haiti's Bad Press*. Rochester, VT: Schenkman Books, 1992. 73. Print. shows that Voodoo, alternately spelled vaudou, vaudoun, vudu, vodun, vodoun, really describes a type of dance emanating out of Africa. More, the naming and description of that dance, from the Dahomean (Benin), was penned by a White foreigner. Hence, the origin of the term may be a non-indigenous construction from its very start.

41 Lawless (56).

42 Lawless (109).

43 I use the spelling "Voodoo" just as the films discussed in this book do. In doing so, I work to distinguish entertainment fiction's depiction of evil rituals performed by Blacks from discussion of the Haitian religion Vodou or the West African religion Vodun. American horror films have largely depicted the Louisiana version of the religion, "Voodoo."

44 Rhodes, Gary D. *White Zombie: Anatomy of a Horror Film*. Jefferson, NC: McFarland & Company, Inc., 2001. 78. Print.

45 Seabrook, W.B. *The Magic Island*. New York: Harcourt, Brace and Company, 1929. 42. Print.

46 Seabrook (310).

47 Seabrook (324).

48 Seabrook (93).

49 Rhodes (15–16).

50 L.N. "The Screen. Beyond the Pale." *New York Times*, July 29, 1932: 8. Print.

51 Cited in: Rhodes (46). Later the line was changed to "zombies stole a White girl … the fury of hell broke loose."

52 In another scene, near the end of the film, Neil visits a White doctor/minister, Dr. Bruner (Joseph Cawthorn), to get help for his entranced Madeline. Dr. Bruner advises that they visit his friend, a native witchdoctor and "great old fellow," named Pierre (Dan Crimmins), for help. The audiences' introduction to Pierre establishes him as good, rather than the (stereotypical) wicked witchdoctor. He is seen traveling along a road by mule, coming upon a Black man herding an ox. Pierre senses danger

enveloping the area (due to Murder's recent misdeeds) and stops the man to give him a protective amulet. Pierre then provides the man with a second one, this time to protect the man's ox as well. The witchdoctor, unfortunately, is portrayed by the White actor Dan Crimmins, who is made to look Haitian through dark make-up. Such a racist erasure is devastating to the character's possibilities. See: *White Zombie*. Dir. Victor Halperin. Perf. Bela Lugosi. United Artists Corp., 1932. Film.

53 Seabrook (94).

54 Tony Williams sees Muse's performance as a stereotypical scared-Negro performance. See: Williams, Tony. "White Zombie Haitian Horror." *Jump Cut* 28 (April, 1983): 18–20. Print. Rhodes (321) was the target of criticism from Johanne Tournier in the liner notes accompanying the laser disc release of *White Zombie* for being too effusive regarding Muse's portrayal. Muse's character is scared, and he is a Negro, and together the two carry the baggage of stereotypical treatment. However, in this particular representation he plays his fear rather straight, and certainly far from the popular scared-Negro performances that have dominated film before, and which will take center-stage in Chapter 3 through the performances of Stepin Fetchit and Sleep 'n' Eat.

55 As cited in: Noble, Peter. *The Negro in Films*. New York: Arno Press & the New York Times, 1970. 8. Print.

56 Rhodes (178).

57 Dayan, Joan. *Haiti, History, and the Gods*. Berkeley: University of California Press, 1988. 175, 178. Print.

58 Soister, John T. *Up From the Vault: Rare Thrillers of the 1920s and 1930s*. Jefferson, NC: McFarland and Company, 2004. 183. Print.

59 Muse, Clarence. "When a Negro Sings a Song." *Celebrity Articles from the Screen Guild Magazine*. Ed. Anna Kate Sterling. Lanham, MD: Rowman & Littlefield, 1987. 13. Print.

60 Bogle, Donald. *Toms, Coons, Mulattoes, Mammies, & Bucks: An Interpretative History of Blacks in American Films*. New York: Continuum, 1993. 54. Print. Muse's astuteness has often been attributed to his intelligence. Muse was a graduate of Dickinson School of Law (PA).

61 Bogle (*Toons Coons* 54).

62 Schroeder, Caroline T. "Ancient Egyptian Religion on the Silver Screen: Modern Anxieties about Race, Ethnicity, and Religion." *Journal of Religion and Film* 2.3 (October 2003). Web. November 8, 2009. www.unomaha.Edu/jrf/Vol7No2/ ancientegypt.htm.

63 The film was released under a number of titles in the US and abroad—*Drums of the Jungle, Love Wanga, The Love Wanga*, and *Ouanga*. The Canadian release, *The Love Wanga*, is readily available for purchase today, and is the same running time as the U.S. version. Hence, there is likely little difference between the two films. I viewed both versions of the film, but years apart, and could not secure the U.S. version to compare side-by-side against the Canadian. My notes and memory have the two versions as being the same. The film's opening credits boast that *The Love Wanga* was filmed in its entirely in the West Indies.

64 Orbe, Mark and Karen Strother. "Signifying the Tragic Mulatto: A Semiotic Analysis of Alex Haley's Queen." *Howard Journal of Communications* 7 (April 1996): 113–126. Print.

65 *The Love Wanga* is the second zombie film in what quickly becomes a string of such movies.

66 Dayan (37–38)

67 The film industry's content was regulated by the Hay's Office, which presented "the Code" or rules for Hollywood on issues of morality in film. Forbidden by the Code in the 1930s: "Miscegenation (sex relationships between the White and

Black races.)" Sexual perversion, semi-nudity, dancing representing sexual action, and "racial and religious prejudices" were also "immoral," but none of these latter issues seemed to apply to representation of Blacks. See: Hays, Will H. *Annual Report of the President*. New York: Motion Picture Producers and Distributors of America, 1936. Print.

68 Dayan (174).

69 Guerrero, Edward *Framing Blackness: The African American Image in Film*. Philadelphia, PA: Temple University Press, 1993. 23. Print. Guerrero also observes that the Big House provided Depression-era audiences with an insider view of aristocracy.

70 As cited in: Everett (246).

71 Bishop, Kyle William. *American Zombie Gothic: The Rise and Fall (and Rise) of the Walking Dead in Popular Culture*. Jefferson, NC: McFarland & Co, 2010. 60. Print.

72 Lawless (10).

3 Horrifying Goons and Minstrel Coons: 1940s

1 Jaffray, Norman R. "The Spine Chillers." *The Monster Show: A Cultural History of Horror*. Ed. David J. Skal. New York: Faber and Faber, Inc., 1993. 174. Print.

2 Jones, Alan. *The Rough Guide to Horror Movies*. New York: Rough Guides/Penguin, 2005. 24. Print.

3 According to Jones (24). The horror film took a particularly devastating hit in Britain, with only four films making it to the screen between 1940 and 1945.

4 The film is loosely based on Charlotte Brontë's *Jane Eyre* (1847), and as a horror film with a non-horror literary heritage (i.e. compared to Shelley's Frankenstein) it has attracted its fair share of critical attention.

5 Humphries, Reynold. *The American Horror Film*. Edinburgh: Edinburgh University Press, 2002. 48–49. Print. Later, in 2009, Humphries would hail *I Walked With a Zombie* as one of the most significant contributions to the horror genre. *Zombie* is credited for being "dense, complex, and multilayered" thanks to a "brilliant script" which also offers an "exceptionally subtle analysis of repression in every sense." See: Humphries, Reynold. "I Walked With a Zombie." *101 Horror Movies You Must See Before You Die*. Ed. Steven Jay Schneider. London; Quintessence, 2009. 85–86. Print.

6 Hutchings, Peter. *The Horror Film*. Harlow, England: Pearson, 2004. 111. Print.

7 In Vodou, the spirit Carrefour controls the "crossroads," or path to death.

8 Often, there was little exploration into Blacks' stories. They are simply natives or servants and are often not given names in films, or, worse, the actors who portray them receive no credit. As late as 1968, with *Night of the Living Dead*'s Ben, little is known about the lives of horror films' Black stars. That would change with *Blacula* (1972), in which the Black character Mamuwalde's life history is carefully laid out. Later, over the course of two films, *Candyman* (1992) and *Candyman: Farewell to the Flesh* (1995), the Candyman/Daniel Robitaille story emerges.

9 Hutchings (111).

10 Crowther, Bosley. "Old Black Magic." *New York Times*, June 13, 1943: sec. X3. Print.

11 In the last few minutes of the film, when Mumbo Jumbo has to explain to the White men that he saw the pongo carry off a White woman, his character is suddenly fluent in English and without an accent (no 'me boy, you Bwana' type talk). In reference to the ape, Mumbo Jumbo seriously observes, "I certainly hope his disposition improves." It is a nice peek into what Fluellen could have brought to such a character. However, in this extremely low-budget film, Mumbo Jumbo's sudden, inexplicable fluency comes across as if the film's director, Sam Newfield, simply forget that Mumbo Jumbo started the film speaking in very limited, broken English.

12 The film featured the famed man-in-an-ape-suit actor Ray Corrigan from the horror films *White Pongo* and *Nabonga* as the white gorilla.

13 "A Battle for Jungle Supremacy" was a tagline in the film's trailer. See: "The White Gorilla." *YouTube*. YouTube, LLC. 2010. Web. July 26, 2010. http://www.youtube. com/watch?v=n_c47ZGZ5I8.

14 Cripps, Thomas. *Slow Fade to Black: The Negro in American Film, 1900–1942*. New York: Oxford University Press, 1993. 374. Print.

15 Cripps (*Slow Fade* 374).

16 Bogle, Donald. *Bright Boulevards, Bold Dream: The Story of Black Hollywood*. New York: Ballantine One World, 2005. 126. Print.

17 Muse, Clarence. "What's Going on in Hollywood." *Chicago Defender*, December 28, 1940: 21. Print.

18 Cripps (*Slow Fade* 376–378).

19 Leab, Daniel J. *From Sambo to Superspade: The Black Experience in Motion Pictures*. Boston, MA: Houghton Mifflin Company, 1973. 130. Print.

20 Cripps (*Slow Fade* 376).

21 On the point of treatment, Reddick identified 19 stereotypes he wanted buried: the savage African, the happy slave, the devoted servant, the corrupt politician, the petty thief, the social delinquent, the vicious criminal, the sexual superman, the superior athlete, the unhappy non-White, the natural-born cook, the natural-born musician, the perfect entertainer, the superstitious church-goer, the chicken and watermelon eater, the razor and knife "toter," the uninhibited expressionist, and the mental inferior.

22 Reddick, Lawrence D. "Educational Programs for the Improvement of Race Relations: Motion Pictures, Radio, the Press, and Libraries." *Journal of Negro Education* 13.3 (1944): 369, 382. Print.

23 Fifty years after *Son of Ingagi*, films focusing on the Black wedding remain novel, and are often hailed as positive, such as the romantic-comedies *The Wood* (1999) and *The Best Man* (1999).

24 hooks, bell. *Reel to Real: Race, Sex, and Class at the Movies*. New York: Routledge, 1996. 167. Print.

25 Cripps, Thomas. *Making Movies Black: The Hollywood Message Movie from World War II to the Civil Rights Era*. New York: Oxford University Press, 1993. 133. Print.

26 Sobchack, Vivian. *Screening Space: The American Science Fiction Film*. New Brunswick, NJ: Rutgers University Press, 2001. 30. Print.

27 Cripps, Thomas. *Black Film as Genre*. Bloomington: Indiana University Press, 1978. 90. Print.

28 Cripps (*Genre* 90).

29 Manatu, Norma. *African American Women and Sexuality in the Cinema*. Jefferson, NC: McFarland & Company, Inc., 2003. 53. Print.

30 Cripps, Thomas. "The Films of Spencer Williams." *Black American Literature Forum* 12 (1978): 131. Print.

31 Creed, Barbara. *The Monstrous-Feminine: Film, Feminism, Psychoanalysis*. London: Routledge, 1993. 37. Print.

32 See: Gibson, Gloria J. "Cinematic Foremothers: Zora Neale Hurston and Eloyce King Patrick Gist." *Oscar Micheaux & His Circle: African-American Filmmaking and Race Cinema of the Silent Era*. Eds. Pearl Bowser, Jane Gaines, and Charles Musser. Bloomington: Indiana University Press, 2001. 195–209. Print. See also: Gibson-Hudson, Gloria. "Recall and Recollect: Excavating the Life History of Eloyce King Patrick Gist." *Black Film Review* 8 (1994): 20–21. Print.

33 Gibson-Hudson (20–21).

34 Gibson (200).

35 Gibson-Hudson (20–21).

36 Gibson (203).

37 Gibson (203).

38 Gibson (203–204).

39 Gibson-Hudson (20–21).

40 The Library of Congress: American Memory, Library of Congress. 2010. Web. July 26, 2010. Out of sequence fragments for *Hellbound Train* are held by the Library of Congress; a fire destroyed the remaining associated materials/documents related to the Gists' lives and careers. Gloria J. Gibson (Hudson) made an effort to decipher the order of the fragments, as she discusses in detail; see: Gibson (195–209).

41 The summary of this film comes in great part from: Senn, Bryan. *Golden Horrors: An Illustrated Critical Filmography 1931–1939*. Jefferson, NC: McFarland & Company, Inc., 1996. Print.

42 Cripps (Films of Spencer Williams 132).

43 Holland, Sharon Patricia. *Raising the Dead: Readings of Death and (Black) Subjectivity*. Durham, NC: Duke University Press, 2000. 33. Print.

44 The Black filmmaker Charles Burnett would build an entire movie around modern rituals of watching over the dying, at their home bedside, in his haunting film of good and evil *To Sleep With Anger* (1990). In *Anger*, the almost dead, Gideon (Paul Butler) struggles to return to the living, while an evil thrives, distracting and wreaking havoc among those who should be gathered at his bedside in prayer.

45 Clover, Carol. "Her Body, Himself: Gender in the Slasher Film." *The Dread of Difference: Gender and the Horror Film*. Ed. Barry Keith Grant. Austin: University of Texas Press, 1996. 78. Print.

46 Cripps (*Making* 141).

47 Cripps (*Making* 134, 330).

48 Razaf, Andy. "A Colored Movie Fan." *New York Amsterdam News*, January 6, 1940: 16. Print.

49 Coleman, Robin Means. *African American Viewers and the Black Situation Comedy: Situating Racial Humor*. New York: Garland, 2000. 35. Print.

50 Coleman (45).

51 McCaffrey, Donald W. "The Golden Age of Sound Comedy." *Screen* 11 (1970): 27–40. 33. Print.

52 Reid, Mark A. *Redefining Black Film*. Berkeley: University of California Press, 1993. 23, 25. Print.

53 Denzin, Norman K. *Reading Race*. London: Sage, 2002. 18. Print.

54 Koppes, Clayton R. and Gregory D. Blacks. "What to Show the World: The Office of War Information and Hollywood, 1942–1945." *Journal of American History* (1977): 87–105. Print.

55 Cripps, Thomas R. "The Death of Rastus: Negroes in American Films since 1945." *Phylon* 28 (1967): 269. Print.

56 Nesteby, James R. *Black Images in American Films, 1896–1954: The Interplay Between Civil Rights and Film Culture*. Lanham, MD: University Press of America, 1982. 222. Print.

57 Noble, Peter. *The Negro in Film*. New York: Arno Press & the New York Times, 1970. 181–182. Print.

58 Bogle, Donald. *Toms, Coon, Mulattoes, Mammies, and Bucks: An Interpretive History of Blacks in American Films*. New York: Continuum, 1993. 74. Print.

59 Guerrero, Ed. *Framing Blackness: The African American Image in Film*. Philadelphia, PA: University of Temple Press, 1993. 123. Print.

60 *Revolt of the Zombies* (1936), for example, recast the zombie mythology away from Black Voodoo to the purview of a fanatical "Oriental" priest from Angkor Wat, Cambodia, whose power could be used to raise a zombie army, tipping the scales of military power, and thereby bringing "the destruction of the White race."

61 Leab, Daniel J. "The Gamut from A to B: The Image of the Black in Pre-1915 Movies." *Political Science Quarterly* 88 (1973): 63. Print.

62 Nesteby (222).

63 *The Scarlet Clue* (1945).

64 Robinson, Cedric J. *Forgeries of Memory & Meaning: Blacks & the Regimes of Race in American Theater & Film before World War II.* Chapel Hill: University of North Carolina Press, 2007. 376–378. Print.

65 Robinson (376–378).

66 Kliman, Bernice W. "The Biscuit Eater: Racial Stereotypes: 1939–1972." *Phylon* 39 (1978): 92. Print.

67 Noble (181).

68 Bogle (*Toms, Coons* 72); Bogle (*Bright* 118).

69 *Spooks on the Loose* presents one of the oddest endings to a film. The character Glimpy (Huntz Hall), after fighting with the Nazis, comes down with the German measles, which are represented, seemingly comically, as dozens of tiny Swatikas all over his face.

70 Neuert, Richard. "Trouble in Watermelon Land: George Pal and the Little Jasper Cartoons." *Film Quarterly* 55 (2001): 18. Print.

71 Neuert (18).

72 The scene bears strong resemblance to the 1929 Mickey Mouse short *Haunted House*, in which Mickey calls for his mammy, in blackface, in tribute to Al Jolson's 1927 performance in *The Jazz Singer*. Mickey is then forced by a ghost to play piano while skeletons dance.

73 Neuert (16, 21).

74 Neuert (16, 21).

75 "Little Jasper Series Draws Protest from Negro Groups." *Ebony*, January 1947: 27. Print.

76 Neuert (23).

77 Cripps (Films of Spencer Williams 133).

78 "Oregon Station Drops 'Little Jasper' Series." *Los Angeles Sentinel*, June 4, 1959: C1. Print.

79 Bogle (*Bright* 278).

80 "Boris Karloff Joins Fight For Race Equality." *Atlanta Daily World*, September 30, 1947: 1. Print.

81 Coleman (81).

4 Black Invisibility, White Science, and a Night with Ben: 1950s–1960s

1 *Invisible Man* was published as a whole in 1952, and it has been often reprinted. I cite the March 1995 edition here: Ellison, Ralph. *Invisible Man*. New York: Vintage International, 1995. 3. Print.

2 Metress, Christopher. *The Lynching of Emmett Till: A Documentary Narrative.* Charlottesville: University of Virginia Press, 2002. 227. Print.

3 Ellison, Ralph. 1952. *Invisible Man*. New York: Vintage International, 1995. 94. Print.

4 Phillips, Kendall R. *Projected Fears: Horror Films and American Culture.* Westport, CT: Praeger, 2005. 7. Print.

5 For its cinematic innovation, *Invasion* has been inducted into the United States National Film Registry by the National Film Preservation Board. Library of Congress. January 25, 2010. Web. June 17, 2010. It took 47th place, out of 100, on the American Film Institute's (AFI) list of the most-scary films.

6 The term pod is used to describe cookie-cutter suburban enclaves inhabited by bored individuals (see: Duany, Andres, Elizabeth Plater-Zyberk, and Jeff Speck. *Suburban Nation: The Rise of Sprawl and the Decline of the American Dream*. New York: North Point Press, 2000. Print).

7 Wood, Robin. "An Introduction to the American Horror Film." *Movies and Methods: Volume II*. Ed., Bill Nichols. Berkeley: University of California Press, 1985. 195–220, 198–199. Print.

8 Cripps, Thomas. *Making Movies Black: The Hollywood Message Movie from World War II to the Civil Rights Era*. New York: Oxford University Press, 1993. 257. Print.

9 Roth also portrays the gorillas in the movie. Presumably Taro is another exotic trophy of Dan's.

10 Sontag, Susan. "The Imagination of Disaster." *Commentary*, October (1965): 45. Print.

11 In the spoof comedy-crime caper film *The Gristle* (2001), the Black character "Tar" (Michael Dorn) mocks the continued, obsessive concern over threats to White womanhood by Black (sexually attractive) men by offering this line, in faux-racist Black voice, to a group of White men.

12 Gonder, Patrick. "Like a Monstrous Jigsaw Puzzle: Genetics and Race in Horror Films of the 1950s." *The Velvet Light Trap* 52 (2003): 39. Print.

13 Humphries, Reynold. *The American Horror Film: An Introduction*. Edinburgh, UK: Edinburgh University Press, 2002. 63. Print.

14 Gonder (Monstrous 39).

15 Gonder, Patrick. "Race, Gender and Terror: The Primitive in 1950s Horror Films." *Genders* 40 (2004). Web. June 18, 2010. http://www.genders/org/.

16 Goldsby, Jacqueline. "The High and Low Tech of It: The Meaning of Lynching and the Death of Emmett Till." *Yale Journal of Criticism* 9 (1996): 250. Print.

17 Butters, Jr., Gerald R. *Black Manhood on the Silent Screen*. Lawrence: University of Kansas Press, 2002. xvii. Print.

18 Schneider, Steven Jay. "Mixed Blood Couples: Monsters and Miscegenation in U.S. Horror Cinema." *The Gothic Other: Racial and Social Constructions in the Literary Imagination*. Ed. R. Bienstock Anolik and D. L. Howard. Jefferson, NC: McFarland & Company, Inc., 2004. 78. Print.

19 Romero directed *Night of the Living Dead*, and co-wrote the screenplay with John Russo. The film was produced by Image Ten, a group of filmmakers that included Romero and Russo, who also contributed to the script, acted in the movies, and worked on lighting and make-up.

20 Hervey, Ben. *Night of the Living Dead*. New York: Palgrave Macmillan, 2008. 63. Print.

21 Stein, Elliott. "Night of the Living Dead." *Sight and Sound* 39 (1970): 105. Print.

22 Wood, Robin. *Hollywood from Vietnam to Reagan*. New York: Columbia University Press, 1986. 114. Print.

23 Becker, Matt. "A Point of Little Hope: Hippie Horror Films and the Politics of Ambivalence." *The Velvet Light Trap* 57 (2006): 58. Print.

24 Becker (42, 51, 58).

25 Stein (105).

26 Hervey (110). According to Hervey, these scenes made Romero and his film seem even more radical and rebellious as he used the police themselves to make a statement about the Establishment.

27 Becker, Michael and Mike Carbone. "Tony Todd." *Reel Horror*. Episode 25. June 2, 2010. http://legacy-content.libsyn.com/vidhack/reel_horror-ep25-070306.mp3. Radio.

28 Hervey (112).

29 Hervey (113–114).

30 Hervey (118).

31 Dyer, Richard. "White." *Screen* 29 (1988): 45. Print.

32 Heffernan, Kevin. "Inner-City Exhibition and the Genre Film: Distributing Night of the Living Dead." *Cinema Journal* 41 (2002): 59–77. 59. Print.

33 Humphries (*The American Horror Film* 115).

34 Because *Night*, due to an error in the copyright, is a public domain film, it is difficult to gauge its profits. However, according to IMDb.com and BoxOfficeMojo.com, those profits that have been recorded exceed $30 million.

35 Heffernan (Inner-City 59); Heffernan, Kevin. *Ghouls, Gimmicks, and Gold: Horror Films and the American Movie Business 1953–1968*. Durham, NC: Duke University Press. 2004. 207. Print.

36 "Horror Films Debut Soon." *Daily Defender*, November 12, 1957: B10. Col. 5. Print.

37 "Triple Horror Films Electrify Fans at Regal." *Daily Defender*, May 4, 1960: 16. 5. Print.

38 "'Paranoia' Horror Film Debuts at the Oriental." *Chicago Daily Defender*, August 16–22, 1960: 1+. Print.

39 "Two Horror Films Bow at Drive-Ins." *Chicago Defender*, April 18, 1970: 28. 6. Print.

40 Heffernan (Inner-City 60).

41 Heffernan (Inner-City 74).

42 Hervey (7).

43 Dyer (62).

44 Heffernan (Inner-City 9).

45 Ernest Dickerson was the second unit camera operator on this film, according to Mark Reid in *Black Lenses, Black Voices: African American Film Now*. Lanham, MD: Rowman & Littlefield, 2005. 76. Print. Dickerson, an African American, would go on to cinematographer and/or directing acclaim with *The Brother from Another Planet*, *Tales from the Darkside*, *Tales from the Crypt*, *Def by Temptation*, *Bones*, and *Masters of Horror*, to name a few spooky offerings.

46 Horror Hound Weekend. March 26–28, 2010. 7202 East 21st Street, Indianapolis, IN, 46219.

47 Dyer (62–63).

48 I have found no claims that Eugene Clark's casting was color-blind casting.

49 Dyer (59, 62–63). In *Land of the Dead*, the cast is particularly diverse. Though there are Blacks seen living in the restricted, gated high-rise community, a community in which "spics" like one of the forgers are not allowed, the investment in classism and in a sort of effete, enlightened Whiteness is clear.

50 Winokur, Mark. "Technologies of Race: Special Effects, Fetish, Film and the Fifteenth Century." *Genders OnLine Journal* 40 (2004): 6. Web. January 20, 2006. http://www. genders.org/g40/g40_winokur.html.

51 Mailer, Norman. "The White Negro." Fall 1957. *LearnToQuestion.com: Resource Base* 2008. N.p. Web. June 20, 2010. http://www.learntoquestion.com/resources/ database/archives/0.

52 Goldsby (247).

53 Heffernan (Inner-City 75).

5 Scream, Whitey, Scream—Retribution, Enduring Women, and Carnality: 1970s

1 Holly, Ellen. "Where Are the Films about Real Black Men and Women?" *New York Times*, June 2, 1974: 127. Print.

2 Motion Picture Association of America Site. Motion Picture Association, 2005. Web. April 2, 2010. The Hays Code (1930–66), which presented organizing principles for U.S. filmmakers associated with major studios, warned against things such as: criticizing religion, showing childbirth, showing "lustful" kissing or "suggestive" dancing. These principles were replaced by a voluntary ratings system in 1968 which changed three times between 1968 and 1983: G, M, R, X; G, GP, R, X; and G, PG, R, X. There have been further revisions since the early 1980s.

3 Young, Elizabeth. *Black Frankenstein: The Making of an American Metaphor*. New York: Routledge, 2008. 219. Print. In 1977 a comic book called *Black'nstein* "featured a white Kentucky slave owner, Colonel Victah Black'nstein, who builds a black monster-slave"; 1976's *The Slave of Frankenstein* novel presents "Victor Frankenstein's son as a white abolitionist who challenges an evil pro-slavery monster"; George Clinton/Parliament released in 1977 "The Clones of Dr. Funkenstein," focusing on the creation of a Black doctor of funk.

4 Denzin, Norman K. *Reading Race*. London: Sage, 2002. 27. Print.

5 Bogle, Donald. *Toms, Coons, Mulattoes, Mammies, & Bucks*. New York: The Continuum Publishing Company, 1993. 232. Print.

6 Crane, Jonathan. *Terror and Everyday Life*. Thousand Oaks, CA: Sage Publications, 1994. 48. Print.

7 Benshoff, Harry M. "Blaxploitation Horror Films: Generic Reappropriation or Reinscription?" *Cinema Journal* 39(2) (2000): 34. JStor. Web. January 20, 2005. http://www.jstor.org/pss/1225551.

8 Null, Gary. *Black Hollywood: The Negro in Motion Pictures*. Secaucus, NJ: Citadel Press, 1975. 209. Print.

9 Leab, Daniel J. *From Sambo to Superspade: The Black Experience in Motion Pictures*. Boston, MA: Houghton Mifflin Company, 1975. 254. Print.

10 Null (209).

11 Holly (127).

12 Exploitation films, according to Eric Shaefer in his dissertation *Bold! Daring! Shocking! True!: A History of Exploitation Films, 1919–1959*, emerged during the "classical era," 1919–1959, paralleling Hollywood cinema but also made outside of it by indie producers. The films, writes Schaefer, "were rooted in an early, exhibitionistic 'cinema of attractions' and relied on forbidden spectacle at the expense of the more costly system of narrative continuity and coherence favored by mainstream movies." Shaefer, Eric. *Bold! Daring! Shocking! True!: A History of Exploitation Films, 1919–1959*. Austin: University of Texas, 1995. Dissertation. Print.

13 Benshoff (37).

14 Rhines, Jesse Algeron. *Black Film/White Money*. New Brunswick, NJ: Rutgers University Press, 1996. 46. Print.

15 Worland, Rick. *The Horror Film: An Introduction*. Malden, MA: Blackwell, 2007. 97. Print.

16 Benshoff (34).

17 In the film, Luva is entombed with her prince. Her death isn't shown.

18 In the film, it is explained Dracula has been killed by his nemesis Dr. Van Helsing.

19 Sharrett, C. "The Horror Film in Neoconservative Culture." *Journal of Popular Film and Television* 21:3 (Fall 1993): 107. Print.

20 Sharrett ("Neoconservative" 107).

21 Sharrett ("Neoconservative" 100–110).

22 Wlodarz, Joe. "Beyond the Black Macho: Queer Blaxploitation." *The Velvet Light Trap* 53 (Spring 2004): 11. Web. January 20, 2006. http://muse.jhu.edu/login?uri=/journals/the_velvet_light_trap/v053/53.1wlodarz.html.

23 Gateward, Frances. "Daywalkin' Night Stalkin' Bloodsuckas: Black Vampires in Contemporary Film." *Genders OnLine Journal* 40 (2004): 10. Web. June 20, 2005. http://www.genders.org/g40/g40_gateward.html.

24 Medovoi, L. "Theorizing Historicity, or the Many Meanings of Blacula." *Screen* 39 (1998): 14. Print.

25 Baldwin, J. *Notes of a Native Son*. Boston: Beacon Press, 1955/1984. 115, 122. Print.

26 Young (*Black Frankenstein* 189).

27 Medovoi (14).

28 Benshoff (36).

29 Lawrence, N. "Fear of a Blaxploitation Monster: Blackness as Generic Revision in AIP's *Blacula*." *Film International* 39 (2009): 24. Print.

30 Lawrence (18).

31 Stenger, Josh. "Mapping the Beach: Beach Movies, Exploitation Film and Geographies of Whiteness." *Classic Hollywood, Classic Whiteness*. Ed. Daniel Bernardi. Minneapolis: University of Minnesota Press, 1996. 31. Print.

32 Gent, G. "Black Films Are In, So Are Profits." *New York Times*, July 28, 1972: 22. Print.

33 Gent (22).

34 Stenger (31). AIP are also responsible for the distribution of an astonishing number of other "Blaxploitation-era" films, such as *Black Mama, White Mama* (1973), *The Mack* (1973), *Coffy* (1973), *Hell Up in Harlem* (1973), *Foxy Brown* (1974), *Truck Turner* (1974), *Sheba, Baby* (1975), *Cornbread, Earl, and Me* (1975), *Cooley High* (1975), and *Friday Foster* (1975).

35 Stenger (46).

36 Lawrence (18).

37 Young (*Black Frankenstein* 190).

38 Young (*Black Frankenstein* 191).

39 Young (*Black Frankenstein* 196).

40 The 2004 documentary film *The 50 Worst Movies Ever Made* cites *The Thing with Two Heads*. The DVD documentary was produced by Dante Pugliese for the studio Passport Video. *Heads* is frequently included in various fan-developed listings of horror such as Blackhorrormovies.com.

41 Worland (97).

42 In the film, it is never explicitly made clear that the home is in a White neighborhood, or that the prostitutes his mother cleaned for are White. Rather, Dr. Pryde alludes to the prostitutes' race by calling them, with ironic emphasis, "ladies of the evening," while Black street prostitutes working in Watts are "hookers" and "hoes." They do not work in brothels. In addition, the film works to show the great socioeconomic distance between Watts and where Dr. Pryde lives by presenting sequences of neighborhood changes. The homes get bigger, the cars nicer, the streets cleaner, and the Black faces disappear.

43 "Domestic Violence: Domestic Violence in the African American Community." Nabsw.org. National Association of Black Social Workers, 2002. Web. April 9, 2010.

44 Cleaver, Eldridge. *Soul on Ice*. New York: Dell Publishing, 1968. 191. Print.

45 Cleaver (28).

46 Pinedo, Isabel Cristina. *Recreational Terror: Women and the Pleasure of Horror Film Viewing*. Albany, NY: SUNY Press, 1997. 53. Print.

47 Wallace, Michele. *Black Macho and the Myth of the Superwoman*, New York: Verso Classics, 1999. 66. Print.

48 Wallace (67).

49 Bogle (*Toms, Coons* 240).

50 This scene is a precursor to the life-through-death decision made by the characters Thelma and Louise in the movie of the same name.

51 Clover, Carol. *Men, Women, and Chainsaws: Gender in the Modern Horror Film.* Princeton, NJ: Princeton University Press, 1992. 35. Print.

52 Clover (*Chainsaws* 37).

53 Clover (*Chainsaws* 39).

54 Of course, when these movies became franchises, peace could not be had.

55 Diawara, Manthia, and Phyllis Klotman. "*Ganja and Hess*: Vampires, Sex, and Addictions." *Black American Literature Forum* 25.2 (1991): 299. Jstor. N.p. Web. June 21, 2005. http://jstor.org/. Diawara and Klotman cited other kudos for the film. According to the authors, the film was hailed in the *Amsterdam News* as "the most important Black produced film since *Sweet Sweetback's Baadasssss Song*," as well as it being described as a "great underground class of Black film [...] If *Sweet Sweeback* is *Native Son, Ganja and Hess* is *Invisible Man*."

56 Diawara and Klotman (300).

57 Hasan, Mark. "Ganja & Hess [Review]." *Rue Morgue* (2007): 47. Print.

58 Sharrett ("Neoconservative Culture" 100).

59 Diawara and Klotman (299).

60 *Black Mama, White Mama* (1973); *Coffy* (1973); *Scream, Blacula, Scream* (1973); *Foxy Brown* (1974); *Sheba, Baby* (1975); *Bucktown* (1975); *Friday Foster* (1975).

61 Dunn, S. *'Baad Bitches' and Sassy Supermamas: Black Power Action Films.* Urbana and Chicago:University of Illinois Press, 2008. 109. Print.

62 Hill Collins, Patricia. *Black Feminist Thought.* New York: Routledge, 2009. 91. Print.

63 Hill Collins (89).

64 Dunn (111).

65 Dunn (113).

66 Lawrence (18).

67 Clover (*Chainsaws* 65).

68 Bogle (*Toms, Coons* 252–253).

69 Clover (*Chainsaws* 35, 36).

70 As for *The Exorcist*, Warner Bros. thought that the film served as more than a template for the Black horror film *Abby*, and a court agreed.

71 Benshoff (40).

72 Weiler, A.H. (1974). "'Abby', About a Black Family and Exorcism." *New York Times*, December 26, 1974: 53. Print.

73 Sharrett, Christopher. *Mythologies of Violence in Postmodern Media.* Detroit, MI: Wayne State University Press, 1999. 103. Print.

74 "Black-oriented Films Produced since Mid-1970s." *Jet* 42 (1972): 58–59. 58. Print.

75 Guerrero, E. *Framing Blackness: The African American Image in Film.* Philadelphia, PA: Temple University Press, 1993. 86. Print.

76 Dunn.

77 Semedi is a keeper of the dead, a "great lover," and a greedy spirit who values money, gifts, and women. In the film, his name is pronounced Baron Samdi.

78 Benshoff (32).

79 Murray, J. "Now a Boom in Black Directors." *The New York Times*, June 8, 1972: D11. Print.

80 Harris, M. "Scary Sistas: A Brief History of Black Women in Horror Films." *Pretty-scary.net.* Pretty Scary: For Women in Horror By Women in Horror. June 4, 2006. Web. March 17, 2010.

81 Yearwood, Gladstone L. *Black Film as a Signifying Practice: Cinema, Narration and the African-American Aesthetic Tradition.* Trenton, NJ: Africa World Press, Inc., 2000. 44. Print.

82 Null (219).
83 Marlene Clark became a bit of a horror icon, appearing in *Ganja & Hess* and *The Beast Must Die*, as well as two other English-language, Philippines films, *Night of the Cobra Woman* (1972) and *Black Mamba* (1974).
84 Benshoff (39).
85 Rudy Ray Moore. "Petey Wheatstraw, the Devil's Son-in-Law," *The Cockpit*. Kent Comedy Series, 1973. CD.
86 The *Kung Fu* TV series (1972–1975) presented a young martial arts student "Grasshopper" being trained by his Shaolin Priest Master Po.
87 Rudy Ray Moore, in the documentary *Macked, Hammered, Slaughtered, and Shafted* (2004).
88 Cripps, Thomas. *Black Film as Genre*. Bloomington: Indiana University Press, 1978. 129. Print.
89 Cripps (*Genre* 129).
90 George, N. *Blackface: Reflections on African Americans in the Movies*. New York: HarperCollins, 1994. 87. Print.
91 West, Hollie I. "Black Films: Crossovers and Beyond Blaxploitation." *Washington Post*, February 8, 1976: 119. Print.
92 West (119).
93 West (119).
94 West (119).

6 We Always Die First—Invisibility, Racial Red-Lining, and Self-Sacrifice: 1980s

 1 Harris, Mark. "Yelling at the Screen: The Black Die Young." *PopMatters*, September 6, 2005. 1999–2009 PopMatters.com. August 13, 2010.
 2 Nama, Adilifu. *Black Space: Imagining Race in Science Fiction Film*. Austin: University of Texas Press, 2008. 137. Print.
 3 Sobchack, Vivian. "Cities on the Edge of Time: The Urban Science Fiction Film." *East–West Film Journal* (December 1988): 4–19. Print.
 4 Avila, Eric. "Dark City: White Flight and the Urban Science Fiction Film in Postwar America." *Classic Hollywood, Classic Whiteness*. Ed. Daniel Bernardi. Minneapolis: University of Minnesota Press, 2001. 68. Print.
 5 Avila (53).
 6 Venkatest, Sudhir Alladi. *American Project: The Rise and Fall of a Modern Ghetto*. Cambridge, MA: Harvard University Press, 2000. 7. Print.
 7 Even pop music exploited the trend, with Paul McCartney and Stevie Wonder buddying-up to sing "Ebony and Ivory" (1982), an ode to cross-racial teamwork.
 8 Guerrero, E. "The Black Images in Protective Hollywood's Biracial Buddy Films of the Eighties." *Black American Cinema*. Ed. M. Diawara. New York: Routledge, 1993. 237. Print.
 9 Avila (65).
10 Jamieson, Kathleen Hall. "Context and the Creation of Meaning in Advertising of the 1988 Presidential Campaign." *American Behavioral Scientist* 32 (1989): 416, 417. Print.
11 Crane, Jonathan. *Terror and Everyday Life: Singular Moments in the History of the Horror Film*. Thousand Oaks, CA: Sage, 1996. 8. Print.
12 Benjamin, Rich. *Searching for Whitopia: An Improbable Journey to the Heart of White America*. New York: Hyperion, 2009. 1. Print.
13 Clover, Carol. *Men, Women, and Chainsaws: Gender in the Modern Horror Film*. Princeton, NJ: Princeton University Press, 1992. 222. Print.

14 Mathijs, Ernest. "Threat or Treat: Film, Television, and the Ritual of Halloween." *Flow TV*, University of Texas at Austin. October 30, 2009. Web. March 6, 2010.

15 Crane, Jonathan. *Terror and Everyday Life*. Thousand Oaks, CA: Sage Publications, 1994. 8. Print.

16 Rathgeb, Douglas L. "Bogeyman from the Id: Nightmare and Reality in Halloween and A Nightmare on Elm Street." *Journal of Popular Film and Television* (Spring, 1991): 36–43. Print.

17 Riley, Michael J. "Trapped in the History of Film: Racial Conflict and Allure in *The Vanishing American*." Eds. Peter C. Rollins and John E. O'Connor. *Hollywood's Indian: The Portrayal of the Native American in Film*. Lexington: The University of Kentucky Press, 1998. 64. Print.

18 Maddery, Joseph. *Nightmares in Red, White, and Blue: The Evolution of the American Horror Film*. Jefferson, NC: McFarland & Company, Inc., 2004. 71. Print. This presses the point that the film was more about the family's "economic unease" than ghosts. That is, their lives are disrupted long before the horrors show up as they have sunk everything into this suburban home. The stress leaves them angry and vulnerable.

19 Maddery (73).

20 Freeman, Lance. *There Goes the 'Hood: Views of Gentrification from the Ground Up*. Philadelphia, PA: Temple University Press, 2004. 51. Print.

21 In 1975, funk/soul band Parliament released the album *Chocolate City*. The album's title song famously talks about Washington, D.C. being a "chocolate city," that is, predominately Black in population, but also in politics, culture, and resources. It also acknowledges the rise of neighboring "vanilla suburbs."

22 Williams, Tony. "Trying to Survive on the Darker Side: 1980s Family Horror." *The Dread of Difference: Gender and the Horror Film*. Ed. Barry Keith Grant. Austin: University of Texas Press, 1996. 164. Print.

23 In "Blacks in horror" sequels later in the decade, which were regularly severely panned by critics, there are minor Black characters who see the end of horror films, such as *A Nightmare on Elm Street 3: Dream Warriors* (1987) or *Jaws: The Revenge* (1987).

24 The pictures are oddly incongruous to Dick's character. However, they may function to reaffirm that his interest in Danny is truly "safe" and non-sexual.

25 Pinedo, Isabel Cristina. *Recreational Terror: Women and the Pleasure of Horror Film Viewing*. Albany, NY: SUNY Press, 1997. 53. Print.

26 Hughey, Matthew. "Cinethetic Racism: White Redemption and Black Stereotypes in 'Magic Negro' Films." *Social Problems* 56 (2009): 544. Print.

27 Hicks, Heather J. "Hoodoo Economics: White Men's Work and Black Men's Magic in Contemporary American Film." *Camera Obscura 53*(18) (2003): 18. Print.

28 Hicks, Heather J. (28).

29 Clover (*Chainsaws* 86).

30 Heffernan, Kevin. *Ghouls, Gimmicks, and Gold: Horror Films and the American Movie Business, 1953–1968*. Durham, NC: Duke University Press, 2004. 225. Print.

31 Heffernan (*Ghouls* 225) .

32 Mesbur + Smith Architects. *Multiplex Cinema and Theater Architecture*. May 29, 2008. Web.

33 Harris, Martin. "You Can't Kill the Boogeyman: Halloween III and the Modern Horror Franchise." *Journal of Popular Film and Television* 32(3) (Fall, 2004): 98. Print.

34 Crane (3).

35 Mercer, Kobena. "Monster Metaphors: Notes on Michael Jackson's 'Thriller.'" *Screen* 27 (1986): 31. Print.

36 "The Academy of Science Fiction Fantasy & Horror Films." *Saturn Awards*. January 26, 2010. Web. saturnawards.com.

37 Lapeyre, Jason. "The Transformation: Filmmaker John Landis Created a Monster with Michael Jackson's *Thriller*." *Wax Poetics* 37 (October–November 2009). 77. Print.

38 Certainly the 1950s were not all about sock-hops for Black Americans, who were fighting to gain their civil rights.

39 Jones, Steve. "Michael King of Pop dies; Music icon, 50, helped shape a generation." *USA Today*, June 26, 2009. Web. March 6, 2010. usatoday.com.

40 Lapeyre (77).

41 "MTV Video Music Awards." MTV.com. January 26, 2010. Web. mtv.com.

42 Lapeyre (78).

43 Avila, Eric. "Dark City: White Flight and the Urban Science Fiction Film in Postwar America." *Classic Hollywood Classic Whiteness*. Ed. Daniel Bernardi. Minneapolis: University of Minnesota Press, 2001. 59. Print.

44 "MTV Music Television Profile." Cabletvadbureau.com. January 26, 2010. Web.

45 Skal, David J. *The Monster Show: A Cultural History of Horror*. Revised ed. New York: Faber and Faber, Inc., 2001. 230. Print. Skal.

46 Skal (318). Mercer (40) also makes such a connection to Chaney.

47 Mercer (29).

48 The groundskeeper immediately recognizes that the dog is a "white dog," a dog trained to harm Blacks. He reveals that such dogs are fairly common by revealing his scars from a long ago, similar attack.

49 The film is based on the 1970 fiction book *Chien Blanc* [White Dog] by Romain Gary. The book, written in French, is an indictment of White liberals' (particularly Hollywood celebrities') participation in the American Civil Rights movement of the 1960s.

50 Scott, Vernon. "Minority Group Wins Cancellation of Television Movie." *UPI Hollywood Reporter*, January 12, 1984: sec. Domestic News. Print.

51 "NBC Drops Plan to Show Film 'White Dog.'" *New York Times*, January 20, 1984: sec. C23. Print.

52 Katzman, Lisa. "'White Dog' Is Set Loose at Last." *New York Times*, July 7, 1991: sec. 2.17. Print.

53 Katzman (sec. 2.17).

54 Hicks, Chris. "Wide Release of 'White Dog' Is Long Overdue." *Deseret News*, January 23, 2009. Web. http://www.deseretnews.com/article/705279597/Wide-release-of-White-Dog-is-long-overdue.html.

55 In 2009, the film was released on DVD.

56 Guerrero, Edward. "AIDS as Monster in Science Fiction." *Journal of Popular Film & Television* 18.3 (Fall 1990): 88. Print.

57 Doherty, Thomas. "Genre, Gender, and the Aliens Trilogy." *The Dread of Difference: Gender and the Horror Film*. Ed. Barry Keith Grant. Austin: University of Texas Press, 1996. 181–199. Print.

58 Clover, Carol J. "Her Body, Himself: Gender in the Slasher Film." *The Dread of Difference: Gender and the Horror Film*. Ed Barry Keith Grant. Austin: University of Texas Press, 1996. 79. Print.

59 Hutchings, Peter. *The Horror Film*. London: Pearson, 2004. 18. Print.

60 Guerrero ("AIDS").

61 Sharrett, Christopher. "The Horror Film in Neoconservative Culture." *Journal of Popular Film & Television* 21.3 (Fall 1993): 100–110, 108. Print.

62 Hudson, Dale. "Vampires of Color and the Performance of Multicultural Whiteness." *The Persistence of Whiteness: Race and Contemporary Hollywood Cinema*. Ed. Daniel Bernardi. New York: Routledge, 2008. 134. Print.

63 Pinedo (111).

64 Crane (9).

65 Foley, Kevin. "Spike Lee Speaks to Spring Fest." *The University of Vermont, University Communications* 24 (April 2002). Web. January 5, 2010. http://www.uvm.edu/~uvmpr/?Page=article.php&id=409.

66 Sharrett ("The Horror Film," 100).
67 Snead, James. *White Screens, Black Images: Hollywood from the Dark Side*. New York: Routledge, 1994. Print.
68 Neale, Steve. "Masculinity as Spectacle: Reflections on Men and Mainstream Cinema." *Screen* 24(6): 2–17. 19. Print.

7 Black Is Back! Retribution and the Urban Terrain: 1990s

1 Benjamin, Walter. "A Small History of Photography." *One-Way Street and Other Writings*. Ed. Edmund Jephcott and Kingsley Shorter. London: NLB, 1979. 256. Print.
2 Abbott, Stacey. "High Concept Thrills and Chills: The Horror Blockbuster." *Horror Zone*. Ed. Ian Conrich. London: I.B. Tauris, 2010. 29. Print.
3 Abbott (29).
4 Ndalianis, Angela. "Dark Rides, Hybrid Machines and the Horror Experience." *Horror Zone*. Ed. Ian Conrich. London: I.B. Tauris, 2010. 1. Print.
5 Kaufmann makes these comments in a President's message (which he often offers on Troma films) at the start of the VHS release of *Temptation*. *Def by Temptation*. Dir. James Bond III. Perf. James Bond III, Cynthia Bond, Samuel L. Jackson. Bonded Filmworks, 1990. Film. As Jones succinctly explains, "there are bad movies and there are Troma movies." Admittedly, it isn't hard to be the best at Troma. This is the company that takes a film, "for peanuts," and starts "counting the cash." See: Jones, Alan. *The Rough Guide to Horror Movies*. London: Penguin, 2005. 42. Print. Still, *Def By Temptation*, a rather well-done, smart film, seems out of place among Tromas exploitation/horror films titles.
6 Reid, Mark A. *Black Lenses, Black Voices: African American Film Now*. Lanham, MD: Rowman & Littlefield, 2005. 66. Print.
7 According to Gregory M. Herek, "in March–April of 1989, the *San Francisco Examiner* commissioned Teichner Associates to conduct telephone interviews with a gay and lesbian national sample ($n = 400$) as well as a sample of gay residents of the San Francisco Bay Area ($n = 400$). Approximately 27,000 calls were made to obtain 800 responses; 6.2 percent of the national respondents and 10 percent of the Bay Area respondents identified themselves as lesbian, gay, or bisexual to the interviewer (Herek). Although the sample is biased by the willingness of respondents to identify themselves as gay to a telephone interviewer, the poll represents the first published study of its kind in the United States." See: Herek, Gregory M. "Stigma, Prejudice, and Violence Against Lesbians and Gay Men." *Homosexuality: Research Implications for Public Policy*. Eds. John C. Gonsiorek and James D. Weinrich. Newbury Park, CA: Sage, 1991. 60–61. Print.
8 In Spencer Williams' *The Blood of Jesus*, Martha is similarly out of place, and her Temptation, Judas, has to even provide her with the appropriate city attire.
9 Hill Collins, Patricia. *Black Feminist Thought*. New York: Routledge, 2009. 197–198. Print.
10 Picart, Caroline Joan and Cecil E. Greek. "The Compulsions of Real/Reel Serial Killers and Vampires: Toward a Gothic Criminology." *Monsters in and Among Us: Toward a Gothic Criminology*. Eds. Caroline Joan Picart and Cecil E. Greek. Cranbury, NJ: Associated University Presses, 2007. 236. Print.
11 Gateward, Frances. "Daywalkin' Night Stalkin' Bloodsuckas: Black Vampires in Contemporary Film." *Genders Online Journal* 40 (2004): n.p. Web. July 19, 2010. http://www.genders.org/g40/g40_gateward.html.
12 Harrington, Richard. "Def by Temptation." *Washington Post*, June 5, 1990. Web. July 20, 2010. http://www.washingtonpost.com/wp-srv/style/longterm/movies/videos/defbytemptationrharrington_a0aae9.htm.

13 Harrington.

14 Guerrero, Ed. "Framing Blackness: The African American Image in Film." Philadelphia, PA: Temple University Press, 1993. 179. Print.

15 Yearwood, Gladstone L. *Black Film as a Signifying Practice: Cinema, Narration and the African-American Aesthetic Tradition.* Trenton, NJ: Africa World Press, Inc., 2000. 135. Print.

16 Yearwood (113).

17 Avila, Eric. "Dark City: White Flight and the Urban Science Fiction Film in Postwar America." *Classic Hollywood, Classic Whiteness.* Ed. Daniel Bernardi. Minneapolis: University of Minnesota Press, 2001. 53. Print.

18 Forman, Murray. *The 'Hood Comes First: Race, Space, and Place in Rap and Hip-Hop.* Middletown, CT: Wesleyan University Press, 2002. 65. Print.

19 Welch, William M. "Former Senator Thurman Dies." *USA Today,* June 26, 2003. Web. August 12, 2010. http://www.usatoday.com/news/washington/2003-06-26-strom_x.htm.

20 See: "Jesse Helm's 'Hands' Ad." YouTube.com. YouTube, LLC, 2010. Web. August 9, 2010.

21 Pinedo, Isabel Christina. *Recreational Terror: Women and the Pleasures of Horror Film Viewing.* Albany, NY: SUNY Press, 1997. 128. Print.

22 Denzin, Norman K. *Reading Race.* London: Sage, 2002. 112. Print.

23 NWA describe themselves as a "gang" in their title track *Straight Outta Compton* (1988).

24 Fulmer, J. "Men Ain't All"—A Reworking of Masculinity in Tales from the Hood, or, Grandma Meets the Zombie." *Journal of American Folklore* 115(457/458) (2002): 423. Print.

25 "Demon Knight." IMDb.com. Box Office Mojo, n.d. Web. July 23, 2010. Also: Reid (*Black Lenses* 69).

26 "Def by Temptation." IMDb.com. Box Office Mojo, n.d. Web. July 23, 2010.

27 For financial estimates, see: "Vampire in Brooklyn." IMDb.com. Box Office Mojo, n.d. Web. July 23, 2010. Ebert, Robert. "Vampire in Brooklyn." *Chicago Sun-Times,* October 27,1995. Web. July 20, 2010. For a collection of the film's reviews, see: "Vampire in Brooklyn." Metacritic. CBS Interactive Inc., 2010. Web. July 20, 2010.

28 Hutchings, Peter. *The Horror Film.* Essex, England: Pearson, 2004. 109. Print.

29 In a fairly significant gap in the script, it is never explained who these women are or what they are, except that they have power, through religious ritual, to talk to the dead and drive out bad spirits. The credits for the film list one of the women as a Yoruba priestess; however, the film does not assert this.

30 Yearwood (95).

31 Scott, Ellen C. "The Horrors of Remembrance: The Altered Visual Aesthetic of Horror in Jonathan Demme's *Beloved.*" *Genders Online Journal* 40 (2004): 6. Web. August 8, 2010.

32 Wardi, Anissa J. "Freak Shows, Spectacles, and Carnivals: Reading Jonathan Demme's *Beloved.*" *African American Review* 39 (Winter 2005): 513. Print.

33 Scott, Ellen.

34 Wardi (525).

35 In *Predator* (1987) the targets are Brown people—usually South Americans.

36 Pinedo (112–113).

37 Based on the Clive Barker story "The Forbidden," which appears in *Books of Blood.* London: Penguin Group, 1984. The story is set in modern Britain and has no Black focus. Making Candyman Black was Rose's idea.

38 Lott, Eric. *Spirit of the Ghetto: Postindustrial City Space and the Specter of Race.* American Research Seminar, University of Leeds. Leeds, UK. Lecture. February 5th, 2007.

39 *Candyman*. Dir. Bernard Rose. Perf. Tony Todd, Virginia Madsen, Xander Berkeley. Special Edition. Polygram, 1992. DVD.

40 Pinedo (131).

41 However, it was Candyman who fans loved, and he returned for three more films. *Candyman 3* (1999) went straight to DVD. At the time of this writing, a fourth installment is rumored, with a working title of *Candyman: The Tribe*.

42 Creed, Barbara. *The Monstrous-Feminine: Film, Feminism, Psychoanalysis*. London: Routledge, 1993. 69. Print.

43 Helbig, Bob and Mark Edmund. "Family of Konerak Sues City." *Milwaukee Journal*, January 20, 1995. NEWS: 1. *NewsBank*. Web. August 12, 2010; Stanford, Gregory D. "A Paper Trail of Intolerance." *Milwaukee Journal*, January 25, 1995. OPED: 11. *NewsBank*. Web. August 12, 2010; Davis, Don. *The Milwaukee Murders: Nightmare in Apartment 213—The True Story*. New York: St. Martin, 1995. Print.

44 Oates, Joyce. *Zombie*. New York: Plume, 1996. Print.

45 Crane, Jonathan. *Terror and Everyday Life: Singular Moments in the History of the Horror Film*. Thousand Oaks, CA: Sage, 1994. 113. Print.

46 There is a similar fate for the Black superhero Hancock (Will Smith) in *Hancock* (2008). In the film, Hancock says goodbye to his former wife and her suburban life. While he can live anywhere, as long as it is not near her, lest their powers cancel each other out, he opts for the grittier streets of New York.

47 Sobchack, V. "Bringing It All Back Home: Family Economy and Generic Exchange." *The Dread of Difference: Gender and the Horror Film*. Ed. B.K. Grant. Austin: University of Texas Press, 1996. 150. Print.

48 Hutchings (109).

49 Sharrett, Christopher. "The Horror Film in Neoconservative Culture." *Journal of Popular Film and Television* 21 (Fall, 1993): 107. Print.

50 Abbott (39).

51 Schneider, Steven Jay. "Mixed Blood Couples: Monsters and Miscegenation in U.S. Horror Cinema." *The Gothic Other: Racial and Social Constructions in the Literary Imagination*. Eds. Ruth Bienstock Anolik and Douglas L. Howard. Jefferson, NC: McFarland & Co, Inc., 2004. 85. Print.

52 Sharrett (104).

53 Jones, Alan (46).

Conclusion

1 Public Enemy. "Louder Than a Bomb." *It Takes a Nation of Millions to Hold Us Back*. Def Jam, 1988. CD.

2 According to Box Office Mojo.com, *The Blair Witch Project*'s (1999) total domestic gross is $140,539,009, while *Snakes on a Plane* (2006) has a total domestic gross of $34,020,184. "The Blair Witch Project." "Snakes on a Plane." Box Office Mojo.com. IMDb.com Inc., n.d. Web. August 10, 2010.

3 These remakes were joined by increased serialization. For example, eight *Halloween* movies were made before director Rob Zombie started over with his *Halloween*. The narrative effect of serialization was that the audience came to expect that, no matter what happened, the monster was never really dead, a narrative tool that could either be viewed as clichéd "cheating" to market more films, or postmodern innovation disrupting death and even (anti)heroism.

4 Bowles, Scott. "Horror Glut Killing off Part of the Pack." *USA Today*, April 30, 2007: D1. Print.

5 Hutchings, Peter. *The Horror Film*. Essex, England: Pearson, 2004. vii. Print.

6 Fischoff, Stuart, Joe Antonio, and Diane Lewis. "Favorite Films and Film Genres as a Function of Race, Age, and Gender." *Journal of Media Psychology* 3.22 (Winter 1998). Web. August 10, 2010.

7 Carvajal, Doreen. "How the Studios Used Children to Test-Market Violent Films." *New York Times*, September 27, 2000: A1, A21. Print.

8 The testing was met with protest by the Federal Trade Commission, and the studios, through the Motion Picture Association of America, promised to rethink their methods. See: Carvajal, Doreen. "How the Studios Used Children to Test-Market Violent Films." *New York Times*, September 27, 2000: A1, A21. Print.

9 Giroux, Henry A. *Fugitive Cultures: Race, Violence, and Youth*. London: Routledge, 1996. 55. Print.

10 For an extraordinarily comprehensive accounting of Black horror films and films featuring Blacks, see: Mark Harris. Web. July 25, 2010. blackhorrormovies.com. blackhorrormovies.com. 2005–2009.

11 "Are You Ready for Freddy?" by the rap group the Fat Boys, played during the end credits. "A Nightmare on Elm Street 4: The Dream Master." IMDb.com, IMDb.com Inc., 1990–2010. Web. August 12, 2010.

12 Notably, horror is now rife with all manner of Black (often male) monster slayers, especially in straight-to-DVD films. For example, *The Breed* (2001) co-starred Bokeem Woodbine as a cop/vampire hunter in an alternate universe with, ironically, a vampire as his partner on the force. *Vegas Vampires* (2004) brings back 1970s Blaxploitation-era icons Fred Williamson, Richard Roundtree, and Bernie Casey, teaming them up with known "urban" Black film stars Tiny Lister and Glenn Plummer as well as rapper Kurupt to attract a range of audiences. The movie *Vampire Assassin* (2005) was a fairly low-budget affair, but drummed up attention with a cameo by 1970s Blaxploitation/horror icon Rudy Ray Moore and through DVD cover art that presented a Blade lookalike who did not appear in the film.

13 Jones, Eileen. "Will Smith's *Hancock* Fiasco." Alternet.com. Alternet. July 5, 2008. Web. July 25, 2010. http://www.alternet.org/story/90473/will_smith/27s_%27hancock%27_fiasco

14 There are also *Soy Leyenda* (1967) and SyFy's *I am Omega* (2007).

15 Harvey, Ben. *Night of the Living Dead*. New York: Palgrave Macmillan, 2008. 10. Print.

16 *Urban Gothic*. Dir. Michelle Palmer. Perf. Ernest Dickerson, Adam Simon. Automat Pictures, 2002. Film.

17 "Bones." Box Office Mojo.com. IMDb.com Inc., n.d. Web. July 26, 2010; "Bones." IMDb.com, IMDb.com Inc., 1990–2010. Web. July 26, 1020.

18 *Urban Gothic*. Dir. Michelle Palmer. Perf. Ernest Dickerson, Adam Simon. Automat Pictures, 2002. Film.

19 Reid, Mark A. *Black Lenses, Black Voices: African American Film Now*. Latham, MD: Rowman & Littlefield, 2005. 74. Print.

20 Denzin, Norman K. *Reading Race*. London: Sage, 2002. 113. Print.

21 Alexander, George. *Why We Make Movies: Black Filmmakers Talk about the Magic of Cinema*. New York: Harlem Moon, 2003. 114. Print.

22 Hopes for the film were high, with all involved in the project hoping to turn the film into a franchise of the likes of *Crypt* or the more recent *Scary Movie* series. The additional goal, according to co-producer Christopher Tuffin, was to "push the envelope combining humor and gore." "Snoop Scraps: Rapper to Produce/Star in Horror Pic." Eurweb.com. Eurweb.com. April 20, 2006. Web. July 25, 2010.

23 Richards, Chris. "Va. Slayings Spur Harder Look at Horrorcore." *Washington Post*, September 25, 2009. Washington Post Company. Web. July 25, 2010.

24 Actually, the quality of *Now Eat* is rather low, and Lynch delivers his raps in his bedroom in a low-quality, plug-in microphone. Hence, I had to get the lyrics from

the *Now Eat* soundtrack CD. See: Brotha Lynch Hung. *Now Eat*. Siccmade Records, 2000. CD.

25 Bulwa, Demian. "Bay Area Suspect Allegedly Bludgeoned Victims." *San Francisco Chronicle*. Hearst Communications Inc. September 23, 2009. Web. July 25, 2010.

26 Arnold, Thomas K. "Coming Back for Seconds, Thirds…" *USA Today*. usatoday. com. September 26, 2005. Web. July 26, 2010. Apart from full theatrical releases, there are also film festivals and on-demand rentals.

27 Bick, Julie. "Attack of the Sequel King!" *Fast Company* 77 (December 1, 2003). 33. Print.

28 Goldstein, Gregg. "Filmmakers Take Direct Flight to DVD." *Hollywood Reporter* 393 (March 30, 2006). 1, 10. Web. July 26, 2010.

29 Hoag, Christina. "Maverick Entertainment Reaches Direct-to-Video Urban Movie Market." *Knight Ridder Tribune Business News*, September 25, 2005. 1. Print.

30 Kurutz, Steven. "The Star Rapper Paul Wall's New Video: The iPhone 3GS." *Wall Street Journal*, September 24, 2009. Web. August 12, 2010.

31 "Holla' for Halloween: Urban Horror Film Weaves in Comedy for a Scary Time." Eurweb.com. Eurweb.com. October 29,. 2007. Web. October 29, 2007.

32 Horror Dance Film Festival Director's Choice; Denver International World Cinema Film Festival Best Feature and Best Actor; Chicago Horror Film Festival 2nd Place Best Director, all 2006.

33 Sobchack, V. "Bringing It All Back Home: Family Economy and Generic Exchange." *The Dread of Difference: Gender and the Horror Film*. Ed. Barry Keith Grant. Austin: University of Texas Press, 1996. 148. Print.

34 Skal, David J. *The Monster Show: A Cultural History of Horror*. Revised ed. New York: Faber and Faber, Inc., 2001. 294. Print.

35 In *Predator 2*, the male hero received a valuable antique gun. Here, Alexa is marked by the Predator as being "his"—on his team, part of his clan—on her face.

36 Zimmerman, B. "Daughters of Darkness: The Lesbian Vampire on Film." *The Dread of Difference: Gender and the Horror Film*. Ed. B.K. Grant. Austin: University of Texas Press, 1996. 385. Print.

37 At the very end of the film, the "White boy" is shown with the killer's mask in his backpack, alluding to the fact he may have been a killer alongside "Carlton."

38 Fulmer, J. "'Men Ain't All'—A Reworking of Masculinity in Tales from the Hood, or, Grandma Meets the Zombie." *Journal of American Folklore* 115(457/458): 433. Print.

39 Fulmer (433).

40 New York International Independent Film and Video Festival Winner 2006.

41 *Barackula: The Musical*. Dir. Mike Lawson. Barackula.com, 2008. Web. July 25, 2010.

42 Klein, Aaron with Brenda J. Elliott. *The Manchurian President: Barack Obama's Ties to Communists, Socialists and Other Anti-American Extremists*. Washington, DC: WorldNetDaily Books, 2010. Print.

43 *Jason Mattera on Obama Zombies*. Simon and Schuster Videos. YouTube.com. YouTube LLC, 2010. Web. July 27, 2010.

44 "Barakula Full Latex Mask." Halloween Express.com. Halloween Express, 1999–2010. Web. July 27, 2010.

45 Delonas, Sean. Cartoon. *New York Post*. February 18, 2009: 12. Print.

46 *HorrorHound Weekend 2010*. 11320 Chester Rd, Cincinnati, OH 45246. March 26, 2010.

47 Watkins, Craig S. *Representing: Hip Hop Culture and the Production of Black Cinema*. Chicago, IL: The University of Chicago Press, 1998. 24. Print.

48 *HorrorHound Weekend 2010*. March 26, 2010.

49 Gilroy, Paul. "Race Ends Here." *Ethnic and Racial Studies* 41 (1998): 838–847. Print. St. Louis, Brett. "Post-Race/Post-Politics? Activist-Intellectualism and the Reification of Race." *Ethnic and Racial Studies* 25 (2002): 659. Print.

50 See also: Gallagher, Charles. "Color-Blind Privilege: The Social and Political Functions of Erasing the Colorline in Post Race America." *Race, Gender, Class* 10 (October 31, 2003): 22. Web. February 25, 2008.

51 Hicks, Heather. "Hoodoo Economics: White Men's Work and Black Men's Magic in Contemporary American Film." *Camera Obscura 53* 18 (2003): 28. Print.

52 "Scary Movie." Box Office Mojo.com. IMDb.com Inc., n.d. Web. August 10, 2010.

53 The Wayans are no longer associated with the *Scary Movie* franchise.

54 A June 1, 2009 fire at Universal Studios consumed the *King Kong* set, thereby destroying a historical artifact that was also a monument to the racist treatment of Blacks.

55 Hobson, Janell. "Digital Whiteness, Primitive Blackness: Racializing the 'Digital Divide' in Film and New Media." *Feminist Media Studies* 8 (2008): 111–126. Print.

56 Burnett, Charles. Personal communication, January 29, 2009.

57 Coakley, H.M. Personal communication, November 27, 2006.

BIBLIOGRAPHY

Abbott, Stacey. "High Concept Thrills and Chills: The Horror Blockbuster." *Horror Zone*. Ed. Jan Conrich. London: I.B. Tauris, 2010. 27–44. Print.

"The Academy of Science Fiction Fantasy & Horror Films." *Saturn Awards*. Web. August 14, 2010. Saturnawards.org.

Alexander, George. *Why We Make Movies: Black Filmmakers Talk about the Magic of Cinema*. New York: Harlem Moon, 2003. Print.

Allen, Kimberly. "Sony Wonder Bow 'Matinee' DTV Collection." *Video Store Magazine*, January 16–22, 2000: 11. Print.

Anderson, John. "Once It Was Direct to Video, Now It's Direct to the Web." *New York Times*, October 23, 2005. Web. October 23, 2006. nytimes.com/2005/10/23/movies/23ande.html?ex=1287720000&en=f5e92e85677ade&ei=5090&partner=rssuserland&emc=rss.

Andre, Naomi. "Race and Opera." University of Michigan, 2009. Presentation.

Ariola, Doy. "Weekender Lifestyle: Movies." *Business World*, September 17, 2004: 1. Web. July 18, 2006. proquest.umi.com.proxy.lib.umich.edu/pqdweb?did=694668901&Fmt&clientId=17822&RQT=309&VName=PQD.

Aristotle. *Poetics*. Trans. S.H. Butcher. 350 BCE. N.p. Web. August 3, 2010. http://classics.mit.edu/Aristotle/poetics.html.

Arnold, Thomas K. "Coming Back for Seconds, Thirds…" *USA Today*, September 26, 2005. Web. July 26, 2010. usatoday.com.

——. "DVD Release Pipeline Thins in First Quarter." Home Media Retailing, March 26–April 1, 2006: 1, 32. Web. June 12, 2006. proquest.umi.com.proxy.lib.umich.edu/pqdweb?did=1017921071&Fmt3&clientId=17822&RQT=309&VName=PQD.

——. "Franchise Sequels Send DVD Biz Direct to Bank." *Hollywood Reporter*, September 27–October 3, 2005: 1, 66. Web. June 12, 2006. proquest.umi.com.proxy.lib.umich.edu/pqdweb?did=912595291&Fmt&clientId=17822&RQT=309&VName=PQD.

Avila, Eric. "Dark City: White Flight and the Urban Science Fiction Film in Postwar America." *Classic Hollywood Classic Whiteness*. Ed. Daniel Bernardi. Minneapolis: University of Minnesota Press, 2001. 53–71. Print.

Baldwin, J. *Notes of a Native Son*. Boston: Beacon Press, 1955/1984. Print.

Barker, Clive. *Books of Blood*. London: Penguin Group, 1984. Print.

Barton, Eric A. "Straight to Video, Deerfield Beach Studio Cranks Out Latin Themed Movies That'll Likely Bypass the Theaters." *Miami New Times*, June 12, 2003: Web. July 19, 2006. proquest.umi.com.proxy.lib.umich.edu/pqdweb?did=507536181&Fmt &clientId=17822&RQT=309&VName=PQD.

Becker, Matt. "A Point of Little Hope: Hippie Horror Films and the Politics of Ambivalence." *The Velvet Light Trap* 57 (2006): 42–59. Print.

Becker, Michael, and Mike Carbone. "Tony Todd." *Reel Horror*. Episode 25. June 2, 2010. Web. http://legacy-content.libsyn.com/vidhack/reel_horror-ep25-070306.mp3. Radio.

Behind the Planet of the Apes. Dir. David Comtois, and Kevin Burns. Prod. Kevin Burns. Perf. Roddy McDowell. Image Entertainment, 1998. DVD.

Benjamin, Walter. "A Small History of Photography." *One-Way Street and Other Writings*. Eds. Edmund Jephcott and Kingsley Shorter. London: NLB, 1979. Print.

Benshoff, Harry M. "Blaxploitation Horror Films: Generic Reappropriation or Reinscription?" *Cinema Journal* 39.2 (2000): 31–50. JStor. Web. January 20, 2005. http://www.jstor.org/pss/1225551.

Berenstein, Rhona J. "White Heroines and Hearts of Darkness: Race, Gender and Disguise in 1930s Jungle Films." *Film History* 6 (1994): 314–339. Print.

Bick, Julie. "Attack of the Sequel King!" *Fast Company*. December 1, 2003: 77. Print.

Bishop, Kyle William. *American Zombie Gothic: The Rise and Fall (and Rise) of the Walking Dead in Popular Culture*. Jefferson, NC: McFarland & Co., 2010. Print.

Bogle, Donald. *Bright Boulevards, Bold Dreams: The Story of Black Hollywood*. New York: Ballantine One World, 2005. Print.

Bogle, Donald. *Toms, Coons, Mulattoes, Mammies, & Bucks, An Interpretative History of Blacks in American Films*. New York: The Continuum Publishing Company, 1993. Print.

Booth, Michael. "Straight-to-Video Sales Grow as More Movies Bypass Theaters." *Knight Ridder Tribune Business News*, September 26, 2003: 1. N.p. Web. July 17, 2006. proquest. umi.com.proxy.lib.umich.edu/pqdweb?did=412093691&Fmt&clientId= 17822&RQT=309&VName=PQD.

"Boris Karloff Joins Fight For Race Equality." *Atlanta Daily World*, September 30, 1947: 1. Print.

Bowles, Scott. "Horror Glut Killing Off Part of the Pack." *USA Today*, April 30, 2007: D1. Print.

Bowser, P., and L. Spence. *Writing Himself into History: Oscar Micheaux, His Silent Films, and His Audiences*. New Brunswick, NJ: Rutgers University Press, 2000. Print.

Brass, Kevin. "Trimark to Refocus on Traditional Fare, Downsize Its Staff." *Video Store Magazine*, October 11–17, 1998: 1. Print.

Brown, Sterling A. *The Negro in American Fiction*. New York: Atheneum, 1933/1972. Print.

Bulwa, Demian. "Bay Area Suspect Allegedly Bludgeoned Victims." *San Francisco Chronicle*, September 23, 2009. Web. July 25, 2010. http://articles.sfgate.com/2009-09-23/bay-area/17207386_1_web-design-victims-girlfriend.

Butters, Jr., Gerald R. *Black Manhood on the Silent Screen*. Lawrence: University of Kansas Press, 2002. Print.

Candyman. Dir. Bernard Rose. Perf. Tony Todd, Virginia Madsen. Xander Berkeley. Special Edition. Polygram, 1992. DVD.

"Carey Theater, *The Crimson Skull*." *Afro-American*, May 19, 1922: 4. Print.

Carroll, Noel. *Theorizing the Moving Image*. New York: Cambridge University Press, 1996. Print.

Carter, Everett. "Cultural History Written with Lightening: The Significance of the Birth of a Nation (1915)." *Hollywood as Historian: American Film in a Cultural Context*. Ed. Peter C. Rollins. Lexington: University of Kentucky Press, 1998. 304+. Print.

Carvajal, Doreen. "How the Studios used Children to Test-Market Violent Films." *New York Times*, September 27, 2000: A1+. Print.

Casetti, Francesco. *Theories of Cinema, 1945–1995*. Trans. Francesca Chiostri, Elizabeth Gard-Bartolini-Salimbeni, and Thomas Kelso. Austin: University of Texas Press, 1999. Print.

Clark, Cedric. "Television and Social Controls: Some Observations on the Portrayals of Ethnic Minorities." *Television Quarterly* 8 (1969): 18–22. Print.

Cleaver, Eldridge. *Soul on Ice*. New York: Dell Publishing, 1968. Print.

Clover, Carol J. "Her Body, Himself: Gender in the Slasher Film." *The Dread of Difference: Gender and the Horror Film*. Ed. Barry Keith Grant. Austin: University of Texas Press, 1996. Print.

——. *Men, Women, and Chainsaws: Gender in the Modern Horror Film*. Princeton, NJ: Princeton University Press, 1992. Print.

Colan, Gene. "#13-Gene Colan Interview." Comic Book Artist Magazine, October 26, 2009. N.p. Web. August 13, 2010. Twomorrows.com/comicbookartist/articles/13colan.html.

Coleman, Robin Means. *African American Viewers and the Black Situation Comedy: Situating Racial Humor*. New York: Garland, 2000. Print.

Commission on Civil Rights. *Window Dressing on the Set: Women and Minorities*. Washington, DC: GPO, 1977. Print.

Crane, Jonathan. *Terror and Everyday Life*. Thousand Oaks, CA: Sage Publications, 1994. Print.

Creed, Barbara. *The Monstrous-Feminine: Film, Feminism, Psychoanalysis*. London: Routledge, 1993. Print.

Cripps, Thomas. *Black Film as Genre*. Bloomington: Indiana University Press, 1978. Print.

——. "The Death of Rastus: Negroes in American Films since 1945." *Phylon* 28 (1967): 267–275. Print.

——. "The Films of Spencer Williams." *Black American Literature Forum* 12 (1978): 128–134. Print.

——. *Making Movies Black: The Hollywood Message Movie from World War II to the Civil Rights Era*. New York: Oxford University Press, 1993. Print.

——. *Slow Fade to Black: The Negro in American Film, 1900–1942*. New York: Oxford University Press, 1993. Print.

Crowther, Bosley. "Old Black Magic." *New York Times*, June 13, 1943: sec. X3. Print.

Davis, Don. *The Milwaukee Murders: Nightmare in Apartment 213—The True Story*. New York: St. Martin, 1995. Print.

Davis, T. "Foreword." *Writing Himself into History: Oscar Micheaux, His Silent Films, and His Audiences*. Eds. Pearl Bowser and Louise Spence. New Brunswick, NJ: Rutgers University Press, 2000. Print.

Dayan, Joan. *Haiti, History, and the Gods*. Berkeley: University of California Press, 1988. Print.

Deignan, Tom. "Townsend on a Bad Roll?" Irish Voice, September 24, 2002. N.p. Web. July 19, 2006. proquest.umi.com.proxy.lib.umich.edu/pqdweb?did=469616811&Fmt=3&clientId=17822&RQT=309&VName=PQD.

Denzin, Norman K. *Reading Race*. London: Sage, 2002. Print.

Desjardins, Doug. "Direct-to-DVD Franchises Make Sales 'A' List." *DSN Retailing Today*, March 27, 2006: 24. Web. June 12, 2006. proquest.umi.com.proxy.lib.umich.edu/pqdweb?did=1019569221&Fmt=4&clientId=17822&RQT=309&VName=PQD.

Diawara, Manthia, and Phyllis Klotman. "*Ganja and Hess:* Vampires, Sex, and Addictions." *Black American Literature Forum* 25.2 (1991): 299–314. Jstor. N.p. Web. June 21, 2005. http://jsor.org/.

Dismond, Geraldyn. "The Negro Actor and the American Movies." *Film Theory: Critical Concepts in Media and Cultural Studies*. Eds. Philip Simpson, Andrew Utterson, and K.J. Sheperdson. New York: Routledge, 1929/2004. 167–170. Print.

Doherty, Thomas. "Genre, Gender, and the Aliens Trilogy." *The Dread of Difference: Gender and the Horror Film*. Ed. Barry Keith Grant. Austin: University of Texas Press, 1996. 181–199. Print.

"Domestic Violence: Domestic Violence in the African American Community." Nabsw. org. National Association of Black Social Workers, 2002. Web. April 9, 2010.

Duany, Andres, and Elizabeth Plater-Zyberk. *Suburban Nation: The Rise of Sprawl and the Decline of the American Dream*. New York: North Point Press, 2000. Print.

Du Bois, W.E.B. *Darkwater: Voices From Within the Veil*. New York: Harcourt, Brace, and Howe, 1920. Print.

——. *The Souls of Black Folks*. New York: NAL Penguin, 1903/1969. Print.

Dunn, Stephane. *'Baad Bitches' and Sassy Supermamas: Black Power Action Films*. Urbana and Chicago: University of Illinois Press, 2008. Print.

"DVD Boom Spawns Indie Theatricals Surge." OnFilm, April 2004: 21. N.p. Web. July 13, 2006. proquest.umi.com.proxy.lib.umich.edu/pqdweb?did=620541621&Fmt=3&clientId=17822&RQT=309&VName=PQD.

Dyer, Richard. "White." *Screen* 29 (1988): 44–64. Print.

Ebenkamp, Becky, and Todd Wasserman. "Wayans' Thugaboos Hit Streets; GM Getting a Lift at Sundance." *Brandweek*, January 10, 2005: 8. Print.

Ebert, Roger. "*Vampire in Brooklyn*." *Chicago Sun-Times*, October 27, 1995. Print.

"Ebony Film." Letter to the Editor. *Chicago Defender*, July 1, 1916: 4. Print.

Edison: The Invention of the Movies. Disc 2. Prod. Brent Wood. Kino on Video, 2005. DVD.

Eller, Claudia. "Warner to Proceed Straight to Video." *Los Angeles Times*, May 30, 2006. Web. June 12, 2006. latimes.com/technology/la-fi-warner30may30,1,939409.story?coll=la-headlines-technology.

Ellison, Ralph. *Invisible Man*. New York: Vintage International, 1952/1995. Print.

Erb, Cynthia. *Tracking King Kong: A Hollywood Icon in World Cinema*, 2nd ed. Detroit, MI: Wayne State University Press, 2009. Print.

Erish, Andrew. "Illegitimate Dad of 'Kong'." *Los Angeles Times*, January 8, 2006. Web. June 8, 2010. http://articles.latimes.com/2006/jan/08/entertainment/ca-ingagi8.

Everett, Anna. *Returning the Gaze: A Genealogy of Black Film Criticism, 1909–1949*. Durham, NC: Duke University Press, 2001. Print.

The 50 Worst Movies Ever Made. Prod. Dante Pugliese. Perf. Carlos Larkin. Passport International Entertainment, 2004. DVD.

Fanon, Frantz. *Black Skin, White Masks*. London: Pluto Press, 1986. Print.

"Film/TV Bits: Denzel Taps Peter Jackson; Snoop's 'Horror' Picked Up; Depp May Join Smith's 'Legend'," July 3, 2006. Web. July 3, 2006. eurweb.com/story.cfm?id=27249.

Fischoff, Stuart, Joe Antonio, and Diane Lewis. "Favorite Films and Film Genres as a Function of Race, Age, and Gender." *Journal of Media Psychology* 3.1 (Winter 1998): N.p. Web. January 20, 2006. http://www.calstatela.edu/faculty/sfischo/media3.html.

Fischoff, Stuart, Alexandra Dimopoulos, and Francois Nguyen. "The Psychological Appeal of Movie Monsters." *Journal of Media Psychology* 10.3 (Summer 2005): N.p. Web. January 20, 2006. http://www.calstatela.edu/faculty/sfischo/psychological_appeal_of_movie_monsters1.pdf.

Fisher, Celeste A. *Black on Black: Urban Youth Films and the Multicultural Audience*. Lanham, MD: The Scarecrow Press, Inc., 2006. Print.

Fisher, Tracy. "Warner Freebies and Promos Boost a Duo of DTV Sequels." *Video Store Magazine*, July 19–25, 1998: 10. Print.

Foley, Kevin. "Spike Lee Speaks to Spring Fest." University of Vermont, University Communications 24 (April 2002). Web. January 5, 2010. http://www.uvm. edu/~uvmpr/?Page=article.php&id=409.

Forman, Murray. *The 'Hood Comes First: Race, Space, and Place in Rap and Hip-Hop*. Middletown, CT: Wesleyan University Press, 2002. Print.

Freeman, Lance. *There Goes the 'Hood: Views of Gentrification from the Ground Up*. Philadelphia, PA: Temple University Press, 2004. Print.

Frye, Northrop. *Anatomy of Criticism: Four Essays*. Princeton, NJ: Princeton University Press, 1957/2000. Print.

Fulmer, Jacqueline. "'Men Ain't All'—A Reworking of Masculinity in *Tales from the Hood*, Or, *Grandma Meets the Zombie*." *Journal of American Folklore* 115.457/458 (2002): 422–442. Print.

Gallagher, Charles. "Color-Blind Privilege: The Social and Political Functions of Erasing the Colorline in Post Race America." *Race, Gender, Class* 10 (October 31, 2003): 1–17. Web. February 29, 2008. http://aca.lasalle.edu/schools/sas/sscdept/content/faculty/gallagher/Color_Blind_Privilege.pdf.

Gateward, Frances. "Daywalkin' Night Stalkin' Bloodsuckas: Black Vampires in Contemporary Film." *Genders OnLine Journal* 40 (2004). Web. June 20, 2005. http://www.genders.org/g40/g40_gateward.html.

Gelder, Ken. "Postcolonial Voodoo." *Postcolonial Studies* 3 (2000): 89–98. Print.

Gent, G. "Black Films Are In, So Are Profits." *New York Times*, July 28, 1972: 22. Print.

Gibson, Gloria. "Cinematic Foremothers: Zora Neale Hurston and Eloyce King Patrick Gist." *Oscar Micheaux & His Circle: African-American Filmmaking and Race Cinema of the Silent Era*. Eds. Pearl Bowser, Jane Gaines, and Charles Musser. Bloomington: Indiana University Press, 2001. 195–209. Print.

Gibson-Hudson, Gloria. "Recall and Recollect: Excavating the Life History of Eloyce King Patrick Gist." *Black Film Review* 8 (1994): 20–21. Print.

Gilroy, Paul. "Race Ends Here." *Ethnic and Racial Studies* 41 (1998): 838–847. Print.

Giroux, Henry. *Fugitive Cultures: Race, Violence, and Youth*. London: Routledge, 1996. Print.

Goldberg, D.J. *Discontented America: The United States in the 1920s*. Baltimore, MD: Johns Hopkins University Press, 1999. Print.

Golden, Nathan D. *Brief History and Statistics of the American Motion Picture Industry*. Washington, DC: GPO, August 14, 1936. Print.

Goldman, Ari L. "Dissent Grows among Jehovah's Witnesses." *New York Times*, August 29, 1984: B1. Print.

Goldsby, Jacqueline. "The High and Low Tech of It: The Meaning of Lynching and the Death of Emmett Till." *Yale Journal of Criticism* 9 (1996): 245–282. Print.

Goldstein, Gregg. "Filmmakers Take Direct Flight to DVD." *Hollywood Reporter*, March 30, 2006: 1+. Web. June 12, 2006. proquest.umi.com.proxy.lib.umich.edu/pqdweb?did=1031249691&Fmt=4&clientId=17822&RQT=309&VName=PQD.

Goldstein, Seth. "Warner Family Label Set to Debut Titles on DVD." *Video Store Magazine*, February 20–26, 2000: 8. Print.

Gonder, Patrick. "Like a Monstrous Jigsaw Puzzle: Genetics and Race in Horror Films of the 1950s." *The Velvet Light Trap* 52 (2003): 33–44. N.p. Web. January 20, 2006. http://muse.jhu.edu/login?uri=/journals/the_velvet_light_trap/v052/52.1gonder.pdf.

———. "Race, Gender and Terror: The Primitive in 1950s Horror Films." *Genders OnLine Journal* 40 (2004): n.p. Web. January 19, 2006. http://www.genders.org/g40/g40_gondor.html.

Grant, Barry Keith, ed. *The Dread of Difference Gender and the Horror Film*. Austin: University of Texas Press, 1996. Print.

——. "Introduction." *The Dread of Difference: Gender and the Horror Film*. Ed. Barry Keith Grant. Austin: University of Texas Press, 1996. 1–12. Print.

——. "Taking Back the *Night of the Living Dead*: George Romero, Feminism, and the Horror Film." *The Dread of Difference: Gender and the Horror Film*. Ed. Barry Keith Grant. Austin: University of Texas Press, 1996. 200–212. Print.

Greenberg, Harvey Roy. "*King Kong*: The Beast in the Boudoir—Or, 'You Can't Marry that Girl, You're a Gorilla!'" *The Dread of Difference: Gender and the Horror Film*. Ed. Barry Keith Grant. Austin: University of Texas Press, 1996. 338–351. Print.

Greene, Eric. *Planet of the Apes as American Myth: Race and Politics in the Films and Television Series*. Jefferson, NC: McFarland & Co., 1996. Print.

Gruenwedel, Erik. "Urban: Coming Up." *Video Store Magazine*, December 19–25, 2004: 13. Print.

Guerrero, Edward. "AIDS as Monster in Science Fiction." *Journal of Popular Film & Television* 18.3 (Fall 1990): 86–93. Print.

——. "The Black Images in Protective Hollywood's Biracial Buddy Films of the Eighties." *Black American Cinema*. Ed. Manthia Diawara. New York: Routledge, 1993. 237–246. Print.

——. *Framing Blackness: The African American Image in Film*. Philadelphia, PA: Temple University Press, 1993. Print.

"Haiti Country Profile." *BBC*. BBC. 2010. Web. August 11, 2010. http://news.bbc.co. uk/2/hi/americas/country_profiles/1202772.stm.

Hall Jamieson, Kathleen. "Context and the Creation of Meaning in Advertising of the 1988 Presidential Campaign." *American Behavioral Scientist* 32 (1989): 415–424. Print.

Harrington, Richard. "Def by Temptation." *Washington Post*, June 5, 1990. Web. July 20, 2010. http://www.washingtonpost.com/wp-srv/style/longterm/movies/videos/defbytemptationrharrington_a0aae9.htm.

Harris, Mark H. "Scary Sistas: A Brief History of Black Women in Horror Films." *Scary-Scarynet*, June 4, 2006. N.p. Web. August 13, 2010. http://www.fangirltastic.com/content/scary-sistas-brief-history-black-women-horror-films.

——. "Yelling at the Screen: The Black Die Young." *PopMatters*, September 6, 2005. N.p. Web. November 28, 2005. http://popmatters.com/columns/harris/050906.shtml.

Harris, Martin. "You Can't Kill the Boogeyman: Halloween III and the Modern Horror Franchise." *Journal of Popular Film and Television* 32(3) (Fall 2004): 104–105. Print.

Hasan, Mark. "Ganja & Hess [Review]." *Rue Morgue* (2007): 47. Print.

Heffernan, Kevin. *Ghouls, Gimmicks, and Gold: Horror Films and the American Movie Business, 1953–1968*. Durham, NC: Duke University Press, 2004. Print.

Helbig, Bob, and Mark Edmund. "Family of Konerak Sues City." *Milwaukee Journal*, January 20, 1995, NEWS: 1. *NewsBank*. Web. August 12, 2010.

Hendricks, Bill, and Howard Waugh. *The Encyclopedia of Exploitation*. New York: Showmen's Trade Review, 1937. Print.

Herek, Gregory. "Stigma, Prejudice, and Violence against Lesbians and Gay Men." *Homosexuality: Research Implications for Public Policy*. Eds. John C. Gonsiorek and James Weinrich D. Newbury Park, CA: Sage, 1991. 60–80. Print.

Hernandez, Greg. "Sherman Oaks, Calif., Company Provides Movie Audiences with Urban Fare." *Knight Ridder Tribune Business News*, February 9, 2003: 1. Web. July 14, 2006. proquest.umi.com.proxy.lib.umich.edu/pqdweb?did=285897401&Fmt =3&clientId=17822&RQT=309&VName=PQD.

Hervey, Ben. *Night of the Living Dead*. New York: Palgrave Macmillan, 2008. Print.

Hester-Williams, Kim D. "NeoSlaves: Slavery, Freedom, and African American Apotheosis in *Candyman, the Matrix*, and *the Green Mile*." *Genders OnLine Journal* 40 (2004). N.p. Web. June 16, 2006. http://www.genders.org/g40/g40_williams.html.

Hicks, Chris. "Wide Release of 'White Dog' is Long Overdue. *Deseret News* January 23, 2009. Web. http://www.deseretnews.com/article/705279597/Wide-release-of-White-Dog-is-long-overdue.html.

Hicks, Heather J. "Hoodoo Economics: White Men's Work and Black Men's Magic in Contemporary American Film." *Camera Obscura 53* 18.2 (2003): 27–55. Print.

Hill Collins, Patricia. *Black Feminist Thought.* New York: Routledge, 2009. Print.

——. *Black Sexual Politics: African Americans, Gender, and the New Racism.* New York: Routledge, 2004. Print.

Hoag, Christina. "Maverick Entertainment Reaches Direct-to-Video Urban Movie Market." *Knight Ridder Tribune Business News*, March 19, 2006: 1. Web. July 21, 2006.

Hobson, Janell. "Digital Whiteness, Primitive Blackness: Racializing the 'Digital Divide' in Film and New Media." *Feminist Media Studies* 8 (2008): 111–126. Print.

"Holla' for Halloween: Urban Horror Film Weaves in Comedy for a Scary Time." October 29, 2007. N.p. Web. March 6, 2010. eurweb.com.

Holland, Sharon Patricia. *Raising the Dead: Readings of Death and (Black) Subjectivity.* Durham, NC: Duke University Press, 2000. Print.

Holly, Ellen. "Where Are the Films about Real Black Men and Women?" *New York Times,* June 2, 1974: 127. Print.

hooks, bell. *Reel to Real: Race, Sex, and Class at the Movies.* New York: Routledge, 1996. Print.

"Horror Films Debut Soon." *Daily Defender.* Novemer 12, 1957: B10. Col. 5. Print.

Horror Genre Surges in DVD (Video Business). Web. July 21, 2006.

Hudson, Dale. "Vampires of Color and the Performance of Multicultural Whiteness." *The Persistence of Whiteness: Race and Contemporary Hollywood Cinema.* Ed. Daniel Bernardi. New York: Routledge, 2008. 127–156. Print.

Hughes, Langston. "A Little Song to Put in Your Pipe and Smoke." *Black Film as a Signifying Practice: Cinema Narration and the African-American Aesthetic Tradition.* Ed. Gladstone L. Yearwood. Trenton, NJ: Africa World Press, 2000. 113. Print.

Hughey, Matthey. "Cinethetic Racism: White Redemption and Black Stereotypes in 'Magic Negro' Films." *Social Problems* 56 (2009): 543–577. Print.

Humphries, Reynold. "I Walked with a Zombie." *101 Horror Movies You Must See Before You Die.* Ed. Steven Jay Schneider. London: Cassell Illustrated, 2009. 85–86. Print.

——. *The American Horror Film: An Introduction.* Edinburgh, UK: Edinburgh University Press, 2002. Print.

——. *The Hollywood Horror Film 1931–1941: Madness in a Social Landscape.* Lanham, MD: The Scarecrow Press, Inc., 2006. Print.

Hurston, Zora Neale. "Hoodoo in America." *Journal of American Folklore* 44 (October–December 1931): 317–417. Print.

——. *Tell My Horse.* New York: Harper Perennial, 1938/1990. Print.

Hutchings, Peter. *The Horror Film.* London: Pearson, 2004. Print.

Hyatt, Marshall. *The Afro-American Cinematic Experience: An Annotated Bibliography & Filmography.* Wilmington, DE: Scholarly Resources, Inc., 1983. Print.

Kurutz, Steven. "The Star of Rapper Paul Wall's New Video? The iPhone 3GS." *Wall Street Journal*, September 24, 2009. *Wall Street Journal.* Web. August 10, 2010. http://blogs.wsj.com/speakeasy/2009/09/24/the-star-of-rapper-paul-walls-new-video-the-iphone-3gs/.

"Ingagi Reviews Summary." *New York Times.* NYTimes.com. Web. June 18, 2010. http://movies.nytimes.com/movie/96552/Ingagi/overview.

Jaffray, Norman R. "The Spine Chillers." *The Monster Show: A Cultural History of Horror.* Ed. David J. Skal. New York: Faber and Faber, Inc., 1993. 174. Print.

"'Jango' Filmed in Wilds' of Bronx, 'Cannibal'." *Pittsburgh Press*, March 9, 1930: 15 News Section-Editorial. Print.

Jennings, Tom. "Class-ifying Contemporary Cinema." *Variant* 10: n.p. Web. June 10, 2006. http://www.variant.org.uk/10texts/Jennings.html,

Johnson, Ben. "Some Say Police Dog Is Racist." *New Pittsburgh Courier*, May 14, 2003: A1. Print.

Jones, Alan. *The Rough Guide to Horror Movies.* London: Rough Guides, 2005. Print.

Jones, Eileen. "Will Smith's Hancock Fiasco." *Alternet*, July 5, 2008. Web. June 10, 2009. http://www.alternet.org/movies/90473/.

Jones, G. William. *Black Cinema Treasures: Lost and Found.* Denton: University of North Texas Press, 1991. Print.

Jones, Steve. "Michael King of Pop Dies; Music Icon, 50, Helped Shape a Generation." *USA Today*, June 26, 2009. Web. March 6, 2010. usatoday.com.

Katzman, Lisa "'White Dog' Is Set Loose at Last." *New York Times*, July 7, 1991: sec. 2.17. Print.

Kaveney, Roz. *From Alien to the Matrix: Reading Science Fiction Film.* New York: I.B. Tauris & Co. Ltd., 2005. Print.

Keeling, Kara. *The Witch's Flight.* Durham, NC: Duke University Press, 2007. Print.

King, Stephen. "Acceptance Speech: The 2003 National Book Award for Distinguished Contribution to American Letters." *On Writing Horror.* Ed. Mort Castle. Revised ed. Cincinnati, OH: Writer's Digest Books, 2007. 7–12. Print.

Kipnis, Jill. "No Theater? No Problem: Direct-to-DVD Takes Off." *Billboard*, February 4, 2006: 18–19. N.p. Web. June 12, 2006. proquest.umi.com.proxy.lib. umich.edu/pqdweb?did=980828581&Fmt=3&clientId=17822&RQT=309&VName =PQD.

Klein, Aaron, with Brenda J. Elliott. *The Manchurian President: Barack Obama's Ties to Communists, Socialists and Other Anti-American Extremists.* Washington, DC: WorldNetDaily Books, 2010. Print.

Kliman, Bernice W. "The Biscuit Eater: Racial Stereotypes: 1939–1972." *Phylon* 79 (1978): 87–96. Print.

Koppes, Clayton R., and Gregory D. Blacks. "What to Show the World: The Office of War Information and Hollywood, 1942–1945." *Journal of American History* (1977): 87–105. Print.

Kozol, Wendy. "Relocating Citizenship in Photographs of Japanese Americans during World War II." *Haunting Violations: Feminist Criticism and the Crisis of the 'Real.'* Eds. Wendy Hesford and Wendy Kozol. Champaign: University of Illinois Press, 2001. 217–250. Print.

Kuhn (Erlangen), Andrea. "What's the Matter, Trevor? Scared of Something? Representing the Monstrous-Feminine in *Candyman*." *EESE* (2000): Web. January 26, 2006. http:// webdoc.gwdg.de/edoc/ia/eese/artic20/kuhn/kuhn.html.

Lapeyre, Jason. "The Transformation: Filmmaker John Landis Created a Monster with Michael Jackson's *Thriller*." *Wax Poetics* 37 (October–November 2009): 77–78. Print.

Lawless, Robert. *Haiti's Bad Press.* Rochester, VT: Schenkman Books, 1992. Print.

Lawrence, N. "Fear of a Blaxploitation Monster: Blackness as Generic Revision in AIP's *Blacula*." *Film International* 39 (2009): 14–26. Print.

Leab, Daniel J. *From Sambo to Superspade: The Black Experience in Motion Pictures.* Boston, MA: Houghton Mifflin Company, 1975. Print.

——. "The Gamut from A to B: The Images of the Black in Pre-1915 Movies." *Political Science Quarterly* 88 (1973): 53–70. Print.

Leonard, David J. *Screens Fade to Black: Contemporary African American Cinema.* Westport, CT: Praeger, 2006. Print.

Lewis, Theophilus. "The Harlem Sketch Book." *New York Amsterdam News*, April 16, 1930: sec. 10. Print.

"Little Jasper Series Draws Protests from Negro Groups." *Ebony* (January 1947): 27. Print.

Lively, Adam. *Masks: Blackness, Race, and the Imagination.* New York: Oxford University Press, 1998. Print.

"Living Vodou." *Speaking of Faith with Krista Trippet.* American Public Media. June 28, 2007. Radio.

L.N. "The Screen. Beyond the Pale." *New York Times,* July 29, 1932. sec. 8. Print.

Lott, Eric. "Spirit of the Ghetto: Postindustrial City Space and the Specter of Race." Presentation. American Research Seminar. University of Leeds, Leeds, UK. February 5, 2007.

Loudermilk, A. "Eating 'Dawn' in the Dark: Zombie Desire and Commodified Identity in George A. Romero's *Dawn of the Dead.*" *Journal of Consumer Culture* 3 (March 2003): 83–108. Print.

Loughran, Stephanie. "Retailers Find Success in some Direct-to-Video Niches." *Supermarket News,* October 1, 2003: 43. Web. July 21, 2006.

McCaffrey, Donald W. "The Golden Age of Sound Comedy." *Screen* 11 (1970): 27–40. Print.

Machosky, Michael. "Seeking the Paranormal." *Pittsburgh Tribune Review,* October 18, 2005. *Pittsburgh Tribune.* Web. August 2, 2010. www.pittsburghlive.com/x/pittsburghtrib/s_385041.html.

Maddery, Joseph. *Nightmares in Red, White, and Blue: The Evolution of the American Horror Film.* Jefferson, NC: McFarland & Co., 2004. Print.

Mailer, Norman. "The White Negro." Fall 1957. *LearnToQuestion.com: Resource Base* 2008. N.p. Web. June 20, 2010. http://www.learntoquestion.com/resources/database/archives/0.

Manatu, Norma. *African American Women and Sexuality in the Cinema.* Jefferson, NC: McFarland & Co., 2003. Print.

Mason, Fred. *American Gangster Cinema: From Little Caeser to Pulp Fiction.* New York: Palgrave Macmillan, 2002. Print.

"Mass Meeting to Discuss how to Stop Film: Society for Advancement of Colored People Believes '*The Birth of a Nation*' Can Be Removed with Censorship." *Christian Science Monitor,* May 1, 1915: 4. Print.

Mathijs, Ernest. "Threat or Treat: Film, Television, and the Ritual of Halloween." *Flow TV,* October 30, 2009. Web. March 6, 2010. http://flowtv.org/2009/10/threat-or-treat-film-television-and-the-ritual-of-halloween-ernest-mathijs-the-university-of-british-columbia/.

Mattera, Jason. "Jason Mattera on Obama Zombies." Dir. Simon and Schuster Videos. YouTube.com, LLC, 2010. August 10, 2010. http://www.youtube.com/watch?v=bdHIsax3hSE.

"May Not Release 'Birth' Film, Purchaser Says." *Atlanta Daily World,* May 21, 1959: 2. Print.

Medovoi, L. "Theorizing Historicity, or the Many Meanings of Blacula." *Screen* 39 (Spring 1998): 1–21. Print.

Mercer, Kobena. "Monster Metaphors: Notes on Michael Jackson's 'Thriller'." *Screen* 27 (1986): 26–43. Print.

Mesbur + Smith Architects. *Multiplex Cinema and Theater Architecture.* May 29, 2008. Web. http://www.mesbursmith.com/index.htm,

Metress, Christopher. *The Lynching of Emmett Till: A Documentary Narrative.* Charlottesville: University of Virginia Press, 2002. Print.

"Michael Jackson's 'Dangerous' Mind: The Making of the King of Pop." *Rolling Stone,* January 9, 1992. Print.

Moore, Toby. "This Is America: 'Racist' Police Dogs Got the Wrong Collar." *Express,* June 3, 2002. Print.

Motion Picture Association. "Motion Picture Association of America." 2005. N.p. Web. June 12, 2009. http://www.mpaa.org/ratings.

Murray, J. "Now a Boom in Black Directors." *New York Times*, June 8, 1972: D11. Print.

Muse, Clarence. "What's Going on in Hollywood." *Chicago Defender*, December 28, 1940: 21. Print.

———. "When a Negro Sings a Song." *Celebrity Articles from the Screen Guild Magazine*. Ed. Anna Kate Sterling. Lanham, MD: Rowman & Littlefield, 1987. Print.

Musser, Charles. *Before the Nickelodeon: Edwin S. Porter and the Edison Manufacturing Company*. Berkeley: University of California Press, 1991. Print.

Musser, Charles, Corey K. Creekmur, Pearl Bowser, J. Ronald Green, Charlene Regester, and Louise Spence. "Appendix B: An Oscar Micheaux Filmography: From the Silents through His Transition to Sound, 1919–1931." *Oscar Micheaux & His Circle: African-American Filmmaking and Race Cinema of the Silent Era*. Eds. Pearl Bowser, Jane Gaines, and Charles Musser. Bloomington and Indianapolis: Indiana University Press, 2001. 228–277. Print.

"MTV Music Television Profile." Cable TV. Web. August 13, 2010. Cabletvadbureau. com.

"MTV Video Music Awards." MTV. Web. August 13, 2010. MTV.com.

"NAACP Pickets Close 'Birth of a Nation'." *Chicago Defender*, December 12, 1942: 4. Print.

Nama, Adilifu. *Black Space: Imagining Race in Science Fiction Film*. Austin: University of Texas Press, 2008. Print.

National Association of Black Social Workers. "Domestic Violence: Domestic Violence in the African American Community." 2002. Web. August 10, 2010. nabsw.org.

"NBC Drops Plan to Show Film 'White Dog'" *New York Times*, January 20, 1984: sec. C23. Print.

Ndalianis, Angela. "Dark Rides, Hybrid Machines and the Horror Experience." *Horror Zone*. Ed. Ian Conrich. London: I.B. Tauris, 2010. 11–26. Print.

Neale, Steve. "Masculinity as Spectacle: Reflections on Men and Mainstream Cinema." *Screen* 24(6): 2–17, 19. Print.

Nelson, Angela "From Beulah to the Fresh Prince of Bel-Air: A Brief History of Black Stereotypes in Television Comedy." Unpublished manuscript, 1991.

Nesteby, James R. *Black Images in American Films, 1896–1954*. Lanham, MD: University Press of America, 1982. Print.

Neuert, Richard. "Trouble in Watermelon Land: George Pal and the Little Jasper Cartoons." *Film Quarterly* 55 (2001): 14–26. Print.

Neve, Brian. *Film and Politics in America: A Social Tradition*. London: Routledge, 1992. Print.

Nichols, Peter M. "Home Video: Idea to DVD: A Long Road." *New York Times*, September 12, 2003. New York Times. Web. June 10, 2006. infoweb.newsbank.com. proxy.lib.umich.edu/iw-search/we/In...id=E55H4FVIMTE1MDE0OTc3Ny4xNT U4OTE6MToxNToxNDEuMjExLjE3NS4xMzk6.

———. "Home Video: It's a Sequel? O.K., I'll Take It." July 28, 2000. Web. June 10, 2006. infoweb.newsbank.com.proxy.lib.umich.edu/iw-search/we/In...id=E55H4FV IMTE1MDE0OTc3Ny4xNTU4OTE6MToxNToxNDEuMjExLjE3NS4xMzk:.

Noble, Peter. *The Negro in Films*. New York: Arno Press & the New York Times, 1970. Print.

Null, Gary. *Black Hollywood: The Negro in Motion Pictures*. Secaucus, NJ: Citadel Press, 1975. Print.

Oates, Joyce. *Zombie*. New York: Plume, 1996. Print.

Olson, Catherine Applefeld. "Tried-and-True TV." *Billboard*, February 24, 1996: 68. Print.

Orbe, Mark, and Karen Strother. "Signifying the Tragic Mulatto: A Semiotic Analysis of Alex Haley's Queen." *Howard Journal of Communications* 7 (April 1996): 113–126. Print.

"Oregon Station Drops 'Little Jasper' Series." *Los Angeles Sentinel*, June 4, 1959: C1. Print.

"Oscar.Com—Home." N.p. Web. August 13, 2010. Oscar.com.

"'Paranoia' Horror Film Debuts at the Oriental." *Chicago Daily Defender*, August 16–22 1960: 1+. Print.

Parish, James Robert, and George H. Hill. *Black Action Films*. Jefferson, NC: McFarland & Co., 1989. Print.

Penzler, Otto. *Black Noir: Mystery, Crime, and Suspense Fiction by African-American Writers*. New York: Pegasus, 2009. Print.

Petty, Mariam J. "Passing for Horror: Race, Fear, and Elia Kazan's Pinky." Genders OnLine Journal 40 (2004): n.p. Web. January 20, 2006. http://www.genders.org/g40/g40_petty.html.

Phillips, Kendall R. *Projected Fears: Horror Films and American Culture*. Westport, CT: Praeger, 2005. Print.

Picart, Caroline Joan, and Cecil Greek. "The Compulsion of Real/Reel Serial Killers and Vampires: Toward a Gothic Criminology." *Journal of Criminal Justice and Popular Culture* 10.1 (2003): 39–68. Print.

———. "The Compulsions of Real/Reel Serial Killers and Vampires: Toward a Gothic Criminology." *Monsters In and Among Us: Toward a Gothic Criminology*. Eds. Caroline Joan Picart and Cecil Greek. Cranbury, NJ: Associated University Presses, 2007. 227–255. Print.

Pinedo, Isabel Cristina. *Recreational Terror: Women and the Pleasure of Horror Film Viewing*. Albany, NY: SUNY Press, 1997. Print.

Pomerantz, Dorothy. "On a Script and a Prayer." *Forbes*, March 3, 2003: 115. Print.

Prange, Stephanie. "The Direct-to-DVD Stop-Gap." *Home Media Retailing*, October 23–29, 2005: 81. N.p. Web. June 12, 2006. proquest.umi.com.proxy.lib.umich.edu/pqdweb?did=920534951&Fmt=3&clientId=17822&RQT=309&VName=PQD.

———. "Warner Continues Its Direct-to-Video Push with 'Dennis the Menace' Sequel." *Video Store Magazine*, May 16, 1998: 10. Print.

Public Enemy. *Louder Than a Bomb*. Def Jam, 1988. CD.

"Race Press Ignored by Big Film Interests: Louise Beavers 'on Spot'." *Pittsburgh Courier*, December 15, 1934: sec. A9. Print.

Rathgeb, Douglas L. "Bogeyman from the Id: Nightmare and Reality in *Halloween and A Nightmare on Elm Street*." *Journal of Popular Film & Television* (1991): 36–43. Print.

Razaf, Andy. "A Colored Movie Fan." *New York Amsterdam News*, January 6, 1940: sec. 16. Print.

Reddick, Lawrence. "Educational Programs for the Improvement of Race Relations: Motion Pictures, Radio, the Press, and Libraries." *Journal of Negro Education* 13.3 (1944): 367–389. Print.

Regester, Charlene. "The African-American Press and Race Movies, 1909–1929." *Oscar Micheaux & His Circle: African American Filmmaking and Race Cinema of the Silent Era*. Eds. Pearl Bowser, Jane Gaines, and Charles Musser. Bloomington and Indianapolis: Indiana University Press, 2001. 34–49. Print.

Reid, Mark A. *Black Lenses, Black Voices: African American Film Now*. Lanham, MD: Rowman & Littlefield, 2005. Print.

———. *Redefining Black Film*. Berkeley: University of California Press, 1993. Print.

Rhines, Jesse Algeron. *Black Film/White Money*. New Brunswick, NJ: Rutgers University Press, 1996. Print.

Rhodes, Gary D. *White Zombie: Anatomy of a Horror Film*. Jefferson, NC: McFarland & Co., 2001. Print.

Richards, Chris. "Va. Slayings Spur Harder Look at Horrorcore." *Washington Post*, September 25, 2009. Print.

Richards, Larry. *African American Films through 1959: A Comprehensive, Illustrated Filmography*. Jefferson, NC: McFarland & Co., 1998. Print.

Riley, Michael J. "Trapped in the History of Film: Racial Conflict and Allure in *The Vanishing American*." *Hollywood's Indian: The Portrayal of the Native American in Film*. Eds. Peter C. Rollins and John E. O'Connor. Lexington: The University of Kentucky Press, 1998. 58–72. Print.

Robinson, Cedric J. *Forgeries of Memory & Meaning: Blacks & the Regimes of Race in American Theater & Film before World War II*. Chapel Hill: University of North Carolina Press, 2007. Print.

Rocchio, Vincent F. *Reel Racism: Confronting Hollywood's Construction of Afro-American Culture*. Boulder, CO: Westview Press, 2000. Print.

Rogin, Michael P. *Fathers and Children: Andrew Jackson and the Subjugation of the American Indian*. Piscataway, NJ: Transaction Publishers, 1991. Print.

Rony, Fatimah Tobing. *The Third Eye: Race, Cinema, and Ethnographic Spectacle*. Durham, NC: Duke University Press, 1996. Print.

Roosevelt, Theodore. *African Game Trails: An Account of the African Wanderings of an American Hunter-Naturalist*. New York: Charles Scribner's Sons, 1910. Print.

St. Louis, Brett. "Post-Race/Post-Politics? Activist-Intellectualism and Reification of Race." *Ethnic and Racial Studies* 25 (2002): 652–675. Print.

Sampson, Henry T. *Blacks in Black and White: A Source Book on Black Films*. Metuchen, NJ: The Scarecrow Press, Inc., 1977/1995. Print.

Schneider, Steven Jay. "Mixed Blood Couples: Monsters and Miscegenation in U.S. Horror Cinema." *The Gothic Other: Racial and Social Constructions in the Literary Imagination*. Eds. Ruth Beinstock and Douglas L. Howard. Jefferson, NC: McFarland & Co., 2004. 72–89. Print.

Schroeder, Caroline T. "Ancient Egyptian Religion on the Silver Screen: Modern Anxieties about Race, Ethnicity, and Religion." *Journal of Religion and Film* 2.3 (October 2003). Web. November 8, 2009. www.unomaha.Edu/jrf/Vol7No2/ancientegypt.htm.

Scott, Ellen C. "The Horrors of Remembrance: The Altered Visual Aesthetic of Horror in Jonathan Demme's *Beloved*." *Genders OnLine Journal* 40 (2004). Web. January 20, 2006. http://www.genders.org/g40/g40_scott.html.

Scott, Vernon. "Minority Group Wins Cancellation of Television Movie." *UPI Hollywood Reporter*, January 12, 1984: sec. Domestic News. Print.

Seabrook, W.B. *The Magic Island*. New York: Harcourt, Brace and Company, 1929. Print.

Senn, Bryan. *Golden Horrors: An Illustrated Critical Filmography 1931–1939*. Jefferson, NC: McFarland & Co., 1996. Print.

Shaefer, Eric. *Bold! Daring! Shocking! True!: A History of Exploitation Films, 1919–1959*. Austin: University of Texas Press, 1995. Print.

Sharrett, Christopher. "The Horror Film in Neoconservative Culture." *Journal of Popular Film & Television* 21.3 (Fall 1993): 100–110. Print.

——. *Mythologies of Violence in Postmodern Media*. Detroit, MI: Wayne State University Press, 1999. Print.

Skal, David J. *The Monster Show: A Cultural History of Horror*. Revised ed. New York: Faber and Faber, Inc., 2001. Print.

Snead, James. *White Screens, Black Images: Hollywood from the Dark Side*. New York: Routledge, 1994. Print.

"Snoop Scraps: Rapper to Produce/Star in Horror Pic." April 20, 2006. Web. June 10, 2010. eurweb.com.

Sobchack, Vivian. "Bringing It All Back Home: Family Economy and Generic Exchange." *The Dread of Difference: Gender and the Horror Film*. Ed. Barry Keith Grant. Austin: University of Texas Press, 1996. 143–163. Print.

——. "'Cities on the Edge of Time: The Urban Science Fiction Film'." *East–West Film Journal* (December 1988): 4–19. Print.

——. *Screening Space: The American Science Fiction Film*. New Brunswick, NJ: Rutgers University Press, 2001. Print.

Soister, John T. *Up from the Vault: Rare Thrillers of the 1920s and 1930s*. Jefferson, NC: McFarland and Co., 2004. Print.

Sontag, Susan. "The Imagination of Disaster." *Commentary* (October 1965): 42–48. Print.

Southern Poverty Law Center. 2010. Southern Poverty Law Center. Web. June 8, 2009. http://www.splcenter.org/.

Sporich, Brett. "The Lion Roars: MGM Studio Strengthens Commitment to Video, DVD." *Video Store Magazine*, July 18–24, 1999: 1. Print.

Stanford, Gregory D. "A Paper Trail of Intolerance." *Milwaukee Journal*, January 25, 1995, OPED: 11. *NewsBank*. August 12, 2010. Print.

Stein, Elliott. "Night of the Living Dead." *Sight and Sound* 39 (1970): 105. Print.

Stenger, Josh. "Mapping the Beach: Beach Movies, Exploitation Film and Geographies of Whiteness." *Classic Hollywood, Classic Whiteness*. Ed. Daniel Bernardi. Minneapolis: University of Minnesota Press, 1996. 28–50. Print.

Steward, Theophilus Gould. *The Haitian Revolution, 1791 to 1804: Or, Side Lights on the French Revolution*, 2nd ed. New York: Thomas Y. Crowell Publishers, 1914. Print.

Stewart, Jacqueline Najuma. *Migrating to the Movies: Cinema and Black Urban Modernity*. Berkeley: University of California Press, 2005. Print.

Stokes, M. *D.W. Griffith's the Birth of a Nation: A History of the Most Controversial Film of All Time*. New York: Oxford University Press, 2007. Print.

"Straight-to-Video is Lifeline for Directors." Tonight, January 13, 2004. Web. October 23, 2006. tonight.co.za/index.php?fSectionid=358&fArticleid=324497.

"Team 4: Pittsburgh Ghost Hunters Investigate Paranormal Possibilities." November 28, 2007. Web. thepittsburghchannel.com/news/14717730/detail.html.

Thomson, Ian. "The Black Spartacus." *Guardian News and Media*, January 31, 2004. Web. June 23, 2010. Guardian.co.uk.

Toplin, Robert Brent. "Cinematic History: An Anatomy of the Genre." *Cineaste* 29.2: 34–39. Print. Spring 2004.

Tribbey, Ralph. "Tribbey's Spin." *Video Store Magazine* (February 2002): 16–23. Print.

"Triple Horror Films Electrify Fans at Regal." *Daily Defender*, May 4, 1960: 16.5. Print.

"Two Horror Films Bow at Drive-Ins." *Chicago Defender*, April 18, 1970: 28.6. Print.

Tyler, Bruce M. "Racial Imagery in *King Kong*." *King Kong Cometh!: The Evolution of the Great Ape*. Ed. Paula A. Woods. London: Plexus Publishing, 2005. 175. Print.

"Vampire in Brooklyn." Metacritic. CBS Interactive Inc., 2010. Web. July 20, 2010.

Vares, Tina. "Framing 'Killer Women' in Films: Audience Use of Genre." *Feminist Media Studies* 2.2 (2002): 213–229. Print.

Venkatest, Sudhir Alladi. *American Project: The Rise and Fall of a Modern Ghetto*. Cambridge, MA: Harvard University Press, 2000. Print.

Verney, Kevern. *African Americans and US Popular Culture*. New York: Routledge, 2003. Print.

Wallace, Michele. *Black Macho and the Myth of the Superwoman*. New York: Verso Classics, 1999. Print.

Wardi, Anissa J. "Freak Shows, Spectacles, and Carnivals: Reading Jonathan Demme's *Beloved*." *African American Review* 39 (Winter 2005): 513–526. Print.

Wartenber, Thomas E. "Humanizing the Beast: King Kong and the Representation of Black Male Sexuality." *Classic Hollywood, Classic Whiteness*. Ed. Daniel Bernardi. Minneapolis: University of Minnesota Press, 1996. 157–177. Print.

Wasserman, Todd. "For Marketers to Kids, no Pause in Direct-to-DVD." *Brandweek*, July 11–18, 2005: 10. Web. June 12, 2006. proquest.umi.com.proxy.lib.umich.edu/pqdweb?did=869228571&Fmt=4&clientId=17822&RQT=309&VName=PQD.

Watkins, Craig S. *Representing: Hip Hop Culture and the Production of Black Cinema*. Chicago, IL: University of Chicago Press, 1998. Print.

Weddington, Randy. "Mixing It Up: Direct-to-Video Has Become a Tough Sell for Some Retailers, but Star Power and Good Cover Art Can Help Move Titles off the Shelves." *Supermarket News*, April 23, 2001: 88. Web. July 12, 2006. http://proquest.umi.com.proxy.lib.umich.edu/pqdweb?did=1049469661&sid=3&Fmt=1&clientId=17822&RQT=309&VName=PQD.

Weiler, A.H. "'Abby,' about a Black Family and Exorcism." *New York Times*, December 26, 1974: 53. Print.

Welch, William M. "Former Senator Thurman Dies." *USA Today*, June 26, 2003. Web. August 12, 2010. http://www.usatoday.com/news/washington/2003-06-26-strom_x.htm.

West, Hollie I. "Black Films: Crossovers and Beyond Blaxploitation." *Washington Post*, February 8, 1976: 119. Print.

"What's Hot: Direct-to-Video." *DSN Retailing Today*, 2 April, 2001: 37. Print.

White Boyz. Dir. Marc Levin. Perf. Danny Hoch. Fox Search Light, 2004. DVD.

"The White Gorilla." YouTube.com, LLC, 2010. Web. July 26, 2010. http://www.youtube.com/watch?v=n_c47ZGZ5I8.

White Zombie. Dir. Victor Halperin. Prod. Edward Halperin. Perf. Bela Lugosi. Film. United Artists Corp., 1932.

"Wild Cannibal Turns Out to Be Ex-Janitor: Salary Suit Reveals Harlem as Scene of Fake Movie." *Chicago Defender*, March 15, 1930: 3. Print.

Williams, Delores S. *Sisters in the Wilderness: The Challenges of Womanist God-Talk*. Maryknoll, NY: Orbis Books, 1993. Print.

Williams, Linda. "When the Woman Looks." *The Dread of Difference: Gender and the Horror Film*. Ed. Barry Keith Grant. Austin: University of Texas Press, 1996. 15–34. Print.

Williams, Tony. "Trying to Survive on the Darker Side: 1980s Family Horror." *The Dread of Difference: Gender and the Horror Film*. Ed. Barry Keith Grant. Austin: University of Texas Press, 1996. 164–180. Print.

Wilson, Wendy. "Web Pages Give Direct-to-Video Titles an Online Push." *Video Business*, September 14, 1998: 32. Web. July 18, 2006. proquest.umi.com.proxy.lib.umich.edu/pqdweb?did=34088315&Fmt=3&clientId=17822&RQT=309&VName=PQD.

Winokur, Mark. "Technologies of Race: Special Effects, Fetish, Film and the Fifteenth Century." *Genders OnLine Journal* 40 (2004). Web. January 20, 2006. http://www.genders.org/g40/g40_winokur.html.

Wlodarz, Joe. "Beyond the Black Macho: Queer Blaxploitation." *The Velvet Light Trap* 53 (Spring 2004): 10–25. Web. January 20, 2006. http://muse.jhu.edu/login?uri=/journals/the_velvet_light_trap/v053/53.1wlodarz.html.

Wolf, Jessica. "'Final Destination 3' DVD Lets Fans Direct Hand of Fate." *Home Media Retailing*, April 9–15, 2006: 12. Web. June 12, 2006. proquest.umi.com.proxy.lib.umich.edu/pqdweb?did=1024048321&Fmt=4&clientId=17822&RQT=309&VName=PQD.

——. "'Masters of Horror' Makes Its Way to DVD." *Home Media Retailing*, April 2–8, 2006. Web. June 12, 2006. proquest.umi.com.proxy.lib.umich.edu/pqdweb?did=10196 60381&Fmt=4&clientId=17822&RQT=309&VName=PQD.

Wood, Robin. *Hollywood from Vietnam to Reagan*. New York: Columbia University Press, 1986. Print.

——. "An Introduction to the American Horror Film." *Movies and Methods: Volume II*. Ed. Bill Nichols. Berkeley: University of California Press, 1985. 195–220. Print.

——. *Personal Views Explorations in Film*, 2nd ed. Detroit, MI: Wayne State University Press, 2006. Print.

Worland, Rick. *The Horror Film: An Introduction*. Malden, MA: Blackwell, 2007. Print.

Yearwood, Gladstone L. *Black Film as a Signifying Practice: Cinema, Narration and the African-American Aesthetic Tradition*. Trenton, NJ: Africa World Press, Inc., 2000. Print.

Young, Elizabeth. *Black Frankenstein: The Making of an American Metaphor*. New York: Routledge, 2008. Print.

——. "Here Comes the Bride: Wedding Gender and Race in *Bride of Frankenstein*." *The Dread of Difference: Gender and the Horror Film*. Ed. Barry Keith Grant. Austin: University of Texas Press, 1996. 309–337. Print.

Young, Lola. *Fear of the Dark: 'Race,' Gender and Sexuality in the Cinema*. London: Routledge, 1996. Print.

Zimmerman, Bonnie. "*Daughters of Darkness*: The Lesbian Vampire on Film." *The Dread of Difference: Gender and the Horror Film*. Ed. Barry Keith Grant. Austin: University of Texas Press, 1996. 379–387. Print.

INDEX